On Chester On:

A History of Chester College and the University of Chester

On Chester On:

A History of Chester College and the University of Chester

Graeme J. White

First published 2014
by the University of Chester Press
University of Chester
Parkgate Road
Chester CH1 4BJ

Printed and bound by
CPI Group (UK) Ltd
Croydon CR0 4YY

Cover designed by the
LIS Graphics Team
University of Chester

A catalogue record for this book is available from the British Library

ISBN 978-1-908258-19-9

CONTENTS

LIST OF ILLUSTRATIONS

Front Cover Image
Grosvenor House, student accommodation opened in 2013, with the College Rowing Club from the turn of the century, College Rag Day in 1929 (Chester Archives & Local Studies: ZCR 86/7928) and students in in the science laboratory, from the 1968 prospectus.

Back Cover Image
An extract from Cartoons of College Life by George A. Bamber (student, 1905-07). (Cheshire Archives & Local Studies: ZCR 86/19/4.)

Black and White Illustrations

Colour Plates
Plates 1 and 2: The College badge, post Second World War.
Plate 3: The full coat of arms granted in 1954.
Plate 4: Lithograph of the College, *c.*1847.
Plate 5: The same view in 2014.
Plate 6: The garden in front of the Beswick building.
Plate 7: The Binks building.
Plate 8: Warrington campus.
Plate 9: The ceremonial inauguration of the University in 2005.
Plate 10: An assortment of prospectus covers, 1990–2014.
Plate 11: Kingsway buildings.
Plate 12: The Science and Technology campus at Thornton.
Plate 13: A view of the College's Parkgate Road campus in 1975.
Plate 14: The equivalent view in 2013.
Plate 15: Riverside campus.

ABOUT THE AUTHOR

Graeme J. White, MA, PhD, FRHistS, FSA, is Emeritus Professor of Local History at the University of Chester. He was appointed to Chester College as a Lecturer in History in 1977 and went on to become Head of History and latterly the University's Dean of Academic Quality and Standards, before retiring in 2010. He is editor of the journal *Cheshire History* and President of the Chester Society for Landscape History, which was founded by former students of Chester College in 1986. Among his previous books are *Restoration and Reform: Recovery from Civil War in England, 1153–1165* (2000) and *The Medieval English Landscape, 1000–1540* (2012).

FOREWORD

By the Lord Bishop of Chester, Lord President of the University Council and Pro-Chancellor

As the University of Chester celebrates the 175th anniversary of its foundation as the first purpose-built teaching training college in England, it is an appropriate occasion to reflect on the institution's long history and the many people who have contributed to its success. In my role as the Chairman of the University Council, I can take pride in how the six eminent founders and the Church of England took this innovative step to provide qualified teachers for the vast Diocese of Chester's rapidly expanding network of elementary schools and its diversification and expansion over the subsequent 175 years into a fully-fledged University with international status.

It is particularly appropriate that Professor Graeme White has written this new, intensively researched history as a member of staff between 1977 and 2010, in roles including the Head of the Department of History and Dean of Academic Quality & Standards. His unique perspective on the institution and the people involved during that time builds upon the existing scholarship on the history of the institution and gives an insight into how Chester College developed from its modest beginnings to evolve into a key educational institution in the North West.

The University of Chester's continuing success is due to the students and staff who have contributed to this vibrant and caring community and this book is a great tribute to all those who have played their part in its long and distinguished history.

PREFACE

'The picturesque ... city of Chester is one of those places that outsiders probably always expected to have its own university.'

So says *The Times and Sunday Times Good University Guide* for 2014, before explaining that the Church of England's first diocesan teacher training college, founded in 1839, did not in fact attain university status until 2005 and now ranked – by the newspapers' calculations – 52nd equal among the 121 institutions surveyed.[1] By any standards, the story of Chester College and its successor, the University of Chester, is a remarkable one: of pioneering endeavour, more than one near-closure, and the triumphant negotiation of the recurrent threats, opportunities and policy shifts which have characterised UK higher education, especially since the 1960s.

This book celebrates the 175th anniversary of the College's foundation. This preface is being written on the same date in 2014 that the foundation meeting was held in 1839 and the story has been carried forward to that point. It has been a privilege to offer this version of events and I am most grateful to the Vice-Chancellor and to the University of Chester Press for the opportunity to do so. As a medieval historian, I cannot resist quoting one of my heroes, the great twelfth-century monastic writer Orderic Vitalis – born not far away at Atcham in Shropshire – who brought to a close his magnificent *Ecclesiastical History* by saying that 'worn out with age and infirmity' and 'now in the sixty-seventh year of my age', 'I long to bring this book to an end'.[2] But although, as a post-Second World War 'baby-boomer', I currently share Orderic's age, I do not actually feel the same way about the book: it has not worn me out and I shall miss it!

I am of course conscious of an immense debt to those who have covered this ground before, including Stanley Astbury who produced *A History of Chester Diocesan Training College* in 1946, John Bradbury whose *Chester College and the Training of Teachers* appeared in 1975, Elsie Newton, author of *The Padgate Story* which covers the campus at Warrington acquired in 2002, and the contributors to *Perspectives of Chester College*, a collection of original essays to mark the 150th anniversary in 1989. Particular tribute must be paid to Malcolm Seaborne and Ian Dunn. Seaborne's brief account of the College for the *Victoria County History of Cheshire*, published in 2005, is an excellent summary of developments to the turn of the millennium, while Dunn's relatively-short but copiously illustrated book, *The University of Chester: The Bright Star in the Present Prospect*, which reached its third edition in 2012, is a fine example of how to make institutional history interesting and accessible.

Among all these publications, the closest parallel to the present book is that by Bradbury, who used many of the same sources and who showed a similar concern to set the College's story in a wider context. Bradbury's book was important in its timing, helping to boost collegial confidence when there was turmoil within the sector and very few comparable institutions could boast a scholarly history of their own. However, besides the obvious need to give detailed coverage to the period since it was published, there is room for substantial reinterpretation of several episodes in the College's past, including the proposal to close in 1932–33 and the admission of the first women students in the early 1960s. Bradbury also devoted over half his book to the first 30 years, only moving beyond 1869 on page 140. I have chosen to cover this early period more briefly, and to the charge that the chapters seem to expand the closer we come to the present day I can only plead the growing size and complexity of the institution. The last few chapters are in fact shorter than their immediate predecessors. Although, if those higher education students registered with collaborative partners are included in the calculation, roughly half the students who have ever been enrolled with College and University in its 175-year history have been on the books since the turn of the millennium – so giving the early twenty-first century a claim to inordinate attention – I have not thought it appropriate to analyse the recent past in depth. That task awaits the next historian to take up the challenge.

Among my other debts is one to those who assembled the fine archive of Chester College, deposited at the City Record Office in 1970 and now in the custody of Cheshire Archives and Local Studies. There have been occasional deposits since then but, now that this book has been completed, it is intended that a further substantial transfer of recent material will follow. Obviously, the nature of the sources, and the type of information they convey, have changed over 175 years and this accounts – at least in part – for the shifts of emphasis in what I have chosen to say about the institution at different periods of its history. Having worked at Chester from 1977 until retirement in 2010, I have also found it a salutary experience to produce an account of episodes in which I was an active participant; I am very conscious that many friends and colleagues with whom I shared recent decades will have their 'own histories' of these years which are bound to differ to some extent from mine. Whether or not they agree with what I have written, I do wish to record my gratitude to those among their number who have taken an interest in the project and have offered encouragement, advice and information. They include Ruth Ackroyd, Ned Binks, John Carhart, Brenda Davies, Rob Dawson, Loretta Dolan, Judith Done, Tom Driver, Karen Fisher, Neville Ford, John Fowler, Peter Gallagher, Pauline Harrison, Chris Haslam, Bill Hughes, Caroline Jackman, Peter Jenner,

Margaret Lacey, Christine Lynas, Jenny Mann, Dorothy Marriss, Brian McDermott, Keith McLay, Lesley Needham, Eve Nelson, David Perrin, Arthur Poulton, Pat Ransome, Malcolm Rhodes, Kath Roberts, Sarah Steele, David Stevens, Jo Sykes, Bob Taylor, Maggie Taylor, Colin Taylerson, Miranda Thurston, Glyn Turton, Chris Walsh and Tim Wheeler. Special thanks are due to Tim Grady and to Ian and Diana Dunn for kindly reading virtually the whole of the book in draft form and for offering invaluable comments. All were carefully considered, and the book would have been a better one had I been able to act on them all. As Honorary University Archivist, Diana Dunn has also been most helpful in advising on the availability and location of some of the sources I am also grateful to the excellent staff of Cheshire Archives and Local Studies for so patiently accommodating my requests for material – duly wheeled out on my own special trolley – while I was researching the book. Images referenced by the prefix CALS are reproduced by permission of Cheshire Archives and Local Studies. Mark English of the University's Learning & Information Services (LIS) also took several of the photographs, Matthew Houghton from the LIS Graphics team designed the cover and they and the staff of the University's Corporate Communications Services have been unfailingly supportive while the book has been in preparation; I must thank above all Sarah Griffiths, Managing Editor of the University Press, and Fiona Roberts, Alumni and Development Manager, for their guidance and companionship in seeing this through so efficiently.

When I embarked upon this book I was determined to depart from the practice of previous historians who have covered this ground, with their tendency to devote a chapter to each Principal in turn. I felt that this was liable to give undue weight to the contributions made by the men at the top, at the expense of the staff and student body as a whole. It will be readily apparent that I have only partially succeeded in fulfilling this ambition. Among the Principals, the first one and the last two made such a distinctive input to the institution's history that it seemed only logical to give them separate chapters. There is also no doubt that the historian who relies heavily for the basic story on management minute books will encounter the Principal of the day more often than anyone else! But I have tried to reflect the everyday lives of students and staff, both academic and support, and to mark the achievements of a representative sample of them. Much else could have been included, and if what I have written leads to others researching in depth episodes only touched upon here, I would be delighted. Inevitably, in the selection of material, some people have been mentioned by name while the great majority, including many who were equally deserving, have not. It is to the students, staff, governors and others whose contribution to Chester College and the

University of Chester over the past 175 years has *not* been recorded in the pages which follow that this book is dedicated.

Graeme J. White
25 January 2014

---

1   *The Times and Sunday Times Good University Guide 2014* (Glasgow, 2013), p. 366.
2   *The Ecclesiastical History of Orderic Vitalis*, VI, ed. M. Chibnall (Oxford, 1978), pp. 550–51.

ABBREVIATIONS

Bradbury, *Chester College*: J.L. Bradbury, *Chester College and the Training of Teachers* (Chester, 1975).

Dunn, *Bright Star*: I. Dunn, *The University of Chester 1839–2012: The Bright Star in the Present Prospect* (Chester, 2012).

HEQ: Higher Education Quarterly.

VCH: Victoria County History.

White, *Perspectives*: G.J. White, ed., *Perspectives of Chester College, 150th Anniversary Essays, 1839–1989* (Chester, 1989).

The College and University archives are referenced by the prefix ZCR if in the custody of Cheshire Archives & Local Studies (CALS), Duke Street, Chester and by the prefixes CC or UC if, at the time of writing, it was still in the custody of the institution. CC or UC reflects its status – College or University – at the time the document was produced.

INNOVATION, 1839–85

CHAPTER 1

THE FOUNDATION AND RE-FOUNDATION
OF CHESTER COLLEGE

On 8 December 1885, Revd John Martin Chritchley, Principal of the teacher training college which would eventually grow to become the University of Chester, sat down to write his annual report to the Governing Body. He had tendered his resignation in a brief letter of 17 October, having been offered the rectory of Long Newton, County Durham, and this would be the last such report he would write. So after the customary account of the year just past, he took the opportunity to reflect on all that had been achieved since his appointment in May 1869.

Chritchley made it abundantly clear that, in his view, Chester College's continuous history really began, not with the formal foundation in 1839 but with his own promotion to Principal 30 years later. 'Upon the resignation of my predecessor, Mr Rigg, the Training College was practically dead.' The science school attached to the College was 'dying' but the governors, thinking it could still be rescued, advertised for 'a Principal for the Science School only, making no mention of the Training College'. Although teacher training was 'the chief object for which the college was built' it had been decided 'that life could not again be put into it.' However Chritchley, Vice-Principal for the past five years, had other ideas. 'Upon my appointment … I expressed the strong conviction that … under careful management it would certainly recover. I was allowed to try my hand upon its resurrection and with what result we have abundant evidence today.'[1] There is no reason to doubt the accuracy of Chritchley's version of events. The Diocesan Board of Education had decided to close down the College at Christmas 1869, and had Chritchley not convinced the members that he was worth a chance, this would have been the end of Chester's training college. He therefore deserves as much recognition as any of the luminaries still remembered as the institution's founders today.

In effect, the events of 1869 marked the re-foundation of Chester College. As Chritchley explained in his report, 'the College had fallen into such disrepute that no one would enter it as a student, although candidates were flocking to, and crowding other colleges'. 'No one' was a slight exaggeration: there had in fact been one applicant but he had failed the entrance exam![2] Chritchley invited former students to a reunion in order to drum up support and by February 1870 had managed to recruit 21 entrants; a year later he admitted a further 37, bringing the total (after drop-out) to 53.[3] A public meeting was held in Chester Town Hall on 27 September 1870, with the Lord Lieutenant of the county, Lord Egerton of Tatton, in the chair and several MPs and senior clergy in attendance. It featured keynote speeches from the new Bishop of Manchester, James Fraser, a keen advocate of mass elementary education, and from the now-ageing but highly respected educational pioneer Sir James Kay-Shuttleworth, who stressed the importance of partnership in this field between Church and State. There was much reference to the previous gathering at Warrington in 1839 which had led to the original foundation of the College: the treasurer of the Diocesan Board, Richard Cross, told the assembly that 'I look upon this meeting as a renewal of the meeting at Warrington' while Bishop Fraser lamented that the attendance 'shrinks into very small proportions compared with the great meeting at Warrington' 31 years before. Nevertheless, in the published report of proceedings at Chester Town Hall, some 80 people are listed as present, apart from the platform party, and although Bradbury describes them as 'less influential' than their forebears of 1839 they still counted some distinguished figures among them: none more so than Cross, Conservative MP for south-west Lancashire, who would go on to be one of the great reforming home secretaries of Victorian Britain and would later chair an influential royal commission on elementary education.[4]

The Town Hall meeting was intended to increase support – especially financial support – for the work of the Diocesan Board of Education and embraced the needs of Church schools as well as its two training colleges, one at Chester for men and another, larger, college for women at Warrington. There was a particular focus on the challenges and opportunities presented by the passing earlier in the year of the Forster Education Act, designed to make elementary education accessible to every child through provision for rate-aided non-denominational Board Schools wherever the religious bodies could not fully meet demand; the colleges were seen as essential means to ensure that Church-trained teachers continued to find their way into the schools, including those which were not Church foundations. However, whereas the Warrington college, founded in 1844, had 'prospered exceedingly', it was acknowledged that Chester had had a more chequered history. 'I am afraid that the college at Chester has rather fallen off … the enthusiasm, as is often the case, died out to some extent' declared Lord Egerton from the chair. It had 'experienced some vicissitudes' and had 'sustained a brief and transient eclipse' admitted the Bishop of Chester, while doing his best to accentuate the positive. But everyone agreed that the changing context of elementary education made this the ideal time for

Chester College to 'start again' and that, under Chritchley, it had done so to good effect.[5] For their part, the Governing Body's minutes encapsulate the sense of a new beginning. The first surviving book, commencing in 1854, petered out in 1867 with plenty of blank pages towards the end which were never filled. A new book opened on 8 December 1871, calling itself on the front cover 'Minute Book, Chester Training College, vol. I'. In October 1872, it duly recorded the congratulations of Her Majesty's Inspector (HMI) on 'the complete recovery of the College'.[6]

So although the 30-year period from 1839 has received a great deal of attention in previous accounts of Chester College,[7] it represented in a sense the pre-history of the institution. It is the College as resurrected in 1869, with a clear sense of the part it should play within a largely government-funded educational system, which may reasonably be regarded as the forerunner of the University of today. This is not, of course, to underplay the significance of what had gone before: the College of 1839–69 was a truly pioneering and innovative establishment. But as the next chapter will seek to explain, its unusual, distinctive character made it ill-equipped to survive in the long term, in a context where the requirements of the government became ever more clearly defined. Since 1869, the capacity of the institution to adapt to changing political and economic demands – retaining but reinterpreting its core values – has been one of the key factors in its survival and success.

Chester College had originally come into being at the close of that great reforming decade, the 1830s. This was a time when elementary education for the masses was still patchily provided and a matter of some controversy, although by now there was widespread recognition that a measure of 'education for the poor' was less dangerous to social stability than offering nothing at all. It was also a time when, in practice, such education as was systematically available was almost entirely in the hands of the Anglican and Nonconformist churches, for whom – respectively – the National Society and the British and Foreign School Society had been established as promoting and co-ordinating bodies in the early years of the century. There was, furthermore, growing acceptance in reforming circles that the position of schoolteacher needed to be professionalised if schools were to become effective agents for the good of society.[8] An HMI Report on elementary Church schools in Lancashire, Cheshire and Derbyshire published in 1841 – just as Chester College was getting under way – found that most teachers were neat, kind and well-meaning (contrary to what is often said about posts being held by unsavoury characters unfit for any other occupation) but only the minority who had received some form of training could bring out the potential in their children.[9]

Back in 1700, when the principles behind elementary education were still provoking outright hostility, the city of Chester had become the first place outside London to have a school affiliated to the Society for Promoting Christian Knowledge. As the Blue Coat School, it was to have a new building provided for it in Northgate Street in 1714 and would survive until 1949, after which the premises were leased to a variety of tenants, among them through the 1990s and 2000s the College and University itself. Now, in the early years of Queen Victoria's reign, the city would again prove to be an educational pioneer. It was not the first cathedral town or city to establish a Diocesan Board of Education to further the work of the National Society: several dioceses already had them by the time Chester's was founded at a meeting in the Cathedral chapter house on 8 January 1839. However, the new Board immediately proceeded to convene a public meeting at Warrington, chosen because of its ready accessibility from all parts of a diocese of two million people embracing the whole of Lancashire and Cheshire plus parts of Cumberland, Westmorland and North Wales. This was to be held on 25 January 1839, the hope being 'that a seminary will be instituted for the education of Masters, where their minds will be stored with sufficient knowledge, and their habits and dispositions so trained as to qualify them for teaching properly'.[10]

Figure 1: The Blue Coat School, viewed from Chester's city walls.

At the time, there were only three similar institutions in England, all based in London: the training schools of the National Society and the British and Foreign Society at Westminster and at Borough Road, Southwark, respectively, and the Home and Colonial College on the Gray's Inn Road, another Anglican foundation specialising in the preparation of infant teachers. So the decision at Warrington on 25 January to 'establish at Chester a seminary for the training of masters' was a momentous, groundbreaking, event.[11] Other training colleges soon came along, including three in London: Kay-Shuttleworth himself founded an influential one at Battersea, opened in February 1840, and, stimulated by a fresh government grant for the purpose, the National Society proceeded the following year to establish similar institutions for men at Chelsea and for women at Whitelands. Several other foundations came into being around the country, mostly Anglican diocesan initiatives like Chester, so that by 1858 over 2,000 male or female students were attending some 33 such colleges in England. Among them was the sister diocesan college for schoolmistresses at Warrington, which after various changes of site is now a component of Liverpool Hope University.[12] For comparison, by the beginning of Victoria's reign, France already had 75 similar institutions, Prussia over 100.[13]

The College had originally opened with ten students in temporary premises (now demolished) in Nicholas Street on 1 February 1840, moving in October to Bridge House (later the Oddfellows Hall) in Lower Bridge Street while the earlier property was retained as student accommodation.[14] It would eventually settle into the first buildings in England specifically designed for the training of teachers, opened on 1 September 1842 on a one-acre greenfield site at the junction of Parkgate Road and Chain Lane (now Cheyney Road) about a third of a mile north of the city walls, given by the Dean and Chapter of the Cathedral. The Diocesan Board of Education had initially favoured a more central location near the Cathedral or St John's Church, and latterly a site (close to the one eventually chosen) between the Parkgate and Liverpool Roads; this would have given the College a prominent, elevated position at the gateway to Wirral. However, it was happy to accept a free gift of land, especially since the construction and fitting out of the building itself cost over £10,000, some £2,500 of which came from a government grant but most from public subscription within the diocese itself. The acquisition in 1843 of a field immediately to the west, further along what is now Cheyney Road, offered a recreational area and the prospect of future expansion; the building could be advertised as 'in an open and airy situation a short distance from Chester' with 'spacious grounds'.[15]

The site was welcome but not in every respects ideal, since it had a significant slope, with the land falling away to north and west. The discerning eye can perceive even today that the sides of Senate House facing Cheyney Road and Parkgate Road are on slightly higher ground than the other two sides and the issue became of considerable importance in subsequent decades once the College expanded over neighbouring fields towards the canal to the west and the railway line to the north. A series of levelling operations, culminating in a large landfill scheme in the far north-west of the campus in the early 1990s, have disguised these slopes, although their original extent is apparent from the gradients of the two roads which border the campus, from the level of the houses opposite the College beyond the canal and from the flights of steps which punctuate the campus at various points.[16] It is salutary to reflect, however, that had one of the preferred sites been made available, closer to the city centre or in the wedge between the roads leading towards the two sides of Wirral, there would have been limited room for future expansion. At some stage the College would either have had to move elsewhere or would have been closed as too small to be an economic proposition.

The sheer eminence of the six men generally regarded as the 'founders' of the College – and still commemorated as such in the Founders' Prayer – has often been remarked upon.[17] The diocese of Chester in the 1830s was blessed with a group of enlightened senior clergy fiercely committed to the spread of elementary education, none more so than the Bishop and first President of the Diocesan Board of Education, John Bird Sumner – who left Chester in 1848 to become Archbishop of Canterbury – and his good friend the diocesan chancellor, Henry Raikes. By any standards, Sumner must be regarded as one of the greatest of all Bishops of Chester, a liberal-minded supporter of Catholic emancipation and parliamentary reform (despite much local opposition), who achieved a revival in Anglican worship within his diocese through a vigorous church-building programme alongside campaigns to raise the quality of the clergy and promote lay visiting. In his 19 years as Bishop of Chester, he consecrated no less than 233 new churches and oversaw the building of 671 new church day schools.[18] Along with the rector of Warrington and secretary of the Diocesan Board, Horatio Powys, and the vicar of Bolton, James Slade, Sumner and Raikes were key participants in the foundation meeting at Warrington, where the decision to set up a training college was an expression of their shared conviction that the promotion of learning was a Christian duty.[19] They secured the support of two rising local politicians, both destined to be Prime Minister several times in later life: Edward Lord Stanley of Knowsley Hall, the future 14th Earl of Derby, who proposed the motion at Warrington to found the College in Chester, and William Ewart Gladstone of Hawarden Castle, who – though absent on that occasion – made the principal speech at the ceremonial opening of the College on 1 September 1842 and handed over the keys to the first Principal, Revd Arthur Rigg.

The proceedings on the day of the opening had begun with a service at the Cathedral at which Slade had preached on the text from Luke, chapter 6, verse 39: 'Shall the blind lead the blind?' Slade was a good choice since his 39 years as vicar of Bolton were notable for his hands-on encouragement of working-class education, largely through the promotion of Sunday Schools; his sermons also had a fine reputation and he held the post of king's preacher for the county of Lancaster. His sermon so impressed Gladstone as a justification for the Church's promotion of elementary education, and in particular the training of teachers, that it was subsequently published at his request. For Slade, 'the office of instructor of youth is next in dignity and importance to the clerical office itself' and it was crucial that teachers should be exemplars of Christian morality:

> If it be generally true that more has been learned from example than from precept, it is especially true with regard to children, who possess an extraordinary acuteness in detecting the inconsistencies of a teacher, and when they perceive that he disbelieves his own profession, falsifies his own assertions, departs from his own rules, respect for this teaching is utterly at an end; there may be a verbal acquirement of knowledge, an outward obedience, a cold constraint, but there will be no living impression, no drawing of the soul to God, no formation of Christian principle and Christian character.

It was the purpose of the College to be a 'Christian seminary', and in the published version of the sermon he cited glowing testimonials from the employers of the pioneer students trained since 1840 to demonstrate that it was indeed fulfilling this objective.[20] In today's secularised society, Slade's ideal of the teacher as role model, an example to children of how to behave, lives on in the 'Teachers' Standards' against which they are all appraised: 'demonstrate consistently the positive attitudes, values and behaviour which are expected of pupils'.[21]

However, the printed sermon also contains a footnote in which Slade alludes to 'unfavourable opinions which have been formed respecting this Institution'. He did not elaborate, other than to add that the objections seemed to him 'to be generally founded in misapprehension and error' and would fade away once the real purpose of the College became better known. Whatever the precise nature of the criticisms, these comments are a reminder that the foundation of Chester College was a controversial initiative. There was current political debate about the extent to which the Church rather than the State should lead the way in teacher training and it was therefore very helpful to have on board both Stanley and Gladstone, who though from different persuasions and traditions shared a genuine commitment to the cause of Christian elementary education. In later life, Rigg recalled that his first official act as Principal 'was to meet in private conference a body of Gentlemen interested in the work' among whom 'none were more active than the late Earl of Derby', while 'for many years Mr Gladstone regularly paid an Exhibition for a resident student'.[22] All the signs are that the founders were well pleased with their creation. By 1844, Bishop Sumner was calling it 'one of the bright stars in the present prospect'.[23]

---

1   ZCR 86/12/32: Principal's Annual Report for 1885.

2   ZCR 86/12/22: *Report of a Public Meeting held in the Town Hall of Chester on Tuesday 27 September 1870* (reprinted from the *Chester Guardian*, 1870), p. 46 (Dean of Chester's speech); *First Report of the Chester Diocesan Board of Education for year ending December 1870*, p. 8.

3   ZCR 86/12/21: *Report of the Chester and Manchester Diocesan Board of Education for the year ending December 1869*, p. 5; ZCR 86/12/22: *First Report of the Chester Diocesan Board … 1870*, p. 8; Bradbury, *Chester College*, pp. 144–45.

4   ZCR 86/12/22: *Report of a Public Meeting*, esp. pp. 16, 24–30, 33; Bradbury, *Chester College*, p. 142; *Oxford Dictionary of National Biography*, XIV, pp. 432–34. Ironically, Cross had become MP for south-west Lancashire by defeating another champion of Chester College, none other than W.E. Gladstone, in the general election of 1868; the latter had also stood for Greenwich and it was his success there that had enabled him to become Prime Minister.

5   ZCR 86/12/22: *Report of a Public Meeting*, esp. pp. 6–8, 46; Bradbury, *Chester College*, p. 143.

6   ZCR 86/1/2: 14 October 1872.

7   Esp. Bradbury, *Chester College*, pp. 17–139 (a book of 255 pages in total).

8   M.A. Larsen, *The Making and Shaping of the Victorian Teacher* (London, 2011), pp. 53–73.

9   *Minutes of the Committee of Council on Education, 1840–41* (London, 1841), pp. 312–21.

10 Bradbury, *Chester College*, p. 48; *VCH Cheshire*, III, pp. 63–64.

11 ZCR 86/12/1: *Verbatim Report of the Great Diocesan Meeting at Warrington, 1839*; Bradbury, *Chester College*, pp. 50–55.

12 J.E. Hollinshead, ed., *S. Katharine's College, Liverpool Institute of Higher Education: In Thy Light, 1844–1994* (Liverpool, 1994).

13 Larsen, *Victorian Teacher*, pp. 133, 155–56 n. 1; R.W. Rich, *The Training of Teachers in England and Wales during the Nineteenth Century* (Cambridge, 1933), pp. 55–81.

14 For details of these locations, see Dunn, *Bright Star*, p. 10.

15 Hargreaves, 'Chester College – Site and Setting' in White, *Perspectives*, pp. 19–28, at p. 19; ZCR 86/15/1: file of newspaper cuttings, 1842–43.

16 Cf. *Geodiversity Trail: Walking through the Past on the University's Chester Campus* (Chester, 2007), esp. pp. 5–6.

17 See esp. Bradbury, *Chester College*, pp. 23–28, 32–38; Dunn, *Bright Star*, pp. 3–7.

18 *VCH Cheshire*, III, pp. 63–67; *Oxford Dictionary of National Biography*, LIII, pp. 330–33.

19 For biographies of Powys, Raikes and Slade, see *Oxford Dictionary of National Biography*, XLV, pp. 169, 800, L, pp. 897–98. Raikes was the nephew of the founder of the national Sunday School movement, Robert Raikes; Powys went on to become Bishop of Sodor and Man.

20 ZCR 86/12/4: *A Sermon preached in Chester Cathedral on the Opening of the Training College, September 1st 1842* by Rev. Canon Slade.

21 Department for Education: Teachers' Standards, Part One, section 1, bullet-point 3 (<<https://www.gov.uk/government/publications/teachers-standards>>, accessed 22/1/14).

22 ZCR 86/13/4: letter of Rigg, 30 March 1870.

23 Bradbury, *Chester College*, p. 49.

CHAPTER 2

THE RIGG REGIME

The original College buildings – described as a 'model' for institutions of its type by HMI Moseley in 1844 – were designed by J. and G. Buckler of London in a symmetrical 'Elizabethan' style which, despite additions and alterations, is still evident in the early twenty-first century. Their orientation, however, was different to the one familiar today. Although students could gain access from Cheyney Road, a lithograph of the College of c.1847 presents the eastern wing as the principal, most impressive façade, with an entrance above steps from Parkgate Road, one of the arteries leading into and out of the city (see Plate 1). This remained as a formal entrance to the College until the early 1960s. Within this wing, at ground floor level there was originally a dining room, kitchen, scullery and accommodation for a steward. The Principal's house was at the opposite end of the building, occupying the western wing with views of North Wales. The range between the two, which now faces pedestrians approaching from Chester city centre, housed on the ground floor the 'School for Training Masters' towards the west and a 'Commercial and Agricultural School', with separate access, towards the east. From the middle of this range a 'library and museum' protruded south – in an area behind the Cheyney Road entrance which was added in the 1960s – while a gallery of tiered seating for additional teaching space projected north into what is now the 'Prairie' courtyard. The upper storeys of this range were largely given over to dormitories for the trainee masters at one end and the pupils of the commercial school at the other.[1]

The symmetry was broken in 1844 by the provision of an L-shaped elementary school, taking in day pupils from the city and its immediate vicinity, so that the prospective schoolmasters could practise their teaching;. This had initially been housed in the basement of the College building but the new school was located beyond its north-east corner, abutting on to the eastern wing and with an end-wall overlooking Parkgate Road. Symmetry was broken again three years later when the Chapel was completed at the south-east corner, although when viewed from Parkgate Road these two additions matched reasonably well. The Chapel was funded mainly from donations and was largely built and fitted out by the students and commercial school pupils as an exercise in craftsmanship. Among the donations were specially made decorative, encaustic 'Minton tiles', in which the Burslem firm of that name were only then beginning to specialise. Another gift was the service of the Manchester architect, John Edgar Gregan, who produced his designs free of charge. The stone was quarried from the area immediately south of the Chapel – since infilled as a small garden abutting on to the Cheyney Road corner – and within a few years it had been given a romantic appearance through the planting of ivy, using seeds said to have come from Conwy Castle.[2] The ivy has long gone, but the Chapel remains the only part of the 1840s College structure still fulfilling its original purpose.

Initially, therefore, the College was three institutions in one: a 'training school' for future schoolmasters, an elementary 'model' school where they could practise, and a fee-paying boarding school (the 'Commercial and Agricultural School') which opened in January 1843 to teach boys of eight to 15 years of age a range of subjects from English, Maths, History and Geography to Music, 'Agricultural Chemistry' and Foreign Languages. At the outset in 1842 the intended numbers were 50 teacher trainees, 70 'commercial scholars' and 110 boys in the 'model school'. The presence of the boarding school was not in itself remarkable, since, as explained in a statement which

accompanied the invitation to the Warrington meeting of 1839, 'the institution of Middle Schools … for the education of farmers, tradesmen, and others of that class' was one of the objectives of those establishing Diocesan Boards about that time. In the following year, the National Society reported several similar 'commercial schools', actual or proposed, where middle-class pupils could be given an advanced education, in the cathedral cities of Canterbury, Lichfield, Lincoln and elsewhere.[3]

At Chester, however, the first Principal, Revd Arthur Rigg, a Cambridge Mathematics graduate who had latterly been Senior Mathematical and Philosophical Master at the Royal

Figure 2: The Chapel, completed in 1847 and largely built by the students. Among all the University's older buildings, it is the only one to have retained its original function with a virtually unbroken history, including use by those who occupied the College during periods of closure during the two World Wars.

Institution School in Liverpool, showed an exceptional commitment to the boarding school. By the 1850s it had gained a national reputation as a 'Science College', attracting tutors of the calibre of William Crookes, destined to become (as Sir William) President of the Royal Society, and being provided with a new, specially built, laboratory, later reckoned to be superior to any other outside London University.[4] The curriculum was much wider than this, however, and pupils came from country houses, rectories and upmarket urban addresses across England, Wales and Ireland[5] to an institution advertised as preparing its pupils for Natural Science scholarships at Oxford and Cambridge, for examinations to enter the Civil Service and the Public Works Department in India, and for University of London matriculation which was taken as a qualification for legal, medical or military training. As an example, one of the earliest pupils, Percy Westmacott, went on to a distinguished career in mechanical engineering on Tyneside and eventually became President of the Institution of Mechanical Engineers. Luke Fildes, who was at the school in the 1850s, became an eminent painter and illustrator, knighted in 1906 having painted the coronation portraits of King Edward VII and Queen Alexandra.[6]

Training college and science school were seen as complementary: though taught and accommodated separately, the students and the schoolboys ate simultaneously in the dining room and shared specialist facilities, such as the laboratory and an open-air gymnasium which both appear on a later plan of 1874 occupying the area now known as the 'Prairie'.[7] In 1851 they all went together to visit the Great Exhibition when the Archbishop of Canterbury – as Chester's former Bishop Sumner had now become – put them up for the night in Lambeth Palace. The two enterprises supported one another financially – with the science school often bringing a handsome income to the Diocesan Board of Education – but to some extent they also competed for the same resources. In December 1854 the Governing Body expressed concern that if the full number of funded teacher trainees turned up, it would be necessary to reduce numbers in the 'Scientific School'; six years later, with enrolments at 56 to 33 in the training college's favour, Rigg asked the governors 'that the [science] school should be more generally made known'.[8] Worthy though these different initiatives were, their co-existence made the first three decades of the College's history a period of uncertain mission and purpose.

The absence of minutes before 1854 – by which time the new diocese of Manchester, created out of Chester in 1847, had its own representation on the committee governing the College – makes it difficult to piece together a coherent story of the early years. The first recorded meeting in December 1854 lamented the death of the Honorary Secretary – Chester's diocesan

Chancellor, Raikes – and took the opportunity to revise the arrangements for the keeping of minutes, authorising the purchase of new books so that the affairs of Chester and its sister college at Warrington could be recorded separately.[9] Raikes was a keen historian who helped to found what is now known as Chester Archaeological Society in 1849,[10] but whatever minutes he took, he failed to ensure their long-term survival. However, we do know the names of some of the early staff, including the 'Principal's assistant' Revd G. Kingsford, in place by the time of the opening in September 1842, a steward called Sandfield appointed two months later, a master in the commercial school, James Peel Holliday, who was drowned in the River Dee in September 1844, and Randel Greenhalgh, student 1847–48 and staff member 1850–56, who is credited with planting the Chapel ivy.[11] It is also clear that from the outset there was flexibility in the length of time students spent at the College – though generally between one year and three – and considerable variability in what was seen as appropriate training from one institution to another: Battersea College, for example, was heavily influenced by the Swiss educationist Pestalozzi, while St Mark's Chelsea sought to introduce its students to high culture, through compulsory Latin and elaborate sung services in Chapel.[12] We are informed by a report from HMI Moseley in 1844[13] that the pioneer Chester students rose on weekdays at 5.00 a.m. in the summer and 6.45 a.m. in the winter, with 'studies' occupying six and a half hours a day, prayers at 7.00 a.m. and 8.30 p.m., three meals, about three and a half hours at intervals for 'industrial occupations', private reading and exercise, then bed at 9.00 p.m.; sabbaths were largely given over to organised worship and Sunday school. The curriculum that year, much of it delivered by Rigg in person or by his Vice-Principal – too narrow a tutorial base compared to other colleges in the view of HMI[14] – was dominated by various branches of Mathematics and by the theory and practice of teaching, but did include Reading, Writing, Grammar, History, Geography, Natural and Experimental Philosophy, Drawing, Vocal Music and Bookbinding, alongside Scripture and other Church-related subjects: even the 'industrial occupations' gave way to Psalmody if the weather was bad.

For Rigg, the industrial activity – which he had started in an empty stable in the back garden of Bridge House in 1840 and which by 1844 included various aspects of woodwork, metalwork, masonry and soil-shifting – was a means of providing the technical education which he saw as vital to the country's future prosperity. Both the training college students and the boys in the boarding school engaged in this work. Wearing a leather apron and wielding a hammer, the Principal led by example; the construction of the Chapel was an ideal project on which to focus attention, but his charges also built a steam engine, fashioned tools for their own use and for sale to the public, and mixed chemical compounds for the science laboratory. HMI Moseley never quite made up his mind about the merits of all this. He was initially impressed and observed that students enjoyed the work but by 1845 was expressing reservations about whether they were being deprived of 'healthful recreation'; he also questioned whether the manual labour – by inculcating 'an asperity of manner, an independent bearing and a rude deportment' – was appropriate for aspiring professionals who would have to work with local clergy in Church schools. The activities at Chester, he reported, suggested 'a theory of the schoolmaster diametrically opposed to that on which the system of every other training college with which I am acquainted is found'. Yet he had to accept that the students were fine specimens of manhood who seemed to be thriving on all this physical exertion: as he wrote in 1848, 'they are generally robust and athletic men, four of whom would, I should think, weigh as much as five at Battersea and six at [Chelsea].' And in 1851 he fully acknowledged the benefits of 'the active scene of industry which the workshops present – admirably organised and managed as is that part of the institution', evident from the fact that 'no expense whatever has been incurred during the last year for medical attendance'. No other men's college in the country that year had a clean bill of health![15]

It was the norm for training colleges at this time to keep their students busy with domestic chores like cleaning and cooking; those at Battersea College even built a Chinese pagoda, while at Saltley (Birmingham) they laid out a botanical garden.[16] But Chester outshone all others in the fulfilment which came with craftsmanship and creativity. Twenty-first century universities strive for 'distinctiveness' but early-Victorian Chester College had plenty already. The writer Thomas Hughes – best-known for *Tom Brown's Schooldays* – thought it worth highlighting in his *Stranger's Handbook to Chester* of 1856 that 'in addition to the ordinary details of scholastic training, the students are instructed in various branches of manual labour; they are taught how "to handle the chisel and the saw, the mattock and the spade"'.[17] Rigg might also have argued, with justification, that his 'hands-on' approach was an excellent way of preparing for some of the exams set nationally for training college students by the government's Committee of Council on Education, even though from 1854 they were supposed to follow a common syllabus. At Christmas 1855, for example, the first-year Mechanics paper asked for 'the point at which the steam should be cut off', 'the length of the stroke in an engine being 15 feet, the pressure of the steam 45 lbs, and the resistance of the vapour in the condenser together with the friction of the engine being 5 lbs per square inch of the piston'. The second-year Physical Science paper had the question: 'What is meant by convection, conduction, radiation and reflection of heat? Give instances of each.'[18] Even in the narrow range of compulsory subjects Chester's students do not seem to have suffered, and may even have benefited, from being made to solve practical problems as they went about their workshop crafts. Moseley criticised their 'low standard of attainment' in the Christmas 1851 exams but may have been unduly influenced by an appalling record in English Grammar where not a single student that year managed an 'excellent, good or fair' grade; the rest of the evidence he cited does not support his contention. Chester's results in Arithmetic, for which Rigg's activities would have afforded plenty of practice, were the best of all the seven Church training colleges for men in England and Wales. The same was true, on one interpretation of the figures, of School Management, where students were expected to answer questions about different methods of organising elementary schools ('State which … you yourself prefer and the reasons for that preference') and the relationship between home and school ('What reasonable ground is there for confidence in a good school education even if it be counteracted by the education of the home?')[19] On this evidence, the Chester men, though ignorant of the difference between an adverb and a preposition, were above-average nationally when it came to advancing an independent argument.

Given the merits of Rigg's unusual approach, it is perhaps regrettable that he was so wedded to the College motto he proudly showed a visitor in 1850. 'The principle on which we act here', he explained, was summed up in the words 'without noise, without bustle, without fame'.[20] Had he been as committed to proclaiming the values of the Chester training experience as he clearly was to the promotion of the science school, the early College might have featured more prominently in standard accounts of Victorian teacher education. As we have seen, the students of the 1840s and 1850s appear to have adjusted to the regime very well. This is certainly the conclusion to be drawn from the surviving papers of one of the earliest of them, Peter Calvert from Bury, which reveal a well-rounded individual with apparent enthusiasm for what was expected of him. Calvert, who like his fellow-students sat six three-hour exams and also what we would now call a *viva voce* as part of Moseley's 1844 visit, describes a life of gowns and caps 'of cloth of a blueish-black colour', of 'lines' being set for unpunctuality, and of dimly lit dormitories with partitions between each bed which reached to about a yard below the ceiling. But while the notes he took on pedagogy read like a series of 'tips for teachers', they do show an appreciation of the importance of making lessons stimulating: 'to render the subject really interesting there must be at least an effort on the part of the teacher to infuse life into it'; 'single out the most careless boy for the next question … ask him the same question as you have just got answered – and see if he has heard it'. Marbles were seen as a good vehicle for teaching Arithmetic, since their different colours could stand for different values. Calvert, the son of a whitesmith, went on to teach at Church schools at Warrington and Winwick for more than 25 years, became a pillar of his community as assistant overseer of the poor and local antiquarian, and ended his working life as an accountant and estate agent: an excellent example of the 'self-improvement' which institutions such as Chester College could foster.[21] And the experience was clearly valued: early September reunions of former students were already popular by 1854.[22]

In being drawn from within the diocese of Chester and going on to employment within the diocese as well, Calvert was typical of the students of the nineteenth century, although there were always exceptions. In 1855, for example, those completing their courses went to schools in Brymbo, Ripponden, Cirencester, Whitehaven and Etruria as well as to places in Lancashire and Cheshire.[23] By then, under a scheme introduced in 1846, a growing number of teacher trainees had already served a five-year apprenticeship as pupil-teachers in their elementary schools between the ages of 13 and 18, before embarking on a college course of one to three years (typically two), many having passed an exam to become a Queen's Scholar with eligibility for a government grant. They had much better career prospects than those pupil-teachers who never went on to college, and who could therefore never rise above the rank of 'assistant teacher' unless they managed in their own time to pass the same exams as those set for college students. By 1859, the incentives offered by the Committee of Council on Education meant that about 85% of college students nationally were Queen's Scholars, mostly taking two-year courses.[24] Accordingly, there was sufficient confidence at Chester to be more selective in student recruitment, through a deliberate policy of seeking to fill allocated numbers with the better performers in the Queen's Scholarships exams, 'so that the next year's students may be above rather than below the average'. Indeed, by March 1860 it was being reported that 'the new Queen's Scholars are superior in character and intelligence to their predecessors'.[25] Meanwhile, in 1856, the governors had sanctioned the purchase for £1,000 from the Ecclesiastical Commissioners of a further seven and a quarter acres to the north and west of the College, with one of Joseph Paxton's leading assistants subsequently being brought in to landscape the grounds with gardens, walkways, plantations and an embankment to separate the Principal's house from the terrace below.[26]

Within a few years, all this optimism had evaporated. Growing parliamentary concern that expenditure on elementary education was spiralling out of control led to the establishment of the Newcastle Commission in 1858. Its recommendations three years later were followed by the Revised Code for Education of 1862. The Code is best known for making public expenditure on elementary schooling accountable through 'payment by results' on the basis of tests conducted by HMIs, but it also had a direct bearing on training for the teaching profession. State remuneration of pupil-teachers was withdrawn and Queen's Scholarships were replaced by a less generous scheme, all of which led to a sharp reduction in the numbers applying to teacher training colleges as a whole. Whereas 542 pupil-teachers were admitted to the colleges in England and Wales in 1863, by 1867 the figure was down to 224. The effects of the Revised Code were exacerbated by an accompanying decision to limit the range of grant-earning subjects in the colleges, excluding those not strictly necessary for elementary schoolteachers and severely curtailing the syllabus of the remainder. Among those subjects which had their grants withdrawn or drastically reduced were several dear to Rigg's heart – Higher Mathematics, Algebra, Mechanics, Physical Science – which made way for the repetition from memory of poetry and prose and 'elementary questions in sanitary and other practical science of common application, and in political economy'.[27]

The 57 students in the training college in June 1860 fell to 39 by the end of 1862, 19 by the close of 1865, five by the middle of 1867 – a faster rate than the national decline[28] – while Rigg, deprived by the grant system of the subjects he loved and of the freedom to shape the College in his own image, showed little inclination to battle against the trend. Instead, he devoted the best of himself to the science school, which increased its numbers from 36 in 1862 to 54 in 1866, and – along with the practising school which also remained popular despite the lack of trainees – offered the prospect of the institution and its buildings surviving in some guise even if the training college collapsed. In 1867, the science school was still yielding a handsome profit, when the training college was down to two tutors (plus the Principal), five students and two servants.[29]

A further threat to the College came in the mid-1860s when, with the Ecclesiastical Commissioners selling off its land in the vicinity – hence the spread of the Garden Lane/Bouverie Street suburb between the College and the city walls around this time – a speculator bought land on the west side of Parkgate Road immediately to the north of the College site with the intention of building houses for the well-to-do in a development to be known as 'Exton Park'. The long narrow access to the University campus from Parkgate Road has its origins in the roadway created into Exton Park, with Rutland Villa (now the Porters' Lodge) built to control the entrance in 1865. Had this development proceeded much further, it would have severely curtailed the College's opportunities for further growth.[30] But dealing with this was not an immediate priority. In 1862 Rigg reported to the governors with pride on the fact that science school pupils had secured three of the ten places available nationally for entry to the Engineering Department in India. Five years later, he was unable to tell the current HMI whether any of the most recent outgoing teacher trainees had found employment.[31]

Despite the enduring appeal of the science school, Rigg's disillusionment was evident in a contribution he made to a Society of Arts conference in January 1868. Here, he spoke in support of the promotion of technical and industrial education while bemoaning what he saw as the failure of his experiment at Chester, where the training college students no longer engaged in this activity and all his lathes had been abandoned. He offered to resign as Principal soon after and eventually did so the following year, unfortunately taking with him several key documents relating to his time in office; those still extant were returned by one of his sons in 1913. He moved to London where he remained active in the Society of Arts, contributing to its *Journal* and publishing two books which expressed his commitment to the popularisation of scientific and technical education: *An Easy Introduction to Chemistry* (jointly with W. Hooker, in 1873) and *A Practical Treatise on the Steam Engine* (1878). He also published, in the year he left Chester, an edition of four sermons in which – bravely and controversially, given the tensions between ecclesiastical and scientific opinion at the time – he argued that science was an aid rather than a hindrance to religious belief. Under the title *The Harmony of the Bible with Experimental Physical Science*, he called upon Christians to see Nature as well as the Bible as the basis for their faith. 'Religion is built upon the works of God – the awakening of the Soul is often through the material and visible ones. Natural Religion aptly precedes Revealed'. This only adds to his claim to have been one of the most innovative thinkers resident in nineteenth-century Chester; he was, for example, hostile to smoking at a time when this was fashionable in male society and scolded one of his College tutors for his habit. On his death in 1880 his body was returned to the city for burial in the Old Cemetery on the south bank of the River Dee but the newspaper report of his funeral, which Chritchley conducted, suggests that it was a low-key affair attended by family and relatively few friends. He remains the only former Principal of the College to be buried in Chester and his grave can still be seen. Tellingly, the memorial to him in the College Chapel was erected at the expense not of former teacher trainees but of 'some of his old pupils of the

Figure 3: The grave of the first Principal, Arthur Rigg in the Old Cemetery beside the River Dee, Chester.

Figure 4: Principal Rigg's memorial plaque in the College Chapel. The inscription beneath hails him as 'founder of the first English School for Technical and Practical Engineering'.

Science School' – led by one of the most eminent, Percy Westmacott, whose cousin was the sculptor – and a plaque beneath it continues to pay tribute to him as 'the founder of the first English School for Technical and Practical Engineering'.

Two training colleges, at Chichester and at Highbury (London), closed during the 1860s[32] and by the end of the decade there was every prospect that Chester would be the third. As we have seen – though the circumstances are inadequately recorded – the Diocesan Board of Education advertised in April 1869 for a Principal solely to run the science school, only for Chritchley to persuade them that there was life in the old College yet. According to his farewell report of 1885, he had no doubt where the root of the problem under his predecessor lay.

> The College had fallen into … disrepute … One cause of this bad reputation I saw clearly was the Science School, as it was then conducted. I was strongly of the opinion that the two departments – so different in their aims and objects and in the social condition and age of their respective inmates – could not run together and be equally prosperous. In this opinion I was confirmed by Sir James Kay-Shuttleworth … who strongly advised the encouragement of the training college and the abandonment of the Science School. His advice was practically adopted with immediate and satisfactory results. Since that time the College has continued to advance in prosperity and usefulness.[33]

So from hereon, while Chritchley did all he could to promote teacher training, the science school was clearly to occupy a subordinate role. Following Rigg's departure, it seems to have been empty through 1870 and 1871 and although it was revived at the beginning of 1872 it was never again the force of old, recruiting regionally rather than nationally and finally closing in 1883.[34] The institution now had a different set of priorities to pursue.

1   The plan on which this description is based is reproduced in Bradbury, *Chester College*, plate 3.
2   ZCR 86/13/1: Notes and Transcripts on the History of the College; S. Astbury, *A History of Chester College Chapel* (Chester, 1953).
3   Bradbury, *Chester College*, p. 134.
4   ZCR 86/1/1: 29 March 1855; Bradbury, *Chester College*, pp. 113–14.
5   ZCR 86/3/2: Ledger Book, 1865–72.
6   *The Cestrian* 2008, p. 19.
7   ZCR 86/13/1 pt i: Letter from W.H. Allen of Detroit, 4 May 1913; M.V.J. Seaborne, 'The College Buildings' in White, *Perspectives*, pp. 29–49, at pp. 34–35.
8   ZCR 86/1/1: 7 December 1854, 11 December 1860.
9   ZCR 86/1/1: 7 December 1854.
10 *Oxford Dictionary of National Biography*, XLV, p. 800.
11 ZCR 86/13/1.
12 Rich, *Training of Teachers*, pp. 55–96; P. Horn, *Education in Rural England, 1800–1914* (Dublin, 1978), p. 91; W.A.C. Stewart and W.P. McCann, *The Educational Innovators, 1780–1880* (New York, 1967), p. 179–97.
13 Bradbury, *Chester College*, pp. 102–3.
14 At Chelsea there were already four full-time plus five occasional tutors, and at Battersea three plus six: P. Horn, *The Victorian and Edwardian Schoolchild* (Gloucester, 1989), p. 99.
15 *Minutes of the Committee of Council on Education 1851–52* (London, 1852), I, p. 303; F.E. Foden, 'The Rev. Arthur Rigg: Pioneer of Workshop Practice', *Vocational Aspect of Secondary and Further Education*, XI, no. 23 (1959), pp. 105–18, at pp. 112–13; Rich, *Training of Teachers*, p. 83; cf. Bradbury, *Chester College*, pp. 101–15.
16 Horn, *Education in Rural England*, p. 90; Larsen, *Victorian Teacher*, p. 140; J. Osborne, ed., *Saltley College Centenary, 1850–1950* (Birmingham, 1950), p. 33.
17 Hughes also considered the College 'a noble institution', all three components of which were marked by 'intelligence and liberality' (T. Hughes, *A Stranger's Handbook to Chester*, Chester, 1856, p. 103).
18 *Minutes of Committee of Council on Education, 1855–56* (London, 1856). I, pp. 63, 73.
19 *Minutes of Committee of Council on Education, 1851–52*, I, pp. 291–318. 67.5% of Chester students attained an 'excellent, good or fair' grade for Arithmetic and 15% similar grades for School Management, at the Christmas 1851 examinations;

comparable figures at Battersea were 56% and 12%, at Chelsea 59% and 5% and at Cheltenham 59% and 13%.

[20] ZCR 86/12/12: letter by an Irish gentleman reporting on his visit to the College in September 1850, published in the *Chester Courant*; he was impressed with both the training college and the boarding school, recommending the latter because 'the knowledge [pupils] may gain in the workshops is in my opinion more valuable than any other'.

[21] P.J. Andrews 'The Making of a Victorian Schoolmaster: Peter Calvert at Chester College' in White, *Perspectives*, pp. 55–62.

[22] ZCR 86/1/1: 7 December 1854.

[23] ZCR 86/1/1: 14 June 1855.

[24] Horn, *Education in Rural England*, pp. 99–100; H.C. Dent, *The Training of Teachers in England and Wales, 1800–1975* (London, 1977), pp. 17–24; Rich, *Training of Teachers*, pp. 115–45.

[25] ZCR 86/1/1: 9 December 1859, 29 March 1860.

[26] ZCR 86/1/1: 18 June 1856; ZCR 86/13/1 pt 3: letter of James Rigg to Edward Rigg 23 January 1912; Hargreaves, 'Chester College – Site and Setting', p. 20.

[27] D.W. Sylvester, *Robert Lowe and Education* (Cambridge, 1974), p. 107; J.M. Goldstrom, *Education: Elementary Education, 1780–1900* (Newton Abbot, 1972), pp. 129–31; Horn, *Education in Rural England*, p. 101. There was an accompanying shift in the focus of the Committee of Council's examinations, away from questions which allowed some vestige of subjectivity in the answers ('Give some account of the reign of Edward I'; 'Under what circumstances was Canada acquired by the English?') towards dry, fact-based questions and answers which lent themselves to standardised marking schemes for grading purposes: *Minutes of Committee of Council on Education 1851–52*, I, p. 313; Larsen, *Victorian Teacher*, pp. 172–73.

[28] Horn, *Education in Rural England*, p. 102.

[29] Bradbury, *Chester College*, p. 141.

[30] Hargreaves, 'Chester College – Site and Setting', pp. 20–24.

[31] ZCR 86/1/1: 12 June 1862; Bradbury, *Chester College*, p. 124.

[32] Horn, *Education in Rural England*, p. 102; a new college at Chichester, Bishop Otter, opened in 1873.

[33] ZCR 86/12/32.

[34] ZCR 86/13/1.

CHAPTER 3

THE IMPACT OF THE 1870 EDUCATION ACT

In August 1870, less than 15 months after Chritchley's appointment as Principal, the Forster Education Act, one of the great achievements of Gladstone's first ministry, received the royal assent. Although this Act was not primarily concerned with the training of teachers, it had profound implications for every institution with an interest in the elementary education of the masses. The measure ensured that, from hereon, every child in England and Wales between the ages of five and 12 would have access to elementary education by providing for the election of School Boards to build Board Schools wherever there was a deficiency of school places available; this in turn led to greater demand for teachers to cater for the increased number of schoolchildren. More than this, since Board Schools were essentially secular institutions, providing non-denominational religious education and observance from which parents could opt out, the Church of England – especially – was provoked to redouble its efforts to build or enlarge its own 'voluntary' schools, in the hope that the need for such rivals would not arise. In 1870, average attendance at all voluntary schools in England and Wales stood at 1.15 million, of whom the Church of England accounted for 0.84 million; by 1895, average attendance in Board Schools totalled 1.88 million, but the figure for voluntary schools had soared in the meantime to 2.45 million, with the Church of England's own contribution at 1.85 million.[1] Chester itself is an example of a borough where no School Board was ever elected, since the provision of Church of England and other voluntary schools kept pace with demand. If Chritchley and his Governing Body were

Figure 5: Christ Church National School, Newtown, Chester. The inscription records enlargement in 1872 as part of the Church of England's response to the challenges posed by the 1870 Education Act.

looking for a context to give new focus and vigour to the work of the Diocesan Training College, the Forster Act provided it – as several speakers pointed out at the public meeting of September 1870 in Chester Town Hall which effectively re-launched the College.[2]

In many respects, Chester College now went from strength to strength. It had a clear sense of purpose, training future teachers (normally on two-year courses) as part of the government's grand plan for elementary education: primarily for Church of England schools although those who found employment in the new Board Schools would also earn grant for the institution. The term 'Queen's Scholar' was revived in 1871 to apply to any pupil-teacher whose admissions exam performance was good enough to secure entry to a college and the grants available for them became more generous once again. All this led to rapidly rising demand for places across the country and the opening of several new colleges, not least by the Church of England.[3] In December 1871 the governors endorsed the Principal's suggestion that permission be sought to increase student numbers at Chester from 70 to 80. The following October, HMI Cowie congratulated the College on its enrolment of 82 students, while also proposing some relief for the Principal in Chapel duties, and suggesting 'that the Committee should look forward to the discontinuance of the Science School'.[4]

The appointment of the College's first chaplain duly followed in 1873, when the Bishop of Chester ordained the English master, James Eaves, who had joined the College two years before. Chritchley acknowledged that 'this arrangement has not only given additional dignity and efficiency to the Chapel services, but has proved an advantage to the College and a comfort in many ways to himself'. Eaves was further promoted at the beginning of 1877 to resident Vice-Principal, combining chaplaincy duties with responsibility for student discipline and welfare, before resigning in 1878 because he wished to marry:[5] He was the first Vice-Principal Chritchley had appointed, although the post had been well-established under Rigg.[6] However, HMI's other proposal, to close the science school, took longer to bear fruit. Even with reduced numbers because the increase in teacher trainees took up most of the dormitory accommodation, it continued for a few more years to generate a profit which subsidised the teacher-training work and this was all the more important once the upsurge in voluntary subscriptions and donations in the immediate aftermath of the 1870 Town Hall meeting fell away.[7] However, in 1877 – by which time it was running at a loss – the governors proposed to their respective Diocesan Boards of Education that it be closed at the end of the year; in the event it survived until Christmas 1883,[8] leaving relatively few records from which its detailed history can be reconstructed. In its heyday under Rigg it was an educational enterprise more distinguished than the training college it helped to fund. After his departure, the impetus behind an enlightened, futuristic, project was gone.

In December 1874, Chritchley reported the College's first recorded case of 'academic malpractice' – an otherwise 'amiable' and 'industrious' student who had been suspended for a year for 'copying his mental arithmetic paper' – but also felt able to say that Chester was 'increasingly gaining the confidence of school managers and teachers and rising in public estimation'. His annual end-of-year reports continued in this positive vein. By 1875 he was receiving 'encouraging reports from all quarters of students who have left the College and are now working in National Schools'; 'the educational successes, it is true, have not been exceptionally brilliant, but the College nevertheless has fully kept up its character and position and considering the material on which we have had to work the results have been gratifying and encouraging'. By 1878 there were 93 students and 'we are turning out a host of well-qualified and earnest elementary teachers … the College is satisfactorily doing the work which it was formed to accomplish'. In 1879 – 'a year of prosperity and upon the whole one of steady work and substantial progress' – there were 96, by his departure in 1885, 110. He could also point to the 'added value' of a Chester College education, citing figures in one of his reports to the governors to show that while only 2% of entrants in 1879 had gained a first-class in the Queen's Scholarship exam, 26.5% of those who gained certificates that year were in the first class. This was the most substantial improvement recorded by any of the 13 Church of England male training colleges in England and Wales, and he could not resist pointing out that Battersea and Cheltenham 'which are usually held up to us as models of all that is excellent and praiseworthy in Training College work' were among the five which actually turned out a lower percentage of first-class students (albeit 79.3% and 52.2% respectively) than they admitted.[9]

Trained schoolmasters in this period, armed with a certificate, could advance rapidly in a profession where many of their colleagues still lacked one. John Dobson, for example, born in Westmorland in 1855 and a former scholar and pupil-teacher at his local Bongate National School, spent the years 1874 and 1875 at Chester College and in January 1876 became master – that is, headmaster – of Urswick Grammar School in the Furness peninsula. A reference for him, dated 1 November 1875 and written by Chritchley (albeit for a different school), says much about the qualities looked for in a schoolteacher in this period: someone who – as envisaged by Slade in his sermon at the opening of the College – was to set an example to his pupils as well as impart knowledge. It also conveys an impression of Chritchley rather warmer than the 'harsh and unrelenting' figure portrayed by Bradbury.

> Mr Dobson is a young man possessed of abilities and attainments considerably above his class. He is an accurate thinker, industrious, painstaking and enthusiastic in the pursuit of knowledge … He teaches with … intelligence and vivacity, and his discipline, without a shadow of severity, is very effective. His moral character … stands high in the College, and I have a great personal esteem for him as a high principled and virtuous young man.

Dobson was to remain at Urswick as headmaster until his retirement after 44 years in 1920.[10]

Chritchley, who though born in Cheshire was a graduate of Trinity College Dublin with an LlD (Doctor of Law) degree, comes across as a less original thinker than his predecessor. In 1874, for example, he rejected out of hand a suggestion by HMI that students might learn from visiting a variety of local schools, on the grounds that this would be 'injurious to discipline'.[11] However, the rigours of the grants system, with their emphasis on examinations of facts memorised from a single cheap textbook on each subject, positively discouraged original thinking, by staff and students alike.[12] By the mid-1870s Chritchley had done away with all vestige of Rigg's 'industrial occupations' save for gardening,[13] so freeing up student leisure time, which occupied two and a half hours each day (plus two half holidays per week) and was now devoted to the more recognised pursuits of organised drill (useful because taught in elementary schools), cricket and association football. Prompted by HMI who pointed to the example of other colleges, he also allowed the students to form a Volunteer Corps attached to the 1st Cheshire Royal Garrison Artillery (Volunteers), to such good effect that they shot their way to a gold medal in a gunnery competition in 1876.[14] And from 1882, these students had a formal means of keeping in touch after they left, through the inauguration of the College Club as a vehicle to organise reunions, help those in financial hardship and generally keep alive the fellowship engendered by enforced community living. Ten years later, the students of this era would band together to pay for a memorial bust to Chritchley in the College Chapel, following his death in county Durham.[15]

Yet for all this conventionality, the Principal reserved a place for Science in the curriculum, despite the dispersal of the specialist apparatus accumulated by Rigg, some of which he had taken with him while some had gone overseas.[16] This was not entirely without calculation, since it was possible to earn grant from the government's Science and Art Department to supplement that available from the Education Department for mainstream subjects. Science was also the subject Chritchley had originally been appointed to the College to teach. Despite the spin which he was inclined to put upon his students' results, Chester was generally below average nationally in most measures of attainment. But this was not the case in subjects such as Magnetism, Electricity and Acoustics where they did markedly better than elsewhere; in 1875, they also won over 100 prizes in the Science and Art Department's exams in subjects including Mathematics, Physical Geography and Chemistry.[17] HMIs thought Science took up too much time and would have preferred the students to have been better prepared in the mainstream subjects 'required for Village Schools' but Chritchley robustly defended its continued place in the curriculum:

> It is true that some of these subjects have no direct bearing upon the final examination, but certificates of competency to teach elementary natural philosophy will be of great use to our National Schoolmasters in large towns. This will enable them to open Science classes recognized by the government and this will be of no small advantage to them in their competition with the attraction of Board Schools.[18]

But as we have seen this commitment did not extend to the science school itself. Chritchley was content to preside over its slow demise, which freed up space for the accommodation of the rising number of teacher trainees.

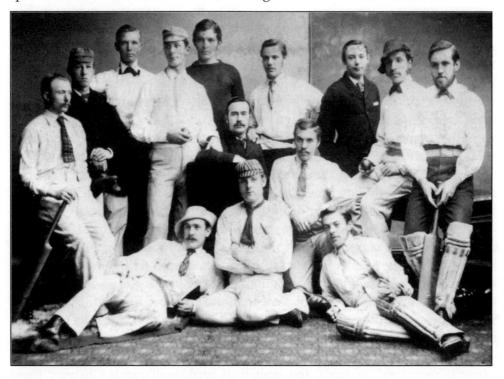

Figure 6: College Cricket team, 1880-81. (CALS: ZCR 86/7928.)

Financial stringency blighted Chritchley's Principalship. Under the system prevailing since 1863, the College received its statutory grant for a student's tuition retrospectively, on successful completion not only of two full years' training but also of a probationary period in a government-funded school. Accordingly, students had to promise on admission 'to labour as an elementary teacher in a Church of England Inspected School or other Inspected School, till I have secured the schoolmaster's certificate from the Committee of Council in Education'.[19] This was no different from other colleges but where Chester suffered was in the level of fees charged to supplement the grant. In the early 1870s, Queen's Scholars at Chester were paying only £4 per year, although others could come as private students for £30. In return for this, students were promised 'education, board, washing, lodging, medical attendance and use of laboratory, harmonium, organ and reference library', plus 'extra instruction in Chemistry, Music, Latin and French' not always available elsewhere. Under pressure from HMI, who pointed out in 1874 that at other colleges £10 or £12 was more usually charged, the governors raised the standard fee to £8 the following year.[20] But this still left Chritchley running the most economical college in England and Wales: on an annual basis, a full £8, 13s. 0d. per resident student cheaper than the next lowest, Carmarthenshire, according to his outraged successor. The consequence was some very basic amenities. Inspectors' reports repeatedly drew attention to dirty, poorly decorated rooms and to the need for more toilet facilities and better ventilation in classrooms and dormitories. The next Principal was appalled to find that there was only one teaspoon to three students, and such a shortage of bedlinen that beds could only be changed once every three to four weeks.[21]

This parsimony extended to the practising school, which inspectors thought understaffed and ill-equipped. In the style of Ofsted today, HMI Sharpe reported in 1883 that it should be aiming to be 'excellent', when it could currently only be graded as 'good'. However, it did have gas installed that year and by 1884, after thorough redecoration, was considered 'a model of cleanliness'.[22] It is worth adding that money was also found in 1882 for the purchase of some extra land near the canal, which though not built upon for several years offered the prospect of future expansion while also forestalling alternative development in this area. It meant that the entire area bounded by Cheyney Road, Parkgate Road, the canal and the access way to Exton Park with its extension down to the canal was in College hands and at an unknown date – possibly the 1890s – this was completely enclosed, partly using existing sandstone walls but mainly through new building in brick, to create an identifiable 'Close'. A surviving stretch of brick wall along Cheyney Road gives the best impression of what this perimeter would have looked like, a very familiar feature to generations of staff and students before most of it was demolished in the 1950s.[23]

One reason for the reluctance to increase fees was almost certainly a fear of poor recruitment, especially from the industrial North West. Although the 1870 Act had restored the concept of Queen's Scholarships, it had allowed 'assistant teachers' to become certificated teachers without attending College, if recommended by their HMI. In the decade following the Act there was rapid growth in the number of pupil-teachers going on to become assistant teachers without further training, with the prospect of earning their way to a certificate in due course. Like other colleges, therefore, Chester faced competition both in attracting students and in finding them positions thereafter, and while numbers held up very well Chritchley was soon expressing concern about employability. In 1877 he reported that 'of 46 students who leave the College at the end of the year, only 29 have yet got schools and even these have had much difficulty – supply clearly exceeds demand'. Two years later he was quite open about what he saw as the reason, while pointing out that the difficulties were 'in line with national trends': 'certificates are being given to teachers not properly trained, so taking jobs from those who have been to the colleges', besides which school managers often preferred the even cheaper alternative of engaging more pupil-teachers instead.[24] Many of these pursued modest careers as 'supplementary' teachers without ever going to college or obtaining a certificate. As late as 1900, 28% of certificated schoolmasters and 51% of certificated schoolmistresses in England and Wales had not been to a training college, while there was a substantial additional number who had never even acquired a certificate.[25]

All this puts the circumstances of a late-Victorian college student into context. He or she had achieved a place in a competitive examination which gave entitlement to a professional education regarded by the government as an expensive investment. The trained teacher emerged with a certificate which made him or her the elite of the profession, with every prospect of rising above other teachers to become a Head sooner rather than later. Indeed, some went straight into a headship, like John Dobson at Urswick in 1876.[26] For young men drawn from working-class households in the north-west of England, Chester College – like its peers elsewhere across the country – was undoubtedly a vehicle for social mobility.

In terms of academic work, HMIs considered Chritchley's students 'rather rough', below average in attainment both when they entered and when they left two years later, and entitled to a more up-to-date library. They also thought there was too much emphasis on lectures at the expense of small

Figure 7: College Smoking Club, 1880–81. (CALS: ZCR 86/7928.)

group work and private study – not conducive to 'cultivating habits of independent thought' – although Chritchley countered by saying that within the hours normally devoted to lectures (8.00 to 12.00 in the morning, 2.00 to 5.00 in the afternoon), one was for singing and another for drawing and he granted exemptions at his discretion.[27] There were recurrent outbreaks of student revolt, including one in November 1876 when virtually the entire student body signed a letter protesting that 'the system of "fines in addition to impositions" is unworthy of you the learned professor of this Training College and we have unanimously resolved not to submit to it': a move which led the governors to demand an apology from the students but also to set up a visiting committee to check what lay behind the unrest.[28] Four years later, the governors again expressed their alarm that 'the general discipline of the College is most unsatisfactory'; two students were expelled and others put on probation.[29] Indeed, it is hard to avoid the impression that Chritchley was less than candid with the governors about the day-to-day conduct of College life. In 1883, when HMI queried why bolts had been put on the doors of cubicles in the dormitories, he replied that this had been 'found convenient', only for it to emerge under his successor that one reason for this was the 'initiatory rite of pulling the men out of bed'.[30] Chritchley's own explanation for disruptive behaviour was the pernicious influence of radical publications such as the National Union of Teachers' own organ, *The Schoolmaster*, and – with reference to the Lancashire catchment area – the fact that 'the bulk of our students are drawn from the very hotbed of strikes and combinations'.[31]

Perhaps the most telling charge against Chritchley was that levelled, with due tact, by HMI Sharpe in a letter of June 1885: 'in the choice of your staff you do not attach sufficient weight to the special qualities required from the post to be filled'.[32] Chritchley almost always defended his staff to the governors whenever there was adverse comment from HMIs and from a modern perspective some of their verdicts may have been unfair. The History lecturer, Mr Deverell, was criticised in 1879 because the lecture he gave in front of the Inspectors was 'somewhat democratic in its tendency'; by 1882 he was 'picturesque in his treatment of history' without sufficient attention to the facts, and by 1883 his teaching was 'not efficient' in terms of achieving results, so he left at the end of that year. Given that the nationally set exams for which he had to prepare his students still had questions like 'Make a table showing the grandchildren and great-grandchildren of Henry the Seventh' and 'Enumerate the chief events of the years 1814–15', it looks as if a preference for analysis and interpretation was not what was required.[33]

Chritchley also acted quickly enough to remove Eaves's successor as Vice-Principal, Revd Alfred Wren, a Cambridge Mathematics graduate whom he acknowledged 'had but little previous experience in educational work'; 'never before having had to deal with large bodies of young men, he has failed entirely in discipline'. He lasted from April to December 1878.[34] Against this, it is difficult to justify the indulgence shown towards Robert Wilkinson, who (under his various titles of 'Model Master', 'Normal Master' and 'Master of Method') was responsible for teaching educational theory and practice, work central to the College's *raison d'être*. Wilkinson was a former Chester student, appointed in 1871 after 12 years as master of Bickerstaffe School near Ormskirk. He divided his time between the College – where he also taught singing – and the practising school but was already receiving criticism from the current HMI as early as 1873. By the following year he had 'altogether improved' but the adverse judgments became more sustained from 1882; by then, as HMI Sharpe explained to Chritchley in his 1885 letter, 'some knowledge of education as a science (apart from a mere code of rules and methods) [had come to be] required from Training College students by the Education Department'. Sharpe went on to say that 'Mr Wilkinson did well enough in former years before the higher requirement was imposed but I feel compelled to say that I have never been satisfied with his lectures on the Science in Education … you will have observed what a low position your College took last Christmas in this subject'. Whatever merits Chester's students had displayed in this subject a generation earlier were no longer in evidence and HMI was moved to threaten loss of grant because the relevant staff did not meet current government requirements; with this went a suggestion that Wilkinson be found alternative employment.[35]

Chritchley's initial response to HMI Sharpe's comments, when he met the governors at the end of June 1885, was to fight Wilkinson's corner. He even suggested lodging a protest to the Education Department and it took a subcommittee of the Governing Body to secure both men's agreement to the redeployment of Wilkinson, as Sharpe had recommended. Henceforth he became a tutor in Music, Geography and Maths; one student, Joseph Maiden of Bury, rated him 'best tutor in College' in verses composed for an autograph book of 1886–87.[36] But reading Wilkinson's lesson notes – a remarkable survival, privately printed in 1885 as *Syllabus of Lectures in Psychology and in the Method Used in the Practising School at Chester College* – it is hard to disagree with HMI's verdict that he was woefully behind the times. At a time when there were scores of educational publications, disseminating theories about the 'science of the mind',[37] his guidance on teaching was heavily reliant on one authority, James Currie's *Principles and Practice of Common-School Education*, first published in 1861, and largely consisted of sequences of instructions to ensure good class management and a series of precepts for teachers to follow. These he acknowledged were, in the main, taken verbatim from the notes of his mentor and predecessor, John Eloy Hardy – incidentally one of the original ten students of 1840 – who had been Method Master between 1852 and 1871 before going on to become Head of Chester's Blue Coat School.

In fairness, there is a good deal here which would still be regarded favourably today:

> Let the children have something suitable to do for every moment of the day.
> Encourage sensible questioning by the children and answer appropriately.
> Use public opinion to condemn wrong actions.
> When the eye of a child wanders, let it see something which will advance it morally or intellectually.
> Don't attempt to make all children alike.
> Brand the deed and not the child.
> Nobly preserve childlike trust, without which there can be no education.

And in amongst these were others which are insights into the day-to-day context in which mid-Victorian teachers worked:

> Have your dusters fixed and your chalk handy.
> Visitors to a school generally notice three things: (a) the writing which they can see, (b) the music which they can hear, (c) the general order, which they cannot avoid not noticing.

Arrange your classes in groups and for grant purposes work at the least advanced group most. NB. This is scarcely fair to the advanced children but unfortunately it has to be done.'[38]

There is a similar set of precepts known from another training college, Westminster, giving six ways of securing good order and eight ways to lose it ('give dry lessons', 'manifest irresolution', and so on) but this dates from 1855, not 30 years later.[39] The problem with all this was not that it was unsound in itself, but that it lacked firm grounding in a coherent theory of education or any assessment of the merits of alternative approaches. As evidence of training at Chester under Hardy in the 1850s, when the profession of elementary schoolteacher was in its infancy, Wilkinson's *Syllabus* is testimony to some enlightened thinking about practice. After 1880, when every child in England and Wales was supposed to be at school, at least to the age of ten, and local teachers impacted upon the lives of every family in the country, a more sophisticated approach was required.

So Chester College reached the mid-1880s with a mixed reputation. It had made a very promising start, as the first purpose-built teacher training college in England, sharing its premises with a boarding school which by the 1850s had become a nationally esteemed centre for science education. In its first two decades, it was also unlike any equivalent college in the stress it laid on 'workshop practice' as a means of promoting technical education. But in the 1860s, this distinctive approach fell foul of government policy, as mediated through the grants system, and by the end of the decade, under a disillusioned Principal, teacher training at Chester had all but disappeared. The appointment of a new Principal in 1869, closely followed by the passage of the Forster Education Act which gave new impetus to elementary education, prompted the revival of the College as a teacher training institution, now with a clear focus on its mission and purpose. With just over 100 students, it had become one of the largest such colleges in the country. But it was a much more conventional place, shorn of its workshops and (after some years in a subordinate role) its science school as well. As a College, it also seems to have settled for a modest reputation, charging lower fees and spending less than the others, falling behind the latest educational thinking, and content to give its below-average students a limited experience – albeit one which turned them out better trained than the assistant teachers and pupil-teachers on whom elementary schools heavily relied. Persistent criticism from HMI of the limitations of his students and staff seems eventually to have persuaded Chritchley to accept the offer of a living in the North East, prompting the resignation at the close of 1885 with which this book began. It was time for a new broom.

1   G. Sutherland, *Policy-Making in Elementary Education, 1870–1895* (Oxford, 1973), p. 350.
2   See Chapter 1.
3   Horn, *Education in Rural England*, pp. 103–4; Dent, *Training of Teachers*, p. 25.
4   ZCR 86/1/2: 8 December 1871, 14 October 1872.
5   ZCR 86/1/2: 3 October, 18 December 1878; ZCR 86/12/23: *Second Report of the Chester Diocesan Board of Education for year ending December 1871*, pp. 13–14; ZCR 86/12/25: *Diocese of Chester Report on the Diocesan Institutions for year ending December 1873*, pp. 39, 41; on the Chester Town Hall meeting, see above, Chapter 1.
6   See Chapter 2.
7   ZCR 86/12/23: *Second Report of the Chester Diocesan Board of Education for … 1871*, pp. 11–14; ZCR 86/12/24: *Third Report of the Chester Diocesan Board of Education for year ending December 1872*, pp. 6–7 (reporting that '89 students and 21 boys in the Science School were as many as the dormitories can possibly accommodate'); ZCR 86/12/25: *Diocese of Chester Report on the Diocesan Institutions for … 1873*, p. 39.
8   ZCR 86/1/7: 16 February 1877; ZCR 86/1/3: 25 September 1884.
9   ZCR 86/1/2: 5 November 1874, 17 December 1875, 3 October 1878, 14 December 1879; ZCR 86/12/32; another case of malpractice – copying during an exam, for which a first-year student was expelled – is recorded in ZCR 86/1/3: 28 March 1887.
10 UC, deposit by Mr B. Thomas (great-grandson of Dobson) of Harborne, Birmingham, 2011; the reference was for another school to which he was applying at the time, at Kirkby Thore near Penrith. Cf. Bradbury, *Chester College*, p. 161.
11 ZCR 86/1/2: 5 November 1874.
12 Rich, *Training of Teachers*, pp. 192–95; Horn, *Education in Rural England*, pp. 104–11.
13 ZCR 86/1/2: 9 September 1875.
14 ZCR 86/1/2: 5 November 1874; A.F. Dawtry, 'All Work and No Play … the Development of Student Leisure Activities at Chester College' in White, *Perspectives*, pp. 75–84, at pp. 78–77. Chritchley was delighted with the 'experiment' of setting up an artillery battery, which resulted in 'moral and physical advantages which he hoped for, but hardly dared to expect': ZCR 86/12/27 (*Diocese of Chester Report on the Diocesan Institutions for … 1875*, p. 44).
15 ZCR 86/1/4: 12 December 1892; Bradbury, *Chester College*, pp. 148–49, 160–61.
16 ZCR 86/1/2: 17 December 1875; Foden, 'Rev. Arthur Rigg', p. 114, who mentions it going to Australia and America.
17 ZCR 86/1/2: 17 December 1875, 14 December 1879; ZCR 86/12/27: *Diocese of Chester Report on the Diocesan Institutions for … 1875*, p. 44.
18 ZCR 86/1/2: 9 September, 17 December 1875; ZCR 86/1/3: 20 June 1883, 12 June 1884.
19 ZCR 86/1/7.
20 ZCR 86/1/2: 4 September 1873, 5 November 1874, 11 March 1875.

[21] ZCR 86/12/33: Report by new Principal, Allen, 1886; until the 1890s students did not even have a chest of drawers beside each bed and had to keep their clothes in boxes (ZCR 86/1/4: 18 May 1893).

[22] ZCR 86/1/3: 20 June 1883, 12 June 1884.

[23] Hargreaves, 'Chester College – Site and Setting', pp. 20, 25; *Geodiversity Trail*, p. 11; cf. Chapter 4.

[24] ZCR 86/1/2: 19 December 1877, 14 December 1879.

[25] Horn, *Education in Rural England*, pp. 111–12.

[26] Dobson's experience was much happier than that of Daniel Lord, a student who left Chester in 1892 to become Head of Newtown Board School, Disley, only to fall foul of the National Union of Teachers because he had taken the job of a predecessor 'unlawfully dealt with' (ZCR 86/1/4: 15 September, 12 December 1892).

[27] ZCR 86/1/2: 16 December 1881.

[28] ZCR 86/1/2: 23 November, 8 December, 15 December 1876.

[29] ZCR 86/1/2: 7: May 1880.

[30] ZCR 86/1/3: 20 June 1883, 20 May 1887.

[31] ZCR 86/1/7: pp. 80–90.

[32] ZCR 86/1/3: 29 June 1885 (inserted letter of 25 June).

[33] ZCR 86/1/2: 25 September 1879; ZCR 86/1/7: 15 September 1882. In fairness, the 1882 exam did contain a few questions which would have suited Deverell better: 'Explain briefly the purposes for which Doomsday [*sic*] Book was compiled' – a topic still much-debated today – and 'Discuss the justice of Elizabeth's behaviour towards Mary Queen of Scots'.

[34] ZCR 86/1/2: 3 October 1878.

[35] ZCR 86/12/22: *First Report of the Chester Diocesan Board of Education for … 1870*, p. 9; ZCR 86/1/2: 4 September 1873, 15 September 1882; ZCR 86/1/3: 17 June, 29 June 1885; ZCR 86/1/7: 15 September 1882.

[36] ZCR 86/13/5: Autograph book of Henry Norris. This amusing little book also includes repeated references to a catchphrase used by Revd James Morgan, Vice-Principal 1879–86 – 'is that not so?' – which clearly had the students in stitches.

[37] Larsen, *Victorian Teacher*, pp. 43–45, 74–103.

[38] ZCR 86/12/32: *School Management Notes: Syllabus of Lectures in Psychology and in the Method Used in the Practising School at Chester College* (1885).

[39] Horn, *Education in Rural England*, p. 108.

CONSOLIDATION, 1886–1932

CHAPTER 4

AN AGE OF ENLIGHTENMENT

In December 1885 the governors interviewed two candidates for the position of Principal, selected from 56 original applicants. However, they were so impressed by the qualifications and testimonials of a third – who had written to say that he was too ill to attend – that he was appointed instead, subject to a satisfactory interview with the Bishop of Chester. The Bishop was the great medieval historian William Stubbs, consecrated the previous year, and he duly accepted the candidate, Revd Andrew James Campbell Allen. Allen had been Senior Wrangler[1] at Cambridge in 1879, at a time when this was seen as the greatest possible intellectual achievement, conferring celebrity status.[2] He retained his fellowship at Peterhouse, Cambridge, throughout his time as Principal so must always have thought that there was an alternative to which he could return if his sojourn at Chester did not go as well as he hoped; in effect, this is what happened. But he deserves credit for leaving the comforts of Cambridge to take on a training college serving the industrial North West and he clearly regarded himself as a man with a mission. As for the governors, they must have regarded him as a tremendous 'catch'.

Allen was dismayed by what he found at Chester and on 10 March 1886 produced a detailed report on what needed to be done: 'considerable alterations are necessary if the College is to be raised to the position which it should occupy among similar institutions'.[3] He went through the teaching staff, which then numbered seven plus himself and his Vice-Principal, considering this sufficient in quantity but criticising disparities in salary, certain anomalies in deployment and a system whereby some were paid partly according to their students' results, leading to 'poaching'. This was not unusual in late-Victorian training colleges,[4] and at Chester one who profited thereby was the Science teacher, John Craig, a man whose abilities Allen rated highly. He also thought very well of Albert Lovell, Wilkinson's successor as Master of Method who combined these duties with the headship of the practising school; one of Chritchley's parting gifts to the College had been to recommend that these posts be combined, and to appoint Lovell to fill them.[5] Other tutors met with Allen's muted approval, but he thought two assistant teachers in the practising school could also do some work in the College and he made an exception of his Vice-Principal, Revd James Morgan. Though 'willing to work and do his best', he seemed plagued by a 'longstanding feud between him and the students which renders him nearly useless as an aid in maintaining discipline'.[6] Allen wanted a different sort of Vice-Principal, better paid than the other tutors, someone who was clearly second-in-command and could deputise for the Principal if necessary; he could also manage the grounds and keep the accounts, tasks currently done by the Principal in time when he should be reading up on the theory and history of education. The household was well run by an 'excellent and conscientious' matron, although he had already added one further servant girl to help her and purchased some extra materials. The buildings were 'on the whole ... satisfactory' but the dining room and Chapel were 'exceedingly draughty' so that the students suffered from cold; conversely, ventilation in the classrooms was poor while the dormitories would benefit from a small outlay on furnishings such as drawers and mirrors. He also recommended an extension of the Easter holiday from Thursday to Wednesday, so students could go home; the existing practice of suspending work from Good Friday to Easter Tuesday but keeping the students in residence could only lead to 'hanging about Chester in companies with nothing to do ... every inducement for falling into evil'.[7]

All this gives us an excellent insight into the College as Chritchley had left it, and Allen recognised that it would take a fundamental change of attitude if deficiencies were to be remedied. He ended his report by acknowledging that his reforms would mean spending money but stressed that the annual cost of a student at Chester College was over £15 below the average for similar colleges[8] and that extra expenditure was an imperative investment. 'It is essential in the interests of Church and Religion that the present system of training colleges be maintained and every effort made to turn out a plentiful supply of qualified teachers'.

The Governing Body duly set up a subcommittee to consider Allen's report and went some way to meeting his demands. Tutors' duties and salaries were rationalised, any links between remuneration and students' results were removed, it was agreed that two teachers from the practising school could help out in the College as well. A bursar was to be appointed from among the teaching staff to assist the Principal part-time with the accounts and the grounds. But the fees were not increased and, rather than sanction all that Allen wanted to spend on new furniture and the like, the governors suggested that he agree contracts with suppliers to achieve some economies. Two victims of all this were the Vice-Principal (despite giving a 'very good' lecture on King Lear when HMI visited in June) and the recently redeployed Wilkinson, who evidently declined an offer to have sole charge of Music at a reduced salary but teach nothing else; both left in the summer of 1886. Allen appointed as the new Vice-Principal David Alexander Stewart, a recent Cambridge graduate in his own image: Belfast-born like himself and the sixth Wrangler of the previous year. In a break with tradition, he was not yet ordained to the priesthood at the time of his appointment. As for the successor to Wilkinson, the man chosen to teach Music, Theodore Ardern, was to become one of the most respected tutors the College ever had.[9]

Clearly, Allen was determined to give the students a better experience than their predecessors had had and tutors such as Ardern – committed to realising potential and extending horizons – were just what he wanted. Lovell was another, 'a very earnest, capable man' according to HMI, who introduced a systematic record of his students' progress, challenged himself academically through taking external degrees of London University while working at Chester, and raised standards to the point where his practising school at last attained an 'excellent' grade in 1888.[10] Meanwhile, with Allen handling some of the Mathematics teaching in person, the students had the benefit of one of the most brilliant practitioners in the country. A student of Allen's time, reminiscing almost 70 years later, described him as a 'tall, slight, ascetic looking man' who was nevertheless 'very affable' and at pains to put him at his ease when meeting him as a candidate for admission. In recalling the 'criticism lessons' which every student had to give to a small class in front of an array of staff and fellow-students – who were invited to pass comment before the Master of Method summed up – he claimed to have brought the house down, at least among the students, by using Allen's pet phrase, 'Why, it's obvious on the face of it'.[11] Quite apart from all this, indications of a more relaxed regime under Allen are evident from the autograph book of 1886, already mentioned, which pokes gentle fun at the various tutors and tells of a 'Jerry Band' striking up after lights out in one of the dormitories;[12] from a complaint by HMI Oakeley in 1889 about students smoking and lounging about in boating or cricketing costumes on the streets of Chester;[13] and above all from the introduction of the *Collegian* as a student magazine where (within reason) they could vent their opinions.

The *Collegian* originally appeared, presumably with Allen's connivance if not his active encouragement, as some loose broadsheets – now lost – written and duplicated by the students. In February 1888, it was re-launched as a printed magazine run by the College Club as a means of keeping old students in touch, though still with heavy reliance on contributions from those currently in residence and also from some of the staff. For most of its first 50 years it was a three-times-per-year publication, although there were periods when it appeared more frequently. It is an excellent source for what mattered most to students, full of in-jokes about College life and a means of tracing the rise and fall of various cultural and sporting activities. The first printed edition in 1888 produced a spoof exam paper with the style of question so familiar at that time: 'Describe and give map of "State of Hungary" (This state is known intimately to most of us)', and 'What is meant by "Soporific Influence"?'. But it also pulled no punches in criticising the failure to keep classrooms and Chapel heated in a current prolonged spell of bitterly cold weather: 'how any man can be expected to study and worship properly on an empty stomach, and with the thermometer standing at freezing point, I do not know'.

In the early years concerts and a debating society were already in being and duly reported upon; sports reports were confined to association football, rugby union and cricket, written in a way which demonstrates that codes of conduct still had some way to evolve. In May 1888 the College cricket team walked off with the score at 60 for 8 in reply to Runcorn's 71 all out because of what were seen as two blatantly bad decisions by the biased Runcorn umpire. In March 1889, the football team lost a second-round Association Shield Tie away to Fifth Liverpool Irish 6–1 but their second goal had been 'palpably offside', their third goal 'appeared to be' and in the second half they 'always fouled the Collegians when their goal was in jeopardy'. That season there were also defeats at rugby both at home and away to Runcorn Shop Assistants, but they unfairly fielded several players from Runcorn Football Club 'assisted by a few shop assistants'. In truth, results were usually much better than this. In the summer of 1894, for example, the cricket team, playing local clubs such as Wallasey, Pontblyddyn and Tattenhall, recorded five wins, four draws and only two defeats. In September and October of that year, the 1st football XI beat Holywell 4–1, Chester Shop Assistants 14–0 and Warrington St Elphin's 3–0, while the 1st rugby XV, though losing narrowly to Warrington Rangers, defeated Port Sunlight by 3 tries to 1 and Mr Benson's Theatrical Company by 1 goal and 2 tries to 1 goal.[14]

Back in the governors' meetings, the Principal kept pressing for more expenditure. Over the years, he succeeded in obtaining some minor adjustments to the practising school (including provision for a private master's room), new seating for the classrooms, 'nine feet long, backed, in pitch pine varnished on iron standards', two extra WCs, a new piano and a new organ for the Chapel, but not in increasing the number of hot-water baths available to resident staff and students, of which there was only one. His requests for a swimming bath and gymnasium were turned down flat, while a decision on a new laboratory was deferred to the point where the College had to sacrifice its grant for the teaching of Chemistry, with the result that the well-regarded Science tutor Craig was given his notice and left in December 1889. A silver tea service presented to Craig by his grateful students, past and present, survives to this day in Canada.[15]

Alongside these disappointments were signs of improvement in discipline and the quality of academic work. In 1886 HMI Oakeley passed favourable comment on all the tutors he observed, none more so than the Geography lecturer, Woodhouse, 'extremely interesting and good in all respects'. The average place of Chester's second year students in the class lists at Christmas that year was 707, compared (among similar colleges) to 250 at Cheltenham, 547 at Saltley and 745 at Exeter, but among first-years the average was as high as 451.[16] Three years later he thought 'the behaviour of the men good on the whole' and, while acknowledging the generally poor standard of students at entry, 'reported very favourably of the work done in the College year by year': thanks partly to Woodhouse's excellent teaching, a student named Halliwell had won fourth prize from the Royal Geographical Society, leading him to conclude that 'when Chester got hold of a good, intelligent student, the progress such a student made was quite equal to what it would have been in a London college'.[17]

Comments such as these would have been music to Allen's ears but it is clear that by the end of the decade he was becoming increasingly frustrated by what he perceived as lack of support from the Governing Body. Having had his request to raise students' fees turned down soon after his arrival, he had had to endure the rejection – at least partly on grounds of expenditure – of one proposed improvement after another. Bishop Stubbs, who had appointed him and was possibly the only person in Chester, in or out of College, whom he regarded as his academic equal, was translated to Oxford in January 1889; it may be no coincidence that relations with the governors deteriorated rapidly from hereon. Tensions between the parties seem apparent from two decisions taken in March 1889: on the one hand, a niggardly response to Allen's practice of sending the students home for Easter by requiring him to pay for any fares in excess of 15s. 0d., on the other a refusal to accept his idea – which smacks of desperation – of building a laundry at his own expense if the College would lease him the land.[18] Later that year, procrastination over building a new laboratory, which ultimately lost the College a grant-earning subject and a good member of the teaching staff, must have infuriated him beyond measure. So on 11 December 1889 he wrote to the governors, asserting that they were out of harmony with each other and in terms which were interpreted as an offer to resign. There was some further sparring over the next few months, with Allen declining a request to withdraw his letter, the governors then accepting his offer, and Allen arguing that he had offered to resign only if requested to do so. This obliged the governors in June 1890 'after full consideration for the fourth time

Figure 8: Staff and students, 1890. The Principal, Andrew Allen, is in the middle of the back row, wearing a mortarboard like his fellow Oxbridge-educated colleagues. Theodore Ardern is third from the right, in a bowler hat; Albert Lovell is between him and Allen. (CALS: ZCR 86/17/26.)

of his letters' to write specifically requesting him to send in his resignation, to take effect at the end of the year.[19]

HMI Oakeley's 1890 report, the last of Allen's Principalship, had been more negative than some of his previous ones, again stressing the low quality of student intake and their modest attainment on leaving: out of 18 colleges, Chester was ranked fifth in Euclid (Algebra and Geometry) and seventh in both Reading and Grammar but 10th in Writing, 12th in School Management and as low as 17th in Practical Teaching. Students' demeanour was 'good on the point of respectfulness, but for the most part they are rough and uncultivated' and they were still smoking in the streets. Even the practising school – which had become a 'higher-grade school' catering for pupils beyond the minimum leaving age – came in for criticism as offering an atypical experience: there were too many students waiting their turn and they would benefit from visiting a variety of other schools. 'The Principal and his colleagues were painstaking and fair: but however earnest the teachers' work, the material to work upon is poor'.[20] Whether the failure to make more rapid progress with student attainment contributed to Allen's decision to leave we cannot say, but given the lukewarm response of the Governing Body to the enterprise and enthusiasm he had brought to his task, disappointing results would have done nothing to convince him to stay. What was needed now was a Principal who would be more comfortable with his situation and who would give the governors the impression that he was working with rather than against them.

On 3 September 1890 the governors gathered at Warrington to confirm their shortlist, on the basis of recommendations made by a subcommittee which had been considering applications. Warrington was chosen ostensibly 'for the convenience of the members of the Liverpool and Manchester contingent' – Liverpool now having its own representation as a separate diocese since 1880 – but it looks as if relations with Allen had become so bad that they either could not, or would not, meet at the College; the subcommittee itself had assembled in Chester, but in alternative premises. The six candidates recommended by the subcommittee (out of 46 original applications) included the Vice-Principals of the training colleges at Battersea, Culham and York, but the full governors' committee had other ideas, relegating the Culham man to the reserve list but selecting two others, one of whom was Revd John Dugdale Best, already Principal of the – much smaller – college for schoolmistresses at Derby which served the dioceses of Lichfield and Southwell.[21] Having thus scraped on to the shortlist, Best triumphed at the interviews on 13 October and took office at the beginning of 1891.

Allen sold his bookcase, desk and safe to the College[22] and returned to Cambridge with his wife and the two children born to them during their time in Chester. From 1892 to 1917 he was vicar of St Mary the Less, the church adjacent to Peterhouse who were patrons of the living, and he went on to publish a number of books, some of them illustrative of his commitment to making widely accessible the best that scholarship could offer. An edition of *The Acts of the Apostles with Notes and Explanations*, 'a commentary for school and family use', appeared in the Nisbet's Scriptural Handbooks series in 1891 and was presumably in preparation while he was still based in Chester. *The Church Catechism: Its History and Contents: A Manual for Teachers and Students*, published by Longmans in 1892, declared itself to be based on his experience in teaching the catechism to first-year Chester students.[23] He revisited the College at least once, in summer 1922, but died in November of the following year near his home in Lewisham, to where he had retired.[24]

Best had been exactly one class below Allen in the Cambridge Mathematics finals of 1879: top Senior Optime (Second-class Honours) to Allen's top First. But as a more rounded character the new Principal succeeded in bringing Chester into line with the lifestyle of other colleges of the time: securing by charm and diplomacy much of what his predecessor had failed to achieve by confrontation.[25] Like Allen before him, within a few months of his arrival Best submitted a report on what needed urgently to be done, but now there was a very favourable reception. The governors clearly found him a more soothing presence, epitomised by the care he took at this juncture to praise the 'true and loyal' manner in which he had been received by staff and students alike. He played down some 'slight changes' he had already made – in reality quite significant ones – relaxing the timetable to allow one hour more of afternoon recreation, permitting the students to leave the precincts in any free time between 1.30 and 6.20 p.m. (as Allen had favoured, he noted!) but asking for – and, he said, partly obtaining – better order and discipline in classrooms and dormitories 'and more restrained and self-controlled behaviour generally'. He had also taken what was, in fact, a radical step in allowing the Vice-Principal to live out of College, so freeing space which enabled all resident tutors to have their own sitting-rooms. He was, in other words, trying to introduce a more civilised and collegial approach to living on site, for students and staff alike. He pointed out that there was still only one bath (for 109 students), asked that supper be provided (because at present there was 'private and irregular provision') and requested a second school to be available where teaching could be practised. Other matters raised included the need for an even better piano, the construction of a perimeter wall along the Parkgate Road side of the campus – possibly the rounding off of 'The Close'[26] – and repairs to his own house. In response, he was allowed to buy the piano and to introduce supper, and was promised further consideration of both his bath and building proposals and the second school. A 'committee of works' was immediately established, soon re-launched as a General Purposes Committee of the Governing Body, to meet once a month in term-time. Its enthusiasm for monthly meetings was not sustained but it did sanction without more ado such improvements as the building of the Parkgate Road wall, repairs to the Principal's house and the provision of six more hot-water baths through the sacrifice of two dormitory cubicles.[27]

There were, of course, limits to the generosity of the General Purposes Committee. In November 1891, a recommendation from the local Fire Brigade Superintendent for an emergency exit from the upper dormitory – ideally with a bridge across to the roof of the Principal's house – was rejected because it would in any case have to be kept locked to prevent students coming and going at will. 'The object of the Superintendent was to enable persons to get out of the College: the object of discipline is to make them keep in college and not to multiply exits', so a trapdoor and ladder from the upper to the lower dormitory were to be fitted instead.[28] Ever tactful, in his first annual report at the close of that year, Best was careful to say how much supper and the new baths were appreciated, and to commend 'the extension of liberty' granted to students as 'beneficial in the development of manliness and self-respect'.[29] By

1893, wooden partitions had been installed to create corridors alongside each classroom.[30] The following year, he obtained permission for students when visiting the city to wear straw hats 'with a proper and plain design upon the ribbon' as an alternative to their College caps, and also secured the building of a new sanatorium, so giving the College facilities for invalid care 'not surpassed in any training college' according to HMI two years later.[31] A students' recreation room (through the conversion of a former workshop) followed in 1897, as did an updated laboratory in 1901 and the first showers, the installation of which (by 1905) alleviated pressure for the fitting of any more baths.[32] Two surviving buildings of Best's era, now named Beswick (the practising school opened in 1901) and Cloisters (of 1907) are dealt with below.

The impression one has of the students in the 1890s, and indeed through to the First World War, is one of great camaraderie, and, despite inevitable

Figure 9: Cartoons of College Life by George A. Bamber (student, 1905-07). (CALS: ZCR 86/19/4.)

jokes about the food and compulsory Chapel, of a genuine pride and a certain enjoyment in being at Chester College. There was a sense of achievement in having risen through the ranks of pupil-teachers to qualify for admission[33] and they had a common goal at which to aim. Best certainly appreciated the importance of this *esprit de corps* and, as President of the College Club (as Allen had been before him), he was instrumental in ensuring its closer association with the College: in 1893, the rules were changed so as to admit all past and present College members automatically, the Music tutor Ardern was elected General Secretary in place of a former student and it began to meet on the campus instead of having to find premises elsewhere.[34] Cartoons sketched by two students in the early years of the twentieth century highlight unpunctuality, disruption in the dormitories, formal and informal music-making and various sporting activities, including rowing on the River Dee and the annual 'Muffs v. Duffs' fancy-dress football match, but give a clear impression of the College experience being a passage to success.[35] The Principal himself played the cello in Ardern's orchestra, along with his son and daughter, and in an interview for the journal, *The Teacher*, in 1905 claimed that the first performance in England of Wagner's *Last Supper of the Apostles* had taken place at the College. As he also told his interviewer, he greatly valued sport – hence the importance of keeping afternoons free of lectures – because it fostered 'friendly rivalry … decision and initiative', unlike the previously favoured military drill: 'such regularised movements may be good enough for the Germans'.[36]

The *Collegian* operated under the slogan 'On Chester On', which appeared on the front cover until the First World War and served in this late-Victorian and Edwardian period as the College motto. In his interview for *The Teacher*, Best explained that it had arisen from a misquotation of Sir Walter Scott's narrative poem, *Marmion*: '"Charge, Chester, charge! On, Stanley, on!"/Were the last words of Marmion'. 'You see' he added, 'Charge, Chester, Charge!' would be so inappropriate: we don't charge enough. Our fees are the lowest in the land'.[37] It was a motto which befitted a more confident institution than that of Chritchley's day. One of Allen's last acts as Principal had been to secure the formation – on the model of an Oxbridge college – of the Amalgamated Club so that the finances of sports and other societies could be controlled under the oversight of College tutors, though with students as committee members.[38] Under its auspices, cultural and sporting activity flourished and the *Collegian* delighted in reporting it all.

The first College athletics day was held in 1891, the same year that the Volunteer force won the National Artillery Association's Queen's Prize at Shoeburyness and returned to cheering crowds through the streets of

Figure 10: College Football team on the steps of the Principal's house, 1898: evidently a squad of 13. The Principal, John Best, is at the back, on the left; the future Principal, Richard Thomas, is the player on the left of the four in the middle row. (CALS: ZCR 86/17/95.)

Chester.[39] Organised gymnastics began in 1892, Cycling, Rambling, Harriers and (as an antidote to all this) Smoking Clubs were formed in the mid-1890s, a Rowing Club by the turn of the century, a dramatic society in 1910, and a branch of the Student Christian Movement in 1911. We read, for example, of the annual Muffs v. Duffs football match in September 1896 being won 6–1 by the Muffs, after a band had led a procession of players from the smoking room on to the pitch, a drum solo on an old biscuit box had been played at half-time, and sticking plasters and bandages had been liberally applied, including to one participant who had scored too many goals. At a more serious level, the College football team benefited from having the future Principal, Thomas – then a newly appointed Science tutor – as the regular left-back from that year; he continued after he had become Vice-Principal, though switching to right-back, playing his last match in an 11–0 victory over Manchester Day Training College in November 1905. The following spring the Rowing Club, by now well-established, was looking forward to a Past v. Present regatta with a series of races between crews drawn from the different cohorts. Meanwhile, the debating society encouraged not only formal debates but talks by guest speakers and 'impromptu speaking' on topics drawn from a hat. In spring 1897 Principal Best contributed two talks on Rome (one 'Ancient', one 'Modern') and the motion 'Is professionalism detrimental to sport?' was carried by 31 to 14. In November 1900, the question 'Is Smoking Injurious to the powers of body and mind?' received a resounding 'no', by 62 to 14.[40]

One important change affecting the rhythm of College life came in 1895, with a nationally imposed switch from a January to December academic year (with holidays only at Christmas/New Year and in the summer, apart from a long Easter weekend) to the now-familiar three terms running from September to July. It meant that the cohort entering in January 1894 left in July 1895 and their successors entering in January 1895 took their end-of-first-year exams after only six months. The normally sanguine Best lamented the 'unusual stress and anxiety' this had caused, exacerbated by prolonged severe frosts at the beginning of 1895 and then an outbreak of influenza which struck down five tutors, six servants and 24 students and necessitated the employment of two temporary nurses.[41] But it is hard to discern any adverse

Figure 11: A turn of the century view of the Rowing Club, with several coxed fours in action on the River Dee.

impact on exam results and in academic matters generally there was slow but steady progress as the old century gave way to the new. In 1892, HMI Oakeley reported that 'the tone of the College and its position in the class lists had much improved', a conclusion borne out by figures which Best made sure were brought to the governors' attention to demonstrate, as Chritchley had done, the improvements wrought by the experience at Chester. These showed that the percentage of students in all colleges nationally obtaining a first-class grade in the admission exam of 1890 had been 60, whereas for those entering Chester it had been only 23; however in the final certificate exams taken by these same students in 1892, the national figure for first-class grades was 51%, Chester's 40%.[42] By 1897, HMI Bennett reported that in most subjects Chester students were now performing above the national average: comments confirmed by results two years later when almost three-quarters of the certificates achieved by the senior students were in the first class.[43] By 1901, the proportions were not quite so good – 32 firsts, 10 seconds, 10 thirds among the seniors – but this still compared well with the national figures of 273 – 185 – 78.[44]

In line with nationwide trends, problems over recruitment and employability receded. The Principal's report for 1901 said that the most recent cohort had had no difficulty in finding jobs and that there were more candidates for admission than hitherto: 130 for 51 places. It is some evidence of the growing repute of the College, beyond its original Anglican and diocesan focus, that while 28 leavers that year found jobs in Lancashire, and four in Cheshire, 19 went elsewhere in the country – with more going to Board schools than Church schools.[45] Of the 1897 intake, 30 came from Church schools, 17 from Board schools, but when they left two years later the proportions were reversed: 16 went to Church schools, 30 to Board schools, including to establishments in Leeds and Bradford.[46] Applications for entry rose to 200 by 1908, for only 50 available places,[47] by which time, to get around the cap on recruitment imposed by the limits of dormitory accommodation, a tiny number of local men had begun to be admitted as non-resident day-students.[48]

HMIs gave much of the credit for these improvements to Best himself. HMI Bennett in 1894 said that 'he and Mrs Best seemed to spread themselves for the good of the students. The Principal showed an intimate knowledge of each individually'. One of his successors, Scott-Coward in 1902, considered him 'an admirable Head, excellent in temper, mind, tact and judgment'.[49] But they also warmly commended Ardern, who in addition to his teaching of Music, organisation of concerts and secretaryship of the College Club, prepared the students for recitations at HMI visits and served as part-time bursar; in 1904 the inspector of music had 'nothing but praise' for the excellent singing.[50] At a time when government thinking on schooling had moved on appreciably – 'payment by results' had finally been abolished in 1897 and the Committee of Council had recently stated that 'a school [was] a living thing … not merely … a factory producing a certain modicum of examinable knowledge'[51] – they were also full of praise for Lovell. In 1901, he was reported to be

> a very good normal master, who does not confine himself to mere perfunctory performance of what is required but by promotion of discussion among the men of subjects such as 'How to teach Geography', 'How to teach Drawing', he brings out what is latent in them and is able to direct and guide and encourage.[52]

It was to Lovell's credit that in his February 1903 report, HMI Scott-Coward reported that the students they had observed teaching 'showed careful training and practice. There had been much advance during the last few years'.[53] Most other staff also fared well: in 1902, for example, Potts was reported to have 'given a delightful lecture on the influence of Italian upon English Literature … very good', while Thomas, later to become Vice-Principal and Principal, was commended for his ability to popularise Science. These comments were generally much more positive in tone than they had been in Chritchley's day. One of the few stars of that period, Woodhouse, was sadly now seen as a weak link – 'well-read, studious … kind, but [of] no influence' – and he eventually left in 1896.[54]

One problem of the 1890s was the growing unsuitability of the practising school, too small for the number of trainees who needed an opportunity to give lessons and also – with its single large schoolroom open to the roof, which sometimes had three classes being taught side by side – seriously outmoded in design.[55] In 1892 Christ Church National School in Newtown, Chester – where the Head was a former College student familiar with Lovell's approach – began to be used as an alternative venue, replaced three years later by St John's, a three-storey school close to where the amphitheatre would later be discovered, built in the previous decade at the expense of the Duke of Westminster.[56] Best, whose former college at Derby had two practising schools of its own for a much smaller number of students, first raised the issue of building a new 'Model School' and converting the existing one into a dining room at a governors' meeting in July 1893. By November 1894, Harry Beswick, who designed several schools in Cheshire, had prepared plans, but the governors thought there was very little prospect of raising the necessary finance. However, the Principal persisted and by the end of the year had persuaded them to try, the matter being referred to the General

Purposes Committee who decided on a fundraising appeal. This was initially launched in 1896, when the Duke of Westminster led the way with a donation; after delays occasioned by the competing demands of the Queen's Diamond Jubilee, it was re-launched two years later, with the College Club being among those who contributed to a total cost in excess of £4,000. Beswick's plans were modified slightly

Figure 12: The Dining Hall as it appeared in the interwar period, clearly modelled on that of an Oxbridge college. (CALS: ZCR 86/7928.)

in the light of HMIs' suggestions and the need to economise, but when it was eventually opened by the Bishop of Chester on 15 December 1900 it gave the College a fine modern building, typical of its time in having a large central hall surrounded by separate classrooms.[57]

The former school duly became a dining room, and after oak panelling had been fitted to the interior walls in 1911, to accompany the existing roof beams, the next Principal could describe it as a 'really fine College hall' as if it belonged in Oxford or Cambridge.[58] The previous dining room became a recreation room in place of the one recently provided. The new building continued as the College School until the 1960s before conversion into an Art & Craft block, then in the 1980s into lecture and tutorial rooms and tutors' offices, initially in part for the Geography department and now for more general use. The usual view of what is known as the 'Beswick Building' today gives a misleading impression because it is the rear of the structure, facing inwards to the campus; the original façade looking out to Parkgate Road, where the main entrance was, was obscured when the Swimming Pool was inserted in 1974.[59] But though it now offered sufficient accommodation for all students to practise therein, almost from the outset it was not the only school used for this purpose. In the interests of broadening experience, schools in Birkenhead and Liverpool were already being used for teaching practice by 1905.[60]

The opening of the new practising school was a high point of Best's time at Chester College and he went on to oversee the construction of one further important building, the red-brick structure now labelled 'Cloisters'. In 1906, HMI Dale stressed the importance of a student common room as part of the 'civilizing influence' which he felt residential colleges like Chester could offer. This was seen as one of their advantages over day colleges attached to universities, which had come into being since 1890, and by the turn of the century were providing about 25% of the teacher training places available in England and Wales, and which from the government's perspective offered a cheaper alternative since they attracted far less grant. They were also regarded as 'secular' alternatives to the Church-dominated residential colleges, while claiming to offer a more stimulating intellectual environment since their students were not spending all their time 'among the same people preparing for the same profession'.[61] So a statement about what was 'different' about a residential college was timely and, when it opened in 1907, this fine new building duly provided on its first floor a spacious common room with a view to North Wales comparable to that enjoyed from the Principal's house. It certainly enhanced the College's appearance and amenities although, with hindsight, it would surely have been better to build a block of study-bedrooms instead. The College at York, for instance, did so in 1903; had the Principal sought inspiration from his own university he would have found recent examples at colleges including Christ's, Gonville & Caius and Trinity Hall.[62] Chester only decided to follow suit – with appalling timing – in the summer and autumn of 1914. The inevitable abandonment of this scheme led to the College having no substantial alternative to the dormitories – other than lodgings – for another four decades.[63]

In his later years, Best found general College affairs more difficult. As early as 1901, he had reported that the tone and discipline of the College 'had involved more care and anxiety during the last few years than heretofore', a circumstance he attributed to the development since the 1880s of pupil-teacher centres, which he felt discouraged loyalty and willing obedience once students encountered the more rigid regime of a college. These centres, mostly run by School Boards, offered what was in effect secondary education distinct from the elementary schools to which the pupil-teachers were attached, and there was a particular concentration of them in south Lancashire.[64] Best also pointed to the more liberal regimes of the rival day colleges, of which students were well aware: the University of Manchester had one from 1890, Liverpool from 1891. He put the best possible face on all this: 'we have been spared the insubordination at many colleges ... mutual relations between masters and students have never been happier than now'. But in 1900 he had been obliged – temporarily – to close down the Smoking Club where some second-years 'had shown mean malice and spite by petty annoyances ... it was becoming an active coterie simply setting all discipline at defiance'.[65]

To add to Best's concerns, as the new century dawned, various governmental reforms presented the College with a more challenging context in which to work. In 1900, the Committee of Council on Education was replaced by the Board of Education as the responsible government department. Two years later a new Education Act established Local Education Authorities (hereafter LEAs), which took over the Board Schools, were encouraged to develop rate-aided secondary education – so giving children an opportunity to progress from their elementary schools for more advanced study at the age of about 11 – and in a minority of cases began to provide their own teacher training colleges which were inevitably seen as rivals to their established peers.[66] Cheshire decided to build one at Crewe in 1908 and it opened four years later, with brand new study-bedrooms as student accommodation, ironically designed by the architect responsible for the recent Chester College school. Its railway links were second to none and it had the added attraction (for some) of recruiting both male and female students.[67] Meanwhile, various measures over the course of the decade, including the abolition of King's (formerly Queen's) Scholarships in 1906, had the effect of drastically curbing the supply of pupil-teachers, a scheme virtually extinct by the First World War although it would linger on in places through the interwar years. Increasingly, students were recruited instead from the secondary schools – usually having obtained some teaching experience in the meantime – with several taking advantage of a 'bursary' scheme introduced in 1907 allowing them an extra year's schooling above the age of 16.[68]

One immediate impact of the 1902 Act was the resignation of the excellent Lovell, who took advantage of the creation of the new Chester LEA the following year to become its first Director of Education.[69] Although there were some 100 applications for his post as 'Normal Master' and Head of the practising school, his chosen replacement, despite fine credentials,[70] was not a success in either respect. Best had to give him his notice in 1907, a move which prompted an end to resistance, by Principal and governors alike, to longstanding pressure from successive HMIs to separate the two elements of the post.[71] Practice among training colleges differed, some (like Chester) favouring the consistency of approach which came with the Normal Master also running the practising school, others following the Education Department's line, mediated through its HMIs, that the burden was too much for one person to carry.[72] So two different men were now appointed, one 'to lecture … on the History, Theory and Art of Education and to superintend the School Practice', the other as Head of the School, and in 1909 HMI Dale duly commended them both.[73]

Best eventually resigned in the summer of 1910 to take up the living of Sandon (near Chelmsford), to which he had been presented by the patrons, his old college of Queens' Cambridge: the first Principal to leave on the best of terms with his governors, who were fulsome in their praise. The advertisement for his successor, agreed in June, neatly summarised how the College saw itself at the time:

> … founded in 1839. There is accommodation for 105 Students (Resident) and there are a few Day Students. The majority of the Staff are Graduates of Cambridge or Oxford. There is a College Chapel, with Daily Services and Celebrations of Holy Communion on Sundays and Holy Days. The College possesses an excellent Model and Practising School.

We also know from a governors' inquiry into domestic arrangements that there were at this time, in addition to the College matron, six female servants – cook, two kitchen maids, scullery maid, between maid and seamstress – and about eight male servants, mostly assigned to the dining halls and dormitories but some doing outside work, in gardening and maintenance.[74] The *Collegian* summed up the general feeling as Best departed: 'his amiability has endeared him to all who know him'. Although both Rigg and Chritchley have busts in the Chapel, Best is the only Principal with a stained glass window in his memory, given after his death in May 1933 by his family and intended to show through the images of Saints Francis and Anselm both the pastoral and the academic sides of the character.[75]

Out of 40 applicants for the vacant Principalship, the governors interviewed four candidates on 20 July 1910. They appointed Revd Richard Albert Thomas, who had attended the King's School, Chester, as a child, had served as Science master and later Vice-Principal after joining the College as Woodhouse's successor in 1896, and had then become Vice-Principal of the Church College at Winchester in 1905; it is indicative of his ambition that he had got as far as an interview for the post of Principal of Bede College, Durham, as far back as 1904.[76] He was of course familiar with his predecessor's approach and the governors were doubtless hoping for more of the same. If so, they were not disappointed, with Thomas soon pursuing several initiatives to foster the collegial spirit. He introduced Founders' Day on Thursday 25 January 1912 as an annual opportunity to celebrate the history and ethos of the institution, with services in the Chapel and an evening dinner and concert. The guests on this first occasion included Lovell and Edward Rigg, son of the first Principal, and they were treated to a new 'Hymn for Founders' Day', with music composed by Ardern and words by the former headmaster of Harrow (now master of Trinity College, Cambridge) Henry Montagu Butler, celebrating 'the love of each for other' in 'this honoured pile'.[77] Thomas also completed in 1911 the installation of electric light throughout the College, a project begun by Best eight years earlier. Other early developments included the extension of teaching practice to schools in Northwich and Wrexham in 1912 and what may have been the first opening up of the campus to outside users when Chester Diocesan Sunday School Association was allowed to hold a training week during the summer vacation of 1913.[78] Nor did the new Principal neglect the support staff, for in January 1911 he pressed ahead with plans for an accommodation block for 'women servants' (no longer extant) and with arrangements to provide the matron with an assistant who would have particular responsibility for nursing the sick and overseeing the cleaning of sanatorium and dormitories.[79]

Clearly, Chester College was a more civilised place by the eve of the First World War than it had been a generation earlier. Under a succession of more enlightened Principals, there were marked improvements in the quality of teaching and in the environment within which students lived and worked. As in every other period there were challenges to be faced, especially those arising from changes to the pupil-teacher system and from the competition posed by new training colleges, but there seems to have been genuine pride and enjoyment in being part of the institution, on the part of students and staff alike. The College did, however, remain a tightly controlled community, as regulations governing student behaviour, issued by Thomas probably soon after his arrival, amply demonstrate.

> No Student may be absent from Lecture, Private Study, Meals or Chapel without the permission of the Vice-Principal … Students may leave the College precincts at all free times between 1.30 p.m. and 4.55 p.m. (Sundays 9 to 11.15 a.m. and 1.30 to 4.55 p.m., Saturdays 1.30 to 5.55 p.m.) but not at other times, except by printed Exeat to be obtained from the Vice-Principal … No Student may visit the Dormitories between first Roll-call and bed-time, except during the two short afternoon periods after dinner and before tea, without permission from the Vice-Principal … If a Student desires exemption from any College obligation, such as Roll-call or Lecture on the ground of sickness, he must not leave the College or College-grounds or engage in sport during the remainder of that day … Students may not smoke in any part of the College except in the Common-room and the College-grounds [or] in the streets of the City, which term includes Cheyney Road and all that part of the City that lies to the south of Cheyney Road … It is expected of all Students that they should exercise due care in the matter of dress, and take responsibility for the order of their bedrooms, desks, etc.'[80]

Within a few years, the students subjected to all this were fighting and dying on the Western Front.

1   Wrangler is a University of Cambridge term for those gaining a First-class Honours degree in Mathematics and the Senior Wrangler gains the highest mark for that year. The Senior Optime gains the highest mark in the Second-class Honours degree classification.

2   ZCR 86/1/3: 11 December 1885; D. Forfar, 'What became of the Senior Wranglers?', *Mathematical Spectrum*, XXIX (1996–97), pp. 1–4. Allen's immediate predecessor and successor as Senior Wrangler, E.W. Robson (1878) and Joseph Larmor (1880) both went on to hold Professorships in Mathematics at Cambridge.

3   ZCR 86/12/33; ZCR 86/1/3: 19 March 1886; ZCR 86/12/33: Allen's report, 1886.

4   Rich, *Training of Teachers*, pp. 196–97.

5   ZCR 86/1/3: 29 June 1885; *Collegian*, Lent 1933, p. 25 (Lovell's obituary).

6   Cf. Chapter 3, note 36.

7   Allen's summary of the establishment under Chritchley may be supplemented by a staff list for 1881 compiled by a former student, James Lyon, and inserted into his scrapbook (ZCR 86/7928). This confirms the seven tutors apart from the Principal and Vice-Principal and mentions also Mrs Thurlow the matron and a waiter called George whose surname the student did not know.

8   Cf. Chapter 3.

9   *Collegian*, Christmas 1933, pp. 109–10 (Stewart's obituary); ZCR 86/1/3: 12 April 1886, 12 June 1886. A window in Wilkinson's memory is in Chester's Cathedral cloisters.

10 ZCR 86/1/3: 12 June 1886.

11 *Collegian*, Summer 1954, p. 12.

12 ZCR 86/13/5.

13 ZCR 86/1/3: 23 May 1889.

14 *Collegian*, February 1888, pp. 2–3, 6; May 1888, p. 8; March 1889; vol. 8, VII, no. 7[1894], pp. 14–16. The popularity of shop assistants' teams arose from the custom of Wednesdays being 'early closing day'.

15 ZCR 86/1/3: 27 March, 23 May, 30 September 1889; *pers. comm.* (via Fiona Roberts) P. Winthrope of Delta, British Columbia.

16 ZCR 86/1/3: 20 May 1887.

17 ZCR 86/1/3: 23 May 1889.

18 ZCR 86/1/3: 27 March 1889.

19 ZCR 86/1/3: 27 March, 21 April, 5 June 1890.

20 ZCR 86/1/3: 5 June 1890.

21 ZCR 86/1/3: 24 July, 3 September 1890. In 1893, Derby had 44 students compared to Chester's 108: *Report of the Committee of Council on Education, 1893–94* (London 1894), pp. 146, 190.

22 ZCR 86/1/4: 13 October, 11 December 1890.

23 *The Acts of the Apostles*, ed. A.J.C. Allen (London, 1891); A.J.C. Allen, *The Church Catechism: its History and Contents: A Manual for Teachers and Students* (London, 1892), pp. vii–viii; Allen's last book was *The Christ of the Future: A Criticism and a*

Forecast (London, 1920), a spirited defence of orthodoxy against modern liberal theology.

24   <<http://www.tolliss.com/gedview/family.php?famid=F4637>>, accessed 18/3/13; *Collegian*, December. 1923 (obituary), p. 33.

25   Horn, *Education in Rural England*, pp. 97–98.

26   See Chapter 3.

27   ZCR 86/12/39; ZCR 86/1/4: 13 April, 14 May 1891.

28   ZCR 86/2/1: 2 November 1891.

29   ZCR 86/12/39.

30   ZCR 86/1/4: 12 December 1892, 18 May 1893.

31   ZCR 86/2/1: 25 June 1894; ZCR 86/1/4: 30 April 1896.

32   ZCR 86/1/5: 19 February 1897; ZCR 86/1/8: 24 March 1905; Bradbury, *Chester College*, p. 180. Showers had been suggested by HMI Scott-Coward in 1900; there had been scepticism at the governors' meeting over whether the students would use them but HMI had confirmed that their introduction had proved popular elsewhere (ZCR 86/1/5: 16 March 1900).

33   *Pupil-Teachers' Classified Examination Questions* (London, 1895), pp. 17, 91, 107, includes the following as examples of what students of this period would have had to master before entry to the College: 'Find the exact difference between the simple and compound interest on £6,072 for 3 years at 3 ½ per cent per annum … Explain the meaning of each of these terms and make sentences containing illustrations of their use: passive, antithesis, co-ordinate, apposition, infinitive of purpose, demonstration, ellipsis … State the requirements of the Code in geography for the Fourth and Fifth Standards and say how geography may be made useful and interesting to children.'

34   ZCR 86/8/1: 7 October 1893; ZCR 86/1/5: 9 December 1901; Dawtry, 'All Work and No Play', pp. 77–79.

35   ZCR 86/19/3; ZCR 86/19/4.

36   ZCR 86/13/1, pt. 1: *The Teacher*, 7 January 1905, pp. 16–10; *Collegian*, 1985, p. 46. Best managed to avoid mentioning in his interview an 'invasion of rats which had been repulsed with some difficulty', reported to the governors just over a year earlier (ZCR 86/2/3: 16 November 1903).

37   Cf. for low fees, ZCR 86/1/5: 9 October 1899.

38   Bradbury, *Chester College*, p. 174.

39   *Collegian*, August 1891, p. 2; Dawtry, 'All Work and No Play', pp. 76–77.

40   *Collegian*, November 1896, March 1897, November 1900, March 1906, pp. 11, 13; Dawtry, 'All Work and No Play', pp. 77–78.

41   ZCR 86/5/1; ZCR 86/12/43: Principal's Reports, July and December 1895.

42   ZCR 86/1/4: 20 May 1892, 10 April 1893; for Chritchley's figures showing 'added value', see Chapter 3.

43   ZCR 86/1/5: 5 April 1897, 9 October 1899.

44   ZCR 86/5/1: 1901.

45   ZCR 86/1/5: 9 December 1901.

46 ZCR 86/5/1: 1897–99.

47 ZCR 86/1/8: 5 October 1908.

48 ZCR 86/1/8: 24 March 1905, 8 October 1906.

49 ZCR 86/1/4: 25 May 1894; ZCR 86/1/5: 20 March 1902.

50 ZCR 86/1/5: 20 June 1904.

51 *Report of the Committee of Council on Education, 1897-98*, pp. xv–xvi, quoted in Goldstrom, *Elementary Education*, p. 162.

52 ZCR 86/1/5: 14 March 1901.

53 ZCR 86/1/5: 27 February 1903; G.J. White, 'Three Great Tutors: Lovell, Ardern, Morrell', in White, *Perspectives*, pp. 63–74, at p. 66.

54 ZCR 86/1/5: 20 March 1902; ZCR 86/1/4: 25 May 1894, 30 April 1896. According to the reminiscences of a former colleague published in the *Collegian*, Christmas 1949, pp. 80–82, Woodhouse was 'the mystery man of the College', very able but 'to the students … a sealed book', better regarded by Allen than by Best.

55 *Collegian*, Summer 1954, p. 12; M.V.J. Seaborne, *Primary School Design* (London, 1971), pp. 13–28.

56 ZCR 86/1/4: 20 May 1892, 20 February 1895, 30 April 1896.

57 ZCR 86/1/4: 10 July 1893, 16 March, 15 June 1896; ZCR 86/1/5: 13 December 1897, 22 June, 12 December 1898, 14 October 1901; ZCR 86/2/1: 12 November 1894; ZCR 86/12/48; *Collegian*, 1983, pp. 38–41; Seaborne, 'The College Buildings', pp. 36–38.

58 ZCR 86/13/1 pt 1: interview with Thomas in *Cheshire Observer*, 17 December 1932.

59 Seaborne, 'The College Buildings', pp. 37–39.

60 ZCR 86/1/8: 16 October 1905.

61 Rich, *Training of Tearchers*, pp. 215, 221–33; J.B. Thomas, 'Victorian Beginnings' and 'Day Training College to Department of Education' in J.B. Thomas, ed., *British Universities and Teacher Education: A Century of Change* (London, 1990), pp. 14, 19; P. Gardner, 'Higher Education and Teacher Training: A Century of Progress and Promise' in J. Furlong and R. Smith, eds, *The Role of Higher Education in Initial Teacher Training* (London, 1996), pp. 35–49, esp. pp. 38–45. There were 16 day training departments attached to British universities by 1902 (W.A.C. Stewart, *Higher Education in Postwar Britain*, Basingstoke, 1989, p. 25). The quotation is from O. Browning, *The Importance of the Training of Teachers* (Cambridge, 1906), p. 12; Browning was Principal of the day training college at Cambridge.

62 G.P. McGregor, *A Church College for the 21st Century? 150 Years of Ripon & York St John* (York, 1991), p. 101; N. Pevsner, *The Buildings of England: Cambridgeshire* (2nd ed., Harmondsworth, 1970), pp. 54, 81, 181; C. Hartwell, M. Hyde, E. Hubbard and N. Pevsner, *The Buildings of England: Cheshire* (New Haven and London, 2011), p. 312.

63 See Chapters 5, 7.

64 Rich, *Training of Teachers*, pp. 236–45; W. Robinson, *Pupil Teachers and their Professional Training in Pupil Teacher Centres in England and Wales, 1870-1914* (Lampeter, 2003), pp. 36–40, 253–54, 256.

65 ZCR 86/1/5: 12 December 1900, 9 December 1901.

66 Cheshire was one of the pioneers; by 1914, only 20 out of 146 LEAs had founded their own teacher training colleges (B. Collins and R. Morgan, *Celebrating a Centenary: Teacher Education at Sheffield Hallam University*, Sheffield, 2005, p. 9).

67 This is now the Crewe campus of Manchester Metropolitan University.

68 Dent, *Training of Teachers*, pp. 47–56: Robinson, *Pupil Teachers*, pp. 40–42.

69 White, 'Three Great Tutors', pp. 64–66.

70 ZCR 86/1/5: 12 October 1903. Taylor, the successful candidate, was son of the Normal Master at Battersea and Head of St George's School, Hanover Square; however, HMI Dale (ZCR 86/1/8: 6 December 1906) considered his manner 'rough and repellent' and criticised his work in both aspects of the post.

71 ZCR 86/1/8: 11 March, 17 June, 7 October 1907.

72 ZCR 86/2/2: 11 December 1899, where Best reports the results of his enquiries of other colleges. At Battersea the posts were combined (as at Chester); at Peterborough they had been separated in accordance with the government's wishes but the result had not been favourable; at Saltley and Exeter the separation of the posts was working well, but required vigilance.

73 ZCR 86/1/8: 4 March 1909.

74 ZCR 86/1/8: 11 October 1909, 20 June 1910.

75 *Collegian*, June 1910, p. 1; ZCR 86/1/9: 7 December 1934, 15 March 1935; ZCR 86/12/59: Assistant Matron's duties, 17 January 1911.

76 ZCR 86/1/8: 20 June 1910; ZCR 86/2/3: 16 November 1903, 16 February 1904.

77 *Collegian*, March 1912, pp. 2–4; White, 'Three Great Tutors', p. 63; *Chester College Song Book* (1939), p. 20 (author's copy).

78 ZCR 86/1/8: 22 June 1903, 12 June 1911, 18 March 1912, 10 March 1913.

79 ZCR 86/12/59: Assistant Matron's duties, 17 January 1911; Letter of New to Board of Education, 10 January 1911.

80 ZCR 86/12/58.

CHAPTER 5

THE FIRST WORLD WAR AND ITS AFTERMATH

Limited-circulation publications such as the *Collegian* are invaluable evidence of the grass-roots public mood at the outset of the First World War. The September 1914 edition strikes a tone not of foreboding but of defiant optimism, with mention of plans to form a College Company for Home Defence and an old students' 'Pals' unit, neither of which proved to be feasible. There was news of individuals who had enlisted (all still alive, although one was a prisoner of war) and the reproduction of Thomas Hardy's 'Song of the Soldiers': 'March we to the field ungrieving/In our hearts believing/Victory crowns the just'. Also featured was a College Greeting 'to all those Old Students who represent the College in this greatest of all wars and who set so fine an example of intelligent and devoted patriotism … the College … will follow their fortunes with affectionate interest. Floreat Collegium!'[1] Despite the circumstances, virtually all places were filled for the autumn of 1914 and in June of that year Thomas proposed the building of a new student hostel, intended for 120 study-bedrooms; accordingly, in October, the governors agreed to buy a further two acres of land to the north of the campus, roughly in the area now occupied by the University library, while acknowledging that fundraising for the new building would have to await the end of the War.[2] However, they simultaneously authorised the Principal to spend £50 on a miniature rifle range if he wanted to and it was not long before the dire consequences of a prolonged armed conflict became all too apparent.

With recruitment falling, and existing students leaving to join the forces, the National Society proposed a concentration of the Church of England male training colleges. Among these, St Mark's Chelsea, Culham and Winchester all closed in summer 1914, Cheltenham, Exeter and Peterborough a year later, with such students as continued their training being found places elsewhere.[3] By October 1915, the number of Chester students still in College was down to 58, but they had been supplemented by 39 incomers from Cheltenham; one member of staff from Cheltenham, and two from Exeter, had also arrived. This only delayed matters. In the early months of 1916 staff were given notice in case the College closed down in the summer, and arrangements were made for the Principal's wife – who had been the country's first female head of a co-educational secondary school[4] – to take charge if Thomas was called up as an army chaplain. By August, with a further concentration plan in place and a supplementary grant available as an inducement to accept it, the governors reluctantly agreed 'temporarily to close the College' and to its occupation for the rest of the War by St Lawrence's College, Ramsgate, then a boys-only boarding school.[5] The practising school continued under LEA management but most of the staff seem to have dispersed, with Thomas himself later receiving an OBE for his sterling work as Acting Chaplain General to the Fifth Army which faced the German Spring offensive in 1918. Seventy-seven past and present College students lost their lives in the War. They were commemorated through a major refurbishment of the library (now the Senior Common Room) in 1924 and the placing three years earlier of a war memorial tablet in the Chapel, where one line left blank is said to reflect the initial inclusion of a man who survived.[6]

One indirect victim of the First World War was Ardern, who suffered a major breakdown in 1919 following the loss of his eldest son, not to mention so many of his former students, and was off work for some two years. The College Club – of which he was still secretary – raised funds for him to have specialist treatment and a recuperative holiday but having returned to his duties he died of pneumonia and pleurisy in May 1923, after being soaked by heavy rain on a visit to supervise teaching practice at Backford school. A further appeal by the Club raised the funds for a memorial window to him in the College Chapel, the place enriched by his music for over 35 years. It is an irony that in 1922 the government's Board of Education had made it clear that it now expected all College tutors to have at least a Second-class Honours degree:[7] Ardern, who had arrived via the teacher-training route through St Mark's Chelsea, was by then one of only two members of the teaching staff who were not University graduates. Yet he had given the College a subject, and an activity, in which it was nationally recognised as excellent. Sir John Stainer, then serving as the government's Inspector of Music, had afforded Chester a better report in 1898 than any other training college and he produced a special arrangement of his Sevenfold Amen for use in the College Chapel.[8] His successor Arthur (later Sir Arthur) Somervell had written in 1907 that 'both individually and collectively the men attain a high standard; it is no small thing that in a College of 110 students, there should be an orchestra of 33, many members of which have learnt their instruments since they came to College'.[9] One of Ardern's enduring legacies is the tuition he gave to William Ferrier, who left College in 1890 with a testimonial praising his 'good voice … excellent ear and … ready knowledge of the theory of music', attributes he would later pass on to his world-famous daughter Kathleen.[10] Fittingly, Ardern remains the only College tutor – outside the ranks of Principals – to have his own stained-glass window in the Chapel and a memorial within the nave rather than the antechapel. The *Collegian* of June 1923 devoted over eight pages to tributes following his death.[11]

In August 1918, as the War drew to a close, the Fisher Education Act received the royal assent. Among its provisions was the raising of the minimum school leaving age from 12 (where it had been since 1899) to 14, although it took a further Act in 1921 to bring this into force. As we have seen, 'higher-grade schools' such as the College School had already been catering for pupils in their early teens in the closing years of the nineteenth century. As 'higher elementary schools' they continued to do so under the revised arrangements introduced by the 1902 Act and in the years immediately after the War several were converted to 'central' schools, specifically for those of 11 years and upwards; this was the case with three in Chester, one of which was the College School. These 'central' schools, though 'elementary' in their classification were clearly 'secondary' in the level of their work.[12] This meant that by the interwar period, the College, though its roots were in elementary teacher training, was actually covering ground we would now regard as more appropriate for 'secondary' level, in terms of both professional practice and academic study. Students emerged as suitable for both 'primary' and 'secondary' work: practice in their own College school was with older boys, while other schools were found to give them experience teaching younger children. In 1936, Astbury responded to a Board of Education query by reporting that all 101 students who had left the previous summer had taken the course for 'general practitioners' – as opposed to those for 'specialists' or

Figure 13: The College orchestra, with Ardern seated in the middle of the front row, shortly before the First World War. The picture is undated, but several students appear in group photographs of those who left in 1913 and 1914. (CALS: ZCR 86/17/66.)

'infants teachers' – but an HMI report in the same year noted that most Chester students taking Science were actually aiming for secondary schools.[13]

With this 'secondary' target in mind, colleges like Chester in the 1920s and 1930s offered an advanced curriculum. The Physics syllabus a few years before the Second World War embraced Ohm's, Joule's and Faraday's laws, electromagnetism, relative motion and the refraction of light, while Chemistry ranged over the properties of metals, non-metals and carbon compounds and included practical work in volumetric analysis using various acids and alkalis. English Literature, to take one other example, offered Henry V, Hamlet and Antony and Cleopatra as 'Shakespeare', a selection from Chaucer, Milton, Pope, Shelley and Tennyson as 'English poetry', and works by Bacon, Johnson, Hazlitt and Arnold ('Culture and Anarchy') as 'representative prose'.[14] Bradbury testifies from personal experience to the high calibre of many members of the College during this interwar period, eminently suitable for any university of the time had they had the financial means.[15] In an era when less than 2% of Britain's 18-year-olds attended university, usually reliant on highly competitive scholarships if parental help was not available, the grants from the Board of Education to those engaged in teacher training provided a very welcome alternative route into the closest approximation the colleges could offer to 'higher education'.[16]

At a political level, the Church training colleges prepared for the changed post-war environment by forming an overarching General Council of Governing Body representatives, so as to protect common interests. It met only occasionally and in practice delegated its functions to a Board of Supervision, whose executive comprised representatives of the National Society, college governors and the Church of England Central Board of Finance. The College itself reopened in September 1919, though it needed extra financial help from the Board of Supervision and the government's Board of Education in order to do so.[17] There were initial concerns, at Chester as throughout the sector, about poor recruitment. A 'new illustrated prospectus' which 'it is hoped … may prove useful in recruiting candidates' was introduced in spring 1921; even so, prospects for that September looked so bleak that Thomas sent out an appeal to the clergy of the diocese, to former students and to others with influence, asking for their help in persuading suitable candidates to consider teaching in preference to careers in business.[18] These initiatives must have been successful, since by the start of the academic year there were in fact 121 residential and six day-students, with those in residence who could not be accommodated in dormitories having to be found lodgings instead; some 70 were ex-servicemen, several of whom – to the

Principal's evident anxiety – had had to take out a loan in order to meet their fees.[19]

Numbers steadily increased thereafter – by 1922 to 150, by 1924 to 160, by 1929 to 183 – with Thomas declaring his opinion in 1925 that 'a College which held 200 students could be worked to the greatest economical advantage'.[20] This figure was soon revised upwards. At the end of the decade, Ramsay MacDonald's minority Labour government declared its intention of raising the school leaving age to 15 from April 1931, so creating a demand for yet more trained teachers, with colleges being invited to bid for extra places. In response, the governors agreed in March 1930 to request Board of Education permission to have 220 as a 'permanent' figure and duly recruited that number in September. Even this meant that the College was only one-fifth of the size of its LEA competitor at Crewe.[21] Behind the College's drive for expansion was a wish for financial security; an increased volume of students with their attendant government grants and fees being seen as a more reliable source of income than fluctuating subventions from the Church of England Board of Supervision. In a clear reversal of policy under previous Principals – and with a view to generating a surplus which could be spent on new buildings – the raising of the fee to £25 per annum in 1925 made Chester the highest-charging of any Church college, with above-average expenditure on each student as well.[22]

More students meant, of course, a need for more land and buildings. A further purchase of over 10 acres to the north of the campus in 1928, financed by bank loans,[23] ensured that the College got its hands on all the land extending west to the canal and north to the railway embankment – erected in the mid-1880s to carry a line from Chester Northgate station to Hawarden – save for two strips of housing, running along and inwards from Parkgate Road, which were all that the development intended to become upmarket residential 'Exton Park' had managed to accomplish.[24] In 1931, the students threw themselves into an earth-moving scheme for levelling part of this area for use as playing fields, a purpose for which Thomas purchased '120 yards of miniature railway, a turntable and 8 tipping wagons';[25] even so, the slope down towards the canal in the north-western corner – where the main staff and students' car park was eventually sited in the 1990s after a major landfill operation – was so steep that it drew the comment from surveyors that it 'will probably never be utilised for any other purpose than grazing'.[26] The area beyond Exton Park would not be built upon for another four decades, but at a time of financial stringency these purchases were remarkably far-sighted, fundamental to the College's growth in the last third of the twentieth century. As Thomas put it in the *Collegian* of summer term 1928, 'I venture to prophesy that the value and significance of this large open space in time to come will be incalculably great'.[27]

There was no success, however, with another intended purchase, that of Abbot's Grange, lying between Parkgate Road and Liverpool Road, opposite where the Tower block now stands. This included two large houses suitable for accommodating students currently in lodgings but was otherwise a vacant plot where a hostel of study-bedrooms could be built: a revival of the hope that the dormitories could be replaced, as envisaged back in 1914. Thomas first raised the possibility of buying this late in 1925, the year when the diocesan training college in Birmingham (St Peter's Saltley), a men's college of similar size to Chester, set about planning a fine new hostel ('South Wing') duly opened by the end of the decade. But at Chester, despite a special meeting of the General Purposes Committee, a decision was deferred. He urged it upon the governors again in June 1928, only for a decision again to be put off. Thomas claimed to have been promised that he would be informed if the land was likely to be sold to another party, so he was doubtless shocked to learn in May 1929 that it had been bought by a local builder for housing. Only now were the governors induced to make an offer for the land, but this time to the builder who wanted an exorbitant price.[28] So construction went ahead with the semi-detached houses which still ring Abbot's Grange and the College, having missed an opportunity, was left to look elsewhere for a hostel site.

Attention turned instead to an area just outside 'The Close', immediately north of the access way from Parkgate Road, with Theodore Fyfe, Head of the School of Architecture at Cambridge, being engaged to design a new gymnasium and a four-storey block of 100 study-bedrooms to occupy the site. According to a plan of June 1931, the gymnasium was to be placed just east of the present location of the Binks building – although this would have involved buying two houses and adjoining land in Exton Park – while the hostel was to be built where the modern Seaborne Library stands.[29] Fyfe also produced plans for the conversion of the dormitories in the original College building, providing on the top floor both laboratories and (with future ambitions to increase their numbers in mind) 'research rooms for degree students'.[30] The enlargement of the Chapel was also mooted. However, lack of funds meant that these schemes did not proceed. They might have done had the Governing Body been willing to borrow heavily to finance building projects, as some other Church colleges such as York decided to do,[31] but prudence prevailed with near-disastrous consequences in the following decade, as we shall see in a later chapter. In the event, Fyfe's plans for a new west gallery to provide extra space in the Chapel did eventually bear fruit in

1936. A two-storey Arts, Crafts and Science block, now known appropriately as the Thomas building, was also opened to Fyfe's design in 1931, although this was only completed to his original scheme in 1939.[32] In the meantime, for student accommodation, the College had to be content with the purchase for £1,175 of no. 4 Exton Park, which being outside 'The Close' became known as the 'College Annexe'.[33] This appears to have been accommodating five 'Extonians' by 1933, a number increased to 16 through some rearrangement of the rooms at the end of that year.[34]

Through the 1920s, the shadow of the First World War hung over the College, as over society in general – seen, for example, in the foundation of student branches of Toc H (a Christian social service group which had originated for the benefit of troops in Belgium in 1915) and of the British Universities League of Nations. As for the routine of College life, much of it bore a superficial resemblance to that of pre-war days. The curriculum was delivered by the same number of tutors as before, seven plus the Principal and Vice-Principal; at least three of these, apart from Thomas, were resident at any time. Studies encompassed Education (that is, Principles and Practice of Teaching with teaching practice both built into the weekly timetable through the practising school and in blocks using schools elsewhere), English, History, Geography, Religious Knowledge, Mathematics, Science, Nature Study, Art, Handwork, Hygiene, Music, French and Physical Training (PT), the latter a subject the government was keen to improve in schools after the shocking revelations about the nation's physical health made apparent by wartime recruitment campaigns. When Thomas took over, the College had a poor reputation for PT but by the early 1920s good HMI reports were being received, despite the enforced use of the central hall in the practising school in the continued absence of the gymnasium for which inspectors had been pressing since at least 1905.[35] Among these subjects, both English and Principles and Practice of Teaching were compulsory and four or five others had to be taken as well,[36] so a 'shared curriculum' common to everyone was largely but not entirely the case.

The retention of the dormitories with their open-topped cubicles – essentially the pattern of the 1840s – meant that students continued to enjoy, or endure, only limited privacy, although since the maximum capacity of the dormitories was little over 100 here again there was inevitably some dilution of the 'common experience': increasing numbers came to be accommodated elsewhere, mostly in lodgings but with the addition of an army hut to cope with some of the 220 students expected for 1930.[37] Sport remained very prominent – with the timetable still mostly suspended on weekday afternoons to facilitate it – although the annual fancy-dress football match

Figure 14: The College Harriers' Club, 1928. (ZCR 86/7928.)

between the 'Muffs' and the 'Duffs' seems not to have survived the War. It disappeared without any explanation in the *Collegian*, but it may be that the spectacle of students bandaging one another as 'walking wounded' was now in poor taste.[38] Meanwhile, a matron continued to govern domestic arrangements, and the postholder from 1919 to 1936, Miss Wills, received warm tributes in the pages of the *Collegian* from one outgoing cohort to the next, never more so than at her retirement, when she was acclaimed for her 'great influence on the whole life of the College … her kindliness and care … energy and cheerfulness'.[39] And the old concern to control students' freedom of movement persisted. When the building of a new lavatory block in 1924 had the unintended consequence of making it easy for students to enter and leave the campus at unauthorised times, a 'reasonably high wall with a door in it' had to be built.[40]

But within all this there were several changes. In the early 1920s, elected prefects oversaw student life and a Students' Council – partly composed of the same people – discussed matters of common interest and occasionally raised issues with the Principal; this was replaced in 1925 by an amalgamated 'Guild Council of Prefects' which combined both roles. We do not have to agree with the *Collegian* that 'the inauguration of the Guild Council is one of the biggest landmarks in College history' but it did have enhanced powers to control expenditure on 'all … matters pertaining to the welfare and comfort of the students' – making grants, for example, to the Amalgamated Sports

Figure 15: Dramatic Society, 1930. The two women on the front row are (left to right) Mabel Thomas, wife of the Principal, and Nellie Waywell, whose husband taught PT. They are flanked by the Principal (in clerical collar) and the future Vice-Principal and College historian, John Bradbury. (CALS: ZCR 86/7928.)

Committee – and it had an immediate impact, improving the appearance of the dining hall and securing the abolition of Sunday morning roll call.[41] As for organised leisure activities, these continued to diversify. A billiard room was provided in the basement of the original building in 1924, a pavilion and hard tennis court in 1928–29.[42] The *Collegian* of Lent Term 1930 carried reports of rowing, football, the harriers, rugby, boxing, hockey, swimming and tennis, of a concert given by the senior year, of Parnassus (for play-readings), the Student Christian Movement, Toc H, the League of Nations Society, Photographic, Wireless, Dramatic and Literary Societies and of Societies devoted to Modern Languages, History, Music and Natural Sciences. The activities of the Wireless Society had embraced both a lecture on television ('which we trust will bear fruit in a very short while') and broadcasts open to all College members, ranging from the football results to reports on an international naval conference in London. The Dramatic Society – reinforced by the wives of both the Principal and the PT lecturer to play the female roles – had performed Pirandello's 'The Man with a Flower in his Mouth' and Shaw's 'The Admirable Bashville', also contributing Schnitzer's 'The Mate' to the British Drama League festival at Liverpool.[43]

One of the most notable introductions of the interwar period was the College Rag, which, following on from an intermittent series of street-collections in fancy dress – possibly a substitute for the tomfoolery of 'Muffs v. Duffs' – became an annual event in 1923: complete with procession into the city, music performed from a lorry parked in the Town Hall Square and stunts throughout the afternoon and early evening. The *Chester Chronicle* reported (approvingly) that 'peaceful citizens were held up by weirdly attired nondescripts who demanded money in no mild or half-hearted way' while the *Collegian* considered Saturday 26 May 1923 to have been a great success, with over £146 collected for Chester Royal Infirmary and Chester Council for Social Welfare through the efforts of a motley crew of 'pianists, violinists, singers, organ grinders, handcuff manipulators, hypnotists, artists, elocutionists, etc.'. The following year Tutankhamun emerged from his (recently discovered) tomb to watch a medieval tournament and by 1925 students were jumping into the River Dee off the suspension bridge.[44]

A staff contract which survives from this period gives a glimpse of prevailing expectations. It was signed by Eric Pickup, appointed to teach French as from 1 January 1929, who as a 'resident assistant teacher' was required 'to reside in College during term-time receiving board, rooms, medical attendance and laundry', with vacations at Christmas, Easter and in the summer totalling at least 12 weeks. His duties apart from covering his academic subject included 'some supervision of resident students, some supervision of students' studies and some supervision of teaching practice'. In the event, he was to remain on the staff until 1969, by which time he was Head of a department of Linguistics which embraced English Literature, French and Drama.[45]

Pickup's appointment was one of a number of significant staff changes during the 1920s, including the appointment of a private secretary to the Principal in 1928: the person concerned, Douglas Jones, was the only full-time administrator on the College staff until after the Second World War and as such handled salaries and wages, accounts and record-keeping. He continued in a central administrative role, save for five years' war service (which included fighting in North Africa and Normandy) right through to 1970, when he retired as College Registrar.[46] Among the departures, both the Vice-Principal, Revd David Boyle, and the longstanding lecturer in History, Latin and English Literature, Andrew Potts – who had served for over 38 years since his appointment by Chritchley – retired in 1922. Of these two, Potts was sufficiently well-regarded to have a plaque in his memory installed in the antechapel. A serious-minded scholar who had won prizes after graduating from Oxford and had helped Allen with his *Church Catechism* book, he also

Figure 16: Rag Day, 1929, with students outside the gateway leading into Abbey Square, Chester. (CALS: ZCR 86/7928.)

served for a time as a meticulous College bursar and in his retirement contributed a remarkably forward-looking article for the *Collegian*, challenging current orthodoxies on the post-Roman 'English settlement' and championing the role of archaeology and philology to the advancement of knowledge of the period. Nothing could be further from the dry, memorise-the-facts-in-the-text-book approach which had prevailed when he arrived.[47]

The withdrawal of these two senior members of staff allowed the engagement – at an initial salary saving of £500 per annum, Thomas was delighted to note![48] – of a pair of young tutors destined to be among the longest-serving and most devoted of the twentieth century. They were John Bradbury to teach English Language and Literature and Frederick Hooper to teach Science. Bradbury would eventually become Vice-Principal in 1951 and after retiring in 1965 would write his book on the history of the College, while Hooper would have a long and distinguished career teaching various branches of Science until his retirement in 1961. At the end of 1929 came the first Professorial appointment, when Robert Newstead, who had been first curator of Chester's Grosvenor Museum and was now an Emeritus Professor of Liverpool University, was appointed part-time to teach the newly introduced subject of Rural Science[49] – an arrangement which continued until summer 1934. Meanwhile in 1922, Herbert Morrell, who had joined the College staff as assistant Method Master and tutor in Maths and Science 11 years earlier, was promoted to Master of Method, immediately making his mark in an area which was once again attracting criticism from HMI for being outmoded in its approach. He informalised the lectures to encourage more discussion, put renewed focus on 'criticism lessons' as regular features of the weekly timetable and added schools in Ellesmere Port, New Ferry and Port Sunlight to those in and around Chester, in Liverpool and in Birkenhead which were already being used for teaching practice. The College school itself came to be called the 'Practising and Demonstration School' – or simply the College School – because it was here that Morrell personally showed groups of students how to teach children, as Lovell had done in the past. In 1924 he also became Vice-Principal, the first layman to hold the post if we discount Stewart's appointment prior to ordination in 1886. This position had been left vacant for the past two years presumably as an economy measure, but he went on to combine these posts, along with a role (in succession to Ardern) as secretary of the College Club, until his retirement in 1951. For his 40 years of outstanding service, and for the profound influence he had on generations of schoolmasters and headteachers active from the 1930s to the 1980s, Morrell has a strong claim to be regarded as the greatest of all among the College's fine sequence of tutorial staff.[50]

1   *Collegian*, September 1914, pp. 49–56.
2   ZCR 86/7/3: *Annual Report on Chester Training College, 1914*, p. 9; ZCR 86/1/ 8: 21 October 1914.
3   ZCR 86/7/4: *Annual Report on Chester Training College, 1915*, p. 5.
4   *Cheshire Observer*, 18 November 1939 (her obituary); the school was at Newport, Isle of Wight.
5   ZCR 86/1/8: 19 July, 28 July, 20 October 1915, 21 January, 22 March, 11 August, 18 October 1916.
6   *Collegian*, December 1921, p. 17; the memorial in the Chapel was unveiled by former Principal Best, who would have known most of those whose names appear.
7   ZCR 86/1/8: 13 December 1922.
8   CC, *Chester College Songs*, 1913, p. 32.
9   White, 'Three Great Tutors', p. 68; cf. *Collegian*, Summer 1954, p. 12, for reference to Stainer's admiration for Ardern's work as early as 1888.
10 ZCR 86/13/1, pt. 2.
11 *Collegian*, June 1923, pp. 2, 12–19.
12 *VCH Cheshire*, V (ii), p. 284.
13 ZCR 86/12/85: Letter of Astbury to Board of Education, 6 May 1936; Report of Inspection of Chester Diocesan Training College held in session 1935–36.

14 CC, Hooper deposit: *Training College Examinations Board: Regulations and Syllabus, 1935–1937*, pp. 28, 46–49.

15 Bradbury, *Chester College*, pp. 195–96.

16 C. Dyhouse, 'Going to University: Funding, Costs, Benefits' at <<http://www.historyandpolicy.org/papers/policy-paper-61.html#students>>, accessed 27/11/13.

17 ZCR 86/1/8: 23 April 1919, 16 June 1920.

18 *Collegian*, March 1921, p. 11; ZCR 86/1/10 (paper kept with minute book).

19 ZCR 86/1/8: 29 July, 12 October 1921; Bradbury, *Chester College*, pp. 198–99, testifies to Thomas's passionate concern that students should not fall into crippling debt.

20 ZCR 86/1/8: 19 March 1924, 17 June 1925; ZCR 86/1/9: 16 October 1929, 4 March 1930; ZCR 86/2/5: 27 January, 4 March 1930.

21 <<www.cheshire.mmu.ac.uk/aboutus/history.php>>, accessed 1/11/13.

22 ZCR 86/1/8: 18 June 1924, 5 January 1927.

23 ZCR 86/1/9: 13 April, 20 June 1928, 20 March 1929.

24 Hargreaves, 'Chester College – Site and Setting', pp. 22–24.

25 ZCR 86/1/9: 9 October, 4 December 1931.

26 ZCR 86A/227: survey by W.E. Brown, 11 April 1928.

27 Bradbury, *Chester College*, p. 189.

28 ZCR 86/1/8: 16 December 1925, 17 March 1926; ZCR 86/1/9: 20 June 1928, 17 May, 3 July 1929; ZCR 86/2/5: 21 April 1926; Osborne, *Saltley College Centenary*, pp. 48–49.

29 ZCR 86/1/9: 3 July 1929, 3 June 1930, 5 June 1931; ZCR 86A/231, 232. Fyfe would have been known to the governors as the Chester cathedral architect; he had also worked on the Deeside Regional Planning Scheme (incorporating what was in effect a 'Chester town plan'), published in 1923, on which see below, Chapter 15.

30 ZCR 86A/240.

31 McGregor, *A Church College for the 21st Century?*, p. 128.

32 ZCR 86/2/5: 27 January 1930; *Collegian*, Lent 1936, p. 9; Seaborne, 'The College Buildings', pp. 40–41.

33 ZCR 86/1/9: 4 December 1931, 4 March, 3 June, 7 October 1932.

34 ZCR 86/2/6: 5 December 1933.

35 ZCR 86/1/8: 24 March 1905, 4 March 1909, 11 October 1921; ZCR 86/12/59: HMI report on 'Physical Exercises', 26 June 1911; ZCR 86/12/71: HMI report, 5 May 1923. In July 1911, following the poor HMI report, Thomas had advertised for a tutor to teach History, English, Latin and/or French, 'a churchman, young and athletic' who would also have the opportunity if suitable 'to become an expert teacher of Physical Training': ZCR 86/12/59.

36 Bradbury, *Chester College*, p. 195.

37 ZCR 86/1/9: 4 March 1930; Seaborne, 'The College Buildings', pp. 31–33.

38 However, 'Muffs v. Duffs' still featured at King Alfred's Winchester in 1929: M. Rose, *A History of King Alfred's College, Winchester, 1840–1980* (Chichester, 1981), plate 24.

39 *Collegian*, Summer 1936, p. 53. A previous (un-named) matron appointed in July 1908 had also been commended, this time in an HMI report (ZCR 86/1/8: 4 March 1909).

40 ZCR 86/1/8: 18 June 1924.

41 *Collegian*, Christmas 1925, p. 31.

42 ZCR 86/1/8: 13 June 1923, 22 June 1924; ZCR 86/1/9: 20 June, 31 October 1928, 20 March 1929.

43 *Collegian*, Lent 1930, pp. 12–21; Dawtry, 'All Work and No Play', pp. 79–80.

44 *Collegian*, June 1922, p. 13; June 1923, pp. 2, 4; 1987, pp. 40–42.

45 ZCR 86/6/1; *Collegian*, Summer 1969, pp. 7–8.

46 ZCR 86/1/10: 24 June 1955; *Collegian*, Spring 1971, pp. 108–9, a tribute to Jones written by Pickup, including reference to the fact that 'the College owes him a great debt for preserving from decay or even destruction many valuable archives of the past'. This would have been a thinner book without him.

47 *Collegian*, December 1922, p. 25; Lent 1926, pp. 10–13. In his preface to *The Church Catechism* (p. viii, see Chapter 4) Allen thanks Potts for compiling most of the sample exam questions appended to the book and calls him his 'friend', not an accolade one imagines was lightly bestowed.

48 ZCR 86/1/8: 11 October 1921.

49 ZCR 86/1/9: 11 December 1929.

50 White, 'Three Great Tutors', pp. 69–72.

CHAPTER 6

AFFILIATION TO THE UNIVERSITY OF LIVERPOOL

The raising of academic standards which came with the appointment of tutors such as Newstead and Morrell was nowhere better demonstrated than through the College's developing relationship with the University of Liverpool. This is a story which has its origins before the First World War, but may conveniently be dealt with discretely at this point.

Ever since 1897 a small number within each cohort of Chester students had taken advantage of the opportunity to extend their course over three years and read for a University of London external degree. According to HMI Bennett, the original seven 'all passed very well and in some subjects surpassed Borough Road', the British and Foreign Society College which had moved from Southwark to Isleworth in 1889 and was then the largest in the country. Thereafter, one to three London external students per year seems to have been the norm and Bradbury, who taught these men in the 1920s, notes the distinction of their later careers.[1] In 1899, HMI Scott-Coward, echoing current thinking about the importance of exposing teacher trainees to the higher branches of learning, had recommended closer association with a local university – such as Victoria University, Manchester, which had been founded in 1880 and encouraged college affiliations – although he added that 'there should not be the desire to let men rush through the course in order that they may put BA [to] their names, which so often was mere humbug'.[2]

Scott-Coward's proposal had not been followed up, but Best had sought instead to broaden the horizons of all students through initiatives such as sending them to public lectures on British birds given by Newstead at Grosvenor Museum in 1904.[3] Thomas was more enterprising, initiating a scheme in 1924 whereby students over the course of two years would attend four short courses of lectures by distinguished academic visitors. Thus, in autumn 1924 James Johnstone, Professor of Oceanography at Liverpool, gave the same lectures on 'Oceans of the World' as he had at his own University. In Spring 1925, the Cambridge scholar E.M.W. Tillyard lectured on 'The Romantics', 'Poetry' and 'Literature and the Arts'. Another to appear was the Oxford medievalist F.M. Powicke.[4] But for an institutional link we must look to the arrangements made in 1906 whereby the University of Liverpool – founded three years earlier, having previously been an affiliated college of Victoria, Manchester – agreed to conduct the teachers' certificate examinations for students of Chester, Warrington and Edge Hill Colleges. The immediate prompt for this had been a decision by the Board of Education in

1904 to end the classification system for teachers' certificates, which after 1905 would be determined on a 'pass/fail' basis only, though with an option for colleges to provide their own classifications. A scheme involving Chester and the two other colleges whereby classification was retained through examination by an independent university was approved by the Board of Education as a credible alternative.[5]

The first results reported under these arrangements, in October 1909, showed 16 second-year students in the first class, 38 in the second and four in the third: not such good figures as had been attained under the Board of Education's own examinations, but a balance in the classifications which suggests appropriate rigour.[6] There was disquiet however. That summer, Best had been obliged to report to the governors 'the desire of the College staff to cease preparing students for the Liverpool University examination'; the reasons were not specified but they were probably connected with inadequate remuneration for additional work. In March 1910 the governors decided to seek a meeting with the University's Board of Examiners. They objected to the expense, which (at over £98) had turned out to be far greater than the 'third part of £50' which had been expected; to the greater stringency in awarding first-classes; and (notwithstanding this concern) to the dangers inherent in College tutors knowing the contents of the exam papers in advance. 'The Committee seemed on the whole to doubt whether the advantage gained by entering for this examination (which could not be considered entirely independent of the College staff or exterior to the College) could be said to be worth its cost'.[7] In 1911 application was made to the Board of Education, jointly with the sister diocesan College for women at Warrington, for a grant towards the cost of the Liverpool exam. This was turned down, but at least the tutorial staff seem to have been placated by new agreements on pay. A list of proposals dated December 1911 shows that those acting as internal examiners on behalf of the University of Liverpool would receive fees ranging from £1, 1s. 0d to £3. 10s. 0d., depending on the length of the exam papers. It is interesting to note, as an indication of the weight given to different subjects, that History and Principles of Teaching both involved three-hour exams, optional subjects (which must have included Geography and Science) also three hours, English Literature and Arithmetic two and a half hours, Hygiene, Algebra and Geometry two hours, and English Language, English Composition and Music one hour each.[8]

In the event, the Liverpool scheme would continue – albeit with a break during the War – until 1923, after which the College once again prepared students for Board of Education examinations. In 1929, these arrangements in turn gave way to a Joint Board for colleges local to the Universities of

Liverpool and Manchester, one of eleven such regional Boards established across England and Wales at that time, under a government initiative designed, among other things, to foster closer links between the different institutions.[9]

Accordingly, Chester College had a well-established relationship with the University of Liverpool when a new Board of Education regulation in 1920 gave permission for those training colleges affiliated to a university to offer four-year courses to some of their students. Thomas, and at least some of the governors, may have had wind of this in February 1919 when the subject of increasing opportunities for students to pursue degree courses was raised at a meeting of the General Purposes Committee and he undertook to consult Liverpool about it. In any event, it was on the agenda of the full governors in June 1920 and by October he was writing both to other college principals to seek their experience of affiliation to their local universities, and to several universities asking the terms on which colleges were affiliated to them.[10] Indeed, so keen was Thomas on an affiliation with Liverpool that he was even prepared – in a confidential statement to the governors in February 1921 – to consider the relocation of the College 'to a Liverpool site in order that the students may be within easy reach of the University', possibly with Warrington College moving to occupy the Chester buildings instead. In fairness, however, this was not the only option, and a more prosaic suggestion was simply to provide a College motorbus to meet the trains at Rock Ferry![11]

Be that as it may, Thomas was clearly well prepared when on 3 May 1921 he sent off to the Vice-Chancellor of the University of Liverpool, the eminent pathologist J. George Adami, a letter requesting a meeting about possible affiliation. Adami was an ebullient character, with a belief that Liverpool could become 'the most live and active, the most representative and most sought university in the British Isles'; the purchase of several houses in Abercromby Square is one of his legacies.[12] He duly came over on the train eight days later, accompanied by his Registrar, Edward Carey, and met the Principal and General Purposes Committee for an hour or so before they proceeded to lunch with all the resident members of the academic staff. The College pitched for a one-two-one arrangement. In their first year, students would remain in Chester, taught by those College tutors whom Liverpool was prepared to recognise as University lecturers; in the second and third years, students would commute to Liverpool for lectures there, but the fourth year would be devoted solely to professional training back in Chester. Adami replied that he fully recognised 'the ferment which was working in the Training Colleges' and that with his fellow Vice-Chancellors he was giving active consideration to what could be done with 'outlying' colleges. He was supportive in principle, but everything would depend on the University's Regulations and Ordinances, on approval by the faculties of Arts and Science – who would doubtless want to scrutinise the College's library and other facilities – and on the consent of Senate and the University Council. He advised the College 'not to ask for any special privileges outside existing University ordinances, which would lead to delay', but thought – in the manner of Vice-Chancellors – that although it was rather late in the summer it might be possible to complete all the negotiations 'by the end of this term'.[13]

One problem with all this was that there was not unanimous approval for the affiliation among the governors themselves. E.M. Sneyd-Kynnersley, who had been added to the General Purposes Committee for the purposes of overseeing negotiations for University affiliation, sent a circular letter to his fellow-governors, objecting in the strongest terms. Sneyd-Kynnersley had been associated with the College since Chritchley's time, making annual visits to the practising school as an HMI; in 1894, Lovell had lodged a formal complaint about his conduct when he had provoked an argument in front of a class. He had joined the Governing Body on his retirement, becoming the College's representative on the Liverpool Board of Examiners when the certificate scheme had been set up in 1906. In his letter, he lamented the prospect of second- and third-year Chester students being at a loose end in Liverpool in between their lectures: 'homeless in a proctorless city' as he put it, even though Bradbury (who quotes this letter in full) rightly points out that many of them had seen service in the First World War. He also questioned the cost involved, the value of being taught by lecturers who did not know the students personally, and the relevance of a four-year course to students' future careers. 'The object of our College is to train masters for elementary schools: the aim of the affiliated student is to obtain a place in a Secondary School.'[14] The last sentence says everything about his perspective, wedded to a view of the College and its role which was rooted in the past. The governors as a whole agreed with the Principal that it was time to move forward.

So it was that a letter was drafted to the Council and Senate of the University of Liverpool in the names of Thomas and of the secretary to the Governing Body, J.M. New, making formal application for affiliation. A draft was sent in advance for comment to Carey, the University Registrar who had been present at the 11 May meeting, but he restricted his advice to the comment that the address to 'My Lords and Gentlemen' was unnecessary: since 'we have no Lords on our Senate', 'Gentlemen' would be sufficient. 'Everything will depend on the result of the inspection', he stressed, 'so the exact form of the application is not really material'. Even so, the final letter, dated 19 May 1921, was very carefully composed. It 'respectfully' sought 'the fullest measure of affiliation which is possible in the light of the Statutes and existing Ordinances of the University' involving 'complete exemption for the University students of the College from the first year of attendance upon Courses of Study in the University for degrees in Arts and in Science'. Latin, French, English Literature, Modern History, Philosophy, Economics, Geography and Mathematics were given as the Arts subjects, Pure Mathematics, Applied Mathematics, Physics and Chemistry as those in Science, even though some of these went beyond what was currently being taught for the teachers' certificate. It ended with a little gentle pressure on the University's political antennae and social conscience.

> We submit this proposal with the greater courage, knowing that the University is keenly alive to the demand made by many representative bodies in this country, notably the world of Labour and by the teachers themselves, that in increasing measure our future teachers including those in Public Elementary Schools should be graduates of a University.[15]

The submission came to the University's Senate on 1 June 1921. The Faculty of Science expressed its willingness to send a committee of three to visit and inspect the College, the Faculty of Arts wanted more time to consider the issue of affiliation in general. On 16 June, the Dean and two other professors from the University's Faculty of Science – among them Joseph Proudman, a former pupil-teacher in Farnworth who was now a leading authority on oceanic tides – duly visited and their report was sufficiently favourable, once Thomas had sent full details of his staff's academic qualifications, for affiliation to be granted: up to a point. The letter sent by Carey to Thomas on 6 July confirmed that the University's Council had approved the affiliation on the previous day, but only for the first year's courses in Chemistry, Physics and Mathematics, and only for one year; Thomas himself was recognised as a teacher of Mathematics, Morrell as a teacher of Physics and Chemistry and another member of staff, John Campbell Hill, a Durham graduate who had become an Associate of the Institute of Chemistry in 1919 before joining the College staff in 1920, as a further teacher of that subject. To that extent, the University had fulfilled the Vice-Chancellor's promise that matters could be sorted out before the end of term, but it was of course a long way short of what had originally been asked for. Quite apart from the wholesale omission of Arts subjects, the rejection by the University of another proposed teacher in Mathematics virtually ruled that out as well, since Thomas as Principal did not have time to deliver it on his own. Beyond this, as Thomas pointed out to the Vice-Chancellor in letters of August and November 1921, the grant of affiliation for one year only created a most unsatisfactory situation, since the

College could not promise its students that the scheme, once embarked upon, would continue through to the completion of their studies.[16]

In the event, the University did renew the affiliation in Science throughout the 1920s – by 1924 for a further five-year term – although according to Bradbury, who lived through this episode, only one Chester student actually took advantage of the scheme as proposed. He duly spent 1921–22 studying at the College, 1922–24 commuting to Liverpool where he attained his degree in Science, then 1924–25 undertaking professional teacher training at Chester.[17] Thomas was clearly unhappy that a wider range of subjects could not be offered and in May 1925, evidently on his own initiative without consulting the governors, wrote to Henry Bond, the Master of his old college, Trinity Hall, to ask whether there was any possibility of Chester affiliating to Cambridge University. He gave some details of the College ('a Residential Training College for 160 men'), explained that a few of the best students currently aimed for London degrees over three years concurrently with their professional training, but set out his four-year scheme, suitably adjusted from that discussed with Liverpool, as a much better alternative. The students would have ended up with Cambridge degrees, the first year's teaching for which would have been undertaken at Chester, and with either the Board of Education certificate or the Cambridge Teacher's Diploma following their fourth year back in Chester. Omitting any reference to issues such as how Chester students would be financed during two years' residence in Cambridge – there would have been no daily commuting under this version! – he offered to pay a visit for a full conversation and expressed the hope that all this could start in the coming September. Bond graciously volunteered to take this up with his old friend the University registrar – John Neville Keynes, father of the most famous British economist of the twentieth century – but the following month received the briefest of replies, which was duly forwarded to Thomas. 'My dear Bond. I enclose a copy of the present Regulations relating to Affiliated Colleges. There is, I regret, no possibility that Mr Thomas can obtain recognition for his College.'[18]

With that avenue abruptly closed off, it was back to negotiating with Liverpool. Thomas wrote to the Faculty of Arts in May 1925 – the correspondence overlaps with that to Cambridge so he clearly had two balls in the air at the same time – but found it more resistant to affiliation than Science had been. He was rebuffed on the grounds that no other affiliated college exempted its first-year students from attendance at the University, and in any case the College's lecturers – other than in Mathematics, treated for this purpose as an Arts subject – did not meet the University's requirements. He tried again in November 1928, proposing 'a generous measure of affiliation' across the two faculties for delivery of four-year courses on the same basis as before, but again only Science accepted the College, renewing the affiliation for three years from March 1929 with a new Mathematician, Lewis, among the 'recognised tutors', plus Hooper for Chemistry and Physics, alongside Thomas himself for Mathematics. Eventually, with different personnel in charge, the Faculty of Arts agreed to pay a visit in March 1932 – to include observation of lectures in French and Geography – and when affiliation was renewed yet again in June of that year, it at last included Arts as well as Science. Bradbury (English Literature), Pickup (French) and Stephens (Geography) all received recognition, although the College was required to buy some extra books and maps and to accept input from the Faculty of Arts to the determination of the curriculum. It had been a long struggle, and the University had understandably been cautious: for the Faculty of Arts non-attendance for the first year had been a major concession, a 'new principle' as they put in their 1932 Annual Report despite Science's decade-long acceptance of it.[19]

In practice, affiliation at this time meant relatively little to students. No others took advantage of Thomas's controversial scheme for the first and fourth years to be spent at Chester and those in between at Liverpool, so academic contact was confined to the examinations conducted by the Joint Board from 1929, for which institutional affiliation was not in itself a requirement. Affiliation was periodically renewed through the 1930s and 1940s, although in 1947 the next Principal, Astbury, had to be prompted twice by the University since he forgot to submit the application. When in January 1955 his successor as Principal, Price, sent in some new names for recognition as University lecturers – Milton and Vincent in History, Pollard in English Language and Literature – he observed that this was the first such request for about 20 years; the University Registrar did not reply until July, and when he did so it was to say that the matter would be considered by a Senate committee not meeting until October.[20] None of this suggests that the arrangements were high on the priorities of either institution; with no students combining their studies at College and University, as originally envisaged, this is understandable. But 'recognised' tutors could of course use Liverpool's library and affiliation to a leading University did give the College formal contact with, and access to the guidance and support of, a prestigious academic institution. Looking ahead, Chester's most meaningful link with Liverpool through the third quarter of the twentieth century would be via the area training organisation, which replaced the Joint Examinations Board in 1949 and came to be based at the University's Institute of Education in 1954. However, this was a relationship shared with several other regional colleges.

It was only with the demise of the Institute in 1975, and the establishment of a Board of College Studies in its place, that the full benefits of affiliation were to be realised, as the basis for the late-twentieth-century diversification which would prove vital to the College's survival.[21]

Notwithstanding initiatives such as this, the years from the mid-1880s to the early 1930s were essentially a conservative period in the history of the College. It continued to do the same thing – train elementary schoolmasters in an environment where the only resident women were the matron and some of her domestic staff along with members of the Principal's family – but became much better at doing it. It was transformed from a College of below-average attainment to one of the strongest institutions of its type in England. A succession of Principals whose own undergraduate years had been spent in Cambridge, supported by an increasingly Oxbridge-educated tutorial staff, succeeded in raising academic standards and in fostering the collegiate spirit they themselves had known, so that a much more liberal regime developed, with ample time for sporting and cultural activity. But in 1932, as in 1886, nearly every student took a two-year course. Most of them slept in unheated dormitories – the same dormitories, minimally redesigned, as had been used in the 1840s – as all had done in 1886: plans to build a proper student hostel had so far come to nought. Although some new buildings had appeared, notably the practising school in 1900, the College was only just beginning to address its need for up-to-date teaching space and still lacked a proper gymnasium to do justice to its growing reputation for Physical Training: Thomas did not mince his words when in his February 1921 memorandum to the governors about possible relocation to Liverpool, he wrote that: 'the buildings at Chester … bear tragic evidence of the wisdom of making changes or additions without reference to a comprehensive, well-thought out plan'.[22] Apart from the 'College Annexe' bought at the end of 1931, these buildings were confined to a compact area bounded by Exton Park to the north, Parkgate Road to the east, Cheyney Road to the south and a terrace created by levelling to the west – over twice that built upon when Allen had taken over, to match the approximate doubling in student numbers since his time, but still a tightly knit complex of structures, beyond which a mixture of landscaped grounds, playing fields and unimproved pasture stretched to the canal and railway line to north and west. The area south of Exton Park, reaching down to the canal – part buildings, part playing fields – was surrounded by a wall to create 'The Close', a feature in existence for most, possibly all, of the period since 1886. Beyond 'The Close', further purchases of land, more than enough for the foreseeable future, offered the potential for significant development but – as Thomas fully realised with his persistent pleas for expansion – there was no room for complacency amid the political and economic upheavals which characterised the interwar period. This was what the rest of the College was about to discover.

---

1 ZCR 86/1/5: 5 April 1897, 9 October 1899; ZCR 86/5/2: Examination Record Book, e.g. Christmas 1912, Summer 1925, Summer 1939; Bradbury, *Chester College*, p. 197 note 12.

2 ZCR 86/1/5: 26 May 1899.

3 The extent to which trainee teachers should be educated beyond immediate 'elementary' requirements was much debated in the late-Victorian and Edwardian periods. A witness before the Cross Commission in the 1880s had called for 'a closer approximation of our teacher training system with the liberal culture of the universities, so that all that is best in modern education may be brought within the reach of those to whom the teaching of the great mass of children … will be entrusted' (quoted in Gardner, 'Higher Education and Teacher Training', p. 36); day colleges attached to universities had come into being as a response to this argument. At the opening ceremony of Sheffield City Training College in 1905, a junior minister had asserted that colleges' main role was to train students to teach, but six years later, the Liberal Lord Chancellor, opening new buildings, stressed the importance of teachers extending their own education in order to instil a love of lifelong learning in others (Collins and Morgan, *Celebrating a Centenary*, p. 12).

4 ZCR 86/1/5: 14 May 1904; ZCR 86/11/1: Letter of Thomas to Field, Dean of University of Liverpool Faculty of Arts, 11 June 1925; Bradbury, *Chester College*, p. 186.

5 ZCR 86/1/5: 14 March 1904; ZCR 86/1/8: 18 June 1906.

6 ZCR 86/1/8: 11 October 1909; cf. e.g. ZCR 86/1/5: 9 October 1899.

7 ZCR 86/1/8: 14 June 1909, 7 March 1910.

8 ZCR 86/1/8: 6 March, 11 December 1911.

9 Bradbury, *Chester College*, p. 195; Dent, *Training of Teachers*, pp. 98–101.

10 ZCR 86/2/5: 25 February 1919; ZCR 86/1/8: 10 June 1920; ZCR 86/11/1: Letters of Thomas, 1925.

11 ZCR 86/1/10: Statement by the Principal of Chester Training College, 9 February 1921 (loose paper); on the eagerness of the Warrington governors at this time to relocate 'to healthy and attractive surroundings', see Hollinshead, *In Thy Light*, p. 28.

12 T. Kelly, *For Advancement of Learning: The University of Liverpool 1881–1981* (Liverpool, 1981), p. 191.

13 ZCR 86/11/1: Letters of Adami, 4 May, and of Thomas, 6 May 1921; ZCR 86/2/5: 11 May 1921.

14 Bradbury, *Chester College*, pp. 187–88; White, 'Three Great Tutors', p. 66. Sneyd-Kynnersley's book, *HMI: Some Passages in the Life of one of HM Inspectors of Schools*, published in 1908, is an amusing if rather patronising insight into the conduct of school inspections in the late-Victorian period.

15 ZCR 86/11/1: Letters of Carey, New and Thomas, 19 May 1921.
16 ZCR 86/11/1: Letters of Adami, 2 June, of Baly, 10 June, of Carey, 6 July, of Thomas, 2 August, 21 November 1921.
17 Bradbury, *Chester College*, p. 186.
18 ZCR 86/11/1: Letters of Thomas, 5 May, of Keynes 18 June 1925.
19 ZCR 86/11/1: Letters of Thomas, 5 June 1924, 26 November 1928, 5 March, 30 May 1929, of Field, 25 May 1925, of others at University, 3 March and 14 June 1932; *University of Liverpool Annual Reports, 1932* (Liverpool 1932), p. 26.
20 ZCR 86/11/1: Letters of Astbury, 20 June 1947, of Price, 17 January 1955, of University Registrar, 15 July 1955.
21 Below, Chapters 8, 10.
22 See note 11.

MODERNISATION, 1933–74

CHAPTER 7

RESPONSE TO CRISIS

Despite all his efforts to have a hostel of study-bedrooms built at Chester College, Thomas never lived to see one completed. He died in 1943, almost three decades after he had initially proposed a residential hostel on the eve of the First World War, but it was to be another ten years before the first one was opened. It was quickly followed by another, in 1954. In his speech at the opening ceremony of this second hostel, on 1 July, the Bishop of Chester, Douglas Crick, reflected on an episode over 20 years earlier which he described as 'a milestone in the history of Chester College'. He named the hostel 'Fisher House' in honour of the Archbishop of Canterbury at the time, Geoffrey Fisher – famous for having crowned Queen Elizabeth II and present on this occasion – because 'it was largely due to Bishop Fisher's appeal to the Church Assembly that the College was saved'.[1] The earlier hostel had been named 'Astbury House' after the man who had succeeded Thomas as Principal, and in his own short *History of Chester Diocesan Training College*, written at the request of the Church of England's Central Board of Finance in 1946, Astbury had been even more emphatic about Fisher's contribution to saving the College: 'it is doubtful whether the battle could have been won without his very able and active leadership … indeed the Assembly had seldom, if ever, been so stirred and its opinion so completely reversed by a single speech'.[2] But there was an element of illusion to the ceremonial opening of Fisher House. Since it was not quite finished, the main door had to be opened by a workman hidden inside, in response to the Archbishop inserting the key.[3] The argument which follows here is that Fisher's claim to have been the principal 'saviour of the College' is equally an illusion: although in fairness it should be added that it was really a claim foisted upon him by others and, helpful though the episode was in boosting his popularity within city and diocese, it was not one in which he took any particular pride.[4]

The crisis to which Crick and Astbury were referring represented the biggest threat to the College's existence since the resurrection masterminded by Chritchley in 1869–70. It blew up very suddenly, following the return of a National Government under Ramsay MacDonald in October 1931 and the cancellation – in the context of severe economic depression – of the previous Labour administration's plans to raise the school leaving age to 15. In anticipation of the greater demand for teachers which these plans would require, the College had responded to government encouragement to increase its student numbers, which as we have seen had risen to 220. But by the

85

summer of 1932 the College had been told that it must have no more than 160 students in training in the following academic year – a figure which could only be achieved by drastically curtailing the first-year intake, leading to a severe imbalance between the two years in 1932–33. Far more seriously, at a time when there were still nearly 8,000 elementary school classes in England and Wales with a pupil-to-teacher ratio in excess of 50,[5] the Board of Education in autumn 1932 demanded a further cut of 10% in training college numbers for the year to come. In response to this, the Board of Supervision alerted the Church of England Assembly – set up in 1919 and forerunner of the General Synod – when it met on 16 November, presenting it with the alternatives of spreading the cut across the board or 'suspending' – that is temporarily closing – a few colleges so that the rest could remain at full strength: a version of the 'concentration' policy last applied in the First World War but also seriously considered when a 5% cut had been imposed because of over-supply of trained teachers in 1923.[6] The Board of Supervision expressed a clear preference for concentration but, having not had time to work up a detailed scheme, did not press for a resolution at that stage. There was no debate on this occasion, so no expression of opinion from the floor for or against the principle of suspending any colleges.[7]

Full discussion of the issue took place instead at a meeting on 24 November of the General Council of Church Training Colleges, the consultative body composed of Governing Body representatives from all the Church colleges, and this did pass some (inconsistent!) resolutions. One approved a policy of concentration 'in the highest interests of the group of the Church of England colleges'. Another sought to defend 'small Colleges and … Colleges in outlying districts' by affirming their 'special value to the Church'. Yet another – proposed by Chester's own Principal, Thomas, though he later claimed to have had no special interest in doing so – asked the Board of Supervision to work on a recommendation to the Board of Education for an adjustment of numbers in each college so that none would have to close. Meanwhile the Council of Principals, meeting after the General Council had finished, devised its own proposal to the Board of Supervision, asking for a phased introduction of any concentration scheme to minimise disruption to second-year students and saying that they could all live with a 5% cut in order to bring this about. The fairest conclusion to be drawn from these conflicting propositions is that concentration was accepted in principle but alternative solutions were to be explored. However the Board of Supervision, which was not bound in any case by recommendations from a consultative body, could reasonably conclude that it had been left with considerable discretion to act in the best interests of the colleges as a whole. Crucially, it seems that no-one had openly objected to a policy of concentration, either during informal discussions through the autumn or at the November meetings of the Church Assembly and General Council of Training Colleges.[8]

In the event, the Board of Supervision, meeting the following day, 25 November, decided that three colleges should undergo 'suspension' in the interests of saving the others. They fixed on one men's college in the Province of York, Chester with its 160 students, and two women's colleges in the Province of Canterbury, Lincoln and Fishponds (Bristol), with 250 students between them, as those to be sacrificed. That evening, Thomas received a telegram conveying the news, with the promise of a letter to follow, though with an invitation to meet the Board of Supervision before names were sent to the Board of Education. His initial response was one of defiance – 'this is not the end'[9] – but the fact remains that no-one associated with the College appears to have seen this coming. Chester was a larger-than-average men's college, the only Church college in the industrial north-west of England. The general expectation seems to have been that if any colleges would have to close, it would be the smaller ones – hence the resolution at the General Council in their defence – although this would of course have inflicted more widespread pain in order to achieve the required reduction in numbers. It is tempting to speculate that Chester's somewhat limited relationship with the Board of Supervision since its inception in 1917 might have had a bearing on the decision; the College did not have one of its own members on the Board and had preferred to incur capital expenditure from internal resources where possible. It had benefited from grants made by the Board on behalf of the Church Assembly[10] but had not raised significant loans, through the Board, for building development from the Church's Central Board of Finance. In any event, battle would now be joined.

The Board of Supervision's case has been given short shrift in previous histories of the College but at this distance of time a more balanced assessment can be attempted. In a pamphlet issued to explain the decision[11] and in speeches made at the Church Assembly, the main argument was that it was better to maintain quality at a reduced number of fully resourced colleges than to jeopardise it by expecting every institution to scrimp and save. Assurances had been given by the Board of Education that money would continue to be spent on the upkeep of the closed colleges, with a view to their reopening after a gap of three years, when it was hoped that the worst of the crisis would be over. Severe time constraints in the autumn, with the Board of Education pressing for the Church's decision, had curtailed the consultation process, but even so there had been no principled objection to the closure of colleges; only when their identities had been made known had there been an outcry against the whole idea. As for the selection of the three colleges concerned, factors taken into account were equitable distribution between the two provinces and between colleges of men and women, the need to avoid closing colleges which had heavy debts on building schemes to repay to the Ecclesiastical Commissioners, and the desirability, if any premises were to be left empty, of their being 'inferior' to those left open elsewhere. It was also thought that all three being sacrificed were in a relatively strong financial position – ironically because they had not borrowed heavily to improve their buildings – so were well placed to reopen in due course. The rationale for saying that the women's colleges should come from the Province of Canterbury and the men's from the Province of York never seems to have been properly explained but had this principle been openly declared at an earlier stage then Chester would have been seriously worried, for it would have known that it was competing for survival not against men's colleges across the country but against only two others: York and Bede, Durham. As the Archdeacon of Richmond, a member of the Board of Supervision, explained to the Church Assembly, 'Durham offered a special course different from any of the others, and was, therefore, impossible to close': presumably a reference to the arrangements in place since the 1890s for their teacher trainees to read for BA and BSc degrees of their prestigious local University as an integral part of their studies. York 'had embarked upon a large scheme of building and was, therefore, impossible to close' because of the repayments it had to find on what had been borrowed. That left Chester, 'and frankly, in the opinion of the Board, the buildings at Chester were not so satisfactory as at some other Colleges'.[12]

When he heard this advanced as a reason for Chester's selection, Thomas would have been forgiven for silently cursing some of his past governors for their dilatory response to his building schemes. In truth, it was not the continued use of dormitories which was seen as the main problem – the male students at Cheltenham, for example, only lost theirs in the early 1950s, at about the same time as those at Chester[13] – but the significant reliance on lodgings. No other Church college had a single permanent student in lodgings at this time but Chester had 40 and this was regarded as weakening the collegiate residential experience. Of course, there was much to be said against the Board of Supervision's case and this duly appeared in letters to the press, in pamphlets and in speeches at the Church Assembly debate: the obvious unfairness of penalising institutions for not going heavily into debt, the effective withdrawal of Church of England teacher training from key parts of the country (of which the removal of the only men's college in Lancashire and Cheshire was seen as the most serious), the intrinsic merits of the colleges under threat. A key issue was an understandable fear that temporary closure, at a time of falling national birth rate, uncertain economic future and expansionist plans among rival LEA colleges as soon as opportunity allowed, could easily become permanent. Despite conveying to the Church Assembly such assurances on all this as he had been able to secure from the Board of Education, the chairman of the Central Board of Finance, Earl Grey, never quite managed to convince the members that there was nothing to worry about on this score.[14]

In selecting 'strong' colleges for the axe, the Board of Supervision had of course guaranteed that there would be a very forceful reaction from their many stakeholders, especially those associated with Chester. December of 1932 was devoted to urgent meetings of the Governing Body and deputations to both the Board of Education and the Board of Supervision. It should be remembered that, following the establishment of Blackburn Diocese which first sent members to the Governing Body in March 1932, Chester was the men's training college for not one diocese but four: it was the Bishops of Manchester and Blackburn, along with Canon Thicknesse of Liverpool – rector of Wigan – who travelled to Whitehall to meet the Board of Education on behalf of the governors on 7 December, and representatives of all four dioceses were in a party sent to tackle the Board of Supervision on 23 December.[15] The Board of Education's position, understandably, was that it would accept whatever solution for its colleges the Church of England came up with, provided that the overall reduction was achieved, and in the circumstances it deserves some credit for its forbearance while the infighting took place. A refusal by the Board of Supervision to change its mind, despite visits by representatives of all three threatened colleges, must have made for a very grim Christmas. However, the trio could at least cling on to the argument that under Board of Education regulations no college could be closed without the consent of its Governing Body so the Board of Supervision had arguably exceeded its powers: sufficient grounds for the colleges to take their case to the Church Assembly for further debate, if there was the stomach to do so.

There now followed a critical week at the very beginning of 1933 which has been glossed over in previous accounts of the crisis. A difficulty for all senior clergy associated with Chester College was that they had loyalties to the wider Church – and, being human, to their own reputations within it – as well as to the institution on Parkgate Road. On 15 December 1932, for example, the Bishop of Blackburn, in sending his apologies for absence from a special meeting of the governors in advance of the deputation just before Christmas to the Board of Supervision, expressed the view that whatever came out of that encounter should be regarded as final: he was not in favour of rocking the boat any further. Essentially, by the turn of the year, this was Bishop Fisher's position as well. On 30 December he wrote to the Bishop of Gloucester (who was defending Fishponds), asking to be released from his undertaking to write to *The Times* on their joint behalf. It would only wash the Church's dirty linen in public, to no avail. 'I am bound to admit the force of the financial arguments for the policy of closing' and nothing could now be done to change it, especially since both archbishops were in favour; in particular, the Archbishop of York had gone into matters at length and could see no alternative. 'We have made our protest and died fighting.' More appropriate than a letter to *The Times*, he suggested, would be 'a discussion in the Church Assembly … though (I suspect) it would not affect the issue'. Copies of the letter were enclosed with a circular note to all the governors, discouraging them from holding a meeting scheduled for 10 January 1933, since 'there remains no effective method of delaying or altering the decision'.[16] The governors took the message and chose not to gather on the appointed day; indeed, having last met on 20 December they did not reconvene until 10 March, a month after the crucial Assembly debate. So if anyone 'saved the College' at this critical juncture, it certainly was not the governors acting as a corporate body. Nor – at this stage – was it the much-lauded Bishop Fisher, who was for giving up the fight.

It was now that some hitherto-unsung heroes came to the rescue. One was Tom Scott of 38 Bouverie Street, a stalwart of the College Club Executive who had served as treasurer since 1924. He had completed his student career in 1906 and had for many years been headmaster of Holy Trinity School in a deprived area of Chester. Since he lived so close to the College, and was a trusted figure whose school was frequently used for teaching practice, Principal Thomas doubtless kept him as fully informed as he dare.[17] On 10 December, immediately on learning of the College's plight, he had prepared a one-page SOS with the headline 'The College is in the Gravest Danger', calling for a 'monster petition' signed by former students, and having obtained his Executive's consent by telegram had sent it out two days later. This had generated over 2,000 signatures in a matter of days.[18] Now, at the very beginning of January, he prepared another statement to the

Figure 17: Tom Scott. (*Collegian*, Christmas, 1937.)

effect that 'the Executive of the Club is of the opinion that the matter should be brought before the Church Assembly and that that body should be urged to reverse the decision'; arguments in defence of the College followed.[19] In cold reality, the Church Assembly, as a deliberative body, had no authority to overturn a decision by the Board of Supervision, but it was entitled to pass an opinion and the hope was that so much opposition would be generated that the Board would feel obliged to back down; in effect, this was what eventually happened. It is hard to believe, however, that Scott would have decided to involve the Church Assembly unless Thomas had suggested it to him. As 1933 dawned, neither man would have known whether anything would come of such an approach but they must have thought that there was nothing to lose. And by letting the College Club loose to bang the drum all over the North West and beyond, with the declared intention of in some way influencing the Church Assembly, Scott and Thomas were creating a groundswell of pressure which more cautious ecclesiastical dignitaries could not ignore.

By 4 January, Scott's statement, along with four copies of a one-page petition against the closure of Chester College, was in the post to every former student in the North West and every incumbent in the dioceses of Manchester, Liverpool, Blackburn and Chester. The clergy of Carlisle and the Isle of Man received theirs a few days later, once addresses had been obtained. The College Club abounded in head teachers and Directors of Education, by no means confined to the North West, who were well used to playing politics, at least at the local level, and in the weeks which followed some 38,000 signatures, including those of 28 local mayors, from Appleby to Stockport to Wallasey, were obtained for this petition. Beyond this, the Club's connections also helped in securing resolutions or letters of support from nearly 30 LEAs, many of which went direct to one or other of the Boards concerned. Old students were also supplied with the names of Church Assembly members in their dioceses, who were duly lobbied, often in person, in support of the College.[20] There were some grounds for hope in that, with Chester now serving four dioceses, to add to the dioceses of other threatened colleges plus Carlisle which was perceived as a North West ally, around one-fifth of the Assembly's membership might be expected to be naturally sympathetic to their colleges' cause. Not everyone would necessarily vote to save their local college – in the event, the Bishops of Liverpool, Manchester and Blackburn declined to do so[21] and a Blackburn lay member, Mr R. Assheton, was against, as 'an opponent of borrowing and a firm advocate of economy'[22] – but there was here a solid platform on which to build.

Figure 18: Frank Bennett, Dean of Chester Cathedral 1920-37. (By permission of Chester Cathedral.)

The other 'unsung hero' was the Dean of Chester, Frank Bennett, who had revolutionised the Cathedral by abolishing admission charges and successfully repairing much of the fabric.[23] As Thomas put it in a revealing letter dictated from his sickbed on 6 January, when the idea was being mooted of calling for a debate in the Convocation of the Province of York, 'I do not know if our new Bishop will want to plunge openly into this painful subject on his first experience of the House. The Dean of Chester is tremendously keen and concerned about the College. As soon as I am fit for it, I hope to collect opinions about actions in the Church Assembly' although he was aware of its complexities over *'standing orders'*! *By 9 January, the idea of* going to Convocation had been dropped as a futile gesture but he was being urged by his correspondent, an influential Manchester incumbent, to approach the Church Assembly without delay if he wanted the matter discussed at the next session in early February, with a resolution sponsored by either a bishop or a dean.[24] From here, the formal submission to the Church Assembly gathered momentum. The Assembly's secretary, Sir Philip Baker-Wilbraham, wrote from his home at Rode Hall, Scholar Green in the east of Cheshire to explain that a preliminary resolution needed to reach him by 18 January, though confirmation that it would actually be moved could wait until the Assembly opened on 6 February. On 17 January, therefore, Dean Bennett met at the College with other local members of the Church Assembly, including the Archdeacons of Chester and Macclesfield, to draft the resolution, which he said he was willing to propose, and it was posted to Baker-Wilbraham the same day. He also wrote to the Bishop of Gloucester, who had responded to Fisher's failure to write on their joint behalf to *The Times* by submitting his own letter protesting about the proposed closures, published the previous day; Bennett explained that shortage of time had meant that they could not consult him and offered to withdraw the resolution if he had a better one. 'If you are willing to be the spearhead we shall do all we can as a phalanx of pushers.' Only then did he write to Bishop Fisher himself, enclosing the resolution and the letter to the Bishop of Gloucester, expressing delight that he was now recovering from influenza and giving himself an escape route if the Bishop blew his top. 'Of the resolution nothing may come but we thought that we had better secure the right to raise the whole matter in the Assembly if it seems wise to do so when the time comes. I only write just to let you know what we have done and not to worry you with it.' He signed off 'yours very obediently and sincerely'.[25]

Bennett, who was one of the College governors, had presumably been egged on by Thomas, himself an Honorary Canon of the Cathedral. But the Dean showed courage and cunning in taking the initiative after Fisher – now conveniently indisposed – had let it be known that he did not wish the campaign to go any further. Apart from his willingness to raise his head above the parapet at the Church Assembly, Bennett also deserves credit for the skill with which the resolution itself was crafted. It avoided any provocative criticism of the Board of Supervision and merely urged the postponement for twelve months of the closure of any Church training college, to allow for reconsideration with the college authorities of the concentration policy and exploration of alternatives.[26] Despite his expressed willingness to withdraw the motion, it duly went ahead, although in the event Bennett's own illness meant that it had to be moved on his behalf by another governor, Canon Thicknesse the rector of Wigan. It is probably his absence from the Church Assembly debate which has led to Bennett's key role in the affair being largely ignored. By then, the College Club's campaign had agitated the North West and Thomas – besides sending a few helpful suggestions on what to say to those he hoped might speak – had issued a printed appeal to every member of the Church Assembly, dated 30 January, answering points made by the Board of Supervision in its own printed statement released three days earlier. As for Bishop Fisher, he had evidently been so moved by the swirl of opinion with which he was engulfed that he had at last decided to join in and submit his long-delayed letter to *The Times*; this also appeared on 30 January, in time for Thomas to quote it. The letter did precisely what Fisher had previously been reluctant to engage in, namely criticise in public the actions of the Board of Supervision, which he described as 'callous and autocratic'.[27] When the Church Assembly gathered at Church House, Westminster, on 6 February, both petitions organised by Scott against the closure of Chester College were presented,[28] and the stage was set for the fateful debate itself.

The debate, on 9 February, was a highly charged affair, unusually well-attended and with large contingents from the north of England watching from the public galleries to give their representatives moral support. 'Assembly Revolt: Many Northern Speakers' proclaimed the *Yorkshire Post* – which treated Lincoln as well as Chester as a 'northern' college – pointing out how unusual it was for the Church Assembly to reject a plan brought forward with the authority of the Central Board of Finance. For the *Manchester Guardian*, 'today made ample amends for yesterday in the Church Assembly; from its beginning this morning until late in the afternoon the debate moved on a really high level'.[29] Thicknesse of Wigan did an excellent job as deputy for Bennett, although the previous speaker, Sir Walter Buchanan-Riddell, Chairman of the Board of Supervision, also drew high praise for a measured statement explaining from the Board's perspective how the present situation had arisen. Even so, he comes across as a man on the back foot, seeking to defend himself against the barrage of criticisms he had already received from many in the audience before him. In fact, twice as many speeches in the ensuing debate were made in favour of Bennett's motion as against, although it had some distinguished opponents, not least the Bishop of Chichester, George Bell, who during the Second World War would speak out bravely against the area bombing of German cities. In mid-afternoon the Archbishop of York, William Temple – a passionate advocate of the Church training colleges but a reluctant supporter of the concentration scheme – moved an amendment, the effect of which was to support the Board of Supervision's decision but insist that in future there be full consultation over any proposed college closure with relevant governing bodies. At the end of the day, Cosmo Gordon Lang, in the chair as Archbishop of Canterbury, summed up prior to putting matters to a vote, in terms which betray his own opposition to the motion: asserting his confidence in the Board of Supervision and Central Board of Finance, whose expertise had been brought to bear on the recommendations that had been made, and reminding members that they had had the chance to object to a policy of concentration when the matter had come before the Assembly in November. But such was the strength of feeling that Temple's amendment was defeated by 217 votes to 161. That paved the way for the substantive motion to be carried without further ado.[30]

Clearly, this analysis calls into question the long-held opinion that it was Bishop Fisher of Chester who deserves most of the credit for saving the College. He had only recently been consecrated, on 21 September 1932, having been headmaster of the all-boys public school, Repton, since 1914, and can hardly be blamed for taking the position he had reached by the end of December. Newly arrived in the diocese, he was being called upon to rise up in defence of a much-loved, worthy but far from outstanding institution when the ecclesiastical establishment, including his immediate superior the

Archbishop of York, was convinced that the best interests of the Church as a whole would be served by its temporary closure. But after others had taken the initiative in forcing the issue on to the agenda of the Church Assembly, he played his hand there very well indeed: bravely, since the only other bishop to speak in defence of the colleges was Gloucester, and effectively, with a speech – on his debut appearance – which was free of any sonorous pomposity and offered something new. He eschewed any sentimental words about all that the colleges had done and were doing for the Church and focused on two matters: whether closure could be avoided and whether the one year's delay called for in the motion was worthwhile. On the first of these, he presented an over-simplified but superficially impressive account of selected figures to demonstrate that there was sufficient funding available to the Church colleges as a whole for the 10% cut to be absorbed without any having to close. On the second, he argued that delay for further consultation would add greater credibility and acceptability to whatever was ultimately decided: 'if a year was allowed in which a full inquiry was made, and then Chester was closed, for his part he would take it with the utmost good will'. If one has a criticism of the speech, it is that he needlessly introduced towards the end his preference for a two-year delay: a departure from the motion, which was possibly intended to signal that he had had no part in drafting it.[31] This gave his critics some ammunition later in the day and would have been a matter for bitter regret had the result turned out differently.

Fisher was fortunate that he was called to make his speech towards the end of the pre-lunch session. It clearly made an impression because several later speakers made reference to it, for or against. His exposition of figures led to the secretary of the Board of Supervision, Canon Frank Partridge of Chichester, having to come before the Assembly to show that financial matters were much more complicated and precarious than Fisher had suggested. However Partridge's speech was delivered in the 'graveyard slot' of the early afternoon and his detailed exposition of the sums involved is hard to follow even from the printed page: it badly needed a summary at the end, refuting Fisher in headline terms. Archbishop Temple asserted in his own speech that the Bishop of Chester's key contention – that means could be found to maintain all Colleges in existence – 'had been so fatally shaken by Canon Partridge's outline of the financial situation that he could not himself risk following that policy further'.[32] For the *Manchester Guardian*, 'the Bishop of Chester met the financial argument with a muster of figures which were at least plausible, though later Canon Partridge was equally plausible in demonstrating their untrustworthiness'. However, this was clearly not the majority opinion, probably because few managed to understand much of what Partridge said. Fisher deserves full credit, as a novice bishop, for taking on both archbishops and combating the Assembly's natural inclination to support those, such as the 'experts' on the Board of Supervision, whose special area of responsibility was in focus. It was probably this embarrassment to the establishment, through the use of dubious figures, that prompted the outspoken Bishop of Durham, Hensley Henson, to tell Fisher as they left the hall at the end of the day that he should be thrown into the Thames.[33]

But impressive though Fisher's speech was, is it right to regard it – in Bradbury's words – as 'by universal consent … decisive' in achieving the desired result? The Principal of one of the spared colleges, Lincoln, told Thomas that she thought Fisher's speech 'the triumph of the day'. Dean Bennett modestly underplayed his own role by writing in the *Diocesan Gazette* that 'the very able speech of our own Bishop … carried the day'. But while most newspapers thought his speech sufficiently important to deserve an honourable mention, none went so far as the *Church Times*, which admitted to having changed its mind on the matter 'after considering the arguments put forward … and particularly those ably advanced by the Bishop of Chester'. For his part, Principal Thomas, writing in the *Collegian* in the immediate aftermath of events – admittedly in circumstances where he was at pains to thank former students for all they had done – was more cautious in his verdict: Bishop Fisher 'delivered at the Assembly what was regarded as the most decisive speech' but his contribution was one among many. Privately, he was especially grateful to the Conservative MP for Bolton, Sir John Haslam, to whom he wrote on 13 February; as an observer from the gallery, he had feared that the Archbishop of York's authoritative contribution had 'crushed' the debate, but Haslam's speech, which came next, had 'just made the difference and by rescuing the debate and forcing it back on an even level' had done 'our cause a service of quite inestimable value'.[34]

In reality, it is likely that many people already knew how they wanted to vote before the debate started. Indeed, Thomas was told this just before the Assembly gathered by a correspondent from Penzance – far from the immediate scene of conflict – who had been contacting the members; of four replies received, one was definitely going to vote to save the colleges, two were inclined to do so, one was undecided.[35] Credit for this must go to the campaign which prepared the ground in the two months prior to the Assembly's vote, a campaign which the other colleges acknowledged had been led by Chester with its exceptionally strong College Club. Fisher himself recognised as much, for when the governors met again in March he proposed that thanks be conveyed to the College Club Executive, and through them to the old students as a whole, for the great help they had given.[36] His real achievement – 'decisive' in its way – was not to persuade significant numbers to vote against their original intentions but to give those who wanted to save the colleges reassurance, through his financial arguments, that this was a reasonable and responsible thing to do, despite what they were being told by the establishment. That in itself is a matter for congratulation, but the plaudits should rightfully be shared with several others, not least Thomas himself.

On 16 February the Principal was able to inform his governors that the Board of Education had confirmed that the College would be open for business in 1933–34, bearing its share of the 10% cut with 144 students in all.[37] We shall never know whether Chester's temporary suspension in 1933 would in fact have led to its permanent closure. There would have been a concerted campaign for its reopening in due course, almost certainly a more determined one than would have applied to the two women's colleges, but at best some momentum would have been lost, with development opportunities passing to rivals. Any continued suspension beyond the initial three years would have made reopening increasingly unlikely; we can be certain that closure would have been permanent had it persisted into the Second World War. But the triumph in the Church Assembly ensured that these scenarios could be relegated to 'counter-factual history'. The reality was that the Church Assembly, as the logical outcome of its decision, asked the Board of Supervision to set up a Committee of Enquiry to scrutinise all Church of England training colleges – and Thomas made sure that he was a member, as a representative of the men's training colleges. This reported to the Board of Supervision in December 1933. The Report acknowledged differences of opinion – the advocates of 'concentration' had not been silenced – but on balance recommended that all colleges should remain open until the end of 1936–37, so giving time for general economic conditions to improve. It also recommended that all colleges increase their fees, contribute to a central pool to assist those in difficulty, and where necessary work with the Board of Supervision to obtain finance to improve their buildings. All this was subject to a further financial review by the Board of Supervision towards the end of 1935–36, with the threat of concentration thereafter. In the event, three small women's colleges, at Brighton, Peterborough and Truro, were closed for good towards the end of the decade, while the others responded as best they could to the call for modernisation.[38]

In his own speech at the hostel-opening ceremony in July 1954, Fisher recalled that 'once the crisis was averted [we] decided to keep going by reforming the old order', comments which omit to mention the threat from the Committee of Enquiry but are a fair reflection of his own commitment, as chairman of the governors, to modernising the College's facilities and lifestyle. The crisis was clearly a shock to the system – with inadequate buildings specifically cited as an argument to close the College down – and hence a spur to put things right. The Enquiry's own findings show how far Chester had fallen behind in terms of student accommodation: study-bedrooms were the norm in LEA colleges as well as universities but Cheltenham had none, Culham one and Chester five (in Exton Park) at a time when the other six Church of England men's training colleges had between 64 and 138 each. It is fair to add that provision of study-bedrooms was not seen solely as a matter of comfort and privacy but as a reflection of an approach to learning: the dormitory system assumed that students would almost always be working together under supervision, even in the library, while study-bedrooms gave more opportunity to retire for private study whenever time allowed. Most Principals assured the Enquiry of the benefits of study-bedrooms: students' 'strivings towards self-expression became more immediately evident, their initiative was increased, and their sense of responsibility deepened'. Others felt that they were suitable for second-year students but not those straight from school and the Enquiry had some sympathy with this opinion, concluding that 'the time is not far distant when no College will be regarded as fully efficient in respect of its buildings unless provision is made for study-bedrooms for at least one-half of the students, so that every student may be given the opportunity of living in a study-bedroom during his second year'.[39] There could not have been a clearer statement of where Chester's building priorities should lie.

Thomas would have appreciated the changed stance on the part of his governors but left for the Trinity Hall living of Gazeley and Kentford (Suffolk) in April 1935. Less than three years later, poor health obliged him to retire to Waterbeach (Cambridgeshire), where buses to his beloved Cambridge passed his front door.[40] Having served the College in different capacities 'over almost a lifetime' as Bishop Fisher put it at Thomas's last governors' meeting, he had richly earned the warm tributes which came from all quarters.[41] One suspects, however, that he had enjoyed his time as a footballing tutor and Vice-Principal rather more than he had his Principalship, when through anxious striving he had steered the College through a series of threats and challenges. It was his successor who would preside over his long-sought building campaign. His valiant colleague in the campaign to save the College in 1933, Tom Scott, was another quickly to depart the scene. Sadly, illness forced him to resign the treasurership of the College Club in September 1936 and he died just over a year later.[42]

One indication of changing times was that the governors – who had altered their name to the College Council at the height of the crisis in December 1932 – decided to be more flexible over what we would now call the 'person specification' of the new Principal. 'A man in Orders' – that is, an ordained priest – should be appointed 'if possible': in modern parlance, this was no longer 'essential' but 'desirable'. Moreover, 'experience in Training College work should not be made a, rigid condition', let alone any limitations on age.[43] In the event, all four candidates interviewed early in 1935 were in Holy Orders, but two were working in public schools – Bishop Fisher's own background – two in training colleges. The successful candidate, Revd Herbert Stanley Astbury, was an assistant master at Charterhouse: the fifth Principal in six to graduate from Cambridge (having attended Rigg's old College, Christ's) and like Thomas a former army chaplain in the First World War, when he had won the Military Cross. In introducing his successor to students and ex-students through the pages of the *Collegian*, Thomas was careful to stress Astbury's enthusiasm for sport, and in particular that he was 'a rowing man'.[44]

In the years down to the Second World War, sport was one area which did indeed continue to thrive. A 'house' system introduced in the summer term of 1933 as a means to increase participation made an auspicious start when each house won once: Rigg's at tennis, Chritchley's at cricket, Allen's at athletics, Best's at swimming.[45] But it is clear that as numbers fell in subsequent years there was some inconsistency in the competitions held, and it did not survive the War. At College level, however, there was some excellent sport: annual Past v. Present matches, begun in the 1890s, remained as popular as ever and the Rowing Club acquired an eight-man boat, enabling it to compete for the first time in the North of England Head of the River Race on the Dee in March 1936. It was also in 1936 that we find the *Collegian* reporting the revival of the Musical Society (under the presidency of Mrs Astbury), more consistent activity on the part of the League of Nations branch (hitherto 'somewhat spasmodic' but now holding discussions on 'The Present Rhineland Dispute' and 'The Position of the Individual on the Outbreak of War') and fresh initiatives by the Debating Society, which for the first time hosted debates against two other local societies, from Chester and from Hoole and Newton respectively. Meanwhile, the Rag went from strength to strength, without ever quite achieving its target of £500. Even so, the last one before the Second World War, held on 11 February 1939, raised one of the highest totals to date, £428. 10s. 0d., a sum which was distributed between 17 local charities headed by Chester Royal Infirmary (£110), Chester Council of

Social Welfare (£100), Chester District Nursing Association (£45) and the Chester Police Court Poor Box (£40).[46]

The academic work of the College was also creditable. An HMI Report of 1936 had much good to say about every subject in the curriculum and concluded that 'Principal, staff and students alike are combining to maintain a high level of work and progress ... the outlook for the future is promising'. It considered Morrell 'a most able and experienced Vice-Principal ... whose enlightened and beneficial influence is apparent in every aspect of the College life and work' and praised his lectures on educational theory and his oversight of teaching practice; this was 'distinguished by the care with which it is arranged, the effectiveness with which it is supervised and the soundness of judgment shown in assessing the teaching marks on the result of it'.[47] Physical Training, so important in the eyes of the government for the health and wellbeing of the nation, was another area of growing repute. The tutor, Captain Arthur Waywell, left in summer 1936 to become a government inspector in the subject, but not before he had earned a commendation in the HMI report for the 'consistently good' work of his students during nine years in the post; if anyone deserves credit for establishing this subject (and its successors under different names) as one of the College's leading lights, it is him. He was succeeded on a temporary basis by a former student, Hedley Simms, at the time PT master in the College School, and from September 1937 by another ex-student and ex-College Schoolmaster, Ralph Staines, who had more recently been teaching at Bangor Normal College.[48] Staines spent the year 1936–37 prior to starting at Chester as a student at Carnegie Physical Training College, Leeds, opened in 1933 as a specialist centre for the education of male PT teachers, all of whom had to already have a degree or teachers' certificate. The syllabus here covered anatomy, physiology and the theory of gymnastics, as well as practical work, and could properly have been called 'Physical Education'; indeed, by the outbreak of War three former Carnegie students were holding newly created posts as Directors of Physical Education at the Universities of Liverpool, Birmingham and Leeds.[49] On his arrival at Chester, Staines immediately embarked on the delivery of an Advanced Physical Training course for the more able students, approval for this having been given by the Board of Education in 1937; the fact that this had been sanctioned when the College was still having to share the School hall for use as a gymnasium speaks volumes for the quality of the work being undertaken. By summer 1939, 16 of the 72 first-year students were taking this Advanced PT course.[50]

For his part, Astbury patiently set about his updating of the College, evidently with Fisher's approval and support. In 1935–36, his first full year in office, he made it his business to visit a host of schools – mostly secondary schools – in Chester, Cheshire and Wirral, so as to compare their teaching with the work done in College; various adjustments, especially to the delivery of practical subjects such as 'Handwork',[51] were introduced as a result. A confidential report by the Board of Supervision, following a visit at the end of March 1936, praised the 'friendly spirit which seemed to prevail throughout the College', for which Astbury received due credit, noted his commitment to giving students more freedom and recommended some relaxation of the rules regarding compulsory Chapel attendance.[52] Accordingly, in the summer term of 1937 two changes were made which for the student body as a whole were as significant as any in the history of the College to that point. On the one hand, the system of 'prefects' to assist in welfare and the keeping of good order was abolished, having been a feature of College life – under that title or as 'monitors' or 'orderlies' – since Rigg's day; 'I have always felt that this title was too reminiscent of School', explained Astbury in his Annual Report. Henceforth the Guild Council would play an enhanced role, with its President liaising between students and Principal. On the other, daily attendance at Chapel – compulsory ever since it had been built – became 'completely and really voluntary', although students were still expected on Sunday mornings.[53] As Astbury explained the following year, this was all part of granting what he saw as

> increased liberty and self-government within the College … our students are like other people – the more they are trusted the better they respond … I am convinced that the Chapel services have gained immeasurably. One new point I must mention is that on one evening in the week the Service is entirely conducted by the students, to the great gain of all concerned.

So while daily services were no longer full, they had become more devotional.[54]

There is no doubt, however, that the period immediately following the crisis of 1933 was a challenging one for Chester College, as for all the others. The Board of Education's cap on numbers meant that the 220 students of 1931–32 had fallen to 132 by 1934–35, figures which resulted in both a severe drop in income and an awkward imbalance between the size of different cohorts as admissions were managed to meet overall targets. Thus, in 1933–34 there were 103 first-year students and only 41 in their second year (including a few in the third); for 1934–35 the 103 had progressed to the second year, leaving places for only 29 first-years. The ever-resourceful Thomas sought to mitigate the worst effects of all this by admitting a few private students paying full fees, in return for the right to study for University of London external degrees concurrently with their teacher training, and also by negotiating a phased 'equalisation scheme' with the Board of Education whereby numbers achieved equilibrium, within an overall total of 132, by 1937–38.[55] Fees were also increased in September 1934 to £40 per annum – not the £50 recommended by the Committee of Enquiry but higher than that charged by many other Church colleges and the same as leading institutions like Chelsea and Borough Road. In the same year, at Bishop Fisher's suggestion, the governors' General Purposes Committee was reconstituted as a Standing Committee – five of its 10 members to be from the diocese of Chester – to meet monthly and keep a particularly close eye on the College's administration and finances, although in the event enthusiasm for meeting so often soon waned.[56] To its credit, despite its own financial challenges, the College granted bursaries (effectively waiving their fees) to three unemployed people attending a Workers' Educational Association residential summer school held on the campus in summer 1935.[57]

The fall in student numbers had lifted some of the immediate pressure for the construction of new buildings, for which in any case the Board of Supervision acknowledged that there was currently no funding available. However in 1935, in the early months of Astbury's Principalship, an approach was received from a city councillor acting on behalf of the Blue Coat School in Northgate Street, seeking to purchase land at the far north end of the campus acquired seven years earlier. This prompted the governors to re-open the question of future building requirements, an issue made more pertinent by criticism in the 1936 HMI Report of the College's continued lack of study-bedrooms and limited classroom accommodation. Although the Blue Coat School was told that the College did not wish to sell the land, a decision reiterated early in 1937, the prospect must have been tempting as a way to raise money for new building elsewhere on the campus.[58] In October 1937, the Standing Committee of the Governing Body decided to obtain a formal valuation of the seven and a half acres between Parkgate Road and the canal, abutting on to the railway line (purchased in 1928 and now the site of the Downes Sports Hall and Best, Chritchley, Westminster and North West Food Research and Development Centre buildings, with their accompanying car parks) with instructions to Astbury to hold preliminary negotiations with the LEA over its possible sale. Another plot bought in 1915, running down towards the canal beyond Exton Park (now home to the library), was also valued at this time.[59] Nothing came of these negotiations, which obviously threatened to undo Thomas's achievement in extending the grounds, and the College remained free to expand over these areas in generations to come.

By now, efforts to address the building issues were well under way. In March 1936 the Cambridge architect, Fyfe, presented modified plans for a

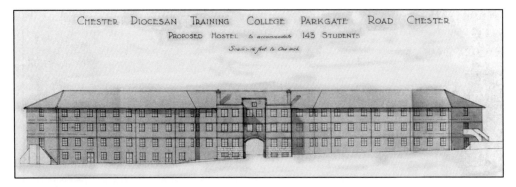

Figure 19: Plans of 1937 for a single hostel of 143 study-bedrooms, shelved the following year. (CALS: ZCR 86A/236.)

student hostel of 100 study-bedrooms, which was to run north-south above the terrace towards Exton Park, concealing the College School behind it.[60] That summer, the Standing Committee, to Fyfe's obvious annoyance, decided to engage a local man instead – 'a practical architect on the spot' – and by the end of the year F. Charles Saxon of the Chester firm of Abercrombie, Saxon and Partners had prepared a plan of the campus as a whole, with some old buildings potentially demolished and new ones pencilled in. In August 1937 he went on to submit plans for a large hostel of three storeys plus basement to accommodate 143 students – a few more than the College was at that time permitted to take – the intention being to build this 'in the north west angle of the Close', that is in the general area where the new hostel for 202 students would eventually be constructed in 2013. He also designed a gymnasium (now the 'Old Gym' and originally seen also as an assembly hall), the site for which was to be immediately north of the Principal's House; this, however, would have involved at least partial demolition of the sanatorium so it was quickly switched to the position it still occupies near Parkgate Road.[61]

The Board of Education duly approved these plans early in 1938, only for a LEA scheme to emerge for the enlargement of the College School, with the potential to intrude upon the area in front of it earmarked for the new student hostel. It was for this reason that Saxon was asked to start again, so in June 1938 he came up instead with designs which effectively split his hostel into two – a north one and a south one, again of three storeys plus basement, each with 70 study-bedrooms plus bathroom and toilet blocks halfway along each corridor. Though two separate buildings, they were conceived as parallel wings of 'the new hostel' in the singular – a term used, for example, in an artist's impression published in the *Collegian* in summer 1939. The twin structures were now to run east-west, projecting out towards the playing fields below the terrace, and aligned with the Art & Craft block now called

103

THE PROPOSED NEW HOSTEL.

Figure 20: Artist's impression of the 'new hostel', with the present Thomas building (before it was extended) in the background. The twin structures are described in the singular because, collectively, they replaced the 143-room hostel designed in 1937. (*Collegian*, Summer 1939.)

the Thomas building so as to create three sides of a courtyard.[62] They were rightly described by Malcolm Seaborne, Principal from 1971 to 1987 and an authority on architectural history, as (at the time) 'among the best of our surviving buildings, with excellent proportions and matching bow fronts' when viewed from the west alongside the canal. Seaborne also pointed out that a layout of study-bedrooms either side of a central corridor leading to communal lavatory facilities – typical of student residential buildings of the interwar period – was essentially a refinement of the old dormitory arrangements which had served from the beginning.[63]

All this construction work, which included the completion to its original design of the Art & Crafts block opened in 1931 and the installation of a new heating system for the whole College (to be based on boilers in one of the hostel basements), was costed at over £58,000. The former students who had acted so heroically in 1933 proved less responsive to a building fund appeal launched by Astbury three years later but the College managed to set aside £9,000 for the purpose and with the Board of Supervision's support to negotiate a loan of £48,000, repayable over 25 years, from the Church of

England's Central Board of Finance.[64] It was a massive undertaking, comparable in scale – up to that time – only with the initial building of the College in 1842. Timing only added to the risks associated with the project, since tenders with builders and the loan itself were being sorted out in the twelve months prior to the outbreak of the Second World War in September 1939. When the foundation stone for the south hostel was laid that summer, the Principal commented that 'if anything happened to stop this building going ahead, this stone … would be known as "Astbury's Folly"', a phrase he repeated in his short *History* in 1946 at a time when the building was still unfinished.[65] Bishop Fisher at the 1939 celebrations preferred to call it 'a great venture of faith for anybody in these days to aim at' but reverted to 'Astbury's Folly' when opening the building 15 years later, adding that it was 'an enterprise at which he, as the then Bishop of Chester, connived'. He paid tribute at this ceremony in 1954 to the Principal's 'unbounded energy, enthusiasm, foresight and vision that kept us all going'[66] but it seems fair to conclude that it was Fisher's own commitment, as chairman of the governors, to the ambitious, multi-faceted and debt-laden building scheme that gave Astbury the confidence to proceed. No sooner had war been declared than Fisher was off to become Bishop of London after only seven years at Chester. Yet his backing for this building programme was at least as important a contribution to the successful development of the College as his wavering but ultimately effective input during the crisis of 1933 had been.

For all the apprehension which clouded the year 1939, it was also the time to celebrate the College's centenary. On the morning of Founders' Day, 25 January, the Chapel was packed out as never before for the commemoration service, with the recently built west gallery full and with seats having to be placed down the aisle. Bishop Fisher then laid the foundation stone of the new gymnasium and the Mayor of Chester, Phyllis Brown, opened the now-completed Art & Craft building. However the highlight for several students seems to have been a somewhat raucous 'mass visit' through the streets of

Figure 21: Mrs Ida Astbury wields a spade at the cutting of the first sod for the building of the (subsequently named) Fisher House, May 1939. Her husband the Principal (wearing clerical collar) is on the left of the picture, with the bespectacled Vice-Principal Herbert Morrell next to him. (*Collegian*, Summer 1939.)

Chester to the Royalty Theatre on City Road for an evening of vaudeville-style entertainment; according to the *Collegian*'s report, the performer who made the most impression was 'a vision (in tights) on the stage: her agility-work moved even the most Advanced PT men to admiration'.[67] On 16 May Mrs Astbury cut the first sod of earth for the new hostel – what we would now call the southern one of the pair – and on 3 June in glorious sunshine the 17th Earl of Derby, grandson of the 14th Earl who had been one of the College's founders, ceremonially laid a foundation stone on the same spot. The second of these occasions, which was attended by about 700 people, was embellished by a Centenary Garden Party, an exhibition of students' work and various tennis, cricket and athletics matches between past and present students.[68]

Both foundation stones are still clearly visible near the corners of their respective buildings, but only the gymnasium was sufficiently far advanced by the outbreak of war for government permission to be granted for its completion. It was duly opened on Founders Day 1940 by the new Bishop of Chester Crick – to the accompaniment of a fine gymnastics display – for use by the College School as well as by students, and was considered to meet the highest specifications of the day; its retractable stage also allowed for dramatic productions.[69] But the two hostels with the accompanying heating system were only in the early stages – the exterior walls completed to a height

Figure 22: The Earl of Derby (in bowler hat) speaks at the laying the foundation stone of Fisher House in 1939, On the left is Principal Astbury; Bishop Fisher is between them. (CALS: ZCR 86/17/132.)

of some four to five feet – so had to be protected and made safe until further notice, work which went on intermittently during much of 1940.[70] The original builders were paid off for the work they had done and the area below the terrace, with the outline of two hostels plus stacks of bricks and other materials, remained as a building site for almost a decade and a half. During the War, the foundations of the two hostels were used as air raid shelters,[71] while everyone associated with the College was left to regret the failure to embark on the scheme long before now.

---

1   ZCR 86/15/1: *Liverpool Daily Post*, 10 July 1954.
2   S. Astbury, *A History of Chester Diocesan Training College* (Chester, 1946), pp. 26, 29.
3   E. Evans, *Those Were the Days: Recollections of Chester College in the Fifties and Sixties* (privately printed, 1989), p. 11.
4   E. Carpenter, *Archbishop Fisher: His Life and Times* (Norwich, 1991), pp. 42–44.
5   Board of Education: *Report of the Consultative Committee on Infant and Nursery Schools* ['Hadow Report'] HMSO, London, 1933, p. xxii.
6   Concentration had been avoided in 1923, when the General Council of Church Training Colleges had advocated 'careful economical management' instead (ZCR 86/1/8: 10 October, 12 December 1923).
7   *Church Assembly: Report of Proceedings 1932* (London, 1932), pp. 486–92; ZCR 86/12/71: letter of Board of Supervision to Thomas, 2 February 1923.
8   *Church Assembly: Report of Proceedings 1933* (London, 1933), pp. 128–30.
9   As related in his obituary by Vice-Principal Morrell, *Collegian*, Christmas 1943, p. 14.
10 As pointed out by Archbishop Temple to the Church Assembly: *Church Assembly Proceedings 1933*, p. 159.
11 ZCR 86/12/81, Letters and Papers, 1933.
12 *Church Assembly Proceedings 1933*, p. 139.
13 C. More, *A Splendid College: An Illustrated History of Teacher Training in Cheltenham. 1847–1990* (Cheltenham, 1992), pp. 11, 14.
14 *Church Assembly Proceedings 1933*, pp. 168–71.
15 ZCR 86/1/9: 20 December 1932.
16 ZCR 86/12/80 pt 2.
17 *Collegian*, Christmas 1937, pp. 120–21 (Scott's obituary).
18 ZCR 86/12/80, pt 2; *Collegian*, Christmas 1932, pp. 123–25.
19 ZCR 86/12/81.
20 ZCR 86/12/81; *Collegian*, Lent 1933, pp. 20–33.
21 ZCR 86/12/81: letter of Haslam, 14 February 1933.
22 *Church Assembly Proceedings 1933*, p. 162.
23 A. Bruce, *The Cathedral 'Open and Free': Dean Bennett of Chester* (Liverpool, 2000).
24 ZCR 86/12/81: letter of Thomas, 6 January, letter of Kerby, 9 January 1933.

25 ZCR 86/12/81: letter of Baker-Wilbraham, 13 January 1933; letters of Bennett, 17 January 1933. Fisher's immediate reaction to being 'bounced' in this way appears not to be recorded but he had – or developed – a very high regard for Bennett, considering him 'a great man' and successfully recommending him to the Archbishop of Canterbury for the award of a Lambeth DD. (Bruce, *Cathedral 'Open and Free'*, p. 221).

26 The precise wording was as follows. 'That the Board of Supervision of the Church Training Colleges be urged by the Church Assembly to take immediately whatever steps may be necessary to postpone for twelve months the closing of any Church Training Colleges, with a view to reconsidering deliberately in the meantime, with the responsible Authorities of the Colleges, its policy of concentration and to exploring with them all possible alternatives to the same.'

27 ZCR 86/12/81: letters of Thomas, 4 February 1933; Bradbury, *Chester College*, p. 202.

28 *Church Assembly Proceedings 1933,* p. 171; this compares with a 10,000-signature petition for Lincoln, but Fishponds did not produce one.

29 ZCR 86/12/82 pt 4: *Yorkshire Post*, 10 February 1933; the *Manchester Guardian*, 10 February 1933.

30 *Church Assembly Proceedings 1933*, pp. 122-72; on Archbishop Temple's commitment to the colleges, see F.A. Iremonger, *William Temple, Archbishop of Canterbury: His Life and Letters* (Oxford, 1948), p. 600.

31 *Church Assembly Proceedings 1933*, pp. 140-43.

32 *Church Assembly: Proceedings 1933*, pp. 150-55, 159.

33 Bradbury, *Chester College*, p. 204.

34 ZCR 86/12/81: letter of Thomas, 13 February 1933, letter of Stewart, 10 February 1933; ZCR 86/12/82 pt 4: *Church Times*, 17 February 1933; Carpenter, *Archbishop Fisher*, p. 43; *Collegian*, Lent 1933, pp. 20-23.

35 ZCR 86/12/81: letter of Forster, 5 February 1933.

36 ZCR 86/1/9: 10 March 1933.

37 ZCR 86/12/81: letter of Thomas, 16 February 1933.

38 ZCR 86/12/82: *Church of England Training Colleges for Teachers: Report of the Committee of Enquiry* (Westminster, 1933), esp. pp. 63-68; Bradbury, *Chester College*, p. 210 (where Peterborough's former role as a men's college is noted).

39 ZCR 86/12/82: *Church of England Report of the Committee of Enquiry*, esp. pp. 27-28, 51-52.

40 *Collegian*, Lent 1938, p. 18.

41 ZCR 86/1/9: 15 March 1935.

42 *Collegian*, Christmas 1936, p. 127; Christmas 1937, pp. 120-21.

43 ZCR 86/1/9: 7 December 1934; adverts were placed in *The Times* and its *Education Supplement* as well as in the *Church Times*.

44 *Collegian*, Easter 1935, p. 4.

45 *Collegian*, Summer 1933, p. 55.

46 *Collegian*, Lent 1936, *passim*; *Cheshire Observer*, 21 May 1939.

47 ZCR 86/12/85; White, 'Three Great Tutors', pp. 70–72.

48 ZCR 86/12/85; *Collegian*, Summer 1936, pp. 52–53; ZCR 86/1/9: 26 March 1936. Simms had the interesting experience of playing in an England Amateur Trial at Chester FC's Sealand Road ground in January 1935, when the FA experimented for the first time with two referees, one for each half of the field: C. Sumner, *On the Borderline* (Harefield, 1997), p. 54.

49 Another former Chester student at Carnegie about this time was Walter Winterbottom, who having left the College with his teacher's certificate in 1933 subsequently used his wages as a part-time Manchester United footballer to finance his course at Leeds, where he then joined the staff; he was destined to be the England football manager from 1946 to 1962.

50 ZCR 86/5/2: Examination Record Book; P.C. McIntosh, *Physical Education in England since 1800* (2nd edn., London, 1968), p. 236; L. Connell, *A Century of Teacher Training in Leeds, 1875–1975* (Leeds, 1994), pp. 215–16.

51 For 'handwork', see 'Handicraft', as it was re-designated, in Chapter 8, below.

52 ZCR 86/12/85: Board of Supervision report, sent 11 May 1936.

53 ZCR 86/7/23: *Report of the College Council for the year ended 31 July 1937*, p. 8.

54 ZCR 86/7/24: *Report of the College Council for the year ended 31 July 1938*, p. 8.

55 ZCR 86/1/9: 20 October 1933, 15 June 1934, 5 October 1934.

56 ZCR 86/1/9: 10 March 1933, 20 October 1933, 15 June 1934; ZCR 86/2/6: 23 May 1933, 22 May 1934, 15 June 1934.

57 ZCR 86/1/9: 14 June 1935.

58 ZCR 86/1/9: 4 October 1935, 26 March 1936, 11 March 1937.

59 ZCR 86/2/6: 14 October 1937; ZCR 86A/227; cf. Chapter 5 for the 1915 purchase.

60 ZCR 86/1/9: 20 March 1936; ZCR 86A/231.

61 ZCR 86/1/9: 8 October, 10 December 1936 (recording assurances to Fyfe that the College would not use his plans!); 10 June, 14 October 1937; ZCR 86A/235; ZCR 86A/ 236; *Collegian*, Lent 1936, p. 19.

62 ZCR 86/1/9: 10 March, 16 June 1938; ZCR 86A/240; *Collegian*, Summer 1939, pp. 62–63, 72–74.

63 Seaborne, 'The College Buildings', pp. 41–42.

64 *Collegian*, Summer 1936, p. 69; Lent 1937, p. 17; ZCR 86/1/9: 23 March, 8 June 1939.

65 Bradbury, *Chester College*, p. 212; Astbury, *History of Chester Diocesan Training College*, p. 33.

66 *Collegian*, Summer 1939, p. 66; *Chester Courant*, 14 July 1954

67 *Collegian*, Lent 1939, pp. 5–10.

68 *Collegian*, Summer 1939, pp. 70–73.

69 ZCR 86/11/2: Letter of Saxon to Astbury, 1 February 1940; *Cheshire Observer*, 14 June 1939.

70 ZCR 86/11/2: Various letters of Astbury, and Saxon during 1940; ZCR 86/11/4: letters of Astbury 20 January, 18 February 1947.

71 ZCR 86/7/26: *Report of the College Council for year ended 31 July 1940*.

CHAPTER 8

THE SECOND WORLD WAR AND THE POST-WAR YEARS

The academic year 1939–40 began with 136 students enrolled, although by December these numbers were beginning to be depleted through call-ups for military service. Two Church colleges, those for men at Chelsea and for women at Cheltenham (St Mary's), had closed almost immediately and the governors fully expected Chester's to be at best reduced in size and at worst shut down under a concentration scheme similar to that which had operated during the First World War. Accordingly, there was ready agreement to the commandeering of the premises as a School for Army Chaplains – the only one in Britain to be run by the Church of England – with Astbury in charge of both that and the scaled-down College. This scheme was in place by June 1940.[1] During 1941–42 he presided over the removal of 1,000 yards of iron railings as a contribution to the war effort[2] while also witnessing a steady diminution in the number of students – from 87 at the start of the academic year to 55 by the end – as a result of which it became clear that some alternative provision for teacher training would have to be made. Arrangements were put in place over the summer of 1942 for staff to find other employment – some went into the forces, others to local schools – and for Morrell, Bradbury and the assistant matron Miss Oakes to move with 45 students to the men's college at Cheltenham (St Paul's), where they met up not only with the local trainees but also those from Exeter and Culham. Somehow, Ginger the College cat managed to make the move as well.[3]

The Chester contingent were housed in their own premises, a large house – actually two houses knocked together – called 'The Priory' on Cheltenham High Street about a mile from the campus, previously occupied by St Mary's. Ironically, they found living conditions superior to those they had left behind. Most second-year students had their own separate bedrooms, first-years shared larger bedrooms accommodating four or five each, bathroom and toilet facilities were 'distinctly good' with an 'excellent supply of hot water', and there was space on the ground floor for three lecture rooms, a dining hall, a common room, surgery and staff sitting room. Cheltenham schools were used for teaching practice and St Paul's facilities were available for sport, with teams generally drawing players from the different colleges combined. Bradbury, who modestly underplays his own role in this episode, rightly stresses that the College retained its separate identity throughout the three-year exile at Cheltenham until 1945, using 'The Priory' as its official address, continuing to issue the *Collegian* (albeit less frequently) and maintaining control of its own admissions, even though student numbers were down to 12 by the end of the War.[4] The 41 former College students who lost their lives in the conflict included two, E.J. Boardman and Ll. R. Davis, who had studied at Cheltenham.[5]

Meanwhile the Chaplains' School – officially the Royal Army Chaplains' Department Reception Centre and Depot – also moved on in autumn 1942 to Tidworth on the edge of Salisbury Plain, with Astbury being replaced as its Head by a former Vice-Principal of Wells Theological College. The School, which is reckoned to have had over 1,000 chaplains through its doors in its two-and-a-quarter years at Chester, offered clergy a fortnight's induction programme covering the basics of army life and discipline – with time being spent in the gymnasium as well as the Chapel – while also tackling issues which might arise and requiring 'specimen sermons' for criticism. It catered for all denominations, apart from Roman Catholics who had their own separate training, and was even open to Jewish rabbis. Astbury found himself summoned to the War Office for permitting inter-denominational communion services, only to be defended both by the student-chaplains themselves and by no less an authority than Temple as Archbishop of York.[6] The departure first of the students, then of the chaplains, meant that all the College buildings could be requisitioned for the Auxiliary Territorial Service (ATS), which treated the premises as accommodation for those working at Western Command headquarters in Queen's Park across the river: thus providing the first cohort of young women the buildings had ever housed. Astbury himself left for service overseas in January 1943, spending most of his time until his release in April 1945 as Assistant Chaplain General in India, and in his absence Morrell was officially deemed to be 'Acting Principal'.[7]

The governors ceased to meet formally for two years from December 1942, but they eventually reconvened towards the end of 1944, confident of a successful outcome to the War. Astbury had been pressing from abroad for the College to reopen the following September and it was agreed to attempt to get the ATS out so that the premises could be recovered.[8] He was able to move back into the Principal's house soon after his return home in the spring but the last College buildings were only vacated by the Army on 5 September 1945. It took an heroic effort by the matron, Nesta Hawthorn, and her domestic staff to have them ready in time for the arrival of students on 1 October.[9] The 1945 intake were a diverse bunch, composed of 62 first-years, another 12 who had completed their first year at Cheltenham and a further 48 on an 'emergency' one-year (four-term) course under a government scheme to meet an acute shortage of teachers; the last group were mostly older men retraining from another occupation. These 122 gradually increased to 160 as servicemen returned to complete the training they had begun before going to war. Tutorial staff also returned, although not all were available immediately and some temporary lecturers had to be hired; Simms once again filled in admirably to teach PT in both the School and the College until Staines returned in autumn 1946, decorated with an MBE after distinguished service in the RAF.[10] An army hut was bought to provide two extra classrooms. Bradbury, writing of course from first-hand experience, only hints at the complexity which all this entailed, as time-honoured practices had to be abandoned to cope with conflicting demands. His focus was on pedagogy and assessment but all aspects of College life were affected, even down to the time-honoured 'initiations' inflicted by second-year students on first-years: these clearly could not survive the change in composition of the student body, especially when in the following September the second-years, all till recently still at school, were considerably younger than the latest batch of ex-servicemen arriving as 'freshers'.[11]

The continued use of early-Victorian dormitories, heated only by electric fires,[12] as the principal accommodation for this eclectic mix of students was an obvious embarrassment. A student of the 1930s later described his experience, recalling 'a small cubicle about the size of a prison cell [with] a bed, a chest of drawers, and a shelf for a tin jug and basin'. 'Each dormitory', he went on, 'had a lavatory and a washbasin from which we filled our jugs with cold water every night. Only the prefects – second-year men, of course – could actually wash at the basin or talk after 'lights out' at ten forty-five, or come out of the cubicles … except in an emergency'.[13] This quasi-monastic regime – without the prefects, terminated by Astbury in 1937 – was re-imposed after the War, on students who entered College having fought the enemy or who (after 1947) were required to have completed National Service before their arrival, and in many cases were married: it was not so much the barrack-like conditions which were a problem as the petty rules considered necessary to regulate behaviour.[14] It is clear from governors' meetings that there was an anxious impatience to be rid of the dormitories as soon as possible, alongside an acknowledgement that modernisation of the buildings should not stop there. The heady days

Figure 23: A dormitory cubicle as it appeared in 1946. (By permission of Arthur Waring.)

of 1945 were a time when the nation looked forward to building a better Britain, liberated from the shackles of the past, and it was just at this point that Principal and governors alike were prepared to 'think the unthinkable': could the building problems be solved by relocating the College elsewhere?

A confidential memorandum on this subject from the Principal, in some respects echoing that of Thomas in 1921,[15] was discussed by the Standing Committee of the Governing Body on 25 July. In this, Astbury anticipated the need for yet further accommodation if three-year courses became the norm, pointed to expectations that closer links would be forged with universities (Liverpool being the obvious, though unspecified, example), and – while not expressing an opinion, merely opening up the question – warned of the dangers of wasting precious building funds 'on a College in the wrong place'. The Standing Committee's response was to affirm that 'the present site is the right place for the College', a view endorsed by the full Governing Body in October. Yet this did not stop the Committee, when it reconvened on 27 November, agreeing to ask the Bishop of Chester to make enquiries about the availability of Eaton Hall 'with a view to transferring the College there'. The ancestral seat of the Dukes of Westminster, rebuilt in the late-Victorian period and set in parkland about three miles south of Chester, had served as a hospital in the early years of the War and since 1943 as a base for the Royal Naval College, Dartmouth. However, the building had never proved satisfactory as a family home, the current Duke was living elsewhere, and in any event a great deal of restorative work would be necessary after the wartime occupation. The Bishop was told that the Admiralty was not yet prepared to release the building, so while keeping this 'in mind as a possibility for the future', the governors turned to focus on the development of the site which they had.[16] Eaton Hall itself passed to the Army for use as an Officer Cadet Training School in 1946 and after its eventual return to the family was largely demolished (save for the Chapel and stable block), to be replaced in 1967 by a smaller modern house, itself remodelled in the 1990s.

The story of the completion of the two hostels is one of repeated frustration. Since February 1945, Ministry grants for the improvement, enlargement or replacement of buildings in voluntary colleges – as those outside LEA control were by now being called – along with renewal of furnishings and equipment therein, had been capped at 50% of total costs; the voluntary body, in Chester's case the Church of England, was responsible for finding the rest. There were many competing claims on public expenditure in the straitened circumstances of the late 1940s and the emphasis within the limited funding available for the expansion of teacher training was towards the foundation of new LEA colleges; there had been over twice as many voluntary as LEA colleges in England and Wales at the start of the War but by 1951 voluntary colleges were in the minority.[17] In these circumstances, Astbury did not have a strong hand to play in his negotiations with both the Council of Church Training Colleges – which had superseded the Board of Supervision – and with the Ministry of Education. When he took up the issue of the incomplete hostels in February 1947 he was told by the Council that plans would have to be resubmitted and by the Ministry that work must be deferred because accommodation for women students was currently a greater priority. He protested in vain that Chester's continued lack of study-bedrooms meant that it had poorer student accommodation than several emergency colleges recently set up as a solution to the post-war teacher shortage.[18] He tried again in 1949, pointing out the steady deterioration of the foundations already laid before the War and the money being wasted on temporary heating arrangements, pending the completion of the hostel within which the new boiler system was to be incorporated. But although the plans being discussed by this stage included not only the progression of the two hostels but also the possible erection of a third to the same design, aligned with them and laid out just to the south, a cabinet decision to cut capital expenditure on educational buildings meant that the College was dropped from the Ministry's 1950 building programme. In a letter to the architect, Astbury likened this news to 'a poke in the eye with a blunt stick'.[19]

Eventually, funding was released to allow work to start on the north hostel – now known as Astbury House – on 1 November 1951. The south hostel – Fisher House – had to wait until the following financial year; the Ministry's original start date was 1 March 1953 but this was brought forward to 1 December 1952 when the College pointed out the savings which would be incurred by using bricklayers and scaffolding still on site engaged in completing the other hostel.[20] Even so, the total cost of each hostel was now in the region of £68,000, a huge increase on the figure negotiated before the War and one to which the Church of England's Central Board of Finance was hard pressed to make its contribution of £75,000 towards the completion of both.[21] The contractors found they had to start again with much of the south hostel, the foundations having deteriorated through years of exposure to the elements, and in the event it emerged that not enough bricks had been stored since before the War; it is for this reason that the top storeys of each hostel use different brick newly bought for the purpose.[22] In the circumstances, the opening ceremonies – 'Astbury' on 23 June 1953 and 'Fisher' on 1 July 1954 (both of them before they were fully ready) – must have been occasions for relief as much as for rejoicing. The second years of 1953–54 were the first cohort to benefit from all this – they soon realised that they could bring their own gramophone records from home – but by 1954–55 the entire student body could be accommodated either in these two hostels or in the 'Annexe' at 4 Exton Park, which was itself given a make-over in the summer vacation of 1954.[23] Not the least of the benefits derived from the Astbury hostel was the long-awaited installation in its basement of a large boiler house as the hub of an oil-fired central heating system serving the whole College. The trained engineer appointed to maintain it, Ernest Evans, remained a key member of the maintenance staff for the next 33 years, retiring in 1986.[24]

By the time the hostel named after him was opened, Astbury had resigned as Principal on the grounds of ill health, moving on to the living of Compton Greenfield, near Bristol, at the end of April 1953. Although he subsequently retired to Devon, Compton Greenfield was to be his last resting place after his death in July 1962.[25] His closing years in office had seen some important developments in the field of education, none more so than the reorganisation of secondary schooling following the passage in 1944 of the Butler Education Act. This set up a Ministry of Education to replace the Board of Education, reiterated the principle of a clear distinction at age 11 between primary and secondary education (though it took several years for 'all-age schools' to be phased out, especially in some rural areas)[26] and provided for free, compulsory secondary schooling to the age of 15 (a rise in the school leaving age actually achieved in 1947). Most LEAs implemented these measures through the introduction of the 11-plus examination, which allowed the minority who passed to proceed to a grammar school and the majority who did not to go to a secondary modern school. The College School was itself re-designated as a secondary modern school, reaffirming the character of the campus as a place where the main focus of teacher training had shifted to the upper age range.

All this had the effect of perpetuating the bipartite system well-entrenched before the War, whereby subject-specialist secondary teachers – especially, now, those destined for grammar schools – emerged with degrees and one year's postgraduate training from universities and their departments of education, while more generalist teachers normally received certificates at the end of two-year college courses. But at least the college-trained teachers were well qualified for the secondary modern as well as the primary sector and the expectation that they might now teach subjects to the age of 15 meant that these had to be studied in some depth. With hindsight, these developments can be seen as significant steps along the road towards the enhancement of the colleges' standing. One indication of this at Chester came in 1950, when the College was chosen by the Ministry of Education to run a 'supplementary course in handicraft', intended after a third year of training to

Figure 24: Students on the supplementary Handicraft course, 1956–57, standing outside the Thomas building (then the Art & Craft block), with their tutor Peter Ainslie (back row, fourth from right). Among them are two Malayan and two Greek Cypriot students. The gables of the Exton Park houses, later demolished to make room for the Binks building, appear to the right of the trees in the background. (By permission of Lionel Jayatilaka.)

equip successful students to become specialist teachers of the subject in secondary modern schools: the subject embraced woodwork, metalwork and bookbinding and represented a focus on a 'practical' specialism to match the 'academic' specialisms found in universities. Six students took the first course in 1950–51, all passing with distinction, and similar results were achieved in subsequent years, with several students recruited, some from overseas, after completing their basic training elsewhere.[27]

The issue of colleges' relationships with universities had been one of the subjects of the McNair Report on the training of teachers and youth leaders, published in May 1944 three months before the Butler Education Act had received the royal assent. This report had sought to bring greater coherence to teacher training by recommending that universities, colleges and LEAs should form what later became known as 'area training organisations' to co-ordinate their work. There was, however, a difference of opinion on the committee, replicated in discussions after the publication of the report, over whether universities should exercise academic leadership of these organisations or should be equal participants alongside others. This 'partnership of equals' model was actually that favoured by the chair, Arnold McNair, who was Vice-Chancellor of Liverpool from 1937 to 1945, but by the end of the decade most universities had accepted a leadership role, housing and servicing the area organisation and overseeing assessment and the curriculum through an Institute of Education. Liverpool, true to its former Vice-Chancellor, was one of three universities which preferred a more independent area training organisation, and after two years' discussion of the respective roles and representation of colleges, LEAs and University this was eventually established in 1949 under the wardenship of the former Principal of Kirkby Emergency Training College. It was a Liverpool – but not University of Liverpool – Institute of Education, although the University did provide offices at no. 1 Abercromby Square. From 1 July it took over the duties of the Joint Examinations Board which had run since 1929, becoming the body responsible for assuring the standards of students' assessed work, and it also revised the curriculum for its constituent colleges, which from 1951 became a combination of compulsory 'Professional Subjects and English', a range of mainstream subjects (of which students had to select two) and a series of options which colleges could choose to reflect their local interests and resources; while the first two groups of subjects were formally examined by the Institute, the local options were continuously assessed by the colleges themselves, which simply returned pass or fail marks overall.

Such innovation went down very well at Chester – as Astbury put it in the *Collegian*, we 'rejoice in our increased responsibility and freedom' – and the same basic scheme continued for the rest of the 1950s; with the advent of three-year courses in 1960 it was amended so that of the mainstream subjects one became a 'main' studied for three years, the other a 'subsidiary' taken for two, but otherwise the essentials remained in place for a further decade. However, the largely independent Institute of Education proved to be of much shorter duration. Following the death of the warden towards the end of 1952, the University took the opportunity to reconsider its position and, after further discussion with the participants, a University of Liverpool Institute of Education – along the lines already established in most of the country – formally came into being on 1 August 1954. This arrangement, which was to prevail until area training organisations were dissolved in 1975, meant that the College's work once again had direct university verification.[28]

Yet despite the changed context in which teacher training was conducted, and despite the inevitable upheaval in the character of the student body, in many respects Chester College remained a deeply conservative institution in the years immediately after the Second World War. Astbury himself, wedded to the theme of 'responsibility and freedom' which he had cited with reference to the Institute of Education's curriculum, would probably not have agreed. In his final Principal's Notes for the *Collegian*, he considered the greater 'freedom and responsibility' given to students as among the most profound changes wrought during his period of office since 1935. As he said to one incoming cohort after another: 'It is not the business of the College to train teachers; it is our business to enable and help students to train themselves'.[29] These were admirable sentiments but the framework within which they were expressed had scarcely advanced. Student numbers stayed roughly where they had been in the late 1930s – 156 in 1947–48, 149 in 1949–50, 151 in 1952–53 – and so did the complement of staff, which in March 1946 still consisted of no more than the Principal, Vice-Principal and nine other tutors.[30] Astbury liked to interview in person as many candidates for admission as he could, favouring 'personality and character' over academic achievement and being prepared to travel to meet those who lived more than 40 miles from Chester.[31] When Hawthorn retired as matron late in 1946, the appointment of Irene MacLeod as her successor perpetuated an arrangement for the supervision of the domestic staff dating back to at least the 1880s.[32] The tutorial staff did increase by one in summer 1946, when a retirement led to the recruitment both of John Milton – later to become Vice-Principal – and Arthur Wigglesworth to cover History and Handicraft respectively; but another additional tutor appointed in February 1947 to teach Rural Science and Nature Study (alongside supervising the College's gardens and grounds) had to be made redundant towards the end of 1950 because of low numbers opting for his subject.[33] Morrell's retirement in summer 1951 created vacancies both for Vice-Principal and for lecturer in Education but the posts were filled internally, apparently without any external advertisement; Bradbury succeeded as Vice-Principal while Staines moved across to Education, to be replaced by a new lecturer in Physical Education (as PT had at last become) in Nicholas Parry.[34] Both promotions were well deserved, but it could be argued that an opportunity was lost to inject some fresh thinking from outside in these critical areas.

Meanwhile, the *Collegian*, now a biannual publication, reported much the same sporting and cultural activities as before the War. The Rag resumed in November 1946, Past v. Present sports day in March 1947, the Music, Literary, Historical, Geographical and Scientific Societies, the Student Christian Movement, and sports clubs from football to rowing to athletics had all revived within two years of VE Day. The biggest achievement of the Guild Council, apart from allowing first-years to be elected in 1947, seems to have been to secure a half-hour extension on Saturday nights (quarter-hour on week-nights) to the time when students were permitted to be off campus.[35] The governors reacted vociferously when HMI expressed the view in 1950 that the College was 'reactionary and old-fashioned in its methods'[36] but all the signs are that this judgment was sound. At a time of such upheaval in the world of teacher training, when the number of students had more than doubled since before the War but voluntary colleges were now outnumbered by their LEA competitors,[37] this was not the moment for a conservative approach.[38]

So the appointment of a new Principal with ideas for modernisation was essential. The advertisement indicated a readiness to cast the net more widely than before: 'applicants … may be either in Holy Orders or communicant lay members of the Church of England', although they had to be graduates of a British university, 'preferably with teaching experience'.[39] Six candidates were interviewed on 12 September 1952. We lack details of the unsuccessful ones but the man chosen, Aubrey Price, was very familiar with the world of training colleges and exceptionally well qualified for the post: a graduate of Jesus College, Oxford, a former boarding school headmaster, Principal of Wymondham Emergency Training College from 1947 to 1950 and currently Warden of Goldsmith's College, London. The post at Goldsmith's was a prestigious one and according to Astbury, introducing his successor in the *Collegian*, the move to Chester involved 'considerable financial sacrifice' on Price's part. But he evidently wanted to run a Church college, professed to have long held Chester in high regard, spoke warmly when meeting the governors of the academic and administrative staff he had met, and repeatedly expressed his delight at having arrived. Apart from being the first Oxford-educated Principal, Price was also the first layman to be appointed, although he had been a licensed lay reader since 1936 and assured his interviewers that he wished soon to be ordained. In the event, he became a deacon (so could be given the title 'Revd') the following December, but never a priest. The original intention was that he would start at the beginning of January but Goldsmith's pleaded to keep him until the end of April. Astbury graciously agreed to stay on, and he eventually took over on 1 May 1953.[40]

Like Allen and Best before him, Price hit the ground running with a series of suggested improvements at his first governors' meeting. He observed that more needed to be spent on the maintenance of buildings and believed the income for this could come from a combination of increased fees and modest growth in student numbers. He thought additional lecturers in English and Education should be appointed. He advocated the taking of a deposit from students when they accepted a place, out of which there should be a levy for the Guild, with the balance – after any damages – being repayable at the end of the course. And he asked for a College coat of arms to fill the spaces which the architect had left over the entrances to the two hostels. There would of course be much more to come, but this initial foray proved very successful. He was allowed to negotiate an increase in fees with the Ministry of Education, which it was agreed would stand for 1953–54 at £154 for tuition and £129 for board, within which £17 was specifically allocated for paying down the College's deficit and repaying its loans. Student numbers for that year were nudged upwards to 158, each 'extra' student, on the basis of these figures, bringing useful additional income. The new financial arrangements with students, over deposits and a subscription to the Guild, went ahead, and although the governors would not sanction two extra appointments, they did allow one, to cover English and Education together. The successful candidate, Hugh Pollard, duly arrived in 1954. His credentials, as an Oxford graduate who had ended his war service by creating a school in ruined Berlin, had spent a year and a half as an assistant professor at Tennessee University and who was completing a PhD on 'Pioneers of Popular Education' at Liverpool, are indicative of a new concern to enhance the academic standing of the tutorial staff. He stayed for only two years before moving on to become assistant to the Director of the Sheffield University Institute of Education, but was considered in that short time to have had a 'quite remarkable' influence on staff and students alike. He subsequently became Vice-Principal of St Mark and St John, Chelsea, and in 1963 (a year before it opened) first Principal of the new Church college later known as S. Martin's Lancaster.[41]

As for the coat of arms, Price's success in this regard fulfilled an aspiration dating back to the 1920s, when there had been at least two approaches to the College of Arms on the subject.[42] Until now, various badges with different emblems had served the College over the years. The *Chester College Song Book* of 1939, for example, was adorned with a shield of four quarters, each bearing devices relating to one of the dioceses represented on the Governing Body: far too elaborate in its conception. An earlier shield, carved in stone with the date 1894, stands between Astbury House and the former College School; this too is an amalgamation from different sources. In October 1953 Price reported that a new coat of arms could be provided for 100 guineas and in the following March the lecturer in Art, Joseph Clarke, who had an interest in heraldry, was asked to prepare sketches for submission to the College of Arms. He worked closely with John Walker, Rouge Croix Pursuivant, to produce a strikingly effective design warmly received by the governors in May and formally granted to the College on 5 July 1954. There are allusions to the cross of St George, the Chester, Cheshire and diocesan wheatsheaf, an open book representative of scholarship, 'the sword of the Spirit' (Ephesians, chapter 6, verse 17) and – in the crest – an episcopal mitre. The motto 'Qui docet in doctrina' is taken from St Paul's Epistle to the Romans chapter 12, verse 7, part of a passage urging the faithful to use their different gifts for the common good: 'he who teaches, in teaching'. This appears not, however, to have originated with the grant of arms, since it had already sometimes featured on College blazers beneath the earlier four-diocese badge in the immediate post-war period. It is not a motto suitable for quoting out of context and, appropriate though it was when the institution was devoted wholly to teacher training, it is perhaps not entirely satisfactory today. Ironically, the new arms were not placed over the entrances to either of the new hostels, as Price had envisaged; both bear those of the Bishop of Chester instead. But visually they serve most effectively as the University's heraldic device to this day (see Plates 1, 2 and 3).[43]

Meanwhile, Price's main concern was the size of the College, against the background of government plans eventually to replace two-year teacher training courses with those of three years' duration, a development expected by the early 1960s. Meetings he attended with representatives of the Church Training Colleges in June and October 1954 recommended that those offering three-year courses should have somewhere between 180 and 240 students, which made 210 a target to aim for. Colleges smaller than this would be deemed not cost-effective and hence vulnerable to closure, so it was essential to prepare sufficient residential and classroom accommodation for these greater numbers.[44] Obtaining Ministry permission to admit more students was not a problem in the mid- to late-1950s since there was a shortage of teachers to cope with the post-war 'baby boomers' making their way through school: in 1954–55 numbers rose to 166 and by 1957–58 had reached 220, a total accommodated partly through the purchase in 1955 of no. 3 Exton Park, which was semi-detached to no. 4 and was knocked through to create an enlarged hostel. As had been the case the last time a total of 220 had been reached in 1931, there was also significant reliance on lodgings.[45] However, while recruitment to women's colleges across the country was buoyant, it was only with difficulty that the College attracted enough suitably qualified male applicants and there was also the issue of how to finance the necessary building schemes.[46] The kitchens, located in a corner of the old College buildings near the dining hall, were remodelled as a matter of urgency in the summer vacation of 1954 and the Christmas break which followed it,[47] but enlargement of the dining hall, conversion of the empty dormitories and provision of new lecture rooms and an assembly hall were all costly projects which could not proceed without Ministry of Education and Church of England funding. It was in this context that in 1957 the governors decided to raise some money on their own account by selling off for residential building development a plot of land in the north-east corner of the campus, close to the railway bridge over Parkgate Road; this plot, recognisable by the presence of modern bungalows out of character with their neighbours, was eventually bought back to serve the University as residential accommodation and may in time be redeveloped as an alternative entrance to the campus.[48]

In due course, sufficient money was available for the expansion of the dining hall and the building of the new lecture room block as projects for 1957–58, although unfortunately Saxon the College architect, who had fulfilled this role since 1936, had designed Fisher and Astbury Houses and had been a willing guest lecturer on aspects of historic Chester, was so dilatory in producing plans that he had to be paid off.[49] Anxious for a completion, Price called in Spooners of Hull to design and build the block of lecture rooms, which, located just beyond the College School, went on to serve in turn as a Geography department, a Primary base and by the institution's 175th anniversary as a Careers and Employability centre). He was so pleased with their speed and efficiency that they were commissioned to build the assembly hall – opposite the lecture block – as well.[50] Both buildings were constructed to modest specifications, since funding was strictly limited, but they have served College and University well for over half a century and the hall in particular would come to have a special meaning for students in coming decades as the place where, on the one hand, they sat their exams and, on the other, began romantic attachments at social events. The hall was ready in time to host the College's first annual Presentation Ceremony on 24 June 1959, when the Vice-Chancellor of Liverpool University Sir James Mountford gave an inaugural address and distributed prizes; the Hawarden Singers performed the first concert there in November 1959 and the Dramatic Society took it over for 'King Oedipus' by Sophocles the following January.[51] Although it is now called the 'Small Hall', it was originally named after Gladstone, the family being approached for their permission at the end of the year.[52]

All this left the redundant dormitories in the upper storeys of the original College building as a major problem to be solved. The ground floor and basement of this structure housed the kitchens, library, teaching spaces and various staff and storage rooms, which made conversion of the area above less than straightforward. To add to the difficulties, the dormitories were of awkward dimensions and lacked any central heating system. Students normally gained access to the building by walking round from a gate on Cheyney Road, down towards the hostels then up again to the 'Prairie' courtyard, from which there were steps (still in place) towards what would now be considered the back of the premises. There was also the original formal entrance up a flight of steps from Parkgate Road, a feature of early-Victorian illustrations of the College but under-used by Price's time and never opened today;[53] from 1955 the Principal was expressing the hope that more welcoming and imposing access could be provided from Cheyney Road. So once the new teaching block had come into use early in 1958,

College representatives met with officers of the Ministry of Education and Council of Church Training Colleges to discuss the future of the 'old buildings'. As reported in the Governing Body minutes, the options were '(a) pull down the buildings and begin again; (b) partially pull down and rebuild; or (c) put them in a complete state of repair and adapt them in the best possible way'.

It beggars belief today that what is now the University Senate House could seriously be considered for demolition, but this was not a 'conservationist' era: the Pontcysyllte aqueduct near Ruabon, now a World Heritage Site, was under serious threat as a redundant structure before it was scheduled as an ancient monument in 1958 and, most notoriously, the iconic Euston arch – well known to rail travellers from Chester as they arrived in London – would come down in 1961. In the event, a consultant architect recommended by the Ministry, W.W. Chapman, travelled up from London in April and proposed option (c) as the most economical.

> The main fabric of the old buildings was good, there would have to be complete refenestration, reflooring, lighting, heating and proper stairs and a lift installed; the adaptations when completed would not provide accommodation as good perhaps as that specifically designed *de novo* but nevertheless the alterations should prove successful.

The governors were happy to agree with this and Chapman was instructed to proceed with his plans; as Price put it, conversion rather than demolition 'would provide much-needed accommodation and return the centre of gravity of the College to the old buildings'.[54] But twelve months later, Chapman had still not submitted his final scheme so the governors looked elsewhere for an architect. Further delays over funding meant that it was not until 1964 that the work was accomplished, to plans prepared by Douglas, Minshull and Company (now the Design Group Partnership).[55]

All this new building went on against a background of ever-rising student numbers and an accompanying increase in the complement of teaching staff, although administrative support lagged behind: when the Ministry's Accounting Director visited to check the books in 1958 he was happy with virtually everything but 'knew of only one other college where there were so few administrative staff'.[56] The College was asked to run a third-year (Supplementary) course in PE from September 1957, to add to that already established in Handicraft, and used this as leverage to ensure funding for the new assembly hall on the grounds that the gymnasium could no longer be made available for multi-purpose gatherings. There was also a meeting with the Ministry in May 1957, when colleges were implored to take more students to meet anticipated demand from school-leavers as National

Service came to an end, through more economical use of their resources. Among an assortment of different solutions across the country, mostly involving a proportion of students being off the premises at any time,[57] Price's response was to offer a 'Mid-Year' entry whereby those admitted at January 1958 could pursue a two-year course ending in December 1959; they were accommodated in lodgings and fed through extra sittings in the dining hall.[58] As a result, there were a record 284 students in the autumn term of 1958–59: 106 in the first year, 97 in the second, 19 'Supplementaries' taking PE or Handicraft and 62 'Mid-Years', who, not having been on National Service, formed a distinctively younger group. The total increased to 338 once a second cohort of Mid-Year students arrived in the following January. The third and final group of 'Mid-Years' was admitted in January 1960, leaving in December 1961.[59]

To cope, the number of teaching staff rose from 13 in March 1956 to 23 in January 1959, with further appointments in Education, PE, English, History, Geography, Art & Craft, Divinity, Physics and Mathematics. Among them were Ian Terrett, the first tutor already to hold a PhD before his appointment (for his work on the Domesday geography project), and a tutor-librarian, Stephen Tillyard, trained at Cambridge University Library and son of the Elizabethan scholar who had been a guest-lecturer at the College in Thomas's day; he was tasked with professionalising the library's service and stock.[60] Until now, the presence of more than one lecturer to cover a subject had been the exception rather than the norm. The increase in numbers enabled staff to enjoy some companionship within their academic disciplines, as well as exposing students to more than one source of wisdom. Extra schools had to be pressed into service for teaching practice, extending not only to Deeside but also to Great Yarmouth and Lowestoft, an arrangement introduced for some second-year students in the autumn term of 1958.[61] Meanwhile, the inevitable loosening of the bonds between all staff and students as the College community expanded was mitigated through the institution of a 'personal tutor' scheme, whereby each student was assigned to a member of academic staff with oversight of his progress and welfare. This was clearly another of Price's reforms and one in which he apparently saw merit even before there was any substantial growth in numbers, since the first reference to it is in March 1955.[62]

On the support side, Price took the opportunity presented by the resignations of the matron and her two assistants in 1954 – for a variety of apparently unconnected reasons – to do away with this Victorian-style approach to running domestic affairs. He appointed a College caterer to run the kitchens and dining hall and manage the catering staff; taking advantage of the refitting of the kitchens, which began later that year, the first postholder Miss A.F. Harris, who arrived in September from the catering department of University College Leicester, proved a great success, improving the meals '100%' according to student opinion while reducing costs. She did in fact move on after only two years to work for the Crown Agents in Tanganyika, but the post was here to stay; after a few short-lived tenures it was to be held from 1961 to 1979 by Diana Ross, previously the Officers' Mess caterer at the Cheshire Regiment's Dale Camp, who would keep staff and students fed and watered during the most dramatic period of fluctuating numbers – outside wartime – to date. Other aspects of the former matron's or assistant matrons' role were fulfilled through an appointment to oversee cleaning and laundry and the engagement of a part-time nurse; from 1956 until 1969, these posts were combined as 'Housekeeper-Nurse' or 'Sister-Housekeeper', with the holder, Miss C.A. Hinds, continuing thereafter as Housekeeper until retirement in 1976.[63] Apart from this, the long-serving Principal's secretary, Douglas Jones, was re-designated as Registrar and in summer 1959 Lt-Col. Arthur Bell, who had retired from Western Command HQ over the river, was appointed full-time Bursar, taking over from Morrell who, as the personification of parsimony, had been doing the job part-time since his own retirement eight years earlier. Bell had read Mechanical Sciences at Jesus College, Cambridge before joining the Royal Engineers and being awarded an MBE; as Price put it to the governors, he had all 'the right experience of buildings, grounds, accounts, roadmaking, etc.' and he would play a major role in overseeing the various projects associated with the expansion of the College through until his second retirement in December 1977.[64]

So through the latter half of the 1950s the College was visibly growing: in staffing, student numbers, buildings and administrative infrastructure. Several new student societies sprang up, ranging from a branch of the Christian Union, as an evangelical alternative to the Student Christian Movement, in 1955, to the College All Stars jazz band in 1958, which had the future TV comedian and presenter Jim Bowen as one of its leading lights and to which the Mid-Year students made a significant contribution.[65] But in many respects, conservatism still prevailed. In June 1957 the Principal raised with the governors the question of the name of the College, which he felt invited confusion across the city with both the College School and the Further Education College. This initially won a favourable reception – 'the consensus of opinion seemed to be that the College should be named after one of the saints' – but the governors repeatedly deferred a decision until Price pressed for one in December 1959. They then plumped for 'Chester College' –

Figure 25: College All Stars, autumn, 1961, featuring its leader, Alan Pirt, who is playing the clarinet. (By permission of Bob Taylor, who stands at the microphone.)

omitting reference to any of the dioceses or to training – because this was what the institution had popularly been known as since the late nineteenth century. It was a decision which failed to meet the Principal's original point but at least it had the merit of concision.[66] Then in June 1959, the governors, on Price's recommendation, unanimously turned down a request from the Guild Council for students to be allowed to stay away from College at weekends, even though this was impossible to enforce on those in lodgings without the co-operation of the landlord or landlady. Under a system which rested on the issue of written permits called exeats, a long weekend away was already allowed at each mid-term, plus one Saturday night in each half-term, but that was enough. To allow a student 'to go away at any weekend whenever he wanted to threatened to destroy the whole value of residential college life and all that it implied and sought to do'.[67] The date when the rule was rescinded appears not to have been recorded[68] but the inevitable cannot have been long delayed. In any case, a far more profound change to the nature of student life was just around the corner.

1   ZCR 86/1/9: 14 December 1939, 7 March 1940, letter of Astbury, 12 June 1940.
2   ZCR 86/11/2: letters of 22 July to 8 December 1941.
3   ZCR 86/1/9: 1 May, 20 August 1942; ZCR 86/7/28: *Report of the College Council for year ended 31 July 1942*; *Collegian*, Christmas 1942, p. 71.
4   *Collegian*, Christmas 1942, p. 71; Bradbury, *Chester College*, p. 213.
5   *Collegian*, Christmas 1947, p. 115.
6   Dunn, *Bright Star*, p. 24; ZCR 86/13/1, pt. 3: *Picture Post* (14 March 1942), which with journalistic licence claims that the School was based 'in the shadow of

Chester Cathedral'; M.F. Snape, *The Royal Army Chaplains' Department: Clergy under Fire* (Woodbridge, 2008), pp. 282, 293–94, where reservations are expressed about the practical utility of the course.

7   ZCR 86/1/9: 17 December 1942; ZCR 86/7/29: *Annual Report for 1946* (including summary 1942–45).

8   ZCR 86/1/9: 18 December 1944.

9   ZCR 86/7/29; *Collegian*, Christmas 1945, p. 12.

10   *Collegian*, Summer 1946, p. 28; Christmas 1946, p. 102.

11   ZCR 86/7/29; ZCR 86/2/6: 27 November 1945; ZCR 86/1/10: *Report of College Council for year ended 31 July 1948*; Bradbury, *Chester College*, pp. 213–15.

12   On heating arrangements in the dormitories, see *Collegian*, Summer 1954, p. 27 and Evans, *Those Were the Days*, p. 9. *The Cestrian* 2008, p. 20, an account by an alumnus of life at the College in the immediate post-war era, reports a student's dentures freezing solid in the glass of water beside his bed during the harsh winter of 1947.

13   Seaborne, 'The College Buildings, pp. 31–33.

14   ZCR 86/2/6: 31 October 1946; *Collegian*, Summer 1946, p. 3, mentions the Saturday morning exodus of students returning to their wives, and also the fact that many wives were accommodated in lodgings 'within the sound of the chapel bell'. Cf. *The Old Collegian*, 1998, where former students of the immediate post-war era, reminiscing about their experiences, express their frustration at having to abide by rules designed for school-leavers rather than ex-servicemen, including a requirement to answer 'Adsum' to their names at the 8 a.m. roll-call. The same point is made in *The Cestrian* 2008, p. 20 and *The Cestrian* 2010, p. 21, where students of 1953–55, the last to experience the dormitories before moving to a hostel for their second year, lament 'the silly rules … tea with the Principal and all the rest of the anachronistic nonsense'.

15   See Chapter 6.

16   ZCR 86/1/10: 19 October 1945, memo re College buildings 1 June 1945 (also ZCR 86/12/94); ZCR 86/2/6: 27 November 1945, 8 February 1946.

17   Dent, *Training of Teachers*, pp. 129–30; Stewart, *Higher Education in Postwar Britain*, p. 69, gives 63 voluntary and 28 LEA colleges in 1939 but 76 LEA and 56 voluntary by 1951.

18   ZCR 86/11/4: letters of Astbury, Ministry of Education and Johnson of Council of Church Training Colleges, 18 February, 21 February, 27 February 1947.

19   ZCR 86/11/5: letters of Astbury, Ministry of Education, Stopford of Church Training Colleges and Saxon (architect), 14 March, 15 March, 28 July, 29 July, 11 October, 26 November 1949.

20   ZCR 86/11/4: letters of Astbury, Saxon and Ministry of Education, 23 September, 26 October, 14 November, 5 December 1952.

21   ZCR 86/11/4: undertakings 13 June 1952, 6 March 1953; letter of Stopford of Church Training Colleges, 10 March 1952.

22 Seaborne, 'The College Buildings', p. 41; Bradbury, *Chester College*, p. 221. The change of brick is most obvious on the north side of Astbury House, even though this was the first to be completed.

23 ZCR 86/1/10: 26 May 1954; *Collegian*, Christmas 1954, pp. 65–68, 71–72, 89–90.

24 Evans, *Those Were the Days*, pp. 1, 4.

25 *Collegian*, Autumn 1962, p. 103.

26 In 1952 almost 16% of children above the age of 11 were still being taught in 'all-age schools': *Hansard, House of Commons, 23 October 1952*, vol. 505, c. 1256.

27 ZCR 86/1/10: 9 June 1950; *Report of College Council for year ended 31 July 1951; cf. Report of College Council for year ended 31 July 1953*; *Collegian*, Summer 1950, p. 29, Christmas 1956, p. 88 (where there is a reference to two Malayan students taking the supplementary Handicraft course).

28 Kelly, *For Advancement of Learning*, pp. 436–40; ZCR 86/1/10: 25 April, 12 December 1947, 4 March, 1 October, 10 December 1948, 6 January, 10 June, 7 October, 9 December 1949, 12 December 1952, 6 March 1953, 25 June 1954; Report of College Council for year ended 31 July 1954; *Collegian*, Christmas 1949, p. 100.

29 *Collegian*, Christmas 1952, p. 95.

30 ZCR 86/1/10: 8 March 1946; *Reports of College Council for years ended 31 July 1948, 1950, 1953*.

31 ZCR 86/12/95: 'Arrangements made for the selection of students for admission to this College', 28 September 1946.

32 ZCR 86/1/10: 13 December 1946; *Collegian*, Christmas 1946, p. 102.

33 ZCR 86/1/10: 7 March, 1947, 9 June, 8 December 1950; the tutor (another former College student) obtained a similar post at Kesteven Training College, Lincolnshire.

34 ZCR 86/1/10: 9 June 1950, 9 March 1951.

35 *Collegian*, Christmas 1946, p. 102; Summer 1947, p. 25; Christmas 1947, p. 102; Christmas 1949, p. 91; Dawtry, 'All Work and No Play', p. 80.

36 ZCR 86/1/10: 9 June 1950 (in the governors' opinion, 'the College was doing good service to the cause of Education by refusing to be carried away by hastily conceived ideas').

37 See note 17.

38 In fairness, it should be said that Chester was not alone in its conservatism. When the Principal of the women's college at Homerton (Cambridge) retired in 1958 after over 20 years in the post, she was said to be 'living … as if all the clocks had stopped in 1939 or even earlier' (E. Edwards, *Women in Teacher Training Colleges, 1900–1960: A Culture of Femininity*, London, 2001, p. 156).

39 *Church Times*, 20 June 1952, p. 457.

40 ZCR 86/1/10: 13 June, 12 September, 12 December 1952, 12 June 1953; *Collegian*, Christmas 1952, p. 73; Summer 1953, p. 28; *Church Times*, 3 October 1952, p. 701.

41 ZCR 86/1/10: 12 June, 1953, 26 May 1954; *Collegian*, Christmas 1956, p. 88; P.S. Gedge and L.M.R. Louden, *S. Martin's College Lancaster, 1964–89* (Lancaster, 1993), pp. 10–11. Under grant arrangements introduced by the Ministry of Education in

1945, each college's agreed tuition fee was paid in full by the government, but students were required to pay part of their maintenance according to means (ZCR 86/1/10: 19 October 1945).

42 ZCR 86/1/8: 15 June 1921; ZCR 86/1/9: 16 October 1929.

43 ZCR 86/1/10: 16 October 1953, 5 March, 26 May 1954; ZCR 86/9/10; *Collegian*, Summer 1954, p. 9; Bradbury, *Chester College*, p. 244, where the full heraldic description is given; The motto may loosely be translated for general purposes as 'let the teacher teach'. There is a representation of the shield in use around the turn of the century on the back cover of this book.

44 ZCR 86/1/10: 25 June 1954 and Principal's report on meeting of Council of Church Training Colleges, 26 October 1954.

45 ZCR 86/1/10: *Report of Chester College Council for year ended 31 July 1955*; 14 October 1955; Bradbury, *Chester College*, p. 227; the building which embraced nos. 3 and 4 Exton Park was later known as Bradbury House; see Chapter 7.

46 ZCR 86/1/10: 7 March 1956.

47 ZCR 86/1/10: 15 October 1954; *Collegian*, Christmas 1954, pp. 89–90.

48 ZCR 86/1/10: 7 December 1956, 8 March, 14 June, 6 November 1957; Hargreaves, 'Chester College – Site and Setting', pp. 23–26; UC, *University of Chester Development Framework* (March 2012), p. 41.

49 ZCR 86/1/10: 6 November 1957; *Collegian*, e.g. Summer 1946, p. 2; Christmas 1948, p. 103.

50 ZCR 86/1/10: 6 November, 13 December 1957, 4 March, 10 October 1958, 6 March 1959.

51 *Collegian*, Summer 1960, p. 36; to judge by the report on the concert, it was briefly known as the 'Great Hall' before Gladstone's name was applied.

52 ZCR 86/1/10: 12 June 1959, 11 December 1959; *Collegian*, Christmas 1959, p. 61.

53 *Pers. comm.* B. McDermott (student, 1954–56), J. Sykes (see Chapter 10, note 45).

54 ZCR 86/1/10: 14 March, 15 June 1958; but cf. 3 October 1956 for an alternative opinion that demolition would be the cheaper option.

55 *Collegian*, Summer 1955, p. 28; ZCR 86/1/10: 12 June, 11 December 1959; below, Chapter 9.

56 ZCR 86/1/10: 10 October 1958.

57 P. Gosden, 'The Role of Central Government and its Agencies, 1963–82' in R.J. Alexander, M. Craft and J. Lynch, eds, *Change in Teacher Education: Context and Provision since Robbins* (London, 1984), pp. 31–45, at p. 37.

58 *The Cestrian* 2007, p. 25 has an article by one of the first intake of Mid-Year students, which includes the following revealing comment. 'National Service was then about to be discontinued and the government gave young men the option of deferring their "call-up" if they applied for teacher training. Eighteen-year-olds in 1958 soon realised that, if they applied for deferment, National Service would be abolished by the time they completed their teacher training, it made the prospect of applying for a two year college course all the more attractive.' The article goes on to explain that the high-profile distinctiveness of this group of 18-year-olds, in

a community of students mostly in their early twenties, was exacerbated by the fact that many were banned from their lodgings during the daytime and there were few on-campus facilities for them to use when not at lectures. (There was always the library, of course.)

59 ZCR 86/1/10: 3 October 1956, 14 June 1957, 10 October 1958, 6 March, 9 October 1959; *Collegian*, Christmas 1961, p. 69.

60 ZCR 86/1/10: 15 June 1956, 14 March 1958; Terrett's *Domesday Geography of Midland England*, jointly edited with H.C. Darby, had been published by Cambridge University Press in 1954.

61 ZCR 86/1/10: 12 June 1956, *Report of College Council for year ended 31 July 1956*, 10 October 1958.

62 ZCR 86/1/10: 4 March 1955; cf. 11 December 1959.

63 ZCR 86/1/10: 26 May 1954, 24 June 1955, 15 June 1956; *Collegian*, Christmas 1956, p. 88; 1980, p. 19; CC, Minutes of Governors, 1975–89: 20 February 1976; CC, Hooper deposit, *Calendar and Diary 1969*, cf. *Calendar and Diary 1970* (which shows a separate nurse to have been appointed). Although there were occasional student complaints about the food during Ross's period of office, the DES's senior catering adviser, visiting the College in 1978, commended 'the good general level of catering and the high standard of cleanliness and hygiene she had observed during her visit to the Dining Hall': CC, Minutes of Academic Council, 1972–81: 8 February 1978.

64 ZCR 86/1/10: 14 March 1958, 6 March, 12 June, 9 October 1959; *Collegian*, 1978, pp. 14–16.

65 *Collegian*, Summer 1952, p. 26; Christmas 1955, p. 74; Summer 1956, pp. 17–18; Christmas 1958, pp. 79–80; Summer 1959, pp. 27–28; *Chester Chronicle* 27 June 2008; *pers. comm.* R. Taylor; cf. *The Cestrian* 2009, pp. 4–5. In his autobiography, *Right Place Right Time* (Lancaster, 2002), p. 20, Bowen – whose surname as a student was Whittaker – explains that the band had originated earlier, as an accompaniment to the Rag procession.

66 ZCR 86/1/10: 14 June 1957, 12 December 1958, 11 December 1959 ; in the College's Annual Report for the year ending 31 July 1959 the institution was headed 'Chester, Manchester and Liverpool Diocesan Training College' (for some reason omitting Blackburn), but this was simplified to 'Chester College' from 1960 (ZCR 86/7/42 and ZCR 86/7/43, *Annual Report and Accounts for 1959* and *1960*).

67 ZCR 86/1/10: 12 June 1959.

68 But see below, Chapter 9.

CHAPTER 9

THE TRANSFORMATION OF THE COLLEGE COMMUNITY

By the close of the 1950s, every teacher training college the size of Chester's had taken on board the message, 'expand or die'. The government was anxious to increase the number of teacher trainees, was willing to fund the building schemes necessary to accommodate them, but let it be known that it was prepared to close those colleges deemed too small to be efficient. For its part, the Church of England Board of Education was prepared to back this expansion as 'an investment of Church money which it would scarcely be possible to better'.[1] When in June 1958 one of the governors reported on a recent meeting of the Council of Church Training Colleges, to the effect that Chester was not among six Church colleges selected by the Ministry for rapid growth over the next three years, there was some alarm; no-one could say what might befall those colleges left out, so a small subcommittee was set up to urge Chester's inclusion on the list. In fact, there was no real cause for concern. A letter from the Ministry the following September envisaged numbers rising on such a scale that a far wider range of colleges could participate and Chester was seen as expanding to some 450 students by 1962. Emboldened by this, the Governing Body submitted a development plan outlining further building requirements, and a small party – the Principal and two governors – duly met Ministry officials to discuss it on 15 December 1958. At the meeting, they were told that the College would indeed be included in the Ministry's plans for expansion, but on condition that Chester became a mixed college of 250 men and 150 women.[2]

This proposal did not come entirely out of the blue, since the government had a well-known commitment to the training of more teachers of both sexes. Back in 1944, the McNair Report had expressed its enthusiasm for co-educational colleges and, more recently, the National Advisory Council for the Training and Supply of Teachers had advocated selecting for growth only colleges with at least 200 students, 'ready to become mixed if they were not mixed already'.[3] A governors' meeting a few days before the encounter with the Ministry, discussing a revised constitution, had indeed raised the possibility that the College might 'become co-educational'.[4] But to say that the idea was unwelcome would be an understatement. Given the immense benefit which the admission of female students has had on the institution – a development vital to the progress made in the last third of the twentieth century – it is difficult nowadays to understand, let alone sympathise with, the attitudes which prevailed at this time. But several other teacher training colleges were allowed to continue as single-sex institutions for many years yet; the Oxbridge colleges only began to admit both men and women during the 1970s. In the view of Price, his more influential staff and most of the governors, the admission of women not only went against tradition and threatened the cohesion of the College, it also posed new challenges in areas such as accommodation, discipline, welfare and the balance between different subjects within the overall curriculum. At a meeting in June 1960, Cyril Jarman, canon of Chester Cathedral and a governor who represented the College at the Liverpool Institute and on deputations to the Ministry, argued that 'since apparently co-education seemed to be the officially approved policy both in schools and colleges, might not the Governing Body be right to accept the situation and to be willing to take in women'.[5] But this seems to have been a lone voice, as all sorts of arguments were marshalled in an attempt to frustrate the Ministry's purpose.

A new factor entered the equation in February 1959 when, hard on the heels of the request to 'go mixed', there came a separate invitation from the Ministry to become a PE 'Wing College' for men. The proposal was a response to the planned introduction from September 1960 of three-year teacher training courses, which would subsume the current third-year 'Supplementary' arrangements within the general provision. Under this scheme, 10 selected men's colleges (and seven women's) were to be recognised as 'Wing Colleges', an odd appellation but one which carried an expectation that they would now offer a specialist PE programme, alongside one other subject and general training, in return for preferential allocation of resources.[6] This was good news indeed, an affirmation of the College's standing in a shortage area and an opportunity, as Price saw it, to counter the 'mixed college' proposal. The Ministry gave short shrift to a letter he wrote arguing that increased numbers of male PE students would create an imbalance if combined with the admission of women as well: he was told that unless the College agreed to both proposals the offer of expansion would go elsewhere. But by June the number of female students had been negotiated down to about 100 'in the initial stages' and by the end of the year it was being suggested to the Ministry that if the College had a Handicraft Wing as well as one for PE it could fill its 400 projected places with men alone. As the Governing Body's minuting secretary could not resist recording it, 'the College should have two wings and no women'. This, too, was rejected. The Ministry wrote in May 1960 ruling out a Handicraft Wing and reaffirming its wish that the College should admit 100 women as soon as possible, eventually rising to 200.[7]

Principal and governors reluctantly accepted this ruling but hoped to delay its implementation for as long as they could, clinging to the vain hope that in the meantime circumstances might change and the College be allowed after all to continue as an all-male institution. Debating the Ministry's letter in June 1960, the governors made the somewhat specious point that there would now be no men's college in the western side of England between St Paul's Cheltenham and the Scottish border, whereas Bede (Durham), York and Saltley (Birmingham) remained in the east: a curious way to partition the country, normally employed only for the weather forecast. Price made the more valid point that he feared a 'most unfortunate dichotomy' arising, with men taking PE, Handicraft, Science and Mathematics while women gravitated towards the Arts subjects, so meaning that there would in reality be little 'co-education' taking place; he failed to mention the mixing at professional classes in Education as well as through social activities. He was instructed to write back to the Ministry 'that if it was a condition of expansion that the College must take in women, the Governing Body had no alternative but to agree' but pointing out that this would have to wait until suitable accommodation was available: 'the Governors could not countenance either of the two hostels … being used for women' because they were 'so close together'. On this point, the Governing Body minutes include a bracketed note, obviously not included in the letter, envisaging that such accommodation might well not be ready for another four years: 'it was felt that it was quite possible that, by that time, the Ministry might again have changed its mind'.[8]

There were of course dangers in resisting the Ministry for too long, because the consequences of a withdrawal of the offer to expand would have been disastrous. Accordingly, Price decided that he had better show willing and in September 1961 duly admitted after interview three mature women students, all married so non-resident on campus; their homes were in West Kirby, in Willaston (both in Wirral) and in the Chester suburb of Hoole. It was agreed with the University Institute of Education, which approved admissions, that they would take a condensed two-year course, rather than the three-year version introduced as standard in the previous year. They had to convince both Principal and Institute, on the basis of qualifications and experience, that they had the aptitude to succeed, since they would take the same final-year exams as the three-year students, and they all duly triumphed in 1963: all three of them in Education and English Literature, with Mrs J.M. Carter and Mrs M.J. Sutton also passing in Divinity while Mrs G. Sharps did so in Art. Always referred to by staff as 'Mrs …', they were among a first-year total for 1961–62 of 136; with a further 113 in the second year and 34 in the

Figure 26: Rag Day, 1963, with Rag chairman Tony Lawton pulling a float through Chester city centre. (By permission of the *Chester Chronicle* and Tony Lawton.)

third year – the latter taking the Supplementary courses in Handicraft and PE – they were also part of a record number of students enrolled to date (339), although that total was reduced when the 55 who made up the final cohort of Mid-Year students left in December.[9]

The *Collegian* of Christmas 1961 lamented the end of the short-lived Mid-Year scheme[10] but made no reference whatsoever to the incoming women, perhaps hoping that their sojourn would prove to be an equally transitory feature of the College's story. But a further 23 arrived in September 1962 – again, non-resident married women 'day-students', though seven enrolled for the full three-year course – and they could no longer be ignored. An editorial in Autumn 1962 offered congratulations both on their serious approach to study and on the 'heartening' contribution they had made to College life. 'Whatever may be the general attitude', said a report in the same volume on the Dramatic Society, its members welcomed 'the arrival of so many ladies into the college; gone are the days when harassed producers had to comb the shelves of local libraries in attempting to find good plays with all-male parts'.

The Student Christian Movement, along with the Country Dancing and Choral Societies, also appear to have benefited and the Rag certainly did:

> This year was memorable, indeed, for the share the women students took in the proceedings, from parodying the worst misgivings of those who dreaded their entrance into College to simply showing charm, energy and skill in gathering contributions.

They also provided much-improved refreshments, tastefully laid out at the Rag Ball: 'a great advance on standing up to a box of crisps'.[11] So in this instance, the way to a man's heart really was through his stomach.

Nevertheless, it took courage and a thick skin to be one of the pioneering women students of Chester College. One of the 1962 mature intake contributed to the *Collegian* an illuminating piece entitled 'A Woman's-eye View of a Man's College':

> That first day we might well have been from another planet; the three of last year had been gradually assimilated, the ripples from their entrance like those from a pebble thrown into a pond, whereas ours was the splash of a boulder – all twenty-three of us. Eyes turned towards us – looked briefly – and slid away again; one could almost read the thoughts: 'She is rather like my Mum – a bit fatter, perhaps – but I can't somehow imagine Mum doing this'. The question was: how to treat us? As fellow-students, or – but – yes, how? Good manners prevailed and we went in through the door first.

She went on to describe 'a little more thawing of that thin suspicion of ice' with each day which passed, and thanked the staff, who had also 'made us welcome and help in every possible way to clear the cobwebs and spur on our minds, full of recipes for home-making, towards more intellectual pursuits'.[12] One of her contemporaries has spoken of the complaint lodged by the women students at initially being given an unheated dressing room in the Gladstone Hall to use as a common room, until space was found in the basement of the old buildings, where they felt 'like Troglodytes'. But she proceeded to gain distinctions in both Art and Divinity, winning the Astbury Divinity prize, and having practised in both primary and secondary schools was Head of the Religious Education department in a girls' secondary modern school a year after leaving College. It was this sort of application and achievement which raised academic standards and won over the sceptics. Even Price, she admits, 'gradually warmed' to the female students he had so reluctantly let in.[13]

The assimilation of women into the College community took a major step forward in September 1963, when the conversion to study-bedrooms of the dormitories in the 'old buildings' meant that 30 unmarried women, most straight from school, could be admitted as resident students. Like their male counterparts, they enrolled for the full three-year course; though the College continued to welcome non-resident mature women, and though a few of these preferred the two-year programme, from hereon they were in the minority. This time, the *Collegian* was at pains to greet the new intake and paid tribute to their predecessors, the day-students, 'who, first, accustomed us to the notion of a mixed college and, second, set a standard of seriousness about their work and an awareness of the social niceties'. Over the next two years, female students became frequent contributors to the magazine, began to lead services in the Chapel and came to enjoy the opportunity to represent the College at sport, through the formation of a rowing four and of hockey and basketball teams.[14] They were also given a dedicated seat on the Guild Council, the first elected representative being Eve Peel, one of the 1963 arrivals whose own recollection of accessing her study-bedroom, before the relevant building work was quite complete, was of having to climb over rubble to reach the spiral stone staircase. She has also commented on the warnings given to male students to curb their language and wear 'appropriate clothing' in their hostels, in case of female visitors.[15]

Meanwhile, student numbers continued to rise. In 1962–63, when the 1960 intake to a three-year course reached their final year and there were consequently three full cohorts to be taught, the figures stood at 356: 78 men and seven women in the first year of the full course, 126 men in the second

Figure 27: College Ladies Hockey team, 1964. (By permission of Eve Nelson.)

year (one of whom was from Sierra Leone), 113 men in the third year, one man and 18 women on the two-year course (including the original trio), one woman on a one-year postgraduate training course, and a further 12 men taking Supplementary courses. By the following year there were 346 men and 65 women students and by 1964–65 the grand total had grown to 443, no less than 120 of whom were women. In September 1965, for the first time, the intake of females (119) outnumbered that of males (101), within a total student body of 558.[16] Alongside this went an increase in teaching and support staff, including female lecturers. The first to arrive, in September 1962, was Barbara Chamier, who had experience of training colleges in Birmingham and Ibadan and was given the remit of ensuring the well-being of the non-resident women students. Strictly speaking, she was not the first woman ever to be appointed to teach at Chester College – that accolade seemingly belongs to Jeanne Queillé, a young graduate of Paris, Caen and Rennes who was engaged as a part-time French tutor in the 1920s[17] – but she was certainly the first to hold a full-time academic post. Chamier moved on within two years to become Head of Geography at Elizabeth Gaskell College of Education, Manchester (now part of Manchester Metropolitan University) but most of the women who followed her over the next few years were to have long careers at Chester. Among them was Charlotte Bowden, formerly headmistress of Brigg Girls' High School, who was appointed in 1963 both as lecturer in History and Education and as 'senior resident woman tutor' to coincide with the first intake of females in residence. A list of staff printed in the *Collegian* at Christmas 1964 has her as 'Dean of Women' – never an official designation – alongside six other female tutors, one of whom was the assistant librarian while the others were teaching between them Primary Education, PE, Art & Craft, English and Linguistics. Even so, they were far outnumbered by the 31 male lecturers who were by then in post.[18]

Alongside this increase in numbers went a major building programme as part of the Ministry's expansion scheme: largely government-funded (in return for the admission of women) but now with a 25% contribution from the Church and the College's own resources. The structures erected in this period are still standing, albeit in modified form. New dining halls and kitchen were built to the south of Fisher House between May 1961 and the autumn term of 1962. By February 1963 the previous dining hall – the practising school of 1844 – could begin to serve as a library, replacing the 'War Memorial Library' on the ground floor of the original buildings next to the Chapel. A new sanatorium and lecture-room block, in the vicinity of the present 'Peace Cross' and above and immediately to the south of the steps which run down to the terrace and Fisher House, were also finished that year.

As we have seen, the study-bedrooms for women on the upper floors of what now began to be called 'Old College' were ready for occupation by September 1963, although the students had to endure further work on the rest of the building for much of the coming year; when finished, this provided Price's longed-for new entrance with foyer looking out to Cheyney Road, a new conference room projecting in unsympathetic concrete above it, a senior common room, administrative offices, and a common room, cloakroom and locker rooms for students not resident on campus.[19] The new entrance subsequently provided a lodge for the College's first porters.

That year also witnessed another significant change to the campus when a newly built Church of England secondary modern school, the Bishops' School, was opened in the nearby Chester suburb of Blacon. Bishops' replaced Hunter Street School (for girls) and the College School (for boys), both 'central schools' of the interwar period which had since been serving as secondary moderns. This meant that, for the first time since the opening of the College, no children were coming on to the premises to be taught: even during the two World Wars the School had carried on while the students were away. In reality, despite occasional shared use of buildings and the need for pupils sometimes to cross to and from some prefabricated 'Horsa' huts near the Exton Park hostel, the School was largely self-contained; it had its own playground and a separate entrance off Parkgate Road, so scarcely intruded on the everyday affairs of students and staff except through its use – like other schools – for practice.[20] But while the departure of the School had less impact on the character of campus life than might be expected, it did free up precious teaching accommodation. The School building itself was duly converted during 1963–64 into an Art & Craft block, with an extra lecture room incorporated within it.

In the same year, what is now known as the Thomas building – the previous base for Art & Craft – had new laboratories and a new lecture room provided, while the 'Cloisters' block north of the sanatorium, opened in 1907, was transformed into what the Principal's Annual Report for 1964 called a 'History school': 'a remarkably attractive group of rooms … now one of the most attractive departments in the College'. By the summer of 1965 there were also a new Music school abutting on to the north of the former College School; a new – second – gymnasium with a climbing wall on its western face; and three new residential hostels for female students, located close to Exton Park where the School's prefabricated huts had been demolished, all given the names of royal women – Catherine, Alexandra and Margaret. The Exton Park hostel itself had been converted into a residence for women a year earlier. All this meant that a rather tired-looking, dual-purpose campus of dated buildings – even Fisher and Astbury Houses were of a pre-War design – had suddenly been modernised. All the buildings were now in the service of higher education, several academic departments had their own dedicated teaching spaces, there were two gymnasia as befitted a PE Wing College, students ate in an airy dining hall instead of a dark, wood-panelled one, and the female students had all the newly furnished study-bedrooms at one or other end of the built-up area.[21]

Facilities were improving, the campus was bustling, but a transformation in students' outlook was evident from declining support for the various societies. The *Collegian* of Christmas 1960 carried reports on no less than 13 different societies, excluding the sports clubs; three years later this had fallen to eight and by Christmas 1966 to four. It is of course possible that some of this reduction was more apparent than real, the product of secretaries' disinclination to write a report. Societies were liable to come and go, to fluctuate in membership and activity, from one year to the next, and the College prospectus in the mid-1960s still claimed that there was wide variety.[22] But there can be no denying an underlying shift of attitude. For three-quarters of a century, since the days of Principals Allen and Best, the societies had been the bedrock of cultural life in the College, vehicles for the pursuit of drama, music and debate and for the exploration of academic subjects beyond the confines of the curriculum. However, they had flourished in a context in which students needed special permission to be off-campus in the evenings and in which they were also confined to Chester most weekends: a College timetable of 1940–41 shows the societies to have had a dedicated slot at 9.00 p.m. every weekday, in the hour before students went to bed.[23] By the early 1960s all this was changing. Such restrictions on students' movements as remained were under severe pressure, it was easy to get away at weekends – some students even had motor cars – and the high proportion of those in lodgings identified with the city and its entertainments as well as with the College, taking others with them. The Summer 1962 edition of the *Collegian* carried an editorial bemoaning poor attendances not only at Chapel but 'at any other optional College function', citing low numbers to watch Dramatic Society productions and athletics events; the Student Christian Movement, the Christian Union, the Choral Society and the Country Dancing Society all mentioned the problem in their reports.[24] That of Autumn 1962 included an article entitled 'The Plight of the Society', which light-heartedly blamed improved transport and poor advertisement of meetings but also mentioned the rival attractions of the bowling alley and the Odeon cinema.[25]

In terms of academic work, increased numbers presented a serious challenge to those responsible for finding schools where students could practise, a problem which became more acute in the mid-1960s when first Morecambe and Lancaster and then Great Yarmouth and Lowestoft, which had in recent years supplemented the places available locally, had to be dropped: the former because they were needed by the new Church college of S. Martin's Lancaster, the latter because supervisors could no longer be released from timetabled duties for four-week stints in East Anglia. But those no longer involved must have missed their invitations to the end-of-school-year Heads' Dinner, inaugurated by Price in 1959 as a celebratory 'thank-you' for their co-operation. These were convivial, well-lubricated occasions and it is hard to believe that the East Anglian contingent which attended in 1960 really had much of an 'educational conference' the following morning: even the Annual Report admitted that it was 'short'.[26]

On a more serious note, the College also had to adjust to a Ministry directive on the 'balance of training' issued in November 1960, which required a shift of focus towards primary instead of secondary work to meet anticipated demand over the coming decade. In Chester's case, it was expected for the coming year to train 105 men for secondary PE, under the Wing scheme, plus a further 30 men in the shortage secondary subjects of Handicraft, Science and Mathematics, but otherwise to prepare students for primary (ages seven to 11) or primary/secondary (nine to 13) work. Similar proportions would apply in subsequent years. Predictably, there were protests – in vain – and because of its timing within the admissions cycle the directive was not fully implemented until 1962–63.[27] But it did mean that there was an inevitable split within the student community, with on the one hand a large group of prospective secondary teachers (all men, mostly taking PE) and on the other various Arts students (both men and women) training for primary schools. This was the sort of dichotomy Price had warned against when he had opposed the opening of the College to women, but ironically these developments must have convinced the sceptics that their admission was the right decision; with such constraints on entry numbers it would have been impossible to meet the targets for expansion, let alone contemplate further growth in the second half of the decade, by recruiting male students alone. The large increase in numbers also helped to reverse the decline of the College societies. Even though they now catered for a smaller proportion of the total student body, and the submission of reports to the *Collegian* became in most cases an intermittent activity – making it impossible to be sure of their unbroken existence – at least there were sufficient recruits each year to keep most of them going.

This boost to social and cultural life was one factor which helped towards the acceptance of women within Chester College. Another was the perception

Figure 28: A female student in her study-bedroom, as shown in successive College Prospectuses of the mid and late 1960s. (CALS: ZCR 86A/327.)

of the early cohorts as a civilising, more academically minded, influence: although there were other factors such as an extension of library hours into the evenings, it cannot be mere coincidence that the number of book-borrowings leapt from 3,414 in 1962–63 to 11,747 in 1964–65![28] By 1965 there were no students left who had known the College before the admission of women; about one-third of the current academic staff had been appointed to a 'mixed' institution. The prospectus that year included a photograph of a female student at her desk in a well-appointed study-bedroom and promised a future in which there would be equal numbers of men and women students resident on campus, and equal numbers within the College community as a whole.[29] A revolution had been accomplished.

One woman whom Price was only too pleased to welcome to the College was HRH the Princess Margaret, who paid the first royal visit in the institution's history on Tuesday 4 May 1965. In the hour between 12.00 noon and 1.00 p.m. – after which she had lunch in the dining hall – she declared the new buildings open by unveiling a plaque in Gladstone Hall and was escorted by the Principal on a guided tour lined by well-dressed students; the Guild President, Michael Perkins, presented her with a cut glass vase adorned with her own and the College's arms and Eve Peel, as 'senior woman student', gave her a bouquet.[30] The occasion was a grand climax to Price's time as Principal and he could retire well-satisfied at the end of the calendar year.[31] He had presided over a transformative period of the College's history, yet it is hard to avoid the impression that in many ways he was a 'reluctant radical' who preferred to run the institution on traditional lines. Although he had advocated some increase in student numbers at his very first governors' meeting, he had not envisaged growth on the scale which would eventually follow and – initially at least – he was clearly unhappy that such growth should be achieved largely through the admission of women. In his early months he was personally giving messages to the maintenance department – often phrased more like requests than instructions – about minutiae such as changing light bulbs in the library, finding some hardboard to repair broken door panels in the Exton Park hostel, oiling the gymnasium floor and mending the door catch to the matron's room.[32] In 1957 he told the governors that administrative support 'should ultimately consist of the Registrar plus a shorthand typist (similar assistance being afforded to himself) together with the domestic administrator; as far as he could see this should suffice for the administrative establishment, unless the College expanded considerably – which was unlikely'.[33] In his final year, to the astonishment of his successor, he was still opening the College mail at his breakfast table.[34]

Price also accepted what had become a tradition during the twentieth century, that his wife should have a fairly high profile on the campus. Mrs Mabel Thomas, besides being seen as a more-than-capable deputy for her husband on occasion, had been founder-President of the College Literary Society and a stalwart of College drama. Mrs Ida Astbury had presided over the Musical Society and had dug the first sod for the foundations of Fisher House. Mrs Jill Price had accompanied her husband to Cheltenham in April 1960 for the Ministry of Education's first conference on college financial and domestic administration and had been one of the main invited speakers; they had learned, incidentally, that Chester was run far more economically than any other college in the country. She also cooked a Christmas dinner for support staff – served by tutors – and made a lasting impression on the College gardens: as the *Collegian* put it 'not merely as planner but with spade and barrow in all weathers and all seasons'.[35] She designed the 'Rockery Steps', built by the College maintenance department to run down to the terrace opposite Fisher House[36] and her planting alongside them shows up particularly well in photographs of the royal visit. Here and elsewhere, Mrs Price's work in the grounds has been maintained ever since.

Essentially, Price was a pragmatist who deserves much credit for skilful management of a transition he did not always welcome but accepted as necessary for the College's future well-being. It is a tribute to the confidence the Ministry placed in him and his institution, despite the difficult

Figure 29: The 'senior woman student', Eve Peel, presents HRH the Princess Margaret with a bouquet during her visit in 1965, watched by (from left to right), the Bishop of Chester Gerald Ellison, the Principal Aubrey Price and Mrs Jill Price. (By permission of Eve Nelson.)

negotiations which had sometimes been conducted, that in February 1963 Chester was one of four Church colleges offered the opportunity of further expansion as part of their plans yet again to increase numbers in teacher training. The governors' acceptance of these proposals, which envisaged 750 students by the closing years of the decade, led to the submission of further building plans, which were given due publicity during Princess Margaret's visit.[37] But as Price departed for his retirement in East Knoyle near Salisbury – he died 13 years later[38] – it would be for his replacement to see them to fruition. The priority for those charged with selecting the next Principal was to find someone with the experience to run an institution much larger than the College of the past, and with the confidence and connections to steer it through the rapids of a fast-changing higher education sector. For this was the time when government, universities and colleges were all coming to terms with the Robbins Report.

This far-reaching publication had appeared in October 1963. It had recommended radical growth in higher education provision, so that courses would be available for all who were qualified to pursue them, not only through considerable further enlargement of the university sector but also through the establishment of a Council for National Academic Awards (CNAA) to award degrees for professional courses pursued in regional and area colleges, many later designated as polytechnics. The teacher training colleges themselves received serious attention, with their three-year certificate courses introduced in 1960 being acknowledged to be of a standard close to that of an Ordinary (though not an Honours) degree. Among the recommendations relating to them were proposals for their expansion to a minimum of 750 students (fortunately the number already offered to Chester), the development of four-year courses leading to Bachelor of Education (BEd) degrees awarded by an associated university, and their re-naming as colleges of education to reflect enhanced status. With commendable foresight, the report also discussed in general terms the possibility of such colleges offering a broader range of courses, in Arts, Science or the Social Services, once demand for trained teachers began to fall in the 1970s.[39] Several aspects of the Robbins Report, such as the idea that these colleges should be financed by grants administered through their universities, never came to pass. Others were implemented but not in the way intended: the CNAA eventually became a degree-awarding body for a wider range of institutions than originally envisaged. But the general thrust of the Report – towards further expansion of higher education and the closer integration of teacher training within it – found favour both with the Conservative government which left office in October 1964 and with its Labour successor. Under the auspices of the Department of Education and Science (DES), which succeeded the Ministry of Education in April 1964, it helped to set the agenda for the coming decade and beyond – and its projections for future student enrolments were soon revised upwards.[40]

For a college such as Chester there were challenges and opportunities in all this. There was an obligation to expand and to conduct itself as an accepted player within the field of higher education. At the same time, there was a possibility that the city of Chester would seek to establish a new university, as happened – alongside rather than as a consequence of Robbins – in 1963 at Norwich and York and in 1964 at Lancaster. There was never sufficient civic enthusiasm for this, despite an offer of land on Wrexham Road (now the site of Chester Business Park) by the Grosvenor Estate, but had it become a live proposition it would have begged the question of what role, if any, the College should play within it. At Presentation Day in June 1964, the principal speaker Lord Leverhulme, then Senior Pro-Chancellor at Liverpool, went so far as to say that he 'looked forward to the creation of a University of

Chester of which the College would be an important part'.[41] This may well have been the first time that the words 'University of Chester' had been uttered at a public occasion on the campus and their implications were bound to exercise the minds of the governors as they sought a successor to Price.

In the event, the man chosen as the new Principal was a quite outstanding individual: descended from Prussian and English aristocrats, knighted three years before his appointment, on personal terms with senior figures in the DES, and one whose experience of the world's hotspots must have made disagreements at Chester College seem very tame indeed. Sir Bernard de Bunsen had accompanied his uncle to Berlin in August 1939 in the hope of salvaging a peace settlement, had served as director of education in Palestine for almost two years prior to the ending of the British mandate in May 1948, and had then spent 17 years in Africa during the closing period of colonial rule. For most of his time in Africa, he had been Principal of Makerere College, Uganda, where he had expanded student numbers to four figures, but latterly he had been the first Vice-Chancellor of the new University of East Africa, of which Makerere had become a constituent part. As a Balliol man, he was the second Oxford-educated Principal in succession. He was also the first never to take holy orders and the first bachelor; he did marry in 1975, four years after his retirement, but the absence of a spouse put an end to the expectations imposed on previous Principals' wives. His *Oxford Dictionary of National Biography* entry – he is the only Principal to have one – describes the Chester years as 'something of an anticlimax', but his own short autobiography, published posthumously in 1995, makes clear his deliberate intention to become involved in English teacher training as the 'last adventure' of his career, at this period of exciting and critical change.[42]

De Bunsen's autobiography suggests that the achievement he was most proud of while at Chester – a tenure of less than six years – was the inauguration of a more deliberative style of College governance, along the lines familiar in universities at the time. The early 1960s had been a time when a college Principal had 'resembled an absolute monarch, unhampered by representative institutions',[43] and de Bunsen's priorities for change tallied with the recommendations for democratisation published not long after his arrival in the government's Weaver Report; he used this Report as an argument to secure his reforms but there is little doubt that he would have sought to introduce them in any case. Indeed, where the Weaver Report recommended the establishment of academic boards in every college, including some provision alongside senior staff for elected representatives of the full tutorial body, de Bunsen was proud to go further and ensure that 50% of the Board was elected in this way.[44]

> My first job as Principal was, it seemed to me, to help release the initiative of my colleagues through the creation of constitutional government for the College, which would remove the Principal from power and put him in a place to which I was more accustomed and happier of 'speaker', enabler and encourager. We launched an Academic Board and other organs of self-government.

When he arrived he found academic staff already arranged into separate departments, each with a designated Head who had some control over a budget: Art & Craft, Divinity, Education, Geography, History, Languages (which embraced English Literature, French and Linguistics, each with its own Head), Mathematics, Music, Physical Education, and Science. He proceeded to ensure that each departmental Head would have a seat on Academic Board, alongside a number of elected staff; total membership including Principal and Vice-Principal came to 25, between a third and a half of the entire academic community at that time. Alongside the Board was an Academic Council, open to all lecturers, which first met on 28 September 1966 and usually about every two months thereafter; elections allowed the first Academic Board meeting to be held a week later on 5 October. This was over a year before they were formally authorised through the approval of the new constitution by the Secretary of State in December 1967. Interestingly, he found that senior staff – such as his Vice-Principal John Milton (whose title changed to Deputy Principal in 1967), and the Heads of Languages and Geography, Eric Pickup and John Stephens, who had joined in 1929 and 1931 respectively – were more sympathetic to his reforms than some of the recent arrivals. The newcomers, he wrote, expected 'Principalian decisions on this and that as if Academic Board was no more than a glorified staff room meeting in which the Principal unfolded his plans'.[45]

To counter this impression, de Bunsen ensured that the Board met frequently – nine times in each of the first two years, at least twice per term in the next two – and that it did, indeed, take worthwhile decisions. He presided, prompted, presented proposals but deliberately fostered the sense that the Board was collectively responsible for whatever was determined. As he wrote in his 1968 Annual Report:

> The decentralisation of authority previously formally vested in the Principal is … important to the Departments. The academic and educational health and vitality of a growing college must spring from a multiplication of its points of initiative and I am certain that an over-reliance on the centre can only be thwarting to the Departments at a time when radical re-thinking … is required of them. The Principal's role must above all be to encourage and facilitate such initiative rather than to direct it. At the same time Academic

> Board ensures that ideas are shared and proposals are subject to the challenges and stimulus of open discussion where policies are involved.[46]

Votes were taken, for example, on the introduction of standard criteria for deciding whether to terminate a student's course (carried by 19 to 1, with 1 abstention), on the adoption of a new timetable (rejected by 9 votes to 8) and even on a proposal to insert the word 'normally' into the process for advertising departmental headships (carried by six to five with 12 abstentions). He encouraged ideas to come forward for the evolution of the curriculum: in 1968, Drama (hitherto taught as a branch of English Literature) was promoted to a main subject; Handicraft (a Chester College specialism since the interwar period) was withdrawn the following year for lack of numbers, other than as a component of Art & Craft; proposals for European Studies and Nautical Studies (the latter suggested by HMI for teachers who were 'qualified mariners' or 'interested in boating') failed to win sufficient support. Subcommittees were established to cover Admissions, Finance and the library and working parties set up to deal with emerging issues. There was real tension in the context of rising student numbers when it came to debate over which departments should have additional staff. The Principal set the parameters, explaining the College's overall entitlement based on a student-staff ratio of 11:1, very generous by today's standards but conducive to the time-consuming deliberative style he favoured; he then let the Heads present their cases before the Board voted for those it favoured. In January 1968, for example, six departments bid for the three appointments available, with Education, Art & Craft and French winning out over Geography, Science and PE, although French only beat Geography by a single vote.[47]

As for Academic Council, its terms of reference were more closely defined in 1970 as being 'to advise the Governors on the welfare of members of the College and to make representations to the Academic Board on general Academic policies of the College'.[48] In practice, before and after this refinement, it was the place where matters of immediate concern to everyday experience could be given a formal airing – and through the decisions which were taken we can perceive the emergence of an institution more recognisable today than the one which had gone before. There was agreement to prohibit car parking on the terrace; to introduce a midweek College service in Chapel for which the timetable would be suspended; to establish a 'College shop' at which Burrells of Chester would sell clothing and sports equipment at the dining hall entrance; to elect a Press Relations Officer (John Edkins of the English department); to introduce a campus bar – designed and built by Scottish Breweries – in a room at one end of the dining hall; to define the working week so that students (who from 1970 attained the age of majority at

18) no longer had to obtain exeats authorising absence; to allow departments, if they wished, to introduce attendance sheets at lectures; to abolish any requirement for students to possess their own gowns; and formally to ban smoking, by invigilators as well as students, during examinations.[49] Issues such as the personal tutorial system, the possibility of more social interaction between staff and students, policy and practice on prizegiving, the unfairness of sending down women students who became pregnant while the men responsible stayed on, and the discrepancy between recorded and actual use of what appears to have been the College's only photocopier ('the Rank Xerox machine') all came before it.[50] But there was also a good deal of discussion of curriculum matters and of the future role of the College in the changing higher education scene of the early 1970s: an opportunity for even the humblest member of academic staff to keep abreast of developments and to make some input to them.

De Bunsen was also sympathetic to moves afoot within the training colleges in the late 1960s to allow student participation in institutional governance. After lengthy discussion of this issue – first raised with the Guild Council in November 1968 – he eventually secured student representation on Academic Council, Academic Board and the Governing Body, not because of any pressure from the Student Guild but because he thought that they should play their part in running the College they belonged to.[51] The first student members of Academic Board, the Guild President Mike Mills – 'a non-militant member of the Welsh Nationalist Party' according to his profile in the *Collegian* – and Vice-President Shirley Browne, were duly welcomed in September 1970.[52] Staff membership of the Governing Body was secured early in 1968, when the long-serving Ralph Staines was elected by Academic Council, along with Nicholas Parry (Head of PE) and Revd John Carhart, a geographer who had arrived in 1963. De Bunsen claimed that he would have welcomed more challenge from his governors but admitted that he found their unfailing support a relief after East Africa. He had a particularly high regard for the chair, the Bishop of Chester Gerald Ellison, who managed to sum up everything in time for lunch to begin promptly at 1.00 p.m. and with whom, outside meetings, he 'unravelled problems sipping beef tea in the Bishop's study'.[53]

The first *Handbook for Students* appeared in 1969, opening with the incontrovertible statement that 'the rapid growth in our numbers in recent years has brought about many changes in our College life and procedures'. It reflected many of the adjustments agreed by Academic Council since its inception three years earlier. At the close of the 1950s, as we saw in the last chapter, a ban on students leaving Chester for more than three weekends per term had been reaffirmed; now, weekends were precisely defined (5.40 p.m. on Friday to 9.05 a.m. on Monday) and students were free between those hours to go wherever they wished. Procedures for reporting absence owing to sickness were explained and the importance of regular contact with the personal tutor affirmed. Predictably, there was a great deal about residential arrangements, including reminders about the damage that could be caused by sellotape on walls and the anti-social nature of 'undue noise in the hostels when others are trying to read or sleep', a ban on visitors to hostel rooms after 10.00 p.m. (11.00 p.m. on Saturdays) and for those in lodgings details about the respective obligations of students and their 'hostesses'. Car parking, for which there were already official College stickers, was restricted to students living off campus and only with the Principal's special permission in spaces allocated by the Deputy Principal; the car parks were next to Gladstone (now Small) Hall and between the old College School and Parkgate Road in the area now occupied by the Swimming Pool. Smoking 'is allowed generally, except where common convenience or usage makes it unsuitable, as in the Gladstone Hall and the lecture rooms'; it was also prohibited in the library.[54]

Of course, a description of procedures does not give the whole story, since in common with higher education institutions (HEIs) all over the country the College did experience its share of student unrest towards the close of the decade. The older voluntary colleges such as Chester have been described at this time as having 'a continuing dedication to a somewhat etiolated version of gracious living'[55] but that only served to make late-sixties radicalism all the more of a shock. In December 1968 the students' Guild Council voted 11:1 in favour of retaining the wearing of gowns on formal occasions such as Sunday Chapel and visits to see the Principal,[56] but this gives a misleading impression of meek conformism. According to the *Collegian*, the Autumn term of 1968 was a time of 'increased discontent … with College courses and College life', memorable for its 'mass meetings and student discussion in general'. As part of this, a new publication, *Crossfire*, appeared on duplicated sheets every three weeks, evidently as a vehicle to challenge the status quo. Even the Guild Council itself came in for criticism as unrepresentative and lacking in transparency.[57] Two years later, the *Collegian* published an article entitled 'Student Opinion on Community Life', critical of the content and style of lectures, of their colleagues' tendency to get by on the minimum of work, and of poor community spirit, attributed to large numbers living off campus and departing at weekends and to lack of social interaction between students and staff; since this was the work of only 10 students who declared no affiliation, it is impossible to know how representative these comments were, but they do at least indicate a readiness to speak out.[58] In the meantime, the Guild organised a one-day demonstration on teachers' salaries in December 1969, leading to lectures and school practice being cancelled. It also participated in a march through Liverpool two years later 'to protest against Mrs M. Thatcher's consultative document on the financing of student unions' – although the President for 1971–72, Ray Marsden, was moved to lament the fact that 'we are still sadly lacking in this sort of national participation in comparison with most of the other colleges in the Liverpool area'.[59]

A rather different issue was plain misbehaviour. The Rag Day of 1968 was marred by a heavy police presence which gave the procession 'a funereal air' and led to several stunts being called off; that year's Rag Mag was banned from sale. There was concern at Academic Council early in 1970 about the bad taste both of the previous year's Rag Mag and of speeches at the most recent College Christmas dinner; the behaviour of some first-years at the next Christmas dinner was such that catering staff could only be persuaded to continue if it was restricted in future to academic staff and third- and fourth-year students. Vandalism also became a matter of concern, not least to the Guild Council which had to contribute to repairs.[60] But while occasional protests continued, the bitterness which characterised some students' attitude at this time – in some ways reminiscent of the eruption of discontent and

Figure 30: Christmas dinner, 1971, with the Principal, Malcolm Seaborne, carrying the boar's head. (*Collegian*, 1972.)

misconduct under Chritchley[61] – was out of character with the stance of the majority of students over most of the institution's history, and it did not endure.

Of far more lasting significance as a legacy of de Bunsen's years is a building which has dominated the Chester campus and featured in the city's skyline ever since – although in presiding over the construction of the tower block he was implementing plans set in train by his predecessor, through the decision in 1963 to expand the College still further. It was later, and most appropriately, named the 'Aubrey Price Tower'. Given the escalation of costs during its construction, it also acquired the nickname 'Price rise'.[62] The appeal to fund the new building programme, with the tower as its centrepiece, was launched in November

1965 with the issue of an illustrated brochure entitled *Chester College: Campaign for Expansion*. This described an 'attractive, modern tower building' between the two gymnasia, which in addition to lecture rooms, tutors' rooms and a language laboratory was originally to have four student common rooms 'invaluable to those 300 or so students who cannot be residentially accommodated in the College'. The *Collegian* of Summer 1964 had promised 10 storeys but the artist's impression in the brochure showed a more reasonable eight, with cladding

Figure 31: Artist's impression of the proposed tower block, which featured in the fundraising booklet *Chester College: Campaign for Expansion* in 1965. (CALS: ZCR 86/17/143.)

to the concrete to give a black-and-white effect. The foundation stone was eventually laid on Presentation Day in June 1967; the inscription refers to this being done 'in the faith of God', a point alluded to by de Bunsen in his speech when he commented that there was currently only enough money to build five of the intended storeys. But by September 1969 it could indeed be occupied to its full height, although it was not formally opened until June 1971. De Bunsen himself became one of the first in a long line of people over the years to be stuck in the lift and (presumably as an economy measure) the concrete walls were – until 2012 – left without any external facing. It was this stark exterior which led Seaborne to describe it as 'best regarded as a legacy of the "brutalist" phase of English architecture in the 1960s'.[63]

The Church of England was a generous benefactor to the College in this hour of need: some £204,000 was granted from central funds towards the new buildings.[64] Even so, lack of finance was a reason why some other projects which featured in the appeal brochure never came about: a fourth hostel of 25 study-bedrooms roughly in the area which now forms a forecourt to the Binks building, and a 'domestic staff residential block' for a 'caretaker' and two others, intended for the Cheyney Road end of the campus, immediately north of the steps leading down to the terrace from the entrance forecourt. There was, however, more success with proposed sporting facilities mentioned in the appeal: new tennis courts were duly provided to the north of the campus in 1973, the promised 'swimming bath' between the former College School and Parkgate Road was also ready that year, and even an all-weather pitch – which had it been laid down in the late 1960s would presumably have been of cinder – ultimately arrived in 1981, paid for entirely from the College's private funds.[65]

One other significant building of de Bunsen's time, a student centre, was erected between Fisher and Astbury Houses at their western end, so completing a loose quadrangle with what was by then officially called the Thomas building on the eastern side. Even this had to be put to a vote at Academic Board, where alternative sites near the dining hall, Gladstone Hall and Exton Park were all considered, before a 14:2 majority won the day. The centre was intended to provide a cafeteria – fitted with vending machines and microwaves, so offering some relief to the dining hall – common rooms and also offices for the Guild, a role it continued to fulfil until new larger premises were built for the Students' Union in 2008, after which it was demolished. Completed in the summer of 1971, just as de Bunsen was retiring, it was appropriately named after him. It had not featured in the 1965 appeal but it reflected his own commitment to ensuring that students should make an active contribution to their community and have a building they could call 'their own'. The College also began to rent a redundant Congregational church and school in Northgate Street (now the Northgate Church adjacent to the Fountains roundabout), used for the teaching of both Drama and Divinity from 1968 and for a Wednesday afternoon pre-school playgroup staffed by students from 1971. The playgroup went on to develop as a Playbus, an old double-decker converted as a mobile facility for children from the Blacon, Lache and Pipers Ash areas of Chester, presented to the city in October 1974 but with students continuing to be involved. The Northgate building itself remained in College use until 1977, when the opening of a new library freed up space on campus instead.[66]

Meanwhile, student numbers continued to rise, reflecting the 'baby boom' of two decades earlier, growth in the proportion of those leaving school with 'A' levels and the government's own plans, post-Robbins, to cater for increased demand. In September 1966 Chester's total stood at 607, with men only slightly outnumbering women. This was, incidentally, the first year that students (29 of them) began to find their own rented accommodation off-campus, rather than rely on approved College lodgings; no less than 255 would be in rented accommodation six years later, a development which by 1974 had prompted the Guild to set up its own advice service to supplement that provided by the College's lodgings officer.[67] In 1967–68 the total figure reached 722, with an overall female majority for the first time; by September 1969 it stood at 890 – 10 less than the 900 target – with two-thirds of the intake being women. In response, Astbury House became accommodation for female students that year, while Fisher next door continued to be allocated to men:[68] a solution expressly ruled out by the governors on the grounds of proximity back in 1960, when arguing that there was as yet no accommodation suitable for residential female students! Conversely, Exton Park – or Ecstasy Park as it was popularly known – reverted two years later to a hostel for men. [69]

The changed balance between the sexes did focus minds. Women students became more assertive. In July 1966, for example, a group of Old College residents, 'bemoaning the fact that everything in the college revolved around MEN … if one was not interested in sport hardly any society was tailored to the needs of women', founded a Needlework Society – unthinkable a few years earlier.[70] By 1970 there was a female Vice-President of the Students' Guild, the aforementioned Shirley Browne, and by 1973 a female President, a former head girl of Blackburn High School for Girls, Lynne Parker.[71] For his part, de Bunsen was clearly embarrassed to be presiding over an academic staff which by 1968–69 still included only 12 women out of a total of 72, explaining this in the *Collegian* as the consequence of too few qualified women applying for posts; ironically, at Edge Hill College in Ormskirk, where the reverse process of admitting male students to a hitherto-all-female institution had begun in 1959, and where women students remained the majority in a much-enlarged community, there were already more men than women on the academic staff by the mid-1960s.[72] De Bunsen did seek a partial remedy by securing a vote at Academic Board in February 1969 in favour of the appointment of a woman 'to an observably senior position' such as Assistant Principal, only for the DES to rule it out as beyond the College's staffing entitlement.[73] In this respect, he had to admit defeat.

One added attraction to recruitment during de Bunsen's short reign was the introduction in September 1968 within the teacher training programme of a strand focusing on the five-to-nine age range, traditionally a specialism of women's colleges – a development which acknowledged that Chester was now targeting a much wider student market than it had been at the start of the decade. Even more significant was the introduction of a four-year BEd programme, which gave an opportunity for students to be assessed for a University of Liverpool degree. Some variant of this was happening all over the country in response to one of the recommendations of the Robbins Report; the University of Leeds, for example, granted its first BEd Honours degrees in summer 1968 to students of local colleges such as Carnegie who had begun their studies in 1964. In common with most universities, Liverpool took a little longer, its first BEds being General (or Ordinary) degrees awarded in June 1969 to 13 of the Chester intake of 1965, for whom the new programme, embracing Education and two other subjects – one of which was studied for all four years, the other for three – was ready by September 1966. Amended arrangements from 1970 meant that Honours degrees could be awarded the following summer; on that occasion, of the 21 students attaining degrees, four did so with Honours. Serious attention was also given in this period to the development of in-service training, with an Education tutor, Bert Briscoe, being made responsible for its co-ordination in February 1968; by 1972, for example, 22 already qualified teachers were registered either full- or part-time for a course on the education of children with special needs.[74]

There were other signs that the College was maturing as an HEI. Closed-circuit television and video-recording arrived in 1967, with the facility not only to record broadcast programmes off-air and replay them later but also to deploy the College's own TV camera to produce material for teaching purposes; a popular scheme was to take the camera into schools, record 'real-life' teaching taking place, then discuss the lessons in seminars. Computing was introduced as an element within the Mathematics course in 1969. The year before, a campus bookshop had been opened by SPCK, using a modular 'terrapin' building erected between what would now be called the Beswick building and the Careers Centre. A bank followed in the spring of 1973, located alongside a shop in the basement of Astbury House. In January 1969 Academic Board agreed to the appointment of the College's first Research Fellow – although in the event the position was not filled – and followed this up in June 1970 by affirming its commitment to sabbatical leave for up to two academic staff at any time, provided that relevant departments covered from their own staffing resources. Tom Driver of the History department, who had recently succeeded the former 'senior resident woman' Charlotte Bowden as College archivist, oversaw the removal of the College archives – on which so much of this book has depended – to the safekeeping of Chester City Record Office during the summer vacation of 1970.[75] And the following year the first, tentative, steps were taken towards the diversification of the College away from its exclusive concentration on teacher training.

This subject had already been mooted in the pages of the *Collegian* in 1968, when Ruth Etchells of the English Literature department used the College's first sponsored 'Long Walk' (30 miles around Wirral to raise funds for the building appeal in April that year) as an opportunity to ask 'But where did we walk to …?' This was an excellently written discussion of the purpose of the College, affirming its Christian tradition but acknowledging – at a time when universities were falling behind the rate of expansion in higher education and colleges were seen as offering a viable alternative – that some students were now arriving not out of a conviction to teach but because they wanted an HE experience. She asked – in the wake of Robbins and with a prescient eye – 'Need every man or woman in a Chester lecture room be a trainee teacher for our role to be properly fulfilled? Wouldn't we be the better for having in some of our courses men and women who would be going on to other things?' In the event, she found the more varied context she was seeking by leaving some months later to become Senior Tutor at Trevelyan College in the University of Durham and in 1979 – at Cranmer Hall within St John's College, Durham – the first female Principal of a Church of England theological college.[76] However, the question she had left behind was picked up at a staff conference in July 1970, when a paper on 'The Future of the College' ranged over options such as developing recognised specialisms in selected aspects of teacher education, fostering expertise in Social Studies, providing Liberal Arts courses, becoming a centre for the recently established Open University and seeking to be some sort of 'outpost' of the University of Liverpool.[77]

Academic Council duly set up as a working party to pursue these and other ideas, leading in turn to a recommendation considered by Academic Board at a special meeting in May 1971: 'explore with the University the possibility of closer association with a view to offering degrees in addition to the BEd degree'. De Bunsen had already had an encouraging private meeting with Liverpool's Vice-Chancellor, Trevor Cawdor Thomas, and Board members looked forward to the development of degree programmes in Liberal Studies and the Social Sciences, in addition to the established focus on teacher training. The precise relationship with Liverpool as a means to achieve this was left unclear, with what look to have been unrealistic, even inconsistent, ideas being entertained:

> the establishment of Chester as a constituent college of Liverpool University should involve the acceptance of the College as a whole as an integral part of the University; it was further hoped that there might be a measure of interchange of both staff and students between Chester and other University institutions.

The Board's minutes also record that 'the question of the prospect of a University of Chester was also raised but considered unlikely in the foreseeable future'. No matter. Issues vital to the institution's future well-being had been given an airing and a small working group was set up, including the Principal and his deputy but chaired by the Head of Divinity, Thomas Fawcett, to pursue them further.[78]

This initiative was one of the last undertaken by de Bunsen, since he retired to live in Hampstead at the end of the academic year. The *Collegian* paid warm tribute both on that occasion and following his death in June 1990; in 1971 his deputy, John Milton, wrote that his greatest attribute was that 'we all trusted him' as he guided the institution through the many changes taking place in his time.[79] He departed a year before reaching the normal retirement age so as to leave his successor a free hand in responding to the major changes in teacher training expected to result from the work of the James Committee, set up by Margaret Thatcher as Secretary of State for Education and Science in December 1970.[80] The remit of his enquiry was to explore all aspects of teacher training in England and Wales, including the role of the colleges and whether more trainees should be educated alongside other students. His committee's Report, in February 1972, recommended the abolition of area training organisations, such as the University of Liverpool's Institute of Education; most of their duties would pass to Regional Advisory Councils (RACs), originally set up in 1946 to co-ordinate further and technical education and hence quite distinct from universities. It was also envisaged that all prospective teachers would in future be taught alongside other students, either on a degree course (normally for three years and certainly not for a BEd) or for a two-year Diploma in Higher Education (DipHE), after which they would receive two years' professional training, the first in a college or a university department of education, the second as a 'licensed teacher' in a school; this would be followed by an entitlement to continuing education throughout a teacher's career, facilitated by paid sabbatical leave.[81] These were radical proposals and many of them, such as systematic sabbaticals, never came to fruition. On the other hand, the notion that teachers would be educated alongside students preparing for alternative careers was in line with ideas being discussed at Chester, as across the rest of the sector. It was not the Report itself, but the government's reaction to it in a context of falling demand for qualified teachers, which would make the next few years one the most uncertain periods in the College's entire history.

De Bunsen's successor, Malcolm Seaborne, was the first Principal in whose appointment members of academic staff played any part. They did so either through their position as governors or through meeting the candidates as participants in Fawcett's working group on the College's future.[82] A History graduate of Gonville and Caius College, Cambridge, Seaborne had a background as a schoolteacher and educational administrator but had spent the previous eight years as Lecturer, then Senior Lecturer, in Education at the University of Leicester. His status as an academic, which would stand him in good stead during negotiations with the University of Liverpool in subsequent years, was affirmed by the publication shortly before his arrival of his magisterial book on *The English School: Its Architecture and Organization, 1370–1870*. He was also the first editor of the *History of Education* journal, volume one of which appeared in 1972, and he delighted in living and working among buildings of various architectural styles, illustrative of different periods in the College's history. Among other, later, publications was *Celtic Crosses of Britain and Ireland*, still in print in the Shire Archaeology series, as much a reflection of his wide-ranging intellectual curiosity as was his discovery on the Lleyn peninsula of a fossil which has entered the official record bearing his name: *Pseudosphaerexochus seabornei*. As for Chester College, his prime achievement would be to accomplish the diversification of the curriculum which had been adumbrated under de Bunsen and which would enable the institution initially to survive and subsequently to thrive, when – as independent entities – most of its peers did not.

In many ways, Seaborne's early years as Principal were a time of steady progress and achievement, facilitated by an Academic Board which remained as busy as ever, though voting less often. An in-service BEd course, which allowed teachers already holding certificates to 'top-up' to a degree, started in January 1972. It was followed in September by the introduction of a postgraduate certificate course, focusing on secondary training in the shortage subjects of Mathematics, Physical Science, English and French, for which a total of 51 students were recruited to the first cohort.[83] Also in September 1972, Nicholas Parry became the first Dean of Students, with oversight of both welfare and discipline, being succeeded as Head of PE by Edward Charlesworth; Parry's new appointment came at a time when the system of hostel tutors (many of them resident) was giving way to student self-management of their hostels, so a senior staff presence on campus (alongside the Principal) was all but essential. Student numbers peaked in 1972–73 at 959, with almost twice as many women as men in each of the first three years; only in the secondary-oriented postgraduate course were male students in the majority. The complement of academic staff, including Principal, Deputy Principal, two librarians and two French assistants, had by then reached 95.[84] In the same year, Old College was converted internally to provide a General Office on the ground floor, providing a support service for academic staff as a whole, with rooms for the accommodation officer and registration secretary above. Discussions were held with HMI over the building of a new library to cope with the greatly increased numbers; the enlargement of Gladstone Hall for this purpose, and its replacement elsewhere on campus by a modern multi-use amenity (in conception not unlike the later Molloy Hall) was one suggested, but rejected, solution.[85] Yet dominating the thoughts of Principal, Academic Board and governors alike was the College's future in the wake of the James Report.

In his first 'Principal's Notes' for the *Collegian* at Christmas 1971 – when James's recommendations were known only through leaks to the press –

Seaborne acknowledged that these were worrying times. There was concern that colleges of education might become a 'third sector' in higher education behind universities and polytechnics, in effect the last resort for staff and students who could not find places elsewhere. There was also a sense that voluntary colleges, dependent on the support of their financially stretched religious bodies, might be more vulnerable than those run by LEAs. So he played up the College's strengths.

> We have the considerable advantage of a large and attractive site in an historic city in whose area we have unrivalled opportunities for the study of history and archaeology, and the natural environment ... we are now ... one of the largest colleges ... in the country as a whole. We continue to attract more first-choice applicants than most colleges and we are well above the national average in the proportion of students we recruit with two or more Advanced level passes ... We embark on a new year, therefore, with some feelings of apprehension about the Government's plans for the colleges of education, but also with a considerable measure of confidence based on our achievements in the past and our strengths in the present.[86]

Over the next three years, the group established under de Bunsen and chaired by Fawcett considered options for the future, Academic Board and the governors debated them, and Seaborne kept open his channel of communication to the University of Liverpool Vice-Chancellor. In the meantime, the government in December 1972 brought out its formal response to the James Report in a White Paper which despite its title – *Education: A Framework for Expansion* – anticipated a reduction in initial teacher training places of at least 38% by 1981, with the colleges set to lose a total of 114,000 places. In the spirit of Robbins rather than of James, the White Paper reaffirmed a commitment to the BEd degree (as three years for an Ordinary award, four years for Honours) and presented various future scenarios for the colleges of education: some would go beyond teacher training to cover a variety of subjects to DipHE or degree level, others would retain their original focus but with increased emphasis on in-service work, some might amalgamate with other institutions, some might have to close. This was followed in May 1973 by the issue of DES Circular 7/73, *Development of Higher Education in the Non-University Sector,* which responded to a declining birth-rate by announcing substantial cuts to the number of future teacher training places and required LEAs to submit to the DES their plans for major reorganisation of the colleges of education within their areas – a move which was to set in train a series of closures and amalgamations over the rest of the decade and made it imperative that the College convince Cheshire County Council as well as the DES of the viability of its future plans. To add to anxiety, recruitment began to fall. Total numbers at Chester were down to 937 for 1973–74 and the target set by the DES for 1975–76 was only 850.[87]

Faced with all this, it was difficult for any institution to steer a consistent course. The early months of 1973 offered the prospect of expansion, the later months of contraction. The County Councils responsible for liaising with the government faced their own reorganisation and redrawing of boundaries, which came into effect in April 1974. There were two general elections in 1974, adding uncertainty to the ultimate thrust of government policy and leaving a great deal of policy-direction to DES civil servants who – according to those who lived through these events – proved secretive and unsympathetic.[88] But through it all, there was a steady conviction at Chester that salvation lay partly in expansion of in-service and postgraduate teacher training and especially in the development of new degrees validated by the University of Liverpool, which would attract students beyond the traditional clientele; in common with most of the sector, only limited interest was shown in pursuing the development of a two-year DipHE. There was fleeting reference at Academic Board in December 1971 to the possibility of making overtures to Keele or of the College awarding its own degrees, and more serious consideration was given at the end of 1973 to an application to the CNAA should negotiations with Liverpool come to nought; but closer association with the University with which the College had been formally linked since Edwardian times always seems to have been the generally favoured option. Proposals for a new three-year Ordinary and four-year Honours BEd, in line with the government's recent *Framework for Expansion* White Paper, were accepted in principle by Liverpool early in 1973; these applied to all the colleges which were members of its Institute. As for a different degree which would bring alternative students to Chester, ideas had by then crystallised into a scheme for a three-year BA Combined Studies Ordinary degree – three subjects in the first year, three in the second, two in the third – in which all academic departments would participate.[89]

Proposals for such a BA were formally submitted to Liverpool on 22 February 1973 and discussed in detail at a meeting involving several University and College representatives the following September. By then, in response to Circular 7/73, Cheshire County Council had accepted in principle that it would like to see Chester College continuing in a diversified role as the only HEI in the western half of the authority's area. But approval of a BA degree was crucial to this, and given Seaborne's own assessment after the Liverpool meeting that there was only a 50:50 chance of securing the University's agreement, it is no surprise that Academic Board was keen to approach the CNAA as an alternative awarding body. Indeed, following an encouraging visit from two of their officers, the Principal on 1 November sent the CNAA a formal Declaration of Intent that a submission would be made. By the time Academic Board met on 9 January 1974, schemes for a DipHE and for a BEd and BA at both Ordinary and Honours level were almost ready to be despatched to the CNAA, only for Seaborne formally to announce to the meeting the good news that Liverpool had after all agreed in principle to validate a College-taught Ordinary BA. Faced with a choice between the two, the Board 'after considerable discussion' voted unanimously to plump for Liverpool, deferring any decision on submission to the CNAA until the summer 'in the hope that by that time University approval will have been received'.[90] The decision had gone in favour of the familiar institution – one which had representatives on the Governing Body, willing to offer informal guidance on how best to proceed – in preference to the one which held out the prospect of Honours BAs. The preliminary submission to Liverpool was refined and re-sent, as a basis for more detailed planning, and was also forwarded to the County Council so as to inform its final submission to the DES.[91] There was a great deal of work still to be done, success could not be guaranteed, but at last an agreed plan was in place: a plan, moreover, consistent with the wishes expressed by Academic Board, before de Bunsen retired, for closer links with Liverpool in the development of alternative degrees.

So Chester College reached the mid-1970s with hopes and fears for the future. Just over 40 years earlier, during another period of government cutbacks in the number of teacher trainees, it had survived the threat of closure – temporary closure which might have become permanent – through vigorous campaigning and with the help of some influential political and ecclesiastical friends. Now, in a fresh crisis, it would owe much to the support of the University of Liverpool and the County of Cheshire. In the intervening period, the College had grown sixfold in terms of student numbers, had revolutionised the appearance of the campus through its building programme and – initially against its will – had become 'co-educational'. But it had retained the exclusive focus on the training of prospective schoolteachers which had characterised the institution ever since the science school had been phased out in the early 1880s. That narrowly defined purpose was no longer an option. An era in the history of the College had come to an end.

---

1   Gedge and Louden, *S. Martin's College, Lancaster*, p. 65.

2   ZCR 86/1/10: 15 June, 10 October, 12 December 1958, 6 March 1959.

3 Edwards, *Women in Teacher Training Colleges*, p. 141.

4 ZCR 86/1/10: 12 December 1958.

5 ZCR 86/1/10: 17 June 1960.

6 McIntosh, *Physical Education*, p. 254.

7 ZCR 86/1/10: 12 June, 11 December 1959, 17 June 1960.

8 ZCR 86/1/10: 17 June 1960.

9 *Collegian*, Christmas 1963, p. 83; ZCR 86/7/45: *Annual Report and Accounts for year ended 31 July 1962*, p. 3 (the 339 total includes one categorised separately as a 'colonial student'; ZCR 86/1/10: 5 October 1961; Bradbury, *Chester College*, p. 231.

10 *Collegian*, Christmas 1961, p. 71, though the tone was tongue-in-cheek: 'the extraordinary quality of the Mid-Years can perhaps be best illustrated by the case of one Samuel Knight, who departed from this establishment well qualified to teach Geography and Music but is now busy teaching metalwork in a grammar school'.

11 *Collegian*, Autumn 1962, pp. 71, 77, 99, 101.

12 *Collegian*, Autumn 1962, pp. 86–87; Fiona Roberts, the University's Alumni and Development Manager, identifies this student as Mary ('Mollie') Hedges of Cliveden Road, Chester.

13 *Pers. comm.* M. Lacey of Thingwall, Wirral, via Fiona Roberts. Both she and Mrs Hedges took the three-year course, receiving their certificates in 1965.

14 E.g. *Collegian*, Christmas 1963, pp. 73, 74; Summer 1964, pp. 32, 33, 37, 38; Christmas 1964, pp. 113, 122–27, 135–38; Summer 1965, p. 23. A slightly later female student, Lin Clark (1968–71), went on to row for Great Britain from 1974 to 1987; her husband Jim, an exact contemporary at the College, also became a Great Britain rower, initially while still a student in 1970 (*Collegian*, 2001, pp. 2.06–2.09).

15 *Pers. comm.* E. Nelson (née Peel) via Fiona Roberts; also *The Cestrian* 2007, p. 30.

16 CC, Hooper deposit: *Calendar 1965–66 Michaelmas Term*; Bradbury, *Chester College*, pp. 235–36 gives a detailed breakdown of the 1964–65 figures; see also ZCR 86/7/47: *Annual Report and Accounts for year ended 31 July 1964*, p. 3.

17 ZCR 86/6/1: Staff Register, 1910–31, which shows her employed for five three-quarter hour periods per week, presumably as an language assistant; she did similar work at the University of Liverpool.

18 ZCR 86/7/45: *Annual Report and Accounts for 1962*, p. 6; *Collegian*, Christmas 1963, p. 73; Summer 1964, p. 6; Christmas 1964, p. 88. The figures for male and female lecturers in 1964 includes the Principal (who taught some Education and Religious Knowledge) but excludes visiting lecturers in Music, Divinity and Anatomy/Physiology (four men, two women).

19 ZCR 86/7/44: *Annual Report and Accounts for year ended 31 July, 1961*, p. 6; ZCR 86/7/45: *Annual Report and Accounts for 1962*, p. 6; ZCR 86/7/46: *Annual Report and Accounts for year ended 31 July, 1963*, pp. 4–5; ZCR 86/7/47: *Annual Report and Accounts for 1964*, pp. 3–4; *Collegian*, Christmas 1961, p. 69; Summer 1962, p. 5; Summer 1963, p. 3; Christmas 1963, p. 73; Summer 1964, pp. 5, 67; Christmas 1964, p. 87. On the 'Peace Cross', see Chapter 10.

20   *Pers. comm.* B. McDermott.

21   *VCH Cheshire,* V (ii), p. 285; ZCR 86/7/46: *Annual Report and Accounts for 1963*, pp. 4–5; ZCR 86/7/47: *Annual Report and Accounts for 1964*, pp. 3–4; ZCR 86/7/48: *Annual Report and Accounts for year ended 31 July, 1965*, pp. 3–4; *Collegian,* Summer 1963, p. 3; Christmas 1963, p. 73; Summer 1964, pp. 5, 67; Christmas 1964, p. 87. According to de Bunsen, each of the three new women's hostels of 1965 were intended for '25 students or so living with their hostel tutors as "family parties"' (ZCR 86/7928: *Annual Report to the Governors on the Year 1967–1968*, p. 3).

22   *Collegian,* Christmas 1960, pp. 105–9; Christmas 1963, pp. 109–12; Christmas 1966, pp. 102–5; ZCR 86/14/37: *Chester College Prospectus, 1965–66*.

23   ZCR 86/12/89.

24   *Collegian,* Summer 1962, pp. 13, 35, 38–39.

25   *Collegian,* Autumn 1962, p. 79.

26   ZCR 86/1/10: 12 June 1959; ZCR 86/7/46: *Annual Report and Accounts for 1963*, pp. 8–9; ZCR 86/7/47: *Annual Report and Accounts for 1964*, p. 7; ZCR 86/7/48: *Annual Report and Accounts for 1965*, p. 8.

27   ZCR 86/7/44: *Annual Report and Accounts for 1961*, pp. 6–7; ZCR 86/1/10: 7 October, 9 December 1960.

28   ZCR 86/7/48: *Annual Report and Accounts for 1965*, p. 7; *pers. comm.* J. Fowler.

29   ZCR 86/14/37: *Chester College Prospectus, 1965–1966*.

30   *Collegian,* Summer 1965, pp. 5–6; ZCR 86/7/48: *Annual Report and Accounts for 1965*, pp. 4–5.

31   *Collegian,* Christmas 1965, pp. 138–39.

32   Evans, *Those Were the Days*, pp. 13–15.

33   ZCR 86/1/10: 8 March 1957.

34   B. de Bunsen, *Adventures in Education* (Kendal, 1995), p. 147.

35   ZCR 86/1/10: 17 June 1960; *Collegian,* Christmas 1965, pp. 83–84; Evans, *Those Were the Days*, p. 10.

36   Evans, *Those Were the Days*, p. 20, cf. p. 23.

37   ZCR 86/7/46: *Annual Report and Accounts for 1963*, p. 5; *Collegian,* Summer 1965, p. 6; Christmas 1965, p. 87.

38   *Collegian,* Christmas 1966, p. 108; 1979, pp. 11–12.

39   *Robbins Report: Higher Education* (HMSO, London, 1963), esp. paras. 311, 313, 319, 333, 339, 341, 351.

40   M. Trow, *The Expansion and Transformation of Higher Education* (New York, 1972), p. 3.

41   *Collegian,* Christmas 1964, p. 89; the Duke of Westminster, as Foundation Chancellor, made reference to his family's offer of land in the 1960s in his address at the inauguration of the University of Chester on 25 September 2005.

42   *Oxford Dictionary of National Biography,* VIII, p. 689; de Bunsen, *Adventures*, pp. 146–47.

[43] T.A. Lockett, 'The Government of Colleges of Education' in T. Burgess (ed.), *Dear Lord James: A Critique of Teacher Education* (Harmondsworth, 1971), pp. 170–88, at p. 170.

[44] DES: *Report of the Study Group on the Government of Colleges of Education* (Weaver Report), esp. pp. 3, 21–22, 26; ZCR 86/7928: *Annual Report to the Governors on 1967–1968*, pp. 1–2.

[45] De Bunsen, *Adventures*, pp. 147–48, 151–52 (for the quotation); ZCR 86/7928: *Annual Report to the Governors on 1967–68*, pp. 1–2; Bradbury, *Chester College*, p. 240; CC, Hooper deposit: *Calendar 1966–67*; CC, Minutes of Academic Board, 1966–70: 5 October 1966, 31 May, 11 October 1967; CC, Minutes of Academic Council, 1966–72: 28 September 1966.

[46] ZCR 86/7928: *Annual Report to the Governors on 1967–1968*, p. 2.

[47] CC, Minutes of Academic Board, 1966–70: 26 October 1966, 1 February, 6 December 1967, 10 January, 24 April 1968, 26 February, 23 April 1969.

[48] CC, Minutes of Academic Council, 1966–72: 7 October 1970.

[49] CC, Minutes of Academic Council, 1966–72: 28 September 1966, 25 January, 15 March, 10 May, 28 June, 30 September 1967, 7 May 1969, 29 April 1970, 10 March, 28 April 1971, 26 January 1972; the sports shop franchise passed to Chester Sports Ltd at the beginning of 1975 (*Collegian*, 1975, p. 36). In practice, students had in recent years only been wearing gowns on special occasions, including chapel services, and there had been no toleration of smoking during exams (*pers. comm.* Revd J.R. Carhart).

[50] CC, Minutes of Academic Council, 1966–72: 22 November 1967, 7 May 1969, 29 April, 17 June, 25 November 1970, 26 January 1972.

[51] The National Union of Students had published a call for student participation in university and college governance in March 1967 (Lockett, 'Government of Colleges', pp. 173–74).

[52] CC, Minutes of Guild Council, 15 November 1968; CC, Minutes of Academic Council, 1966–72: 11 December 1968, 25 June, 24 September, 22 October, 17 December 1969; CC, Minutes of Academic Board, 1966–70: 28 May 1969; CC, Minutes of Academic Board, 1970–73: 23 September 1970; de Bunsen, *Adventures*, pp. 147–49; *Collegian*, Summer 1970, pp. 8–9.

[53] de Bunsen, *Adventures*, pp. 147–49, 151–52.

[54] CC, Hooper deposit: *Handbook for Students*, September 1969.

[55] W. Taylor, 'The National Context, 1972–82' in Alexander, Craft and Lynch, eds, *Change in Teacher Education*, pp. 16–30, at p. 18.

[56] CC, Minutes of Guild Council, 5 December 1968.

[57] *Collegian*, Summer 1968, p. 11; Christmas 1968, pp. 98–99.

[58] *Collegian*, Summer 1970, pp. 15–16 (also ZCR 86/19/11).

[59] CC, Minutes of Academic Council, 1966–72: 17 December 1969; *Collegian*, Christmas 1971, p. 21.

[60] *Collegian*, Christmas 1968; Summer 1979, p. 16; CC, Minutes of Academic Council, 1966–72: 29 April 1970, 10 March, 28 April, 29 September 1971; CC, Minutes of

Academic Council, 1972–81: 29 November 1972. First- and second-year students were provided with a Christmas party in the Gladstone Hall instead of the dinner – nobly organised by Marion Appleton, tutor in charge of Special Needs – until 1979, when arrangements were taken over by the students themselves (CC, Minutes of Academic Council, 1972–81: 31 October 1979).

61 See Chapter 3.

62 CC, Minutes of Academic Council, 1972–81: 30 January 1974.

63 ZCR 86/14/37: *Chester College: Campaign for Expansion*, 1965; *Collegian*, Summer 1964, p. 5; Christmas 1965, p. 85; Christmas 1969, p. 107; Summer 1971, pp. 14–15; Seaborne, 'The College Buildings', p. 44; ZCR 86/15/1: *Cheshire Observer*, 20 June 1967; ZCR 86/15/2: *Liverpool Daily Post*, 14 June 1969.

64 UC, Minutes of Governors, 2005 to date: 29 November 2005.

65 *Collegian*, 1981, p. 48; 1982, p. 7.

66 CC, Minutes of Academic Board, 1966–70: 7 February, 5 June 1968; CC, Minutes of Academic Council, 1966–72: 29 September 1971; ZCR 86/7928: Minutes of Student Centre Committee, 17 June 1971; CC, Minutes of Academic Council, 1972–81: 27 November 1974; *Collegian*, Summer 1970, p. 18; Spring 1971, pp. 112–14; Summer 1971, p. 16; 1975, p. 25.

67 CC, Hooper deposit: *Calendar 1966–67, Michaelmas Term; Calendar and Diary; Michaelmas Term 1972; Collegian*, 1974, p. 18.

68 CC, Hooper deposit: *Calendar and Diary 1967–68* (389 women, 333 men); *Collegian*, Christmas 1969, p. 107. CC, *Annual Report 1967–68*, pp. 30–31, shows a preponderance of women students in Arts & Craft, Divinity, History, English Literature, Drama, Children's Literature, French, Linguistics, Music, Biological Sciences and the History of Scientific Ideas, with men in the majority in Geography, Mathematics, PE, Physical Science and General Science; in the same report (p. 23) the BEd advisor, Charlotte Bowden, regretted that too few well-qualified women students opted for the four-year BEd programme.

69 CC, Minutes of Academic Council, 1966–72: 10 March 1971; on the nickname, see J.L. Bradbury's *Chester College: A Brief Guide to the College Buildings* (privately printed, 1978), p. 7.

70 *Collegian*, Summer 1967, p. 49.

71 *Collegian*, Summer 1970, pp. 8–9; 1974, p. 15.

72 *Collegian*, Summer 1969, p. 5; F.A. Montgomery, *Edge Hill College: A History, 1885–1985* (Ormskirk, 1985), pp. 62–64; cf. for the tendency of male staff to predominate in former women's colleges generally, Edwards, *Women in Teacher Training Colleges*, pp. 164–66, 170 .

73 *Collegian*, Summer 1969, p. 5; CC, Minutes of Academic Board, 1966–70: 26 February, 28 May 1969.

74 CC, Minutes of Academic Board, 1966–70: 7 December 1966, 1 March, 22 March, 29 June, 11 October, 2 December 1967, 7 February 1968; CC, Minutes of Academic Board, 1970–73: 22 September 1971; Minutes of Academic Board, 1973–77: 17 May 1974; CC, Hooper deposit, *Calendar and Diary, Michaelmas Term 1972*; Connell,

Century of Teacher Training, pp. 366–69; A. Ross, 'The Universities and the BEd degree' in J.B. Thomas, ed., *British Universities and Teacher Education: A Century of Change* (London, 1990), pp. 58–72, at pp. 58–59; *Collegian*, Christmas 1969, p. 107; ZCR 86A/329: *Prospectus 1968–69*, pp. 15, 23, 27. Under the original BEd scheme, selected students were given the option of registering for the degree before the start of their second year, and were taught thereafter in small, uneconomical sets; any who failed the more stringent assessments along the way could revert to a certificate. Revised regulations in 1970 allowed for a common certificate and BEd syllabus in the first three years, so all students could be taught together, with the most successful at the end of three years (i.e. from 1973 onwards) having the option of taking a fourth, more specialised, year for the BEd: see *Collegian*, Christmas 1971, pp. 6–10.

[75] CC, Minutes of Academic Board, 1966–70: 13 March, 4 December 1968, 15 January, 28 May, 5 November, 3 December 1969, 4 March 1970; CC, Minutes of Academic Board, 1970–73: 27 May 1970; CC, Minutes of Academic Council, 1972–81: 16 May 1973; *Collegian*, 1974, p. 23; 1975, p. 26; 1982, p. 23. The College archives became the responsibility of the County Record Office, now Cheshire Archives and Local Studies, in 2000; the bank originally opened from 12 noon to 2.00 p.m. on Wednesdays and Fridays.

[76] *Collegian*, Summer 1968, pp. 5–8; Christmas 1968, p. 87; Summer 1969, p. 6; *The Guardian*, 27 August 2012 (Etchells's obituary, which describes her as 'the best female bishop we never had'). On proportions of students entering different sectors of HE during the 1960s, see R. Layard, J. King and C. Moser, *The Impact of Robbins* (Harmondsworth, 1969), e.g. pp. 13, 19, 23–24, 41–44, 61, 72. There were further 'Long Walks' every few years until 1985. For an early twentieth-century exposition of the view that teachers were better trained in company with those preparing for other professions, see Browning, *Importance of Training*, p. 12, cited in Chapter 4.

[77] *Collegian*, Spring 1971, pp. 104–6.

[78] CC, Minutes of Academic Council, 1966–72: 7 October, 25 November 1970, 28 April 1971; CC, Minutes of Academic Board, 1970–73: 10 May 1971.

[79] *Oxford Dictionary of National Biography*, VIII, p. 689; *Collegian*, Summer 1971, pp. 5–8.

[80] Bradbury, *Chester College*, p. 240, derived from comments by de Bunsen himself in *Collegian*, Spring 1971, p. 98, and in Milton's tribute to him, cited in note 79. The Committee's chairman, Lord James of Rusholme, had given the address at the College's Presentation Day in June 1961, telling the then-all-male student audience that the life of a teacher was 'one of three or four finest occupations a man could choose' (*Collegian*, Summer 1962, p. 6); he had become the first Vice-Chancellor of the new University of York the following year, a position he was to hold until 1973.

[81] Dent, *Training of Teachers*, pp. 149–51; P. Gosden, 'The James Report and Recent History' in Thomas, ed., *British Universities*, pp. 73–86, at pp. 73–75; McGregor, *A*

Church College for the 21st Century?, p. 199 (which points out that two members of the James committee publicly dissented from the loosening of ties with universities implicit in the abolition of ATOs).

[82] CC, Minutes of Academic Board, 1970–73: 19 March 1971; *pers. comm.* Revd J.R. Carhart and J. Fowler.

[83] CC, Minutes of Academic Board, 1970–73: 24 June 1970, 13 October 1971, 12 January, 27 September 1972.

[84] CC, Hooper deposit: *Calendar and Diary, Michaelmas Term 1972* (although for total student numbers the statement in Bradbury, *Chester College*, p. 240, is preferred).

[85] CC, Minutes of Academic Board, 1970–73: 27 September 1972; cf. 27 June, 26 September 1973; CC, Minutes of Academic Council, 1972–81: 16 May 1973.

[86] *Collegian*, Christmas 1971, p. 5.

[87] Bradbury, *Chester College*, pp. 240–42; *Collegian*, 1973, p. 5; Dent, *Training of Teachers*, pp. 151–55; Gosden, 'James Report', pp. 75–77; Stewart, *Higher Education in Postwar Britain*, pp. 189–91.

[88] See e.g. D. Hencke, *Colleges in Crisis: The Reorganization of Teacher Training, 1971–7* (Harmondsworth, 1978), esp. pp. 106–28; McGregor, *A Church College for the 21st Century?*, pp. 197–224.

[89] CC, Minutes of Academic Board, 1970–73: 15 December 1971, 22 March , 28 April , 14 June, 27 September, 27 October 1972, 21 February 1973.

[90] CC, Minutes of Academic Board, 1970–73: 28 March, 26 September, 19 October, 12 December 1973; CC, Minutes of Academic Board, 1973–77: 7 November, 23 November, 12 December 1973, 9 January 1974; CC, Minutes of Academic Council, 1972–81: 10 October 1973.

[91] CC, Minutes of Academic Board, 1973–77: 16 January, 20 February 1974; ZCR 86/7928: Chester College of Higher Education, Outline Proposals for the Institution of Courses leading to the award of BEd (Ord.), BEd (Hons), BA in Combined Studies (Ord.) and DipHE, to begin in September 1975 (February 1974).

DIVERSIFICATION, 1975–2004

CHAPTER 10

BEYOND TEACHER EDUCATION

Between 1972 and 1980, in a context of both reduced demand and economic stringency, the number of students admitted to initial teacher training in England and Wales fell from 50,632 to 19,149.[1] During the 1970s as whole, the number of 'public sector institutions' (those outside the universities) engaged in their training declined by almost 100 from a figure of 180 at the start of the decade.[2] Within this total, 27 Anglican colleges of education were reduced to only 13, of which Chester was one of nine which remained fully autonomous and free-standing.[3] Among the other survivors, also located close to cathedrals, were King Alfred's Winchester and Christ Church Canterbury, both of them destined, like Chester, to be raised to university status in 2005. Unlike many of its peers – including the largest of the Church colleges, St Luke's Exeter – Chester neither merged with, nor was taken over by, another institution.[4] Nor did it retain its identity only as part of a federation, as happened to Chester's 'sister' college of S. Katharine's Liverpool, which had begun life as the Diocesan Training College for Schoolmistresses at Warrington and would now become part of the Liverpool Institute of Higher Education (LIHE). Nor was it closed altogether, a fate which befell the Church colleges in Saltley (Birmingham), Bishop's Stortford, Culham and Salisbury.[5]

Chester remained as a separate entity largely because, as the only college of education in the western half of Cheshire and the only voluntary college in the whole of the county, there was no obvious institution with which it could be amalgamated. But this alone would not have been enough to save it. Other factors included the College's good reputation and positive relationship with its local University and County Council, both of whom were willing within reason to offer support in the hour of need; the negotiating skills of the Principal and the enterprise of staff in devising new courses; solid finances and ample space for further building when circumstances changed, making the institution a sound investment for the future; and, with a decently equipped campus in a cathedral city which was itself a 'visitor-attraction', an enviable record of recruiting students with above-average A-level results. In the spring of 1974, after the County had submitted its draft plans for higher education in the wake of Circular 7/73, the DES responded by accepting that Chester could remain discrete, at least for the time being, taking one-quarter of Cheshire's allocated teacher training places, while half went to Crewe and Alsager (about six miles apart and already due to amalgamate) and the remaining quarter to Padgate (at Warrington). The DES used arguments not dissimilar to those advanced by Seaborne soon after he took over. Clearly, they had featured in the College's submission to the County and the County's to the DES, and were now being reflected back.[6]

> We do not foresee an easy future, at least to begin with, for Chester College of Education. However, it does have the advantage that already over half its students have at least 2 'A' levels and, although we would not think it realistic to provide for any expansion at this stage, we would be ready to let it diversify at its present size, in cooperation with the Chester and West Cheshire Colleges of Further Education, and to see what it can achieve on the strength of its character, academic reputation and situation in an attractive city.[7]

In January of the following year, in response to the County's final submission in autumn 1974, a letter from the Secretary of State for Education confirmed Chester's separate status. It accepted the College's plans to remain a major player in initial teacher training (albeit with the reduced numbers set by the government) while developing in-service work and diversifying provision through a new BA degree and the expansion of adult education. The Church Board of Education, convinced that a smaller number of strong colleges was the best way to preserve the Anglican presence in teacher training – a familiar refrain from the 'concentration' schemes during and between the two World Wars – also identified Chester as one which should continue and, following a conference at York in April 1975, submitted a plan to the DES to this effect.

Analysing and reflecting upon the events of 1974–75 for the *Collegian*, Seaborne wrote, with obvious relief:

> There can be no doubt that the situation in teacher training and the world of higher education has rarely before been more difficult … Colleges which only a few years ago were being exhorted to train more and more teachers are now being faced with the prospect of mergers, amalgamations and, in some cases, even closure. Here in Chester we are all extremely thankful that our geographical position and sound academic reputation have saved us from the worst effects of present Government policy. There is no other college of education or polytechnic in the populous West Cheshire and Wirral area, and the Secretary of State for Education has recently told us that we can continue as an independent college training up to 700 teachers at any one time. In addition, the Government is allowing us to admit students preparing for jobs outside teaching so that we are hopeful that we will be able to maintain our present size of about 900 students.

He paid tribute to his academic and administrative staff for their efforts in devising and processing new courses while continuing with their normal duties and also to the governors, especially the Liverpool representatives such as the distinguished late-medieval historian Alec Myers who had played a critical role in steering proposals through the relevant University committees. And he did not forget to mention Bradbury's newly published book as testimony to the fact that the College was accustomed to the successful management of crisis and change![8]

The University of Liverpool's arrangements to accommodate new BA and BEd College-taught programmes included the establishment in June 1975 of a Board of College Studies with Faculty status, accompanied by subject panels to supervise each of the disciplines; Seaborne himself became the first chairman. The area training organisation alias University Institute of Education, set up in the post-war era to oversee teacher training in the colleges, came to an end; in constitutional terms, this meant that Chester College ceased to be a member college of the Institute and became instead an affiliated College of the University, effectively resuming the status which had been negotiated by Thomas in the 1920s.[9] It is one of the ironies of this episode that the government's efforts to reinforce the so-called 'binary divide' in higher education, between universities on the one hand and the 'non-university sector' of polytechnics and colleges on the other – seen for example in the dismantling of university-run area training organisations and in the DES's interim response (quoted above) which envisaged Chester working with further education colleges – led in fact to a stronger relationship between the College and the University of Liverpool. As Stanley Hewett, secretary of the Association of Teachers in Colleges and Departments of Education put it at the conclusion of a conference of Principals in April 1973, called to discuss the implications of government policy: 'I cannot pretend that nobody will get hurt in the process … but … there are rich rewards for those with the courage, resolution and foresight to go out and take them.'[10] As one of those to emerge intact from the 1970s upheaval, Chester was indeed to be richly rewarded in the decades to come.

The development of new BEd and BA programmes, and of various other courses which would all help to compensate for the contraction in initial teacher training numbers, dominated the business of Academic Board and the Governing Body for several years. By June 1974 the University of Liverpool had drafted a scheme for a General (i.e. Ordinary) BA, applicable to all its affiliated colleges, based on a first year in common with the BEd, a second year of three subjects and a third year of two, with input from the colleges to assessment in the first two years and 'a University public examination for the award of the degree' in the third. Thrashing out the content of each subject to the satisfaction of the University was far from easy and there was disquiet at Academic Board over a requirement that students at the different colleges would have to follow a common syllabus and sit a common examination, though provision for options left some room for manoeuvre. The reality was that there was no alternative under a Liverpool scheme and the subject panels eventually agreed the details in time for a cohort of BA students – 48 out of a total intake at Chester that year of 196 – to embark upon the programme in September 1976.[11]

Meanwhile the revised BEd degree – now a three-year course for an Ordinary award with an additional fourth year for Honours – admitted its initial group of students in September 1975, with an option for those who wished to transfer to the new BA to do so at the end of their first year; it was this arrangement which allowed the first BA degrees to be awarded to some 29 Chester students on 1 August 1978. Within a few months of the start of the new BEd, the College had taken the logical decision to cease recruitment to the three-year certificate, since this had effectively become a lesser award for comparable work; the last certificate student left in 1978. There was delight at Academic Board in September 1976 that 'for the first time there was 100% matriculated entry [i.e. holding two A-level passes so qualified for University registration] in the first year'.[12] At a time when the proportion with two A-levels in colleges of education nationally was only 48%,[13] this was a significant achievement which could only help to smooth negotiations for further award-bearing courses in coming years.

Student numbers fell to 854 in September 1974, in line with the government's target, and continued to decline for the next four years.[14] With talk of staff having to be redeployed, retrained or possibly made redundant[15] – the last narrowly avoided for academics during Seaborne's time, except under voluntary arrangements – ideas for further curriculum innovation abounded. In an accompanying marketing drive the prospectus for 1977 became the first to be sent out from Chester to every secondary school in the country. A complication was that the College's overall direction had to meet with the approval of the Church of England Board of Education, while detailed developments could only proceed with the support of the local authority and of HMIs generally more familiar with FE than with HE. They then had to secure the consent both of the North West Regional Advisory Council – one of the 10 such 'RACs' established in 1946 to co-ordinate further and technical education to meet the demands of industry – and finally of the DES, which could exercise the ultimate sanction of withholding grant. The government's decision to entrust to the RACs oversight of the activities of colleges of education, as recommended by the James committee, was an attempt partially to fill the void left by the demise of area training organisations; it was also another indication that, in the eyes of the Department, the future of the colleges lay closer to further education (FE) than it did to universities. But it meant yet more paperwork, with Chester being required to obtain the RAC's agreement to its course proposals (including the subjects within the BA degree) in February 1975 and to repeat the process in 1977 because approval had been given for only two years. Seaborne lamented the necessity for multiple approvals by a variety of organisations in an article for the *Collegian* entitled 'The Bureaucracy of Diversification' and the then-Principal of Bishop Otter College, Chichester, later wrote for wider publication in similar terms.[16]

Needless to say, several ideas for diversification fell by the wayside. Proposals in 1974 to develop a vocationally oriented two-year DipHE in conjunction with Chester College of FE, covering subjects such as 'French with Secretarial Studies' and 'Twentieth-Century Man in the European Environment', were not pursued; this was partly because it risked complicating the validation of the BA (to which it might also have been a competitor) but mainly – and bizarrely given that it chimed with the vision for the College apparently advocated by the DES – because HMI advised against it.[17] By early 1975 Liverpool was being sounded out regarding a College-taught MEd in Special Needs, as recommended by an external examiner in recognition of Chester's expertise in the field, but the advice was not to proceed.[18] There was talk among the governors early in 1976 of the College becoming involved in the training of ordinands and over the next twelve months a motley collection of subjects was considered for possible inclusion within the BA, among them Social Law – seen as a possible way into Social Work training – Urban Studies, Business Administration, German and Ethics; however, the RAC warned against proposals which might conflict with the offering in polytechnics and none were developed further at this stage.[19] Hopes were also vested in an expansion of the College's one-year postgraduate certificate course, launched in 1972 and for which targets were increased in the two following years, but recruitment never got much above the 50 mark with which it had begun and often fell below.

There was more success, however, with in-service training, an area of paramount importance to the Cheshire local authority whose support for the College was essential. After-hours ('twilight') courses in subjects such as Special Needs, PE, Mathematics and French were mounted in 1974–75. A 'preparatory year' for an in-service BEd, designed for certificated teachers who were hoping to proceed to a degree, was also run, leading in turn to the launch in September 1976 of a part-time BEd – after a good deal of pressure on the University to grant permission – delivered after school hours and through a week-long June summer school.[20] Part-time Diplomas for serving teachers in the Advanced Study of Community Education, in Reading and in

Mathematics were also devised in time to start in September 1976[21] and others intended for the general public – a Diploma in Religious Studies and a Diploma in Music – began one year later.[22] Alternative forms of adult education were also encouraged, through the top two floors of the tower being made available from September 1974 for evening classes run by the University of Liverpool Extension Studies, the Workers' Educational Association and the Open University, for which the College became a recognised Centre the following January.[23]

None of this guaranteed the College's survival. Worries about recruitment numbers on the one hand and the vagaries of government policy on the other persisted, especially since unemployment among teachers dissuaded potential students from applying for training and revised DES estimates of demand by schools meant that targets were lowered even further. A story in the *Times Higher Educational Supplement* on 31 December 1976, claiming that the Church Board of Education had been told by the DES that Chester and two other colleges would cease teacher training – though subsequently shown to be untrue – must have ruined many a New Year's Eve celebration.[24] However – such was the roller-coaster ride which had to be endured at this time – there then came a formal announcement from the Secretary of State on 24 January 1977 that Chester would definitely be among the colleges continuing to provide teacher training, alongside diversified courses, with reduced numbers in the short term but the potential for growth in the future. The availability of land as yet not built upon in the northern and western parts of the campus, so carefully accumulated by Thomas and his predecessors, paid dividends at this point.[25] If there was one moment which signalled an end to the worst period of uncertainty, this was it.

Nevertheless, student numbers remained a matter of concern. The permitted total for teacher training, which had exceeded 900 in 1972–73, stood at only 575 for 1977–78, with postgraduate certificate students and those on in-service courses included in the calculation; this was 50 less than expected, following an eleventh-hour decision by Shirley Williams as Secretary of State to reprieve Padgate College, where training had been scheduled to close. A recent shift back towards more emphasis on the secondary age range, in line with trends in the teacher employment market, helped to ensure that these places were filled, but even so the total spread across the three years of the BEd course itself (350) was lower than the first-year intake of five years earlier.[26] Admissions to the three-year programmes in 1977 were down to 173 (47 of them BAs), the lowest since 1962; by 1978–79, although the intake was up, overall College numbers were only 752, the smallest figure for 11 years.[27] But then, aided by an upturn in the number of 18-year-olds with two A-

Levels in the second half of the decade, the tide began to turn.[28] In 1979, much-improved recruitment to the BA brought in 135 first-year students – more than the 125 for the BEd – and total student numbers rose to 876; in broad terms, with only occasional blips, they have been on an upward curve ever since. Seaborne felt sufficiently confident to write for that year's *Collegian* that 'we seem to have weathered the storm and are now set on a new course with – for the present at least – a following wind'. Privately, he was by then looking forward to the prospect of a College with 1,000 students, while his Deputy favoured 1,300, and in the next edition he reflected with some satisfaction, but certainly not complacency, on the success of the diversification policy thus far.[29]

The introduction of the BA degree – quite literally vital to the College at this critical juncture – has rightly been described as 'one of the most outstanding innovations in the history of Chester College'.[30] It was initially delivered alongside the new BEd in half-term blocks, so that students could be taught together as far as possible, taking two of their chosen subjects at any one time. The arrangement whereby the first year was common to both BA and BEd students proved attractive to those who wanted to defer a decision on whether to embark on teacher training until they had had a taste of the experience. The opportunity to combine subjects rather than specialise in one also had its appeal, especially since these embraced the full range of disciplines and offered some combinations not available elsewhere. The College's relatively small size, caring reputation and location within the city of Chester also helped with recruitment.[31] It is worth repeating that the possibility of developing the curriculum beyond teacher training had been under discussion at Chester since the late 1960s, in the context of expansion rather than contraction, so the College was well placed to move quickly when it became part of the strategy for survival.[32] But there was also recognition that offering an unclassified Ordinary degree diminished its appeal and a campaign to persuade Liverpool to sanction a fourth, Honours, year (on the model of the BEd), began in September 1976, as soon as the first full cohort of BA students had arrived.[33]

Meanwhile, measures were taken to ensure that the College had the infrastructure necessary to sustain a more diversified future. In 1975, the academic provision was reorganised into two Schools, Professional Studies (embracing all aspects of the theory and practice of Education) on the one hand and Academic Studies (the disciplines of English, Geography, Science and so on) on the other; Leon Boucher, already Head of the Education Department, and Thomas Fawcett, Head of Divinity, who had led on the BEd and BA submissions respectively, took office as Deans while retaining their departmental headships. New Heads of Primary, Middle and Secondary Studies were also appointed and the following year the Head of French, Barney Emerson, who had already been chairing the In-Service Committee, became Dean of Development and Resources.[34] And the College's second photocopier – an alternative to the one in the General Office – was duly installed in a Resource Centre opened within the Thomas building in September 1975. It was kept under the superintendence of the assistant who held the key, and by the following February – since (at 5p per copy) staff demand was limited and was failing to justify the annual rental charge – its use was extended to students 'through the Librarian, at certain times during the afternoon'.[35]

What gave Seaborne particular pleasure was approval from the DES, secured in April 1975, for the building of a new library on a site opposite the women's hostels opened 10 years earlier. As he explained in the *Collegian*, the current library abutting on to Old College, housed in what had previously been the dining hall (and in the nineteenth century the practising school), was only half the size required for a college of Chester's size and was rapidly running out of space to accommodate any more books. With due acknowledgement to any scepticism during these difficult years about 'joined-up thinking' in the DES, it was obviously an encouraging sign that the Department was willing to sanction expenditure on a new library intended for 900 students. The foundation stone was laid by the Bishop of Chester, Victor Whitsey, in May 1976 and the two-storey building, with provision for 100,000 books and 200 study-spaces, was ready in time for the 1977–78 academic year; the College librarian since 1964, Margaret Bithell, who had overseen an expansion in book stock from 17,000 to 70,000 volumes and an

increase in staffing from one part-time clerical assistant to two assistant librarians, four clerical staff and two part-time auxiliaries, organised the move but then retired three weeks before the official opening in November 1977. Though considerably enlarged since then, it is appropriate that the library still bears Seaborne's name. A new sports pavilion was also built at this time near Cheyney Road, replacing a

Figure 32: Inside the Resource Centre, opened in September 1975. (*Collegian*, 1976.)

wooden structure of 1924 close to the site of the library which was converted to tutors' offices.[36]

Two other developments of the mid-1970s are worth highlighting for their significance within the College's overall story. One was the adoption for the academic year 1975–76, in common with similar institutions, of the designation 'College of Higher Education' in recognition of the commitment to reach beyond teacher training; the traditional name 'Chester College' did, however, continue to be used for most publicity purposes.[37] Then the retirement of the Deputy Principal, John Milton, one of the earliest post-war recruits to the College's staff, led to the appointment from 1 May 1977 of Grace Jones, Head of History at King Alfred's Winchester. Among Milton's legacies was the initiation of staff and student exchanges with the American Universities of Plattsburgh, New Paltz and Chico, which had been a feature of the past decade, and in recent years he had been doing sterling work to maintain the institution's credibility by ensuring that student recruitment targets were met. His successor was not only the first Deputy (or Vice-) Principal in the twentieth century to be appointed from outside the College, and the first since Chritchley to hold a doctorate, she also fulfilled – on merit – the aspiration to appoint a woman 'to an observably senior position' which had been entertained eight years earlier. She would serve for the next 15 years and prove to be warm-hearted, perceptive and decisive in her tenure of the office, detailed in her knowledge of the career aspirations of the staff and concerned where possible to further them.[38]

Opportunities to diversify were constrained by the fact that, with student numbers curtailed, it was no longer possible to broaden expertise by increasing the staffing establishment; the exuberance of 1969, when half the members of staff were so recently appointed that they had been at the College for a shorter time than half of the students, belonged to a distant age.[39] Other than through retraining, the only way to introduce new specialisms was via replacements for those who had left, as happened in History where a vacancy which arose in 1977 was filled by someone with adult education (rather than school teaching) experience who proceeded to develop an evening Diploma in Landscape History, launched the following year.[40] A Diploma in Socio-Legal Studies, aimed at day-release students from social services and the police, began at the same time, although in approving these programmes the University of Liverpool Senate did express some disquiet at potential competition with its own Institute of Extension Studies.[41] Accompanying these developments was a substantial growth towards the end of the decade in the number of staff holding doctorates, either through new appointments or through their acquisition by part-time study while in post; Seaborne himself was awarded a PhD by Cambridge University in 1979, in recognition of his published work on the history of school architecture.[42]

For the student community of the 1970s, Rag Day had effectively become the climax to Rag Week, an annual late-October extravaganza in the name of charity, which included outings to sell Rag Mags up and down the country. Concerns about unruly behaviour and the content of the magazine still surfaced from time to time but £5,400 was raised for distribution to worthy causes in 1976, double the amount two years earlier; by 1984, the figure had risen to £9,000.[43] The Students' Guild made its mark by buying its own house, 15 Cheyney Road, in 1974; a mixed community of four women and four men were the first occupants, each paying rent of £15 per month. The terraced house cost £8,000 and, using profits from the Guild shop and the income from the rents, the mortgage was paid off some six years later, encouraging further purchases thereafter.[44] In demonstrations against education cuts, lectures were boycotted on Tuesday 19 November 1974 and – more spectacularly – the administrative block in what is now the University Senate House was occupied by students at 1.30 p.m. on Friday 28 May 1976; this was followed six days later by a march on County Hall, where there were speeches from representatives of the main political parties and a petition was handed in. The Guild changed its name to the Students' Union in time for the following academic year and went on to strike a blow for democracy in 1981, when securing the warm support of Academic Council for a proposal that students should be represented on departmental committees.[45]

Culturally, most of the special-interest societies had disappeared by the late 1970s – partly a victim of falling numbers – but the performing arts continued to flourish, with both an Opera Group and a Theatre Group still active and several concerts being offered by musicians both internal and external to the College. On the sporting scene, this was a period when rugby union was especially strong. John Carleton, a student of 1974–77, became the first alumnus to secure international honours when he played on the wing for England against New Zealand in November 1979; in all, he would appear 26 times for England and six times for the British and Irish Lions. He was quickly followed by Peter Williams (1977–80), who would go on to represent England at rugby union and Wales at rugby league. The touring New Zealand All Blacks trained at the College during an overnight stay towards the end of 1978, with three of their members trying out the PE department's recently equipped Human Physical Performance Laboratory. Not to be outdone, the College football team won the British Colleges' Cup in 1981. However, the annual spring Past v. Present day, which had originated in the late nineteenth century but had been struggling to raise teams to play one another throughout the decade, was held for the last time in 1979.[46]

With the immediate crisis successfully negotiated, the College could begin to move on to secure its long-term future as a diversified institution. The expansion of the 1960s and contraction of the 1970s had prompted a good deal of debate about the role of Church colleges in an increasingly secular society, not least among ecclesiastical authorities concerned that their claim to be a Christian presence within the firmament of teacher training and higher education was wearing thin. At Chester, the prospectus for 1958 had made no bones about the fact that 'without a spiritual basis, education is lacking its only sure foundation … the aim of the College … is to help men to train themselves as Christian teachers'; students need not be Anglicans, but there was no overt encouragement to unbelievers, since:

> the aim of the College is one with which a member of any of the Christian denominations would find himself in warm agreement. That aim … can best be fulfilled by students playing their proper part in the religious life of the College, just as they do in the academic, social and athletic spheres.[47]

This phraseology continued while Price remained in charge[48] but by 1968 the language had shifted a little, with continuing emphasis on a Christian ethos but a hint that not everyone might share it.

> The Church of England … believes that knowledge without spiritual development is of little worth … Chester is always glad to have students who are members of other churches. Equally, it has been the policy of the Church of England colleges to train students to work in all types of schools. In view of the Church's belief in the essential spiritual basis of all education [there is an] opportunity for corporate worship [in which] it is hoped that all students will feel sufficiently interested to want to be involved.[49]

And by the close of the challenging 1970s, the expectations were clearly expressed as those incumbent upon the institution, rather than its students.

> With the current expansion in the provision of general higher education, the Church is again making a significant contribution. First, because it believes that knowledge without spiritual development is of little worth and, secondly, because it recognizes the value of variety in initiative and control in higher education. Chester College has now, therefore, become a College of Higher Education in which long-established traditions of scholarship and community can be placed at the service of a wider range of students.[50]

But the story is not simply one of ever-more-muted references to the College's Christian origins. During the course of 1984–85 the governors, still with the Bishop of Chester as chair and majority membership drawn from the dioceses, went on to redefine the aims of the College in terms which made no

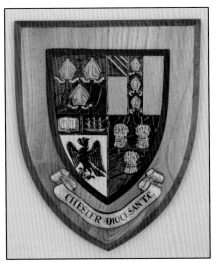

Plates 1 and 2: The College badge in the immediate post-Second World War period, showing the four-diocese design which preceded the formally granted coat of arms. (Blazer badge by permission of Arthur Waring.)

Plate 3: The full coat of arms granted to Chester College in 1954, now used by the University of Chester.

Plate 4: Lithograph of the Parkgate Road frontage of the College, *c.*1847, with the newly built Chapel to the left and the practising school to the right.

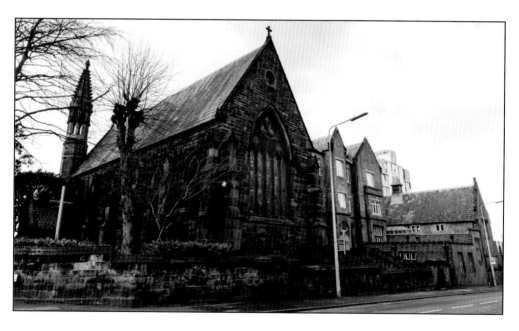

Plate 5: A similar view along Parkgate Road in 2014, with the 1960s tower (recently refurbished) in the background.

Plate 6: The prizewinning garden planted in 2010 in front of the Beswick building, (the former College School of 1900).

Plate 7: The multi-purpose Binks building, which has become one of the main hubs of the Parkgate Road campus since it was completed in 2003.

Plate 8: Part of the University's Warrington campus, showing one of the buildings thoroughly modernised following the acquisition by Chester College in 2002.

Plate 9: Formal procession at the conclusion of the ceremonial inauguration of the University in Chester Cathedral, 25 September 2005. The Esquire Bedell (Head Porter, Ray Williams) leads the Chancellor, the Duke of Westminster, with the Bishop of Chester and members of the senior management team following behind.

Plate 10: An assortment of prospectus covers since 1990, showing changes both to design and to the name of the College in the decade prior to becoming a University. Five of the covers display the now-discarded claret and blue logo.

Plate 11: A view of the Kingsway buildings, in Newton, Chester, in full use by the University for the Faculty of Arts & Media from 2008.

Plate 12: The Science and Technology campus at Thornton, donated to the University by Shell UK in 2013, and now a base for the Faculty of Science & Engineering.

Plate 13: A view of the College's Parkgate Road campus looking north-west from the top of the tower in 1975, with the sloping area towards the canal largely undeveloped except as playing fields. (By permission of David Evans.)

Plate 14: The equivalent view in 2013. Small Hall (bottom left) and the Careers & Employability Centre (opposite it with light-coloured roof) survive from the picture of 1975, as does 'Longfield' (the house bottom right) and Margaret House (beyond the flagpole in the centre). Otherwise, nearly every building which can be seen is a product of the previous 20 years. (By permission of David Evans.)

Plate 15: The 1957 frontage to the former County Hall, which became the University's Riverside campus in 2010; the earlier, neoclassical facade is on the other side of the building.

pretence about mass commitment but clearly affirmed a strong Christian presence. The College existed 'to present human knowledge and experience in the light of Christian truth; to create a community based on and expressive of Christian values' and 'to assist those who attend the College to have the ability when they leave to reflect Christian principles in their life and work'. Around the same time, concern within Academic Board about the importance of multiculturalism would lead to the following statement being inserted into the prospectus, more overt about the Christian basis of the institution than at the beginning of the decade:

> Chester College is a Church of England Foundation. As such it seeks to express Christian values in its daily work and to encourage students to reflect these values in their own lives. It recognises its responsibilities to ensure equal opportunities for members of ethnic minorities and for those with social or physical disadvantages and to educate students for life in a multicultural and multiracial society.[51]

Indeed, a fairly prominent reference to the College's Christian foundation would continue to appear near the front of successive prospectuses until 1997, when the phraseology was as follows:

> The College was founded by the Church of England, and it still maintains close contact with the Church. Among its aims, the College is concerned to present knowledge in the light of Christian belief, to create a community based on Christian values and to encourage students to reflect Christian principles in their life and work.[52]

Since then, prospectuses have conveyed the institution's Christian roots more subtly, mainly through coverage of the chaplaincy as one of the vehicles for student support. But to this day the University's Mission Statement, which appears on public documents such as the Corporate Plan, retains an emphasis on 'Christian values' – and even defines them as 'honesty, integrity and respect for all' – while steering clear of Christian 'truth' or 'belief'.[53]

This excursion into changing phraseology has taken us a long way forward, but it provides a context for the discussion which follows. The adjustments to wording betray growing flexibility over how the Church foundation should best be expressed and some of the implications of this are explored in the penultimate chapter. If we return to the 1970s, the reality was that disappointing Chapel attendances, except on special occasions like the Christmas carol service (inaugurated in 1958), had been causing concern since early in the previous decade. The rapid expansion of the 1960s, at a time when church attendance was in decline, had only been achieved by recruiting staff and students many of whom did not share the religious commitment of their forebears. In turn, the difficulties of the 1970s made it imperative for the

179

College to stress above all its academic credentials, playing down any restrictiveness about its intake. All this raised questions about the institutional ethos.

Revd Arthur Poulton, who was College Chaplain for 20 years from 1964 while also lecturing in the Divinity department, provoked debate at Academic Council in 1973 by stating that he was 'the leader of worship in a College which had not made up its own mind which way it wanted to go' and 'was in a position where it might depart from the intentions of the founders without realising that it had done so'.[54] He also contributed several thoughtful articles to the *Collegian* reflecting on the quality of community life and the nature of a Church college. In 1970, for example, noting that there were by then 'in and around the campus over a thousand ... intelligent people', he called for the creation of 'a social framework ... through which ... sharing of experience would become both more easy and more natural'. In the critical days of 1976, he argued that the future of Church colleges would lie in their distinctiveness as 'Christian centres of higher education' and 'centres of Christian living': 'a Christian College has a unique opportunity, as a united institution of learning embracing many different disciplines, to keep a rounded perspective on the truth'.[55]

He found support from Dr John Gay of the University of Oxford Department of Educational Studies, whose address on Founders' Day in 1980 bluntly asked 'Why should Chester College stay open?' His message, too, was that the future lay in offering a distinctive contribution in the field of higher education, as an unashamedly Christian institution known for the quality of its community life. Seaborne himself was sympathetic, while being anxious that the College should retain a broad appeal to academically able staff and students. The Principal presented papers to Academic Council in May 1975 and January 1976 encouraging the development of courses particularly appropriate to a Church college and in February 1979, in the same forum, 'underlined the urgent need for a hard look at the College's position as an Anglican foundation'; at the turn of the decade he wrote that 'the time may well have come to be more overt about our Christian allegiance ... let us hope that the 1980s will enable us to carry forward the essential elements of our own tradition as a Christian college, and to find new ways of expressing the faith that is in us'. In February 1980 the General Synod unanimously passed a resolution supporting the remaining Church colleges in their diversified role and a staff conference on identity as a Church college was held later that year.[56]

Chester never did nail its colours to the cross to the extent envisaged by Gay but this does not mean that all this discussion was irrelevant. When

Poulton ceased to be chaplain in 1984 – while retaining his lectureship – careful consideration was given to the 'job description' of his successor. Although the post was now envisaged as fixed-term (from three to seven years), requiring residence on campus with a focus full-time on chaplaincy work without lecturing responsibilities, the holder was still expected to discharge the role that Poulton had fulfilled, that of a reflective Christian presence across the institution.

> The main task of the chaplain would not be liturgical or academic but apologetics. He would be responsible for trying to break down the frontiers and open people up to thinking about God and a Christian base for their whole life and academic study. There was also a need to provide some forum for Christians whose faith was being challenged by their academic study and who wanted to share doubts in confidence and security.

In other words, the model of the chaplaincy had changed but its purpose, while being articulated more clearly than ever before, continued to be seen as an affirmation of the College's Christian commitment. The chaplain was certainly more than simply another arm of the College's welfare support network. He was expected to attend – and, if he wished to, speak at – Academic Board, though without voting rights so as to preserve his independence. And the possibility was mooted of one day appointing a deaconess as female chaplain.[57] Several years later a woman priest would indeed be installed as chaplain, in the person of Revd Lorraine Dixon, who held the post in the years immediately before the College became a University.

As for the expectations of the chaplain expressed in 1985, they are not dissimilar to those applicable to the Dean of Chapel in the second decade of the twenty-first century, another period when institutional distinctiveness has come to the fore as a topic for discussion. The immediate task in the mid-1980s, however, was to find a successor to the outgoing Poulton. The solution for the academic year 1984–85 was the licensing of an ecumenical chaplaincy team, composed of academic staff drawn from the Anglican, Roman Catholic and various nonconformist churches, most of whom also held office outside the College as a minister, lay reader/preacher or elder; they were reinforced by part-time assistance from two local curates. Thereafter, Revd Stephen Ridley was appointed full-time resident chaplain but the chaplaincy team, with an evolving membership, has continued in a supporting role ever since.

Offering some 'theological perspectives' for the College's 150th anniversary in 1989, Ridley paid tribute to the 'identifiably caring attitudes' of most academic and support staff, and to the lively spirit of voluntaryism within the community, seen for example in the Chapel Committee's sponsorship of TWIN (Third World in Need). He did, however, observe that the academic work of the College had nothing particularly distinctive about it and summed up the current position as:

> First fairly lively, but voluntary Christian activities backed up by institutional weight, money and personnel. Second, an ethos of caring and professionalism at least in accord with Christian values. Third, central educational and organisational aims which are essentially uninformed by anything specifically Christian.

Alongside this, he pointed to the erection of the large amber glass cross at the top of the Rockery steps in 1982, made and donated by a former Education lecturer, Fred Starkey; to his own appointment as a full-time resident chaplain alongside the chaplaincy team of influential staff; and to the arrival, by the time he was writing, of another Principal in Holy Orders, as indicative of continuing institutional commitment to the College's Christian foundation. He also presented some helpful estimates of the size of the worshipping community:

> The Founders' Day service in the Cathedral, with a massive publicity effort and near three line whip on the staff, will get between a third and a half of the students there. Valedictory [successor since 1979 to Presentation Day] is fashionable at the moment and the Chapel is packed. So too are the Carol services, but realistically, day by day and week by week [Christian Union] and Chapel together probably touch just over 10% of students – perhaps 150 out of 1,000 students, and perhaps 25 out of over 100 academic staff.'

The main College service on Thursday mornings, for which lectures were still suspended, now took place in the Gladstone Hall to allow a variety of experimental formats, moving to the de Bunsen Centre for the summer term when attendance typically dropped from the 60-plus of the autumn and 45 or so of the spring.[58]

Ridley's paper mixed optimism with realism and might, in fact, have been a little more positive about the impact of the College's Christian principles on the curriculum. The introduction in September 1982 of Psychology and Computing as subjects within the BA Combined Studies, initially as two-year options – the former drawing mainly on Education staff, the latter run from within the Mathematics department – was a sensible, pragmatic response to their evident popularity among potential students, using expertise already available. The same could be said about a new Diploma in Computing Across the Curriculum, launched the previous year, however expensive it was to provide the equipment. However, Ecclesiastical History, another Combined Studies option which began in 1980 as a joint venture by the History and Religious Studies departments (as Divinity had now become as part of its own curriculum development), was a worthy attempt to offer something distinctive which reflected the College's traditions.[59] A Certificate in Christian Studies – which, in fairness, Ridley did mention – was also available from 1982 as a Chester College (rather than Liverpool) award, especially for students who wanted an additional qualification to teach Religious Education in schools, and subsequently developed into a collectively recognised Church Colleges Certificate commended by the Archbishops of Canterbury and York.[60] Highly significant was the commencement in September 1980 of the multidisciplinary BA degree in Health & Community Studies, an ingenious compilation of expertise drawn mainly from Biology, Education, Geography and PE, enhanced by outside appointments as vacancies arose elsewhere; this was the College's first named subject degree, a truly unique offering concerned with physical and mental health in the context of physical and social environments. It was initially rejected by the RAC but approved on appeal in 1978 – and by Liverpool early in 1979 – after the focus had been widened from the Natural Sciences to embrace relevant Social Sciences as well. The programme was aimed largely at those already engaged in, or hoping to enter, social services and the caring professions, and attracted healthy recruitment numbers drawn from both school-leavers and mature students; indeed, the timetable was initially arranged so that teaching was over by 3.00 p.m., to help those with childcare responsibilities. By 1982–83, when all three years were running, 54 students were enrolled.[61]

Another development intended to increase the attraction of a Chester BA degree was the introduction of work experience as an integral component. This was first mentioned at a meeting of the Course Planning Committee in March 1979, but not immediately followed up. However, John Stocks of the Education department, whose work both as careers adviser and in visiting schools to advertise the College was highly esteemed, was asked by Academic Board in January 1980 to investigate the possibility of incorporating it into the curriculum. He reported back a year later with various options depending on how far the experience should relate to academic studies, and a working party was set up to pursue the matter further. Given the importance of this activity in the subsequent history of the College, it is worth noting that there was a strong body of opinion at Academic Board in favour of keeping work experience out of the formal curriculum and restricting it to 'short periods ... to take place during the vacations on a voluntary basis'. The instruction to the working party to keep all options open was secured by only 15 votes to 12, with two abstentions.[62] But, as Stocks pointed out in the *Collegian*, LIHE had decided to introduce this to its curriculum for 1981–82; 'work-study attachments' also featured within the final year of Health & Community Studies, due to be reached in 1982–83, and 'industrial attachments' were also built into the new Computing programme launched that year.[63] So the decision was taken to build work experience as a compulsory element into the second year of the BA Combined Studies programme. In the summer term of 1983 Philomena Alston of the Education department was appointed 'work experience tutor', initially on a one-third remission of timetable, and some 110 placements were found in time for the first group of students to undertake it in the spring of 1984, occupying a five-week block when BEd students were on school practice; employers ranged from libraries and record offices to ICI and the Welsh Water Authority. A preparatory lunchtime 'lifeskills' course was added the following year. Alston's work in continuing to build a large network of employers subsequently led to her becoming involved in the work of the Learning from Experience Trust and thereafter to a leading role in a national project on the award of academic credit for Work Based Learning in the early 1990s.[64]

By the early 1980s, diversification had brought student numbers back to the position enjoyed in 1972–73, prior to the cuts in teacher training. Then there had been 959; now, in February 1981, Seaborne was informed by the DES that the College would be grant-aided for no more than 960 full-time equivalent (FTE) students, although the fact that those taking various part-time courses counted only as fractions meant that this represented well over 1,000 individuals. That September, the FTE total itself reached four figures, made up of 372 BA students, 360 BEds, 56 on the Postgraduate Certificate in Education (PGCE) and large numbers of part-timers, equating to 178 on in-service courses and a further 66 on the adult education diplomas. However, during the course of the year the DES recalculated – less generously – the ratio between part-time and full-time attendance, meaning that, retrospectively, total FTE for 1981–82 came down and actually hit the 960 figure exactly: just when everyone thought that the College had topped 1,000 FTE for the first time, it turned out not to have done so! Under these harsher calculations, the 960 target was met again in 1982–83, with 381 BA students, 377 BEds, 42 PGCEs and a host of part-timers whose contribution to the overall FTE was now reduced to 160.[65] Only 63 of the 265 first-year undergraduates were men.[66]

This imbalance between the sexes was not ideal but it did mean that Chester was helping to redress the under-representation of women in higher education at large: it would not be until 1996 that more women than men entered HEIs in England and Wales as a whole.[67] The preponderance of female students was compounded by a further shift in the demand for teachers, this time away from secondary towards primary training.[68] A new National Advisory Body for Local Authority Higher Education (popularly known as NAB) came into being in February 1982 to advise the Secretary of State on academic provision in the non-university sector and that summer, under its guidance, the DES announced a reduction for 1983 in Chester's secondary PGCE numbers from 50 to 20 (retaining English and French but not Science and Mathematics) and also to the BEd intake; this was cut from 120 to 90 for one year and to 110 thereafter, all of whom were to aim for the primary sector. Protests to the DES at a move which brought to an end Chester's cherished position for over two decades as a 'Wing' college for secondary PE were in vain. But at least the College had survived yet again, when others did not: among those in the area to lose all their teacher training were C.F. Mott in Liverpool, De la Salle College in Manchester, Madeley in Staffordshire and (despite its reprieve in 1977) Padgate at Warrington. Seaborne rightly paid tribute to Chester's 'sound academic reputation and excellent recruitment record' in seeing off the latest threat but, even so, Chester was now left in the DES's plans as the smallest non-university provider of teacher training in the North West region; at 130, its projected intake for 1985 to BEd and PGCE together was less than half that of competitors such as Crewe and Alsager, LIHE and Edge Hill.[69] A Voluntary Sector Consultative Council was established in 1984 to represent the interests of the remaining voluntary colleges in negotiations with NAB but there could hardly have been a clearer signal that continued recruitment to alternative award-bearing programmes was imperative.

The last thing needed at this juncture was yet another bout of uncertainty but further government intervention managed to provide it. Through the White Paper *Teaching Quality*, along with accompanying circulars and other publications issued in 1983 and 1984, the DES and the Secretary of State's Advisory Committee on the Supply and Education of Teachers set out new criteria for the accreditation of teacher training courses; a Council for the Accreditation of Teacher Education was established to approve them. As a result, the College was obliged to ensure that the academic content of what by now was an exclusively primary BEd curriculum was relevant to the needs of the schools for which students were being prepared; accordingly, after much debate at Academic Board in May and June 1984, French found itself confined to the BA and to secondary in-service and postgraduate work. There was also a requirement that those teaching the prospective teachers should themselves have recent experience in schools: not in itself a major problem since there were already arrangements for relevant staff to work in schools, but one which helped to reinforce the growing trend for a separation in personnel between those delivering the professional and the academic sides of the College's work. The timely conversion of the Geography block into a largely open-plan Primary base, agreed in spring 1983 and opened in June 1984 by the County's Director of Education, was a brilliant response to the government's expectations: a place where local schoolchildren and their teachers could visit the College to work creatively with students and their tutors.[70] So after a gap of two decades, children were once again coming on to the campus to be taught and there was now a late-twentieth-century version of a 'practising school'. At the same time, the academic content of future teachers' higher education was to be tied more closely to what they would teach. Chritchley, Lovell, Best and their contemporaries would have found the scenario reassuringly familiar.

Alongside all this went a review of the efficiency of the voluntary college sector, conducted by the DES in the context of the Thatcher government's squeeze on public expenditure. Happily, the report, in August 1983, reaffirmed confidence in the College once again, as an institution which recruited well and was economically managed and staffed; while the voluntary sector as a whole was told to reduce academic staff by over 80 in total, Chester's staffing level was to remain the same and a modest increase in student numbers was permitted, to targets just over 1,000. Accordingly, even under the reduced allowance for part-time students in force for the past two years, the College's numbers reached a new record 1,041 FTE in October 1983: indisputably the first time four figures had been attained. A year later they stood at 1,083 and in October 1985 1,072, the last a significant moment because for the first time FTE students registered for a BA or an adult-education diploma (545) outnumbered those engaged in some form of teacher training (527). The pattern was repeated the following year, when teacher training numbers accounted for 518 out of a total FTE of 1,084. A further review of provision in 1985–86 led to the DES switching the PGCE from secondary to primary and allowing some increase to targets in the all-primary BEd, but this was accompanied by a requirement that BA numbers be reduced so there was minimal overall impact on the total College annual intake for the rest of the decade. However, yet another adjustment, whereby BEd students entering from September 1985 were obliged to register for a four-year Honours programme – rather than for three years with the option of a fourth Honours year as hitherto – did have the effect of raising total numbers once there were four full BEd cohorts working their way through. This happened for the first time in 1988–89, when the total College FTE stood at 1,119.[71]

Having presided over a battle for survival as numbers contracted, and then a period of recovery as a plethora of new courses came on stream, Seaborne took the DES's verdict on the College in 1982–83 as a call to enrich what already existed rather than spread resources more thinly. Numbers were capped, both for teacher training and for diversified provision, and despite some tweaking in the subsequent review they effectively remained capped for the rest of the decade. He was just thankful that the cap had been imposed at a record four figures rather than three.

> There is now need for consolidation rather than expansion since the likelihood of obtaining more staff or money is extremely remote ... although we have developed our courses very considerably in recent years, the opportunities for further development are now extremely limited.[72]

So the focus shifted towards renewed negotiation with the University for permission to deliver Honours and higher degrees, seen as essential if the College was to remain competitive with the rest of the non-university HE sector. From October 1980, tiny numbers of selected Chester and LIHE students who had qualified for an Ordinary BA were allowed to proceed to a fourth year for Honours at Liverpool, although this only applied within the Faculty of Arts; a History student, Christine Whittingham, was the first to take the opportunity and nine more were chosen the following year. Then from September 1983, the two colleges were allowed to teach the fourth year of a BA General with Honours themselves; 15 students from the 1980 intake qualified and chose to do so that year and the number had risen to 24 by 1985–86. This arrangement was itself short-lived since, despite approval from the RAC as well as the University, the DES objected to grant-aiding a four-year programme; it took an appeal to the Under Secretary for Higher and Further Education to allow the four-year BA Honours to go ahead, for those students who had in good faith been promised the opportunity to extend beyond their three years, on the understanding that an alternative would have to be found for the future. So negotiations proceeded for a three-year Honours programme instead, duly granted by Liverpool in time for the start of the 1983–84 academic year; the BA students who entered in September 1983 were selected by the University on the basis of their first-year results, the more successful registering for Honours while the remainder stayed on course for an Ordinary degree. This scheme did not last long either: in September 1985 the whole of the BA intake, including that in the named degree of Health & Community Studies, was allowed to register for Honours, which became in effect the standard offering.[73] BA Honours for Chester students had gone from being a four-year commitment open to a tiny elite to a three-year programme available to all in the space of only half a decade.

In the meantime, the University had also sanctioned the delivery of the College's first part-time BA (to be taken over five years), for which seven students registered in September 1984. Five years earlier Seaborne had envisaged part-time BAs 'forming a large part of the future of Colleges of Higher Education' but the fact that this remained a daytime rather than an evening course, with the students simply joining existing sets, meant that it was destined never to attract large numbers. This in turn became an Honours degree (over six years) in 1985.[74] Beyond this, the College's first higher degree, a part-time MEd with alternative specialisms in Religious Education and Curriculum Studies, aimed at serving teachers, was launched in 1984.[75] Two years later, students with the right combination of subjects – drawn from Biology (a department separate from Science since 1982), Mathematics, Computer Studies, Geography, Psychology and PE & Sports Science (as PE had now become) – could register for BSc Honours rather than BA. The only regret here was that study of the Physical Sciences, which had a long and distinguished history going back to the beginnings of the College but was now represented by a lively but low-enrolling option entitled Science in Society, was not admitted to the degree, a decision which led to its being phased out. Then in 1987, the General degree with Honours was re-named as an Honours degree in Combined Subjects, a more accurate description.[76]

One challenge in delivering all this was the profile of the academic staff. Notwithstanding heroic individual efforts to retrain and obtain higher degrees, the fact remained that a substantial proportion of those in place in the early 1980s had originally been appointed because of their expertise in secondary school teaching. With the shift towards a heavy emphasis on primary training and the need for further research-active scholars to underpin the delivery of Honours programmes, a change was essential and – aided partly by a premature retirement scheme introduced in 1982 – this was accomplished despite the constraints imposed by fixed staffing numbers. Ten new members of academic staff were appointed in 1983, a further five in 1985, four more during 1986–87 including Michael Hardstaffe, formerly at Bradford and Ilkley Community College, who succeeded Leon Boucher on his retirement as Dean of Professional Studies. In upbeat mood having steered the College through one crisis after another, Seaborne commented in the 1985 *Collegian* on the sense of 'renewal' he perceived through these appointments. He extended this to encompass the foundation of a well-supported Outdoor Bound Club, the flourishing of the Film Society, musical performances such as Fauré's Requiem, and 'the remarkable revival of sporting activity among the students', congratulating the Ladies Basketball team on becoming British Colleges champions in 1983–84 and commending the achievements of the swimming, football, rugby, cricket and netball teams who all reached the finals or semi-finals of their respective competitions. And he also cited ongoing improvements to buildings as further evidence of this 'renewal'.[77]

In reality, the political and economic context meant that Seaborne's time as Principal was not one of spectacular building development: the library remains as his most tangible memorial. However, though Chester could claim to be one of the leading Church colleges in the country in terms of student numbers – and in 1981 the one with more students enrolled for Religious Studies as a main subject than any other – it was relatively weak in its provision of hostel accommodation and some attempt was made to address this problem.[78] Nos 1 and 2 Exton Park were bought in 1978 and converted into student rooms, to sit alongside nos. 3 and 4; following the deaths of those two stalwarts, successive Vice-Principals Morrell and Bradbury in 1978 and 1981 respectively, the houses were named in their honour. The nearby semi-detached property known as 'Longfield', alongside the access way into the campus from Parkgate Road, was also purchased in 1981, becoming a residence for the Dean of Students; this led in turn to the acquisition as student accommodation of Rutland Court (alias Villa), a house backing on to the campus at the entrance from Parkgate Road, and to the systematic purchase of a line of neighbouring houses along this road as they became available during the course of the decade.[79] More ambitious was a scheme to sell off some of the College's playing fields on Sealand Road so that a developer could build student housing, but local residents objected and planning permission was finally refused early in 1983; an alternative proposal to exchange at least part of the holding on Sealand Road for building land in Chester's 'Northgate Triangle' (close to Liverpool Road and Brook Lane) was also rejected. It was these disappointments which led to the decision to build a 'Student Village' of semi-detached houses on the College campus instead, accessed from Cheyney Road, occupied on a self-catering basis and available as 'holiday lets'; by modern standards, though, with accommodation for about 100 people, it was really a 'student hamlet'. The first sod was cut by the Archdeacon of Chester in December 1986 and it was ready for use by the following September.[80]

As for other new buildings, a 'mobile' was installed in front of the old College School in 1980 (roughly where the prizewinning garden has now been planted) and fitted out as a Professional Centre for Teachers, partly using stock and equipment from the former Centre in George Street, Chester, which the local authority had closed down as an economy measure; under its newly appointed Head, Gordon Taylor, who was also Senior Lecturer in Reading, this fulfilled a valuable role as a base for the College's short in-service courses as well as housing resources and serving as a place where local teachers could meet.[81] In 1981, the roof space of the original College School of 1844, by now serving as a Drama department, was converted into tutors' offices, an administrative staff common room, a classroom and a study area; in the same year, a well-equipped lecture theatre for general College use was created within the other former School, what is now the Beswick building.[82] Approval was also obtained from the DES for the construction of a new Resource Centre as an extension to the west end of the library. The College librarian, Hilda Stoddard, who had recently been awarded an MA of the University of London for a thesis on 'The Response of Libraries to Change in Higher Education' saw this as an opportunity to develop 'a multi-media library as the first stage of an integrated learning resources centre' but when opened in 1983 the Centre was on more traditional lines, with a TV studio on the upper floor and open access workshop below, quite distinct from the adjoining library with its shelves of books and journals.[83]

Among other facilities, a College car and two minibuses were bought in 1979,[84] training lights were installed to allow sports practice on winter evenings in 1981[85] and by 1982 academic departments could purchase their own computers and enjoy access to video-recordings in their own classrooms, using televisions on trolleys supplied from the Resource Centre.[86] The larger of the two dining halls was converted to a cafeteria in 1983.[87] Two years later, a sauna/solarium was introduced adjacent to the Swimming Pool and in 1987 squash courts were built, named after the former Head of PE and Dean of Students Nicholas Parry, both jointly funded by the College and the Students' Union. Another striking student contribution was to be seen in the painstaking restoration of the Chapel east window by Penny Kemp-Jones, dedicated by the Bishop of Chester as part of the valedictory ceremony in June 1987; her comment that, prior to restoration, the workmanship in different parts of the window was of diverse quality supports the claim that Rigg's students were actively involved in the Chapel's construction.[88] One ambitious scheme which never came to fruition, however, was a proposal for the enlargement 'outwards and upwards' of the Gladstone Hall, which was intended for development as a multi-purpose student social centre. Plans were drawn up but spending on the project was repeatedly postponed by the DES even though the College set aside a budget to meet its obligatory 15%. Eventually, in 1989, and on the advice of the DES which was more sympathetic to expenditure on educational buildings, the College decided to build the Molloy Hall adjacent to the library instead. This was not a student centre but a flexible lecturing and tutorial space, with tiered seating in the central hall for 171 people and capacity for over 400 if its partition was opened. New facilities for students' social activities would have to wait.[89]

Much of the credit for the enterprising approach – converting old premises, buying up houses and making minor improvements which cumulatively enhanced the quality of life on the campus – must go to Raymond Downes, formerly Senior Administrative Officer at Didsbury College, Manchester, who had joined as Bursar after Bell had retired in 1977. He continued to serve the College until 1997 and shortly before his own retirement – and as it turned out his death – the next Principal, Ned Binks, paid him a fine tribute for having 'enriched the College' and 'completely transformed the physical environment in which the … community lives and works'.[90] Downes was keen to maximise the income from the College estate so as to pay for the various upgrades and saw increased use of the buildings during vacations as a means to that end. Accordingly, in April 1981, the Catering Officer, Tom Ryan, who had arrived from West London Institute of HE in June 1979, took on the additional role of Conference Organiser and in the academic year 1980–81 some 35 different groups stayed in the College during the vacations, ranging from the American Association of Special Educators and the British Aikido Federation to the Police Clay Pigeon Shooters. Having the campus seemingly as busy during vacations as it was during term-time – as the *Collegian* of 1982 reported, 'the only period not used for conferences is Christmas week' – was a novel experience which sometimes led to tensions especially in the days immediately before the start of term, but over the years this activity has undoubtedly contributed substantially to the College's private funds, for use especially on building improvements.[91]

The development of the conference trade turned College support departments such as Catering and Housekeeping into all-year-round services. By 1987 the Housekeeper, Phyllis Higginbottom, was presiding over a department of two full-time assistants, four full-time male cleaners, 25 part-time female cleaners and one seamstress, but the Bursar admitted that high standards were being maintained despite staffing having failed to keep pace with growth in demand. The porters, too, were kept busy fielding initial enquiries and providing security and assistance out of term as well as in it; they were a team of six based at the Cheyney Road frontage when the *Collegian* reported on their work in 1979, although there was a small increase with the growth in student numbers in subsequent years. Even Academic Records, reorganised at the end of the 1970s in order to meet increasing demand for information from the myriad official bodies with which the College now had to deal, was managing on one full-time and one part-time assistant at the time of Seaborne's retirement in summer 1987.[92] Not the least of the difficulties faced by the College through the 1980s was the tightness of the budget, so the efficiency with which services were maintained owed much to the commitment of various support departments who were entitled to claim that they were under-staffed.

When Malcolm Seaborne ended his tenure as Principal, he was rightly proud of having seen the College through 16 years of almost unremitting challenge. Staff and student numbers were not dissimilar to those prevailing when he had arrived, but in the face of one threat after another he had transformed an institution where most full-time students left with a certificate of education to one in which all were reading for Honours – BA or BEd– or even Master's degrees; various postgraduate, in-service and adult education courses had become important as well. The range of subjects taught at the College had hardly expanded but they were being presented in novel ways and in the context of new awards: Health & Community Studies, Psychology and Computer Studies, for example, though new to the prospectus, were largely derived from expertise which already existed and only gradually acquired their own specialist staff. Academic Board thanked the outgoing Principal for 'his guidance and good humour' in conducting its meetings: testimony to the grace and understated, scholarly determination which characterised his leadership despite the many interested parties, inside and outside the College, whose goodwill had to be secured if initiatives were to succeed. He retired to Mold and kept in touch with the institution, becoming Emeritus Professor of the History of Education in 2005 and receiving an Honorary Doctorate of Letters in 2006, two years before his death.[93] Seaborne was followed into retirement in 1988 by Thomas Fawcett, Dean of Academic Studies, a fine academic in the field of Religious Studies and one whose devising and early co-ordination of the BA Combined Studies degree had been critical to the maintenance of student numbers in the mid- to late-1970s.[94] Taken together with the departure at the end of 1986 of the redoubtable Leon Boucher, these months witnessed the withdrawal from the scene of a triumvirate who had steered the College through the most sustained buffeting it had ever experienced. There was still no guarantee that their achievement would endure: an authoritative assessment of the state of British higher education in the late 1980s saw the colleges as a 'third group' alongside universities and polytechnics among whom some of the voluntary colleges were 'particularly vulnerable to cuts' and shrinkage.[95] But it would be for others now to continue the fight.

1   R.J. Alexander, M. Craft and J. Lynch, 'Introduction' to Alexander, Craft and Lynch, *Change in Teacher Education*, pp. xiii–xviii, at p. xvii.

2   *Collegian*, 1983, p. 11 (figures for England and Wales).

3   J.D. Gay, 'The Churches and the Training of Teachers in England and Wales' in V.A. McClelland, ed., *Christian Education in a Pluralist Society* (London, 1988), pp. 207–29, at p. 214; precise definitions of status mean that different authorities give variant figures.

4   K.E. Shaw, 'Exeter: from College of Education to University' in Alexander, Craft and Lynch, *Change in Teacher Education*, pp. 203–14.

5   CC, Minutes of Academic Board 1973–77: 12 November 1975; the women's Church colleges of Sarum St Michael (Salisbury), and the mixed Church colleges of Culham (near Abingdon) Hockerill (Bishops's Stortford) and St Peter's Saltley (Birmingham) all closed in 1978. Chester purchased library stock from Culham and Hockerill, along with books, audio-visual equipment and a prize fund from Saltley, and also acquired the lease of Saltley's field centre at Murton near Appleby (*Collegian*, 1981, p. 17; CC, Minutes of Academic Board, 1973–77: 22 February, 24 May 1978).

6   See Chapter 9; CC, Minutes of Academic Council, 1972–81: 15 May 1974.

7   CC, Minutes of Academic Board 1973–77: 1 May 1974; CC, Minutes of Academic Council, 1972–81: 9 October 1974.

8   CC, Minutes of Academic Board 1973–77: 26 June 1974; CC, Minutes of Academic Council, 1972–81: 29 January 1975, 12 May 1976; *Collegian*, 1976, pp. 5–7; cf. McGregor, *A Church College for the 21st Century?*, pp. 217–18.

9   CC, Minutes of Academic Board 1973–77: 25 June, 1975; CC, Minutes of Academic Council 1972–81: 3 December 1975; *Collegian*, 1976, p. 8.

10 Quoted in McGregor, *A Church College for the 21st Century?*, p. 203.

11 CC, Minutes of Academic Board, 1973–77: 26 June, 25 September, 20 November 1974 (which reports difficulties during early discussions about the subject-content of a College-taught BA), 29 September 1976; CC, Minutes of Academic Council, 1972–81: 13 October 1976, gives the intake as 194, including 46 BAs. The College's February 1974 submission to Liverpool had envisaged the BA starting in September 1975 but the prolonged approval process delayed this by as year (ZCR 86/7928: Outline Proposals for ... Courses ... to begin in September 1975).

12 The two-year shortened course, which had been an option since the three-year certificate programme had been introduced in 1960 and had been taken by the first three women students who entered in 1961, was also discontinued in 1974: CC, Minutes of Academic Board, 1973–77: 16 October, 1974, 25 June, 1 October 1975, 14 January, 29 September 1976; *Collegian*, 1979, pp. 5–6, 26; 1980, p. 5; Kelly, *For Advancement of Learning*, p. 440.

13 CC, The Future of the Colleges of Education (paper by Seaborne to Academic Board and Governors, February 1977).

14 CC, Minutes of Academic Board, 1973–77: 25 September 1974, 25 June, 1 October 1975; *Collegian*, 1980, p. 5. Figures for September 1974 include 24 on the postgraduate certificate in Education and 23 on the in-service special needs course.
15 CC, Minutes of Academic Council, 1972–81: 12 May 1976.
16 CC, Minutes of Academic Board 1973–77: 26 February 1975, 25 February, 28 April, 17 November, 8 December 1976, 12 January 1977; CC, Minutes of Academic Board 1972–81: 13 March 1974; *Collegian*, 1978, pp. 7–8; McGregor, *A Church College for the 21st Century?*, p. 218.
17 CC, Minutes of Academic Board 1973–77: 16 January, 20 February, 8 March, 5 June 1974, cf. 15 January 1975.
18 CC, Minutes of Academic Board, 1973–77: 11 December 1974, 15 January, 5 February 1975.
19 CC, Minutes of Academic Board, 1973–77: 25 February, 17 March, 28 April, 29 September, 20 October, 17 November, 8 December 1976, 12 January 1977; CC, Minutes of Academic Council, 1972–81: 19 January 1977; CC, Minutes of Academic Board, 1977–82: 23 February 1977; CC, Minutes of Governors, 1975–89: 20 February 1976, 20 May 1977.
20 CC, Minutes of Academic Board, 1973–77: 8 March, 27 March, 1 May, 17 May, 25 September, 20 November 1974, 19 March, 30 April 1975 (which both mention interest in seeking validation of the part-time BEd by Manchester if Liverpool continued to be unwilling), 22 October, 12 November, 10 December 1975, 25 February, 19 May, 20 October 1976; CC, Minutes of Academic Council, 1972–81: 10 October 1973.
21 CC, Minutes of Academic Board, 1973–77: 26 February, 19 March, 30 April, 21 May, 11 June, 25 June, 1 October 1975, 4 February, 9 June 1976.
22 CC, Minutes of Academic Board, 1973–77: 25 February, 23 June, 20 October 1976; *Collegian*, 1979, p. 5.
23 CC, Minutes of Academic Board, 1973–77: 17 May, 25 September 1974; the OU Centre arrangement ended in 1983 but the College briefly collaborated with the OU in providing facilities and tutorial support for local government officers of Cheshire County Council preparing for their awards in the late 1970s and early 1980s (CC, Minutes of Academic Board, 1977–82: 5 October 1977, 15 March 1978, 23 May 1979, 15 October 1980, 13 January 1982; CC, Minutes of Academic Board, 1982–89: 8 December 1982; CC, Minutes of Academic Development Committee: 6 January 1982; *Collegian*, 1982, pp. 28–29).
24 CC, Minutes of Academic Board, 1973–77: 12 January 1977.
25 *Collegian*, 1977, p. 7.
26 *Collegian*, 1979, pp. 5, 12; CC, Minutes of Academic Board, 1973–77: 25 June, 22 October 1975, 17 November 1976; CC, Minutes of Academic Council, 1972–81: 19 October 1977; CC, Minutes of Governors, 1975–89: 11 November 1977, which makes reference to a protest in vain by the Church Board of Education at the decision to take numbers from the voluntary sector to save Padgate, an LEA college.

27 The February 1974 submission to Liverpool had optimistically projected a total of 1,060 students by 1978–79, largely as a result of diversification (ZCR 86/7928: Outline Proposals for … Courses … to begin in September 1975).

28 Layard, King and Moser, *Impact of Robbins*, pp. 90–96, 108.

29 *Collegian*, 1979, p. 6; 1980, pp. 5–6; CC, Minutes of Course Planning Committee: 8 November 1978.

30 *Collegian*, 1977, pp. 8–9 (quotation from Thomas Fawcett)

31 *Collegian*, 1976, p. 8; cf. a survey of student opinion in *Collegian*, 1977, pp. 14–16, which endorses these reasons for applying to the College but adds a few others: 'I heard of the College and its courses through an advertisement in the *Musical Times*', 'I had heard there was a greater proportion of women to men', and 'because I've got a friend in the second-year who said it was a good place and because it's got a good rugby team'.

32 See Chapter 9.

33 CC, Minutes of Academic Board 1973–77: 29 September, 8 December 1976, 12 January 1977; CC, Minutes of Academic Council, 1972–81: 13 October 1976, 19 January 1977; CC. Minutes of Governors, 1975–89: 18 February 1977.

34 *Collegian*, 1975, pp. 7, 16; CC, Minutes of Academic Board, 1973–77: 27 March 1974, 5 February, 11 June 1975, 28 April, 23 June 1976.

35 CC, Minutes of Academic Board, 1973–77: 7 November 1973, 16 January, 27 March, 20 November, 11 December 1974, 26 February, 22 October 1975, 4 February, 25 February 1976. On limited use of the second photocopier, cf. ZCR 86A/1, Minutes of the Educational Technology Committee, 1972–79: 21 January, 5 May 1976; this records academic departments being 'urged to make more use of this facility, which was installed as a result of requests' and suggests that there was more concern about a malfunctioning spirit duplicator which had been provided for staff use in the Senior Common Room. The fact that this Committee had to ask the Estates and Development Committee for permission to put up notices advertising the location of the new Resource Centre is indicative of the extent to which de Bunsen's 'consultative culture' had become embedded by the mid-1970s.

36 CC, Minutes of Academic Board 1973–77: 26 February, 30 April, 22 October 1975, 18 June 1980; CC, Minutes of Academic Council 1972–81: 12 May 1976; *Collegian*, 1975, p. 5; 1976, p. 6; 1977, pp. 4–5; 1978, p. 18.

37 CC, Minutes of Academic Board 1973–77: 1 October 1975.

38 CC, Minutes of Academic Board 1973–77: 8 December 1976; CC, Minutes of Academic Council 1972–81: 14 May 1975; *Collegian*, 1978, pp. 11–12; see Chapter 9. Jones would also raise the College's profile within the city through her work as a JP and for the local Hospice, and was eventually awarded an MBE.

39 *Collegian*, 1979, p. 12.

40 *Collegian*, 1980, p. 12; an unintended consequence of this appointment was that the beneficiary proceeded over three decades later to write this book.

[41] *Collegian*, 1980, p. 13; CC, Minutes of Academic Board 1977–82: 4 October 1978; CC, Minutes of Governors, 1975–89: 16 November 1979.

[42] CC, Minutes of Academic Council, 1972–81: 31 October 1979; *Collegian*, 1980, p. 20.

[43] CC, Minutes of Academic Council, 1972–81: 4 November, 29 November 1972, 31 October 1979; *Collegian*, 1975, p. 23; 1977, p. 18; 1985, p. 25. Formal acknowledgement of 'Rag Week' rather than 'Rag Day' appears to have been granted by Principal de Bunsen in 1969 (CC, Minutes of Guild Council: 14 March 1969).

[44] *Collegian*, 1975, p. 15; 1980, p. 20

[45] *Collegian*, 1975, p. 24; 1977, pp. 14–15; CC, Minutes of Academic Council, 1972–81: 13 October 1976, 18 February 1981; in 1985 it was agreed that there should be at least two departmental committee meetings with student representatives present per annum (CC, Minutes of Academic Board, 1982–89: 16 October 1985). During the 1976 occupation of the administrative block, the students were refused admission to the room where the question papers were stored for the forthcoming exams (*pers. comm.* J. Sykes).

[46] *Collegian*, 1977, p. 19; 1978, pp. 20–21; 1979, pp. 29, 48–49; 1980, p. 29; 1981, p. 53; CC, Minutes of Governors, 1975–89: 15 May 1981; however, reunion matches have not entirely disappeared, an example being 'Old Boys v. New Boys' rugby union at Warrington (*The Cestrian*, Spring 2011, p. 20). Another very distinguished rugby union player who was a student at the College around this time was Gillian Burns, who graduated with a BEd in 1986. She went on to gain a record number of England caps (73), plus two for Great Britain and two for a World XV, before retiring from the sport in 2002; she also became the first female player to be inducted into the Rugby Hall of Fame and in 2005 was awarded an MBE. However, although granted an honorary degree by the University in 2013, she did not actually take up rugby until she had left Chester College.

[47] CC, Hooper deposit, *Prospectus, 1958–59*, p. 20.

[48] E.g. ZCR 86A/327: *Prospectus, 1966–67*, p. 9.

[49] ZCR 86A/329: *Prospectus, 1968–69*, p. 9.

[50] ZCR 86A/330: *Prospectus, 1979*, p. 45 (repeated in ZCR 86A/331: *Prospectus, 1980*, p. 4).

[51] *Collegian*, 1986, p. 6.

[52] CC, *Prospectus, 1997*, p. 4.

[53] See Chapter 14.

[54] CC, Minutes of Academic Council, 1972–81: 20 November 1973, cf. 27 November 1974.

[55] *Collegian*, Summer 1970, pp. 13–14; 1976, pp. 9–11; cf. 1979, pp. 9–10.

[56] CC, Minutes of Academic Council 1972–81: 14 May 1975, 28 January 1976, 21 February 1979, 13 February 1980; CC, Memo, Seaborne to Academic Council, 'Chester as a Church College', January 1976; *Collegian*, 1980, pp. 7–10; 1981, p. 27; CC, Minutes of Governors, 1975–89: 22 February 1980.

57 ZCR 86/7928: Carhart deposit: Reports on Restructuring of Church Colleges: Note (by M.V.J. Seaborne, 14 February 1985) of a Joint Meeting of Governors' Working Party and of Chaplaincy team, 8 February 1985.

58 S. Ridley, 'Theological Perspectives over 150 Years' in White, *Perspectives*, pp. 7–18, at pp. 9–11, 16; an adapted version of this paper appeared as S. Ridley, 'Theological Perspectives over 150 Years' in T. Brighton, ed., *150 Years: the Church Colleges in Higher Education* (Chichester, 1989), pp. 34–49. On the cross, see CC, Minutes of Academic Board, 1982–89: 8 December 1982, where there is agreement to Starkey's request that it be called the 'Peace Cross', and *The Cestrian*, Spring 2011, p. 14.

59 CC, Minutes of Academic Board, 1977–82: 13 December 1978, 28 May, 26 November 1980, 13 January, 3 March 1982; these subjects were also available to selected BEd candidates who accepted that they might then be unable to transfer to a BA. From 1986, Computer Studies and Psychology were available as three-year courses within the BA, with Ecclesiastical History dropping to one year (CC, Minutes of Academic Board, 1982–89: 29 January 1986). Dennis Holman, who later became Head of Computer Science, recalled that when he arrived as a lecturer in 1983 each of the department's 20 brand-new BBC-B microcomputers cost 20% of his annual salary (*Collegian*, 2003, p. 30).

60 Ridley, 'Theological Perspectives', p. 16; CC, Minutes of Academic Board, 1977–82: 25 April 1979; by 1993, when the Church Colleges Certificate underwent a quinquennial review, it had about 1,000 students registered nationwide (CC, Minutes of Academic Board, 1989–93: 12 May 1993).

61 CC, Minutes of Academic Board, 1977–82: 5 October 1977, 12 April, 4 October 1978, 14 February, 14 March, 3 October 1979, 15 October, 1980; CC, Minutes of Course Planning and Academic Development Committees, 1977–85: Emerson paper 16 February 1982; *pers. comm.* Revd J.R. Carhart, who pays tribute to the guidance given by Prof. Mansell Prothero of the University of Liverpool's Geography department in the development of the programme; *pers. comm.* J. Mann (student, 1980–83) via Fiona Roberts; *Collegian*, 1981, p. 16; 1982, pp. 23–24; 1984, p. 26.

62 CC. Minutes of Course Planning and Academic Planning Committees, 1977–85: 21 March 1979; CC, Minutes of Academic Board, 1977–82: 30 January 1980, 28 January 1981.

63 *Collegian*, 1981, pp. 16, 42; 1982, p. 23–24.

64 CC, Minutes of Academic Board, 1982–89: 11 May, 8 June 1983, 6 June 1984; *Collegian*, 1985, p. 33; 1986, p. 35; See Chapter 11.

65 *Collegian*, 1982, pp. 5, 35; 1983, pp. 6–7; CC, Minutes of Academic Board, 1977–82: 13 January 1982.

66 CC, Minutes of Academic Board, 1977–82: 29 September 1982.

67 C. Ianelli, 'Inequalities in Entry to Higher Education: a Comparison Over Time between Scotland and England and Wales', *HEQ*, LXI, 3 (July 2007), pp. 306–33, at p. 314.

68 In anticipation of this change in demand, Academic Board decided in May 1982 to abolish the Junior/Secondary ('Middle') strand within the BEd programme (CC, Minutes of Academic Board, 1977–82: 12 May 1982).

69 CC, Minutes of Academic Board, 1977–82: 29 September 1982; *Collegian*, 1983, pp. 5, 12.

70 CC, Minutes of Academic Board, 1982–89: 23 March 1983, 21 March, 9 May 1984; *Collegian*, 1984, pp. 6, 21–23; 1985, pp. 7, 10–15; Geography moved into the space within the Thomas building vacated by the construction of a new Resource Centre.

71 *Collegian*, 1984, pp. 5–8; 1985, p. 9; 1986, p. 8; 1987, pp. 5–7; CC, Minutes of Academic Board, 1982–89: 6 February, 4 December 1985, 28 February, 23 April 1986, 1 February 1989. By 1985, there were in-service diplomas in Community Education, Special Needs (both of them full- and part-time), French (full-time), Computing, Field Biology, Careers Guidance, and Language & Reading (all part-time), plus adult education part-time diplomas of the Institute of Linguists and in Landscape History.

72 *Collegian*, 1984, p. 5.

73 CC, Minutes of Academic Board, 1977–82: 14 February 1979, 28 May 1980, 25 November 1981, 12 May, 16 June 1982; CC, Minutes of Academic Board, 1982–89: 6 February 1985; CC, Minutes of Academic Development Committee: 5 May 1982; *Collegian*, 1981, p. 7; 1982, p. 5; 1983, p. 6; 1984, pp. 5–8; 1985, pp. 6–9; 1986, p. 39.

74 CC, Minutes of Course Planning Committee: 21 March 1979; *Collegian*, 1985, p. 9.

75 CC, Minutes of Academic Board, 1977–82: 30 September 1981, 12 May, 16 June 1982; CC, Minutes of Academic Board, 1982–89: 23 February, 11 May, 23 November 1983; *Collegian*, 1985, pp. 7, 9.

76 *Collegian*, 1984, p. 31; 1986, pp. 31–32 (where visits by Science in Society students to the Centre for Alternative Technology, British Nuclear Fuels at Capenhurst, the Shell refinery at Stanlow and Greenwich Observatory, among other places, are reported); 1987, pp. 5–7; CC, Minutes of Academic Board, 1982–89: 28 November 1984, 23 April 1986, 4 February 1987.

77 *Collegian*, 1984, p. 6; 1985, pp. 5–8; 1987, pp. 8–23; CC, Minutes of Governors, 1975–89: 15 May 1981, 14 May 1982; CC, Minutes of Academic Board, 1982–89: 1 October 1986.

78 CC, Minutes of Governors, 1975–89: 20 November 1981.

79 CC, Minutes of Academic Board, 1977–82: 3 May 1978, 20 May 1981; *Collegian*, 1980, p. 14; 1981, pp. 48–49; CC, Minutes of Governors, 1975–89: 16 May, 7 November 1980, 20 February, 15 May 1981, 14 May, 19 November 1982, 18 February 1983. Nos. 1 and 2 Exton Park were named after Morrell, nos. 3 and 4 after Bradbury, though both were later said to have 'been built on inadequate foundations' and were demolished to allow the erection of the Binks building on the site (CC, Minutes of Governors, 1990–99: 24 November 1999). Bradbury's obituary in *Collegian*, 1982, pp. 8–9, includes a reference to his 'good humour and … distinctive laugh'; he would therefore have been amused to read in the same

passage that 'faithful throughout his life to Anglican doctrine and practice, he rarely failed to miss worship in College Chapel'.

80 CC, Minutes of Governors, 1975–89: 7 November 1980, 19 November 1982, 18 February 1983; CC, Minutes of Academic Board, 1982–89: 4 December 1985, 26 November 1986; *Collegian*, 1987, pp. 24–25.

81 CC, Minutes of Academic Board, 1977–82: 30 January, 19 March, 18 June, 15 October 1980, 28 January 1981, 29 September 1982; *Collegian*, 1982, p. 30.

82 *Collegian*, 1981, pp. 4, 9; 1982, pp. 6, 50.

83 CC, Minutes of Academic Board, 1977–82: 12 April 1978, 25 April, 23 May 1979; *Collegian*, 1982, p. 30.

84 CC, Minutes of Academic Council, 1972–81: 31 October 1979.

85 *Collegian*, 1981, p. 9.

86 CC, Minutes of Academic Board, 1977–82: 25 November 1981, 3 March 1982.

87 This and other improvements during 1983 are covered in CC, Minutes of Academic Board, 1982–89: 8 June, 28 September 1983; *Collegian*, 1983, p. 6.

88 *Collegian*, 1985, p. 26; 1987, p. 25; CC, Minutes of Governors, 1982–89: 22 May 1987; *pers. comm.* P. Kemp-Jones. In CC, 'Report on the Upkeep of the Great East Window', she estimates that re-leading will again be necessary in 2075.

89 *Collegian*, 1983, p. 22; CC, Minutes of Academic Board, 1982–89: 8 December 1982, 23 February, 23 March 1983, 8 February, 4 December 1985, 4 February 1986, 18 March 1987, 2 November 1988, 1 March 1989; *Campus* 2 (June 1990), p. 1. The Hall was named after Peter Molloy, a property developer who financed the building (*pers. comm.* Canon E.V. Binks).

90 CC, Minutes of Governors, 1990–99: 24 June 1997.

91 CC, Minutes of Governors, 1975–89: 16 November 1979, 16 May 1980; *Collegian*, 1982, pp. 47–49.

92 *Collegian*, 1979, pp. 32–33; 1987, pp. 37–39; CC, Minutes of Academic Board, 1982–89: 21 March 1984.

93 *The Cestrian*, 2005; *The Cestrian*, 2007, p. 5; *The Cestrian*, 2008, p. 23; there is a good obituary of Seaborne in *History of Education*, XXXVIII, no. 1 (January 2009), pp. 1–4.

94 CC, Minutes of Academic Board, 1982–89: 3 April 1987, 11 May 1988; *Collegian*, 1987, pp. 8–9; Fawcett's most influential book is *The Symbolic Language of Religion*, published in 1970.

95 Stewart, *Higher Education in Postwar Britain*, pp. 312–13.

CHAPTER 11

ENTERPRISE AND EXPANSION

In April 1987 the government published its White Paper, *Higher Education: Meeting the Challenge.* This urged greater commitment by the sector to the preparation of students for future employment, advocated more flexibility over admissions, via access courses as well as academic or vocational qualifications, and called for the publication of performance indicators as a means of comparing different institutions' 'value for money'. There was also a promise 'to encourage and reward approaches by HEIs which brought them closer to the world of business' and that December, under the auspices of the Department of Employment, the government launched the Enterprise in Higher Education initiative with the promise of up to £1 million over five years to participating institutions. The Education Reform Act of the following year abolished the University Grants Commission and the National Advisory Body (NAB), known in recent years for their calculated allocations of funded student numbers, and set up in their place the Universities Funding Council (UFC) and its counterpart the Polytechnics and Colleges Funding Council (PCFC). Formally established on 1 April 1989, they were intended from the outset to implement rather than to influence the government's policies for higher education; they proceeded to invite their institutions to bid for student numbers at their own proposed cost, with the clear implication that those which pitched low would have the best chance of growth. All this has been characterised as the 'marketisation of higher education' and it represented the clearest demonstration yet that in the eyes of the government HE was no longer to be seen as an affirmation of Cardinal Newman's dictum that 'knowledge is … an end sufficient to rest in and to pursue for its own sake'. Universities, polytechnics and colleges were now being encouraged to produce 'enterprising' students fit for employment in a competitive world, and being expected themselves to show enterprise in competing for the resources to do so.[1]

This was a prospect which dismayed many academics, in Chester as across the UK, and Seaborne himself, so assured when it came to dealing with senior university colleagues and with local and regional authorities, would not have found it a congenial environment. However the College was extremely fortunate at this juncture to find a new Principal who – not least through having grown up in a highly successful business family in the north-east of England – had the skills and experience to seize the opportunities which went with the fresh challenges now lying in wait. Revd Edmund

('Ned') Binks was a graduate of King's College London and hence the first Principal since Chritchley not to have studied at Oxford or Cambridge; he was also the first since Astbury in 1935 already to be ordained at the time of his appointment. During 18 years as chaplain and then founder Director of the Careers Service he had left his mark on St John's College York, where he had been a key player in the development of vocationally relevant degree courses as part of its own diversification programme.[2] Since 1983, as Head of S. Katharine's College and Pro-Rector of LIHE of which it was a constituent part, he had balanced the need to foster the College's own identity with the promotion of the institution as a whole.[3] He did not initially apply for the Principalship at Chester but after the governors had interviewed nine candidates and decided to make no appointment, he was one of those approached under a 'head-hunting' exercise, eventually being selected from two interviewees in May 1987.[4] His acceptance of the post meant that a College which since the mid-1960s had appointed a former university vice-chancellor to modernise its governance as a credible higher education institution, and an astute scholar when it was imperative to proclaim its academic credentials, had once again secured the man for the times.

Binks's initial report to the governors, at the first meeting he attended in November 1987, was very similar to the opening salvos fired by Best and Price, both of whom, like him, had already been heads of colleges elsewhere. He praised the commitment of the staff whom he had met, thanked the governors for their support and announced that he had already begun to make some changes, in his case the establishment of an Academic Development Fund to promote new initiatives.[5] But within a matter of months he was tackling issues for which there was no precedent in the institution's history: putting together a bid to the Manpower Services Commission for funding under the Enterprise in Higher Education scheme, based on the College's experience in Work Based Learning and his own track record at York; overseeing a proposal to the English National Board for Nursing, Midwifery and Health Visiting, initially to train nurses in teaching and to offer in-service courses; and guiding the College towards a finely judged but critical decision to entrust students' applications to UCCA (the Universities Central Council on Admissions) in preference to PCAS (the equivalent body for Polytechnics).[6] All these measures were to prove of lasting significance, helping to shape the institution as it is today, and with hindsight it is easy to assume that their success was guaranteed. But in his short contribution on 'The Present State of Play' to the collection of essays published for the College's 150th anniversary in 1989, Binks sounded a cautionary note which made it abundantly clear that he saw such initiatives as the best cards he could play in the latest quest to ensure institutional continuity.

> It is … no time for complacency … As we celebrate 150 years of service in Higher Education, we are also having to brace ourselves for the next survival test … The vocational relevance of all our degree courses, not just our teacher training programmes, will have to be demonstrated to ensure continued funding. The College will also need to establish even closer working relationships with local employers and their financial backing be obtained if we are to mount any major new developments.

He went on to 'recognise that if we are to be more cost effective, many of our traditional teaching styles will need to change' and that in this context 'considerable organisational skill will be required if we are to retain that attention to the personal and professional needs of each student, which has been a distinctive characteristic of the College'.[7]

The Principal's calm demeanour concealed the considerable risks involved in the decisions he was having to take and he was only half-joking when he wrote a few years later that 'I frequently caught myself composing a plausible letter of resignation'.[8] The 1988 Education Reform Act required significant revision to the College's Instrument and Articles of Government, resulting in a reduction in the size of the Governing Body from 38 to 25[9] and vesting greater freedom of action in the Principal as, in effect, the Chief Executive of a corporation; it also, incidentally, turned former local authority colleges into corporate bodies by releasing them from direct LEA control, rendering the term 'voluntary college' redundant as a means to distinguish the others. The communitarian style of College government fostered by de Bunsen and largely maintained by Seaborne was no longer what was demanded and it is no coincidence that the number of decisions on which Academic Board held a vote dropped markedly. But with greater autonomy for the Principal in decision-making went greater accountability and, as a pastor as well as a manager, Binks was acutely aware of his responsibilities for the welfare of an expanding staff and student community and the consequences for them if his judgment was awry. In 1989 the Vice-Chancellor of Liverpool, Graeme Davies, estimated that he spent 40% of his time on financial management. A similar fate befell Binks and, like Davies, he set up private companies as a means of diversifying the sources of institutional income – in Chester's case from conferences and from other enterprises, both in 1990.[10] But behind the businessman was a caring and compassionate educational leader, with a genuine commitment to the values of a liberal education.

Chester was in the second group of HEIs to secure a grant under the Enterprise initiative, by which time the scheme had come under the auspices of the Training Agency. The sum involved, £365,000 over five years, was the largest external award – outside its customary government funding – which the College had received up to that time, although less than that awarded to some larger institutions. Formally launched in the newly completed Molloy Hall on 7 June 1990, to the accompaniment of exhibits from academic departments and in the presence of the Duke of Westminster and a host of employers, many of whom already offered work placements, the Chester scheme was based around 10 'characteristics of enterprise', which were to permeate curriculum development and find expression through partnerships with employers and students' work placements: not to the exclusion of other forms of academic activity but certainly as a prominent feature of the work of every subject. These 'characteristics' were carefully crafted, in a context in which many members of staff were uneasy, to say the least, at the prospect of dancing to a Thatcherite tune. In fact, only one of them, 'the recognition of the importance of wealth creation', could plausibly be argued as a concession to a right-wing agenda and even this – which did not specify whether the 'wealth' was individual, corporate or national and in any case would scarcely be controversial within the British Left today – was balanced by another, albeit awkwardly phrased: 'an ability to develop a critique of those aspects of enterprise which are contentious as to values'. The remaining characteristics were really life skills as relevant to successful academic study as they were to making one's way in the world, whatever one's political persuasion: 'a concern to gain maximum effect from time, materials and effort', 'innovation in problem solving', 'an ability to gain the co-operation of others', 'a capacity to deliver to deadlines' and so on. Implementation was monitored by an Enterprise Advisory Board of sympathetic local employers and the project was also subject to annual review by Training Agency representatives and external assessors.[11]

From a twenty-first century perspective, it may seem surprising that the College could persuade a government committed to cutting public expenditure to give it a substantial sum in return for such obvious, incontestable, ambitions. But while these expressions of enterprise were necessary conditions for the bid to succeed, they were not in themselves sufficient. Chester secured funding, and was awarded much more than it had originally hoped for, mainly because of the substantial employer support it had already enjoyed for its student work placement programme. It also offered something distinctive from other universities and colleges: encouragement to students to manage their own 'enterprise' projects rather than merely participate in those arranged for them. Over the lifetime of the scheme, five successive Student Enterprise Managers were appointed on year-long sabbaticals, the first (from August 1990) being Tony Hursey, a History and English graduate, who oversaw ventures such as computer literacy training, travelling drama productions and the provision of sport for disabled people; the College went on to host the first National Student Enterprise Network conference the following January.[12] As for the academic departments, some were more convincing participants than others, with Geography's contribution under its Head Keith Hilton being quite outstanding. From the outset, staff of that department began offering consultancy services in the specialist areas of remote sensing and hazard evaluation, and by summer term 1991 a total of 46 first-year students were working in groups on one of three projects: business cartography for Marks & Spencer Financial Services (based in the city), a survey of 'above the shop' residential accommodation for Chester City Council Conservation Department, and a land-use survey for Cheshire County Council Planning Department.[13] The scheme was also extended to BEd students through provision for at least four weeks' experience beyond the customary practices in mainstream UK primary schools, a requirement which took students into a variety of educational, commercial and community settings, many of them overseas.[14]

When Binks retired in 1998, the Enterprise Manager who had successfully overseen these developments, Maggie Taylor, wrote that the Principal had seen the injection of funding as an opportunity to 'make mistakes' and learn from them. For once, there was a bit of breathing space in the allocation of money, after the severe constraints of the previous two decades. She also stressed how much the College had learned from the experience when it came to submitting other competitive bids, with one of Binks's aphorisms to the fore: 'always bid for projects that will take the college where it wants to be anyway'. Indeed, the College's Enterprise Unit became the centre for drafting funding bids for a wide range of projects, including one supported by CEWTEC (the Cheshire, Ellesmere Port & Wirral Trading and Enterprise Council) to develop study skills provision for unemployed people with a view to widening access to HE.[15] The Enterprise initiative, in other words, became a means to capture the governmental financial support which the College needed to move forward, helping to secure its future far beyond the five-year term for which funding was granted.

The final report on the project in November 1994 stressed how much had been achieved in those five years. Courses were recast into modules, complete with hours of learning activity defined and methods of assessment matched to learning outcomes, and by 1995–96 all three years of an undergraduate degree were arranged into semesters. Several new 'enterprise modules' were introduced for first-year students, adding vocational relevance to academic content: 'The Business of Health Care', 'Heritage Management, Interpretation and Presentation', 'Creative Writing', 'Theatre Communication Skills' and 'Exploring Ecology' were cases in point, and alongside them, under the leadership of Katrina Blythe, Technology modules were devised for BEd students covering science, IT and electronic keyboards. Indeed, Technology became for a time a distinct department within Teacher Education – as Professional Studies in Education was re-named in 1993 – and was one of six 'main subjects' (along with English, Mathematics, Science, Religious Education and PE) within a revised three-year BEd introduced for a short period as an alternative to the four-year version in 1994. Meanwhile, under the auspices of the Learning from Experience Trust, a ground-breaking scheme was devised involving Chester and the two universities in Liverpool, whereby Work Based Learning could earn academic credit through the assessment of definable outcomes; this led in turn to second-year work experience placements being formalised into Work Based Learning modules for which marks counted towards a degree, with students having the opportunity to choose a double module of 'Extended Work Based Learning' if they so wished. Alongside all this, the employment rates of Chester graduates, as measured by first destination statistics, kept increasing and stayed ahead of the national average.[16]

It is of course debateable how much would have been accomplished in any case; the 'work based learning for academic credit' project, for example, the only one in the country, was a separate, parallel initiative, also funded from 1990 to 1994. The very least that should be said is that the Enterprise scheme acted as an important catalyst for change, as the College sought to become more flexible and cost-effective in its delivery of academic programmes and as it learned to sharpen its responsiveness to the government's growing emphasis on the inculcation of skills rather than the acquisition of knowledge. Although the concept of 'enterprise' was sometimes stretched to the margins of credibility, at least in the eyes of some members of the academic community, the extra funding did help to buy out staff time for the development of new modules and, in some cases, new pedagogic approaches and new learning materials as well.[17] Chester could see itself as one of a select group of HEIs which had acted upon a government initiative and had made it work; the College was repeatedly cited by the Training Agency as an example of good practice for what it achieved on less money than was awarded elsewhere. These achievements outlived the period of formal funding when it came to an end in 1994: responsibility for student enterprise projects was transferred to the newly reconstituted Student Guidance and Support Services (SGSS) while, reinforced by the many new employer partnerships forged under the scheme, Work Based Learning continued as a key feature of a Chester BA or BSc degree, as it still does today.

Perhaps the most significant outcome of the developments of the early 1990s – to which the Enterprise initiative definitely contributed – was an end to the notion that, whatever else it did, Chester was 'really' a teacher training college. Back in February 1984, Malcolm Seaborne, who as Principal had striven heroically to ensure the survival of the College through the development of new degrees and diplomas, had assured the Governing Body 'that diversification had been undertaken to complement, and not displace, the teacher training courses'; the governors had responded by agreeing unanimously 'that any proposals which might adversely affect the College's primary role of teacher training should be regarded as an issue of major principle'.[18] In the closing years of that decade, teacher trainees still made up about half the total student body. But there was no future in clinging to this position – ultimately derived from origins as an early-Victorian teacher training foundation – if Chester College was to survive in a competitive, market-oriented environment where BEd numbers were capped (from 1994 by the newly formed Teacher Training Agency) but those for other courses were open to a bidding process. Accordingly, the final report on the Enterprise initiative was proud to proclaim that 'five years ago, the College was seen as a teacher training institution; now it is recognised for its enterprise, influence and the capacity of its students and graduates to take responsibility in the workplace'.[19]

There was in fact another good reason why, by the mid-1990s, Chester College could no longer be seen as primarily engaged in teacher training. Back in May 1983 Seaborne had presented a paper both to Academic Board and to the Governing Body entitled 'Present Situation, Future Developments'. Prompted by links established mainly through Health & Community Studies and the PE department, this had included the possibility of working with Oswestry School of Physiotherapy and Chester School of Nursing in the delivery of what were described as 'full-time diversified courses'.[20] This was not immediately followed up – Academic Board 'received the paper with interest' – but 18 months later the Dean of Professional Studies, Leon Boucher, formally proposed that the College should become a 'centre for the training of orthoptists', an idea which attracted an advisory HMI visit in

February 1985 before petering out.[21] These flirtations with various branches of healthcare became more promising from 1986, when the UK Central Council for Nursing, Midwifery and Health Visiting (forerunner of the Nursing and Midwifery Council) published 'Project 2000', a scheme to raise the status of their professions through vesting training in the higher education sector, with a DipHE as the minimum qualification. The Voluntary Sector Consultative Council, representative at that time of the non-LEA colleges, had already established a working party on nurse education by the beginning of that year and Revd John Carhart, who had led the development of Health & Community Studies since its inception with great success, had the foresight to attend its meetings. This led in turn to discussions being held at the College in April between staff with relevant expertise and representatives of local nurse training schools.[22] Carhart went on to become Dean of Academic Studies in succession to Fawcett in summer 1988 and was thus well-placed to build upon these preliminary overtures once the government in May of that year accepted the thrust of 'Project 2000', and the incoming Principal put his weight behind diversification in this direction.

Discussions duly took place with Chester and Wirral Schools of Nursing from autumn 1988 onwards, leading initially to the College providing some in-service training for small groups of nurses at the Countess of Chester Hospital; in September 1989, after approval from the English National Board, a Nurse Teachers' Certificate was launched as well, extended a few months later to teachers of midwives as well. All this could be seen as a natural extension of the College's traditional role in teacher training – it was Ken Bryan of Education who was applauded by Binks for his development of the Certificate course – but it led to further collaboration over the next two years, with other aspects of training being shared between the College and the Chester and Wirral Schools, plus an extension of activity to the Isle of Man.[23] Meanwhile, Binks secured funding from the health authorities towards the provision of teaching and administrative accommodation for nurse education on campus, which released much-needed space at hospital sites; this was incorporated into a scheme already in hand for a major westward extension to the library, to run parallel to the canal, all of which was ready to be opened by the end of 1991.[24]

These initiatives gave the College a substantial income stream from a new source, ultimately the Department of Health. It was not, however, guaranteed to last. Early in 1991 the Mersey Region Health Authority announced its intention to have a single Nursing School for the whole of its area south of the river, a prospect which, for those HEIs involved so far, appeared to offer a virtual 'all or nothing' outcome to a fresh competition.

This could have spelled the end of the College's active interest in nurse education but the recent provision of dedicated teaching space gave Chester some advantage and in the event it was duly selected. In a highly competitive bidding process, the College's case was presented jointly by Binks and the Principal of the (now-amalgamated) Chester and Wirral College of Nursing, Dorothy Marriss, who argued successfully on the basis of a track record of effective and cost-efficient collaboration and a commitment to further development. Accordingly, from September 1992, the College was offering both a full-time three-year DipHE programme of initial nurse training and a part-time modular programme for qualified nurses and midwives leading to a degree; other programmes soon followed, including a BSc in Professional Practice of Nursing, Midwifery and Health Visiting launched in January 1994 and later an MA in Professional Practice as well. Training staff from the former Chester and Wirral College and, shortly afterwards, those from Crewe and Macclesfield, were transferred to College employment; Marriss herself was appointed as Chester College's first Dean of Nursing & Midwifery. All this involved lengthy and delicate negotiations over funding and staff contracts – not completed with the Regional Health Authority until 1994 – and it entailed complex logistical arrangements, with training embracing midwifery and various specialist branches of nursing being spread across several hospital sites in the county. But alongside the financial benefits to the College went a significant boost to student numbers, just over 1,000 extra by October 1992. Despite some temporary health authority cutbacks to training in the middle years of the decade, there had been only a small decline by the late 1990s.[25]

This major development, alongside the Enterprise initiative which ran parallel to it, called for a change in the College's self-image. The Governing Body acknowledged as much when in June 1993 it acceded to a request to admit a senior member of the local health authority, Marion Needham, and the chairman of the College's Enterprise Board, Andrew Wood, as non-voting advisory members. Three years earlier the College had acquired a new logo, intended to convey a more dynamic institution than that implied by the familiar shield with its red cross, wheatsheaf and Latin motto. However, this claret and blue device, loosely based on the original College buildings with a series of gables which simultaneously evoked 'dreaming spires' and rockets being launched to the skies, always generated mixed feelings and last appeared in 2003; the shield came back into favour for all official documentation as the College chose to stress its long heritage once it had acquired its own taught degree awarding powers in August of that year. More significantly, the mission statement was redrafted early in 1992, evidently with the full approval of the governors, and the stated purposes of the College now made reference to 'widening of access', 'professional training', 'vocational and personal development', collaboration with employers, supplements to central government funding, and 'opportunities to give systematic consideration to the personal and social challenge of Christian teachings'. From hereon, Chester was a College 'founded to prepare students, within an institution guided by Christian values, for careers of service'. 'Christian values' echoed Slade's insistence in his opening-day sermon of 1842 that the College should display 'Christian principles'. 'Careers of service', however, clearly extended the original concept of that service as being that of the teacher.[26] Any reservations the governors had previously entertained about this reinterpretation of the foundational mission had evidently disappeared.

Through the early 1990s, the national student population increased rapidly, in response to funding council encouragement towards institutional expansion. These years have been seen as marking the transition towards 'mass participation' in British higher education, with the age-participation index for young adults in England rising from 16% to 28% between 1989 and 1993,[27] although these headline figures conceal the reality that students from better-off families were the main beneficiaries of the expansion.[28] To its credit, the College did seek to address the issue of widening participation, with Binks taking the lead in establishing a Cheshire Access Federation, designed to facilitate the progression of local FE college students to higher education, and becoming its first chairman early in 1991; the first students on an access route from West Cheshire College (formerly Chester College of FE) arrived in September 1992.[29] But the upward curves in numbers and income could not go on forever. The government's autumn statement of 1992 signalled a reining in of HE expenditure and, even though the College was (unusually) allowed a 10% increase in full-time funded numbers as late as 1994–95, for the rest of his Principalship Binks was wrestling with the impact of curbs on full-time undergraduate numbers (mediated through a scheme known as MASN, or Maximum Aggregate Student Numbers), coupled with significant cuts in funding per student.

Fortunately, part-time and postgraduate recruitment – outside the MASN – continued to rise, with Humanities developing its own part-time BA in 1994 and a plethora of new postgraduate programmes being validated, led by an MSc in Environmental Biology in 1991 and an MA in Victorian Studies in 1992; Master's programmes including Counselling Skills, Exercise & Nutrition Science, Environmental Science, Information Systems, Health & Community Studies, Occupational Health & Fitness, Landscape Heritage & Society,

Applied Theology and Fine Art followed in the next three years, with more to come. By 1998, an additional degree ceremony had had to be introduced, in March, for postgraduates along with Nursing and Midwifery students who had gained a diploma.[30] Meanwhile, PGCE secondary numbers were also increased in 1994, allowing the addition of Physical Education as a strand and hence the partial revival of secondary training in PE which had characterised the institution in its 'Wing College' days prior to 1983.[31]

Another factor behind buoyant student recruitment was the College's decision to enter the UCCA admissions system with effect from the cycle leading to September 1990 entry, after which applications for full-time programmes increased substantially. The choice of whether to allow undergraduate recruitment to be entrusted to UCCA or to PCAS rested on perceptions of whether candidates were more likely to regard the College as an alternative to universities or polytechnics. Accordingly, the decision was a significant statement of how the institution saw its personality within the sector. When in June 1988 Academic Board voted 26:2 in favour of UCCA, with two abstentions, they were still only 'advising' the Principal 'on the basis of the evidence so far available'; the College came under the polytechnics umbrella – the PCFC – for funding purposes and it was necessary to ensure that Chester and LIHE, both affiliated to the University of Liverpool, were of one mind. In the event, Binks took the executive decision to join UCCA – 'following their advice' as Academic Board minutes were careful to record – and it proved to be right.[32] The overall target figure set by NAB for total College numbers for 1989–90 was 1,113 FTE, six less than the actual figure for the previous year. In 1990–91 the FTE stood at 1,800 and in 1991–92 2,144. By June 1993 full-time BA and BSc numbers alone were in four figures, at 1,060, and there were a further 739 full-time BEd and PGCE students, 1,690 part-time Diploma and Master's students and 978 student nurses and midwives. In October 1995 full-time registrations, other than for Nursing and Midwifery, reached their highest level yet, at 2,418; with a further 2,323 part-time registrations and 737 Nursing and Midwifery students, that made a grand total of 5,478, the highest of Binks's tenure. They fell off slightly to 5,173 in 1996 but recovered to 5,325 in his final year.[33] At a national level, total student numbers in Britain almost doubled from 937,000 in 1985–86 to £1.72 million in 1995–96, a fact which prompted the government to implement the policy of retrenchment thereafter.[34] At Chester, as we have seen, the rate of increase had been appreciably higher.[35]

Growth on this scale, facilitated not only by the successful integration of nursing and midwifery but also by a reputation for cost-efficiency, carefully cultivated with successive funding councils, saw the student-staff ratio in most areas of the College rise from 14.5:1 in 1988 to 20:1 two years later, although the inclusion of visiting lecturers brought this down and the appointment of extra technical and secretarial staff also mitigated its effects; there were obviously additional appointments thereafter, including a dozen in 1991 and 1992 funded from the PCFC's permitted extra numbers, but this became generally accepted as an approximate ratio, and one liable to be exceeded in the Humanities. Between 1989 and 1994, while total student numbers rose by 224% (and FTE by 172%), FTE academic support staff increased by 65%, library expenditure by 145% but FTE teaching staff by only 38%.[36] That said, the calibre of academic staff appointed in these years of expansion was impressive. Many of them were scholars early in their careers who brought to the College experience of teaching and research in universities which, in the short term, enhanced the quality of programme content and delivery and in the longer term brought energy and ideas to an institution which would later embark on its own journey towards a more elevated status.

The increased workload implied by the figures in the previous paragraph failed to diminish the enthusiasm of academic staff for devising new programmes of study: apparent not only at postgraduate level, as we have seen, but also in the repackaging of modules into new 'named pathways' of undergraduate study, which made for a more attractive offer than the previous restriction to a degree in Combined Subjects. This in turn was facilitated by a new University Ordinance with associated regulations passed in the autumn of 1995 which introduced 'exit awards' short of a full degree based on the accumulation of credit points – CertHE and DipHE – and permitted a variety of programme titles. Theology & Religious Studies (TRS), as Religious Studies had been re-named under Fawcett's successor as Head, Ruth Ackroyd, had led the way by introducing a Bachelor of Theology degree (initially via a part-time programme) in time for a September 1995 start, ahead of the revision of the generic Ordinance. This initiative was followed in 1996 by the approval of BScs in Applied Biology, Geography & Geomatics, Mathematics & Computer Science and (its reverse) Computer Science & Mathematics. These were, in effect, the College's first 'Single Honours' degree programmes, other than in the specialist areas of nursing and midwifery; their well-established forerunner Health & Community Studies, and the recently introduced part-time BA Humanities, should more accurately be described as multi- and interdisciplinary programmes.[37]

Increased numbers and added complexity necessitated some restructuring of institutional management. When the College librarian Hilda Stoddard retired in summer 1989, her successor Christine Stockton, previously sub-librarian at the University of Sheffield, was appointed Director of Learning Resources, a sign that – with computer use now burgeoning even among the most conservative-minded staff – the more integrated approach which Stoddard had herself called for prior to the opening of the Resource Centre in 1983 was at last coming to pass.[38] In 1992, David Stevens was appointed to the new post of Dean of Administration and Finance, relieving some of the burden upon the Bursar; an Assistant Dean of Teacher Education, Bob Swettenham, was also installed. Two years later, all academic and professional studies were divided between four schools, two already existing (Education and Nursing & Midwifery), two newly created on Carhart's retirement as Dean of Academic Studies (Arts & Humanities and Science & Health). Glyn Turton, Head of English, became Dean of Arts & Humanities, overseeing the departments of Art, Drama, English, History, Modern Languages and TRS. David Cotterrell, formerly Director of the Centre for Human Biology at the University of Leeds, took the equivalent post in Science & Health, a school embracing Computer Science (a separate department since 1987), Mathematics, Biology, Psychology, Geography, PE & Sports Science and Health & Community Studies.[39]

Against this, the post of Dean of Students was not renewed when the holder since 1985, the highly regarded former Head of Mathematics David Hughes, retired in summer 1994.[40] The opportunity was taken to reorganise provision for student discipline, welfare and support, with Lesley Cooke of PE & Sports Science becoming Director of SGSS, initially on a fixed-term contract. This was made permanent in 1997 after she had established SGSS as an 'academic-related … section within the College', proactive in addressing a host of issues relevant to students. In the following year, for example, Andrew Lilley was appointed to a 0.2 post as Disability Co-ordinator and Development Officer but many projects were undertaken by current or former students, as demand for services grew both in volume and in diversity. SGSS was described in the 1998 undergraduate prospectus as providing 'an integrated network of information, advice and support throughout the College' ranging from oversight of the personal academic tutor system to careers guidance, medical liaison, counselling, the student mentoring scheme and 'student rights and responsibilities', the latter eventually enshrined in a Student Charter in 1999.[41] As for the Deans, the net increase in their number meant that, with the Deputy Principal and Bursar, they formed a sizeable senior management team, inevitably distancing Academic Board somewhat from the key decision-making role it had exercised at its inception during the more leisurely paced days of de Bunsen. Even so, the Board still had plenty of committees and sub-committees through which an ambitious member of academic staff could make a mark; in discussion with University of Liverpool representatives who had queried the size and structure of the College's committees, this was defended 'as a consequence of the highly participatory style of College management'.[42]

Meanwhile, new partners were sought wherever there was a shared institutional mission and purpose. Memoranda of Co-operation covering the collaborative delivery of specified programmes were signed with several institutions, including the University of Hong Kong School of Professional and Continuing Education, the Welsh College of Horticulture, Reaseheath College, Isle of Man College (and also with the Manx government), Halton College, Blackburn College of FE, Chester and Ellesmere Port Psychology Service, Cheshire Military Museum and St Deiniol's Library, Hawarden.[43] The MSc in Exercise & Nutrition Science began to be delivered both in Hong Kong and Singapore, with students from Hong Kong, often exceeding 40 per annum, also becoming mainstays of a programme whereby already qualified teachers could obtain a BEd.[44] TRS was particularly successful in forging relationships with external bodies, becoming actively involved – for example – in the Northern Ordination Course, securing scholarships from the Lutheran church for students from Ethiopia, collaborating with the Church of England's Central Board of Education in the validation of lay training programmes, delivering a programme of Reader training with the diocese of Chester through a combination of the Church Colleges' Certificate, a CertHE and – in subsequent years – a DipHE, and joining with various partners both in Cheshire and in London in the delivery of its MA in Adult and Church School Education.[45] There were formal College agreements also in 1993 and 1994 with institutions as diverse as Alverno College, Wisconsin (for staff and student exchanges), with Walbottle High School, Newcastle (to encourage applications from their pupils), and with the city health authority of St Petersburg. This Russian partnership, facilitated by a grant from the European 'Know-How Fund', allowed nurses from the city's Medical College No. 1 to qualify as Nurse Tutors, the first in the country to do so, duly recognised by the award of Liverpool degrees late in 1995.[46]

New buildings were also required, while old ones were adapted to other uses. St Thomas's Vicarage, a late Victorian residence adjacent to the church immediately south of the College, was purchased in 1988 and became a base for the English department; a new student accommodation block was built in the grounds in 1992 and named 'John Douglas Court' after the noted Chester architect who had designed the Vicarage. Bradbury House ceased to be student accommodation in 1988 and was refitted instead as a Student Services Centre, including offices for the chaplain and careers advisor; it also became

Figure 33: Principal Binks helps HRH the Princess Margaret to cut the tape at the opening of the student village in 1989. On the right is Dean of Students, David Hughes.

the base for the Housekeeping department, whose staffing had risen to 35 by the turn of the decade. When Princess Margaret paid her second visit to the College on 17 May 1989, as part of the 150th anniversary celebrations, she laid a foundation stone for the Molloy Hall – completed the following spring – and cut a tape to open the new student village, although she declined a cup of tea from students already living there. An all-year-round income-generating 'Gladstone Short Course and Conference Centre', incorporating the original Principal's house, was also ready for use by the Easter Vacation of 1990, with shops fronting the terrace at the rear of the western wing; 'Bookland' took over the bookshop here in 1992. A new porters' lodge was created in 1991 at the Exton Park entrance through conversion of Rutland Villa, the property at the corner with Parkgate Road. The 'Prairie' courtyard between the rear of Old College and the front of the tower block was landscaped in 1992. The following year the former School was converted from its latest incarnation as an Art and Music block into a base for the Geography department and for more general College use, with a second, 140-seat lecture theatre being created; it acquired the name of its late-Victorian architect, Beswick, at the same time. In 1993 the dining halls were extended through the addition of conservatories. Further purchases of property off-campus included a former stable block at 91 Parkgate Road and land at the bottom of King Street where Powys Court was built, both in 1994, to add some much-needed student accommodation.[47]

Meanwhile, a major landfill project in the north-west of the campus in the early 1990s finished off the various levelling schemes which had been going on intermittently since Principal Thomas's time, enabling this area to serve both as a car park and as a site for further buildings. Planning permission was obtained for a linked group of three to be erected roughly parallel with the canal, first for Art and Technology (now the 'Best building') in 1992 and later for Psychology, Mathematics and Computer Science ('Chritchley') formally opened in October 1995; a Sports Hall, named after the Bursar Raymond Downes, whose financial acumen had enabled so much property development to be accomplished, completed this scheme in 1998, a year after his death from a short illness as he was on the point of retiring. The complex replaced playing fields and, towards the north-western corner a totally undeveloped tract which Bruce Ing of the Biology department described in 1989 as 'the most prolific' area of the campus from the perspective of Natural History, a haven for wild flora and fauna.[48] There was some compensation in 1996 when the steep-sided depression which bisects the car park, where landfill could not take place because of the need to preserve access to a mains sewer below the previous ground level, was converted into a wild area through the work of student conservation volunteers led by Cynthia Burek and Juliet Leadbeater of Biology; although trees have now grown to the point

where it cannot be used, as originally hoped, 'as a restful area on campus', it remains an excellent, albeit smaller, wildlife haven.[49]

The willows, lesser celandines, wrens, rabbits and voles which featured in Ing's paper were not the only casualties of this period of rapid upheaval. Concern to rationalise the

Figure 34: The wildlife area near the north-west corner of the Parkgate Road campus, with a sequence of 1990s buildings to the right: Best (foreground), Chritchley and Downes (in distance). The depression running through the car park indicates the ground level prior to the landfill operation which eradicated the steep slope in this part of the campus.

expenditure of limited academic resources led the Principal to present Academic Board in May 1988 with various proposals relating to departmental size, funding and student-staff ratios, all of which were approved either unanimously or by substantial majorities. Among them were recommendations to cease recruitment to French and Music after the current year's intake and explore alternative avenues for tuition in languages and music within the College. The obvious implication was that these subject departments, which had a long and distinguished history, were identified for potential closure. It was an uncomfortable meeting, with concern being expressed that '"finance-led" policies could lead to a disregard for studies which are intrinsically worthwhile'; Binks had to remind the Board that 'we were not being asked to approve of the values underlying the current educational system, but plan how we would operate within it'. This was, after all, a time when public perceptions of academia, fed by politicians for whom most lecturers did not vote and by a press which followed their lead, were at a low ebb.[50] In the event, the Head of Languages, Mary Best, responded vigorously to the opportunity to diversify into in-service work and short courses for business people, to such good effect that she saved her department; by 1993 both French and German – the latter added to the portfolio in 1990 – had been recognised as modules within all three years of the undergraduate degree and by 1996 French had equal subject status with any other component of the Combined Subjects degree. Music, however, despite attempts to develop skills for the student body as a whole, especially those intending to teach, was eventually closed, with the two remaining members of staff leaving on redundancy terms in summer 1993.[51]

Another victim of changing times was the *Collegian*, which as a stately record of the progress of events and a vehicle for students and staff to publish their poetry and prose, came to an end with Seaborne's retirement, a century after its inception as loose sheets pinned to the dormitory walls and 99 years after the first printed volume in 1888. It would reappear in a different guise a few years later, and 'year notes' from former students continued to be produced, but the preference now was to proclaim the College's achievements through a much livelier, more glossy periodical entitled *Campus*. This was intended primarily for external readership among the local civic and business community, although it was also distributed free to former students for two years after graduation; it appeared biannually, in January and June, from 1990.[52] In 1993 the *Insider*, soon re-named *Insider Bulletin*, was also introduced, as a means to keep all staff abreast of developments, partly because the College was considering a bid for 'Investors in People' status at the time. In recognition of its expanding role, the Print Unit, without which neither these publications nor a mountain of teaching materials would ever have been produced, moved into the ground floor of Astbury House in 1997.[53]

The reality was that as the College expanded and diversified, it was inevitable that some sense of communal identity was lost, and the Corporate Plan submitted to the PCFC in 1989 recognised as much. In presenting it to Academic Board, Binks stressed that 'the most valuable assets of Chester College were its relatively small size and its Christian foundation', as a result of which 'it could offer opportunities to study for a degree in a Christian community on a manageable human scale'. Accordingly, a maximum size of 1,400 undergraduates was favoured – itself higher than previous 'optimum totals' and destined soon to be exceeded – but 'as this is not an economically viable number, it would be necessary for the College to run a number of satellite activities which were related to the undergraduate programme'.[54] Nurse Education was identified as one of these satellites, and clearly, with the advent of nursing and midwifery tutors with a very different background to most academic staff, spread across Cheshire at different hospital sites, it was impossible to retain any semblance of the notion that, even among lecturers, everyone knew everyone else.

As for the student body, these years were a time of growing financial pressure. The introduction of the Student Loans Company in 1990 was a sign that the government had abandoned any pretence that maintenance grants were adequate to meet living costs; even discounting this 'official' loan scheme, by 1993 the average UK student was graduating with a debt in excess of £1,000.[55] Paid part-time work, in term-time as well as vacations, became the only way that many students could finance their way through College and this inevitably meant less time for the 'rounded undergraduate experience' which their lecturers had enjoyed in a previous generation. In June of that year, the Students' Union (SU) President, Pippa Harding, told the governors that in her opinion students were 'becoming more isolated and less involved in community activities'. Similar views had been expressed in the *Collegian* three decades before, but the institution was now so diverse in its activities that it was really several communities, not one.[56] By the early 1990s there were far more students in individual academic departments than there had been in the whole College in Astbury's day; within nursing and midwifery, few of the early intake felt any close affinity with the College, especially if they were based elsewhere in the county. Even so, that great student institution, the College Rag – 'the biggest event in the college diary' according to the Union Handbook of 1985–86 – generated sufficient enthusiasm to raise £26,000 in 1992 and some £30,000, the highest figure ever, two years later;

throughout the 1990s it was still being proclaimed in successive prospectuses as a reason to come to Chester, 'a great deal of fun' and 'an object lesson in organisation and team work'. But even this subsequently went into decline, a victim largely of changing student attitudes and priorities as they themselves were increasingly hard-pressed financially and were having to contribute to their fees. A formal request to the SU towards the end of 1998 that it be moved from its traditional October date to the depths of winter, to occupy the interval between semesters early in the New Year, did nothing to help its cause, nor did a growing tendency for fundraising activities to focus on the student community itself as donors, rather than the general public. It was last mentioned in the prospectus for 1999 and last reported to the governors in 2002: essentially a twentieth- rather than twenty-first century phenomenon, successfully replaced by various volunteering initiatives arranged by SGSS which could be undertaken throughout the year rather than in one concentrated effort.[57]

As the governors recognised in their response to Harding's comments, a changing student outlook was typical of UK higher education as the twentieth century drew to its close. Catering was adjusted from 1997 to meet evolving demand, with the new Catering Manager, Ian White, serving cooked English breakfasts until 11.30 a.m. every weekday and introducing a bistro to the de Bunsen Centre, so restoring the building's original role as a supplementary outlet for refreshments.[58] Choral and Orchestral Societies lived on, and sporting achievement continued to be impressive, facilitated by the resurfacing of the all-weather pitch with AstroTurf and the installation of new floodlights overlooking it in 1994. Ian Tordoff, a third-year Sports Science and Geography student, was called up to the Great Britain Olympics kayak squad in 1991, at a time when Lesley Cooke was the squad's psychologist; he went on to join the staff of the department before moving to a local authority position, becoming National Wildwater Canoeing Champion on several occasions and in 2005 breaking the record for crossing the English Channel in a kayak. Jon Sleightholme (1991–94) was selected to play rugby union as a winger for England against France in January 1996 and went on to represent his country a further 11 times. The College Swimming Club won the British Colleges Championship in both 1991 and 1992 and in the latter year, the men's basketball, men's volleyball and women's water polo teams also triumphed in British Colleges competitions; six years later the rugby league team won the British Universities Sports Association finals, with three players being selected for the England Students squad in the Home Nations Championship. Meanwhile, George Courtney, a Geography student of 1959–61 whose teaching practice report had commended his good positioning in the classroom, refereed the European Cup-Winners Cup final of 1989 and was England's representative referee at the 1990 World Cup Finals, as he had been four years earlier.[59]

Just as the College was bound to be affected by the changing circumstances of its students, so it had to respond to the growing importance attached within the sector to 'quality assurance'. In 1991, Grace Jones as Deputy Principal had to answer the concerns of Academic Board members about a new requirement on each department to produce an annual review of its courses; she also produced a paper entitled 'Achieving Quality Assurance in Course Provision' which was to be inserted into the Staff Handbook. As part of the overall process, departmental quinquennial reviews and annual Dean of School's reviews were also introduced. Jones took early retirement in March 1992 and that summer Binks was asked if he envisaged appointing a 'quality controller' at senior level. His reply was that 'for the time being there was no intention' of doing so, but in reality the new Deputy Principal, Patricia Roberts, who arrived in September from South Bank Polytechnic – soon to be University – London, effectively fulfilled this role. Roberts had been Dean of the Faculty of the Built Environment at South Bank and brought both academic expertise beneficial to a College keen to expand its physical estate and managerial experience in an institution very different from Chester. It is also worth saying that, like her predecessor, she had a keen concern for the interests of all members of staff, those in support departments as well as academics; she personally conducted the staff development interviews for some senior support staff and had a clause written into the College's partnership agreement with the University of North Carolina at Asheville entitling administrative as well as academic staff to apply for an exchange.[60]

At the beginning of the decade, the College was still subject to visits by HMI, with PCFC's readiness to take account of HMI concerns about quality through withholding funds adding bite to the process. Happily, History, Art, Mathematics, Computer Studies and Education all emerged well from inspections between 1988 and 1991.[61] However, once the provisions of the 1992 Further and Higher Education Act came into force from 1 April 1993 – ending the distinction between universities and polytechnics, abolishing the CNAA and replacing the UFC and PCFC with Higher Education Funding Councils for each of the four home countries – only initial teaching training remained under HMI scrutiny. Nursing & Midwifery also retained its own professional inspection regime but the quality of the College's provision in general became subject to review by the new Higher Education Funding Council (HEFCE). The process, initially known as Teaching Quality Assessment, was at first conducted with such lack of consistency that it was bound to arouse scepticism. History in autumn 1993 and Geography a year later were deemed 'satisfactory' with very little feedback, on the evidence of self-assessments alone. Computer Science, however, was given a similar 'satisfactory' rating in spring 1994 only after a visit, the report commending several illustrations of staff commitment to their students but criticising under-investment in equipment when this was largely a reflection of low HEFCE funding. English followed in the spring of 1995 and this time, despite the department under the leadership of its Head, Chris Walsh, modestly claiming to be 'satisfactory', its self-assessment was so impressive that it generated a visit, leading in turn to a well-deserved 'excellent' rating.[62]

Thereafter, HEFCE devoted more resources to the exercise and appointed teams to visit every subject department in every institution, according to its cycle of review, with numerical grades being awarded for each of six aspects of provision (curriculum design, content and organisation; student support and guidance; learning resources; and so on). The first department visited under this revised methodology was Languages in January 1996, when the personal commendation of the Head, Mary Best, was an unusual but particularly gratifying outcome, given her refusal to let this provision go under at the end of the previous decade; Drama, Dance & Theatre Studies – which had only recently added 'Dance' to its title and would later change again to Performing Arts – was also reviewed successfully in February 1998.[63] It was a subject review system which would continue until 2001, surviving even the transfer of responsibility from HEFCE's Quality Assurance Division to the new, independent, Quality Assurance Agency for Higher Education (the QAA) in 1998, and it would give many academic and support staff at the College a taste of the rigours they would face before university status was granted in years to come.

In a bid to secure research funding, the College also entered the competitive 'research selectivity exercise' (or research assessment exercise: RAE) run by the UFC in 1992. It had not entered the two previous exercises, in 1986 and 1989, and on this occasion the results demonstrated that, despite significant work being undertaken by certain individuals, at an institutional level there was a lack of co-ordinated direction. All subject departments entered their research-active staff but only History achieved an income-generating outcome, and that only a '2' rating, defined as 'research quality that equates to attainable levels of national excellence in up to half of the research activity submitted'. Even so, this was sufficient to yield useful funding under different heads of £40,000 per annum for the next four years, a quarter of which was invested in research elsewhere in the College according to competitive departmental bids. By December 1992 the post of Research Co-ordinator had been created on a 0.2 FTE remission of timetable – Roy Alexander of Geography was appointed – and it had been agreed to fund four PhD studentships; the first doctorates resulting from this were awarded in 1998, to Diane Spivey and Neil Thurston, both Geography students.[64] A Research Committee, reporting to Academic Board, was established in 1993, and an Applied Mathematics Research Group and a Centre for Victorian Studies soon followed as focal points for research. The College came to define itself as 'a research-minded teaching institution' and during the next academic year the Research Committee declared its intent to establish its own research degrees subcommittee and to produce its own annual research report distinct from that of the University of Liverpool.[65] All this helped towards improved results in the RAE of 1996, when History, Applied Mathematics and a cluster of staff entered as 'Other Studies & Professions Allied to Medicine' all gained '2' ratings,[66] with more funding being distributed as a result. However, given the long lead-time before research investment was liable to pay off, the benefits were only properly seen in the next exercise, that of 2001.

Meanwhile, relations with the University of Liverpool were further refined. On the surface, this was most apparent in permission being given for degree ceremonies to be held in Chester Cathedral, with the University mace and accompanying dignitaries making a special journey to Chester.[67] This had been mooted as far back as October 1978 but, in that sensitive period, there had been concern that it might be perceived as weakening the ties between College and University and, on advice from the University's Dean of College Studies, who liaised between the two institutions, it had not been pursued. However, the idea resurfaced in 1986, when increased numbers meant that Chester and LIHE had to have their own separate ceremonies in any case.[68] The College's 150th anniversary provided a fitting occasion to take the plunge and the Cathedral degree ceremony on 11 July 1989 rounded off a series of commemorative events which had begun on 25 January with a civic reception in the Town Hall and a pageant-style Founders' Day service the next day, and had then proceeded through various dramatic and musical performances (including a Victorian Music Hall), the royal visit, public lectures by the celebrity botanist David Bellamy and the elder statesman Lord Jenkins, on to a Victorian Open Day and Midsummer Ball.[69] The spectacle of a procession in academic dress making its way past the Chester Cross to the Cathedral after robing in the Guildhall in Watergate Street gave the city a first glimpse of what hosting a university might look like, although this particular piece of exhibitionism was never repeated. The 1989 ceremony itself remained a 'one-off' until it was revived on a regular basis in 1993, following a vigorous campaign by the 1990–91 SU President, Rob Wotton, who secured the support of the Dean and Chapter, police and city business leaders; thereafter, it remained the norm to hold Liverpool ceremonies for the College's graduands at Chester Cathedral until University of Chester degrees began to be awarded in the same venue instead.[70]

Beyond all this, the University had begun to express interest, towards the close of Seaborne's time as Principal, in 'closer constitutional relationships' with its affiliated colleges; even 'merger' had been floated as a possibility at one stage. This was a tribute to the esteem in which the colleges were by now being held, but by 1990 that esteem was being expressed rather differently: not through closer links but through discussions about greater autonomy. An end, after 1988, to the practice of first-year students being 'bussed' to the University for a welcoming reception and the readiness to conceive of a degree ceremony outside Liverpool were symptomatic of this new thinking. In May 1992, after some delay while financial adjustments were agreed, the University Senate gave its approval in principle to the colleges becoming accredited (rather than affiliated) institutions, with much greater devolved authority over matters such as assessment and course approval and review; although an annual report on matters of quality assurance would still have to be submitted, and the University would have the final say on the College's choice of external examiners, for all routine purposes, even including

assessment regulations and procedures for calculating degree classifications, Chester and LIHE could manage themselves. The University duly sent an accreditation panel on 25 and 26 February 1993 but this had sufficient reservations about matters such as the clarity of quality assurance policies and the rigour of programme monitoring for the grant of the new status to be deferred until further meetings had taken place and a comprehensive Quality Assurance Handbook (QAH) had been compiled.

Figure 35: The silver birch tree (right) planted in 1994 to mark the grant by the University of Liverpool of Accredited College status. Beyond the other birch tree (left) is the embankment originally created under the first Principal, Arthur Rigg, as part of a landscaping scheme to separate his own house and gardens from the terrace below.

Irritating though this was at the time, Liverpool's strict approach would stand the College in good stead in the future. Accreditation for undergraduate provision was finally confirmed by the University Senate to take effect from 1 September 1994, and when renewed in 1998, accreditation was formally extended to cover postgraduate programmes as well. At the close of the governors' meeting of March 1994 at which success was reported, the Deputy Principal and her secretary Christine Lynas planted a silver birch tree near the College entrance off Cheyney Road to celebrate the achievement and – as Roberts put it – to make 'some small recompense to the environment' for the amount of paper the process had consumed.[71] Since, in the wild, this is a 'pioneer' species and, as trees go, relatively short-lived, it was an inspired choice.

It is in developments such as these that the first steps in the foothills of the ascent to university status can be discerned. The removal of the distinction between universities and polytechnics in 1992 threatened to diminish the perceived status of those left as 'colleges'. Accordingly, Academic Board in December 1991 had expressed a preference for Chester to become a 'university college' in recognition of its place within the HE rather than the FE sector and the following June, with the polytechnics now looking forward to a future as universities, Binks openly discussed the College's prospects of joining them in the pages of *Campus*. He acknowledged several strengths but also the need to develop research and 'at least one new major area of study'. At the following month's meeting of Academic Board, when Alexander had called for more co-ordination of research, Binks had reiterated that if the College was to receive University status it would be essential that there was a higher research profile.[72]

So in November 1993, after Liverpool had invited the College to use the phrase 'a College of the University of Liverpool' in its promotional material, the governors duly expressed their appreciation, showed some concern about implied loss of autonomy and declared their wish 'to secure the title "University College Chester",' an aspiration which they hoped Liverpool would support.[73] The words 'Chester' and 'university' were now being uttered in the same breath and – as the decade wore on – with increasing confidence. By the close of 1994, some colleges of higher education were already calling themselves 'university colleges' in order to affirm their place in the sector, and there was concern at Chester that, despite official disapproval from HEFCE and the Department for Education and in the absence of any authoritative constructive guidance on the matter, the College was being disadvantaged by declining to use the descriptor. This applied most obviously in terms of prospective students' perceptions of different institutions, but Roberts, who had a good ear for 'quality' issues through her membership of HEFCE's advisory body, the Quality Assessment Committee, also thought lack of the title made it more difficult to secure external funding for research; her reference as part of her argument to the College's aspiration to secure research degree awarding powers is another indication that routes towards university status were already being mapped out.[74] Eventually, in February 1996, after LIHE had adopted the name 'Liverpool Hope University College', towards the end of 1995, the College governors decided that 'the time had come to affirm the nature of its work and protect its recruitment'. Binks was duly authorised to ascertain the opinion of Liverpool's Vice-Chancellor about Chester's adoption of the title, and from 1 May 1996 'University College Chester: a College of the University of Liverpool' formally came into being, albeit not in the eyes of the government.[75]

There were other signs around this time that the institution which would be accorded university status less than 10 years later was taking shape. Back in June 1988 there had been a long and inconclusive discussion at Academic Board over whether it was worthwhile to install an online link to the University of Liverpool Library catalogue. Six years later the Board was welcoming with enthusiasm the forthcoming arrival of a College-wide 'Information Systems Network' which, it was hoped, 'would be easy to use, cost effective to install and which provides secure and reliable service'; an e-mail server was duly provided in the new Chritchley building in 1995 and the whole College, including off-campus departments, had both intranet and internet access by the end of the decade.[76] Meanwhile, in September 1996, TRS moved off campus into former offices in Northgate Street at Vernon Pritchard Court and Chichester House, close to the Northgate church which had been the home of its predecessor, Divinity, in the 1970s. History moved in the same month, abandoning the top of the tower, its base since 1988, for more spacious accommodation in the eighteenth- and nineteenth-century former Blue Coat School, just outside the Northgate itself.[77] The significance of these moves should not be exaggerated: as has been said, TRS had been off campus once before and neither department now occupies these premises. Having sought to capitalise on its high-profile city-centre location, through initiatives such as popular public 'Lunchtime Lectures' series, History returned to the campus – initially with some reluctance – in 2010, after the College decided not to renew the lease from the Blue Coat Foundation on a building which, for all its historical significance, lacked disabled access and was costly to maintain. With more enthusiasm – as the victors in a bidding process – TRS soon transferred to Holly Bank, a well-appointed former school on the opposite side of Parkgate Road from the campus, which had been bought by the College in 1995; this allowed Chichester House to be used instead as administrative offices, mainly for Human Resources and those involved with salaries and finance.[78] Yet with hindsight this departmental diaspora of the mid-1990s can be seen as the early stages of a process, adumbrated in the acquisition of nursing sites across Cheshire a few years earlier, whereby the institution has outgrown the campus to colonise various parts of the city and county: raising its profile, boosting its numbers and diversifying its academic offering in a manner befitting a modern university.

University status would not of course be granted without intense scrutiny and the College had a foretaste of what to expect when it was subjected to a routine quality audit conducted by the Higher Education Quality Council (one of the forerunners of the QAA) in October 1996. Many institutions reviewed during the mid- to late-1990s were found wanting in their handling of processes which, in subsequent years, became embedded as standard practice, and Chester was no exception. Alongside commendations on such matters as staff and student commitment, the development of the QAH and the contributions of SGSS, the Careers Service and the Students' Union, went recommendations about the committee structure, the cumulative effects of resourcing the College's growing portfolio and lack of consistency in the implementation of certain procedures. Essentially, the story was of an institution whose multi-faceted expansion had been impressive but had outrun some aspects of the quality management needed to sustain it. Accordingly, the various recommendations set an agenda for the rearrangement both of committees and of administrative support; in 1997, for example, the Academic Registry was divided into Registry Services on the one hand and a newly constituted Academic Quality Unit on the other, with the latter taking responsibility for revising and updating the QAH.[79] These measures established the structure which would see the institution through to the granting of degree awarding powers – the essential prerequisite of a university title – in 2003.

The context of the College's work began to shift yet again with the publication during 1997 of *Higher Education in the Learning Society*, the report of the National Committee of Inquiry into Higher Education chaired by Sir Ron Dearing. The 'Dearing Report' was the outcome of the most comprehensive investigation into HE in the UK since Robbins had reported in 1963; set up by John Major's Conservative government in 1996, it found itself reporting to its Labour successor after Tony Blair's general election triumph of May 1997. Over the previous two decades, as UK HE student numbers had more than doubled, public funding had risen by only 45%; Dearing was rightly alarmed by chronic under-funding, with the quality of both teaching and research under severe threat, but his recommendations embraced all aspects of the sector's work. There were proposals to foster widening participation; to increase the amount of sub-degree level work (mainly in FE colleges); to establish an Arts and Humanities Research Council and an Institute for Learning and Teaching for academic staff; to give more emphasis to work experience, entrepreneurship and information technology within higher education; to promote students' Progress Files incorporating transcripts of achievement and reflection on personal development; to introduce programme specifications informing students of outcomes at different course stages in terms of knowledge and skills; and to develop a series of subject benchmark statements defining threshold standards.[80]

Programme specifications, with their formulaic descriptions of learning outcomes and module codes, were destined for the same grudging reception at Chester as elsewhere in the sector, but many of these proposals were music to the ears of an institution which already had good access arrangements and close relations with local FE colleges, prided itself on the quality of its teaching and student support, had long incorporated work experience into its provision and had also, through the work at both national and local level of the Academic Registrar Peter Woodhead, been at the forefront in recent years of initiatives to encourage students to keep Records of Achievement. Less welcome, however, was a proposal for more targeted research funding, with the implication that colleges where the main role of research was seen as being to 'underpin teaching' would be marginalised. There was also a call upon the government 'to restrict the use of the title "University College" to those institutions which are in every sense a college which is part of a university under the control of the university's governing body, and to those higher education institutions which have been granted taught degree awarding powers', definitions which certainly excluded Chester. Most controversial were the recommendations on funding. One was to shift the balance away from block grants towards allocations based on student enrolments, a recipe for yet more intense institutional competition. Another was to require graduates in paid employment retrospectively to contribute about 25% of the average cost of HE tuition, through a system administered by the Inland Revenue. It was also proposed that public expenditure on higher education should in future rise in accordance with growth in the country's Gross Domestic Product, but the so-called 'graduate tax' was seen as a means of supplementing this, crucial if the sector was not to continue to subsist on meagre rations.[81] All this signalled a future in which popular institutions would thrive and others potentially go to the wall and in which the beneficiaries of higher education were expected to help pay for the experience, beyond mere maintenance costs.

The recommendations went to various different parties and in one form or another many of them continue to feature in the early twenty-first century landscape of UK higher education. However, on the issue of funding, the incoming Labour government chose to accept the principle of student contributions to tuition but not the methodology set out by Dearing. Instead, through the 1998 Teaching and Higher Education Act, annual tuition fees of £1,000 were to be paid by (or on behalf of) students upfront, albeit with provision through means testing to ensure that those from poorer backgrounds would be exempt. Under the same Act, maintenance grants, already well below subsistence level, were finally abolished except for the least-well-off candidates, to be replaced by extended provision for student loans. All this resulted in the amounts distributed by the Student Loans Company advancing by leaps and bounds. In its first year of operation, 1990–91, the company had loaned out a total of £70 million to some 28% of eligible students, the average sum being £390. By 1997–98, the last year before the new arrangements came into force, it was lending £941 million to 64% of eligible students at an average of £1,530. By 2001–02 these figures had soared: to 81% of eligible students, to an average loan of £3,070, and to a grand total of £2,204 million per annum.[82] Although the government did not relinquish overall control of student numbers through the block grant, in the manner recommended by Dearing, in their own way these measures heralded the fresh era of competitive uncertainty which his Report had envisaged. If students were to be persuaded to apply for higher education when they were being expected to make such a financial commitment, the offering to them would have to be especially attractive.

Just as de Bunsen had considered it right to leave the stage while the James Committee was mapping out a more diversified future – if a future at all – for teacher training colleges, and Seaborne had thought likewise with the advent of a more entrepreneurial, market-driven approach to higher education in the late 1980s, so Binks decided it was time to let someone else lead the College into yet another 'brave new world' of opportunities fraught with challenges and risks – though he might have stayed longer but for health problems. He retired to live in Lewes (Sussex) in March 1998, to the warmest of tributes from colleagues who had all come to admire his skills as business leader, communicator and diplomat, and his capacity to inspire others to give of their best, allied to compassion and self-deprecating humour: he liked to call himself 'just a country vicar', although he became an Honorary Canon of

Chester Cathedral in 1995 (like Thomas and Astbury before him) and was awarded an honorary doctorate by the University of Liverpool in 1998.[83]

Inevitably, some of the projects Binks pursued did not come to pass, for a variety of reasons and not for want of enterprise and commitment on the College's part. Along with the Bursar, Downes, and in the forward-looking spirit of Thomas in the 1920s, he made efforts to buy the green-field site further along Parkgate Road, immediately beyond the railway embankment which forms the northern boundary of the campus; if this was a 'failure' it was only a qualified one, because negotiations did lead to the land being 'zoned' for educational purposes and it was indeed acquired by the institution in the following decade. He sought a stake for the College in Dee House, the Georgian building situated over Chester's Roman amphitheatre, but negotiations eventually came to naught. His hopes for participation with public and private partners in the building of a new performing arts centre in the city ('Chester in Concert'), and for access to the campus from what (in 1992) was described as 'the new Deva Link Road' beyond the canal were also dashed.[84] All would have been beneficial to the College and today everyone who manoeuvres their car through the current Exton Park entrance, or walks through it while avoiding the traffic, could be forgiven for thinking that the last idea, which originated with the Bursar, would have been especially welcome. But alongside the many successful initiatives there were bound to be some which did not turn out as hoped.

Beyond all this, there was a sense in Binks's last years that, because of government policy, the College had to run ever faster just to stand still. For all the new partnerships and new programmes created in these years, total student registrations in October 1997 were only 6% higher than they had been in 1994.[85] But this only bore out the Principal's message, derived from his family business background, that when the market was difficult salvation lay in diversifying the product. Chester College did keep its head well above water through these challenging times, and became in the process an institution where aspirations were fostered and collaboration – internal and external – encouraged. Thus, the last *Campus* magazine of Binks's Principalship, in December 1997, featured stories about links between the School of Education and the Hashemite University in Jordan; a visit by 12 students to Kenya jointly organised by the chaplaincy and Christian Aid; TRS's preparation and publication, helped by external funding, of a series of distance-learning packages and the increasing use being made by the department of St Deiniol's Library, Hawarden, for postgraduate research; three different collaborative projects with Chester City Council involving Computer Science, Psychology and History; the success of the College rugby league team in securing sponsorship from Scruffy Murphy's Irish themed pub and the gift of shirts from the professional Warrington club; the forthcoming Radio Merseyside Christmas morning broadcast from the College Chapel; and the award to the careers service of a national prize for the best university careers resources. Although, as the same issue put it, Binks would be 'a hard act to follow',[86] all this was really a tribute to the energy and enterprise of a multitude of staff and students, who had laid the foundations for even greater achievements to come.

Binks's 11-year tenure as Principal was one of the shortest in the College's history – only Allen and de Bunsen had briefer terms of office – but it was also one of the most significant. He inherited an institution of little over 1,000 FTE students which, notwithstanding the recent development of diversified degrees and diplomas, still regarded itself primarily as engaged in the education of prospective schoolteachers. The prospectus contained little beyond Honours degrees in Combined Subjects and in Health & Community Studies, the BEd and a PGCE (Primary), although in fairness there were other courses which were advertised elsewhere. When he left, despite the government's curb on HE expansion in the second half of the decade after the encouragement previously given to growth, there were over 5,000 students, about two-fifths of them part-time; by then, approaching one in five students was preparing to be a nurse or midwife and only about a quarter of the total intake was for teacher training. Separate undergraduate and postgraduates prospectuses were in circulation, the former listing a dozen 'specialised BA and BSc programmes' in addition to Combined Subjects, the latter covering a score of Master's degrees alongside other award-bearing courses which would appeal to the part-time student market. The College had diversified its income streams, through enterprises such as the expanded conference trade and through a series of successful bids for funding, had raised its profile within the city and beyond and had finally laid to rest the popular notion that it did little more than teacher training. The first research students supervised at Chester had obtained PhDs, and strategies to advance to university status were being actively discussed. It was now time to put them into practice.

---

1   See e.g. R. Shattock, 'Policy Making in British Higher Education, 1980–2006', *HEQ*, LXII, 2 (July 2008), pp. 181–203, esp. pp. 192–93; R. Brown and H. Carasso, *Everything for Sale? The Marketisation of UK Higher Education* (London, 2013).

2   McGregor, *A Church College for the 21st Century?*, p. 239.

3   Hollinshead, ed., *In Thy Light*, pp. 107, 110–11.

4   CC, Minutes of Governors, 1975–89: 17 March, 19 May, 22 May 1987.

5   CC, Minutes of Governors, 1975–89: 20 November 1987; cf. Chapters 4, 8; CC, Minutes of Academic Board, 1982–89: 25 November 1987.

6   CC, Minutes of Governors, 1975–89: 19 February, 20 May 1988; at a time of growing concern about AIDS he also had to deflect the Bishop of Chester's disapproval of the installation by the Students' Union of the College's first two condom machines in the de Bunsen Centre; CC, Minutes of Academic Board, 1982–89: 25 November 1987, 23 March, 8 June 1988.

7   E.V. Binks, 'The Present State of Play' in White, *Perspectives*, pp. 85–87, at p. 86 (sequence of phrases rearranged).

8   N. [E.V.] Binks and P. Roberts, 'A Productive Partnership' in S. Weil, ed., *Introducing Change 'from the Top' in Universities and Colleges* (London, 1994), pp. 71–79, at p. 74; also quoted in Dunn, *Bright Star*, p. 32.

9   The first meeting of the new, slimmed-down, Governing Body took place on 2 March 1990, a few days after their predecessors had held a 'farewell dinner': CC, Minutes of Governors, 1975–89: 17 November 1979; CC, Minutes of Governors, 1990–99: 2 March 1990.

10   S.A. Harrop, *Decade of Change: the University of Liverpool, 1981–1991* (Liverpool, 1994), pp. 47–51; CC, Minutes of Governors, 1975–89: 17 November 1989; *pers. comm.* Canon E.V. Binks.

11   CC, Minutes of Academic Board, 1982–89: 23 March, 8 June, 8 November 1989; CC, *Insider Bulletin*, March 1998, p. 2; CC, *Enterprise in Higher Education: Final Report* (November 1994), pp. 2, 6, 10; *pers. comm.* M. Taylor. The remaining 'characteristics of enterprise' were: a willingness to take personal initiatives and risks; a capacity to sustain self-directed effort; an ability to communicate values, ideas and instructions effectively; and a concern to produce work of quality.

12   T. Hursey and M. Taylor, 'Where do Students Figure in your EHE Equation? The Development of the Role and Function of a Student Enterprise Manager' in J. Gold and R. Holden, eds, *Enterprise in Higher Education: Lighting the Blue Touchpaper* (Bradford, 1991), pp. 30–34; CC, *Enterprise in Higher Education: Final Report* (November 1994), pp. 24–26.

13   R.W. Alexander, 'Assessing a Group-Based Enterprise Project' in G. Clark, ed., *Geography and Enterprise in Higher Education* (Lancaster, 1991), chap. 8.

14   CC, *Enterprise in Higher Education: Final Report* (November 1994), pp. 17–18.

15   CC, *Insider Bulletin*, March 1998, pp. 2, 4; CC, *Campus* 2 (June 1990), p. 2; *pers. comm.* M. Taylor. Taylor, who took up her post in May 1990, had a different academic background to most staff at the time, having previously worked in personnel management, lectured on the subject at the Universities of Western Carolina and Loughborough and most recently been senior lecturer in Management Development at Manchester Polytechnic; like Binks, she held the view that 'Enterprise is the vehicle for bringing about changes we need to address anyway'.

16   CC, *Enterprise in Higher Education: Final Report* (November 1994), pp. 1, 10–16, 31–33; CC, Minutes of Academic Board, 1989–93: 1 April 1992, 17 February 1993; CC,

Minutes of Academic Board, 1993–95: 16 February, 29 June 1994; *pers. comm.* Revd J.R. Carhart. Because of a shift in government funding to support more school-based training, Education also diversified through the development of a certificate for classroom assistants (CC, Minutes of Academic Board, 1993–95: 8 December 1993).

17 CC, Minutes of Academic Board, 1989–93: 13 March 1991.

18 CC, Minutes of Governors, 1975–89: 17 February 1984.

19 CC, *Enterprise in Higher Education: Final Report* (November 1994), p. 4, cf. p. 28.

20 CC, Minutes of Academic Board, 1982–89: 11 May 1983; CC, Minutes of Governors, 1975–89: 13 May 1983.

21 CC, Minutes of Academic Board, 1982–89: 28 November 1984, 6 February 1985; CC, Minutes of Course Planning and Academic Development Committees, 1977–85: 9 January 1985.

22 CC, Minutes of Academic Board, 1982–89: 2 January, 23 April 1986.

23 CC, Minutes of Academic Board, 1982–89: 2 November 1988, 1 February, 1 March, 8 March 1989; CC, Minutes of Academic Board, 1989–93: 21 February, 13 June 1990; CC, Minutes of Governors, 1982–89: 18 November 1988, 24 February 1989; CC, Minutes of Governors, 1990–99: 2 March 1990.

24 CC, Minutes of Academic Board, 1982–89: 1 February, 8 March 1989; CC, Minutes of Governors, 1975–89: 17 November 1989; CC, Minutes of Governors, 1990–99: 19 November 1991; CC, *Campus* 5 (January 1991), p. 1. The library, which had gone over to the Dewey classification system in 1990, was further extended over the winter of 1995–96, with the provision of a new entrance and the development of the basement area for extra study spaces and shelving (CC, Minutes of Academic Board, 1989–93: 31 October 1990; CC, *Insider Bulletin*, September 1995, 4 October 1995).

25 CC, Minutes of Academic Board, 1989–93: 1 May, 12 June, 23 October 1991, 12 February, 28 October 1992; CC, Minutes of Academic Board, 1993–95: 27 October 1993, 16 February 1994; CC, Minutes of Governors, 1990–99: 16 May, 19 November 1991, 18 February, 2 June 1992, 15 June 1993, 15 November 1994, 19 November 1996, 18 November 1997; *pers. comm.* Canon E.V. Binks.

26 CC, Minutes of Academic Board, 1989–93: 12 February 1992; CC, Minutes of Governors, 1990–99: 29 May 1990, 18 February 1992, 15 June 1993. According to the designers of the new College logo, in *Campus* 2 (June 1990, p. 4), 'we wanted to emphasise the College's permanence and tradition, and also to associate it with the city itself'.

27 G. Parry, 'Patterns of Participation in Higher Education in England: A Statistical Summary and Commentary', *HEQ*, LI, 1 (January 1997), pp. 6–28, at p. 12; the index for England was actually lower in both years than those for the other UK countries.

28 Between 1981 and 1999, the percentage of young adults in the UK obtaining a degree rose from 20% to 46% for those in the top quintile of parental income, but from only 6% to 9% for those in the bottom quintile (P. Greenbank, 'The Evolution

of Government Policy on Widening Participation', *HEQ*, LX, 2, April 2006, pp. 141–66, at p. 142).

29 CC, Minutes of Governors, 1990–99: 4 October 1990, 14 March 1991; CC, Minutes of Academic Board, 1982–89: 2 November 1988; CC, Minutes of Academic Board, 1989–93: 31 October 1990, 13 March, 12 June 1991, 1 July 1992.

30 CC, Minutes of Governors, 1990–99: 16 May 1991; CC, Minutes of Academic Board, 1989–93: 12 December 1990, 12 June 1991, 16 December 1992, 17 February 1993; CC, Minutes of Academic Board, 1993–95: 30 June, 27 October, 8 December 1993, 16 February, 23 March 1994 (when Binks's verdict on the 1994–95 allocations was that 'against a significant erosion of the unit of resources across the sector, we emerge as the best treated of all the colleges and as 12th out of 128 HEFCE institutions in the league table for year-on-year percentage funding given'); CC, Minutes of Academic Board, 1996–98: 19 March 1997; CC, *Campus* 11 (Spring 1994), p. 3; CC, *Insider Bulletin*, 16 January, 7 March 1996.

31 CC, *Campus* 8 (June 1992), pp. 1, 3; CC, Minutes of Academic Board, 1989–93: 16 February, 23 March 1994.

32 CC, Minutes of Academic Board, 1982–89: 23 March, 8 June, 2 November 1988.

33 CC, Minutes of Academic Board, 1982–89: 1 February 1989; CC, Minutes of Academic Board, 1989–93: 19 November 1991; CC, Minutes of Governors, 1990–99: 15 June 1993, 18 November 1997.

34 Brown and Carasso, *Everything for Sale?*, p. 81.

35 For 1991–92, for example, the College was allowed a 17% increase in full-time and an 87% increase in part-time funded numbers, at a time when the permitted growth rates nationally were 18% and 15% respectively (CC, Minutes of Academic Board, 1989–93: 30 January 1991).

36 Binks and Roberts, 'A Productive Partnership', p. 73; CC, Minutes of Academic Board, 1989–93: 30 January, 1 May 1991, 1 July 1992; cf. CC, Minutes of Governors, 2000–05: 29 June 2000, where (outside Nursing & Midwifery where lower figures applied) a student-staff ratio of 'between 20:1 to 22:1' was anticipated for the early years of the next millennium.

37 Binks and Roberts, 'A Productive Partnership', p. 73; CC, Minutes of Academic Board, 1995–96: 29 March 1995, 27 March, 26 June 1996; CC, *Insider*, September 1995.

38 CC, Minutes of Academic Board, 1982–89: 1 February, 1 March, 14 June, 8 November 1989; on the last occasion, pressed by the forward-looking Joan Cann of the History department, Board agreed to systematize the provision of College computers and to set aside 'a sum of not less than £25,000 per annum' for the employment of computer support staff.

39 CC, Minutes of Governors, 1990–99: 18 February 1992, 2 November 1993, 21 June 1994; CC, Minutes of Academic Board 1989–93: 12 February, 20 May 1992; CC, Minutes of Academic Board 1993–95: 23 March 1994.

40 See *Collegian* 1999, pp. 20–21, for a warm tribute to Hughes's selfless work as Dean of Students by the former SU President, Rob Wotton.

41   CC, Minutes of Academic Board, 1998–2000: 28 October, 9 December 1998, 23 June 1999; cf. *Collegian*, Freshers' Edition, 1994, pp. 18–19, where Cooke refers to an intention to restructure student services 'through a strong network because the college has expanded so much', while paying tribute to the foundations laid by her predecessor. Lesley Cooke went on to become Dean of Students in 2004, when the post was revived (see Chapter 12).

42   CC, Minutes of Academic Board, 1993–95: 1 December 1993, 29 June 1994; CC, Minutes of Academic Board, 1995–96: 24 May 1995; CC, Minutes of Academic Board, 1996–98: 18 June 1997; CC, Minutes of Academic Board, 1998–2000: 23 June 1999; CC, *Insider Bulletin*, 4 July 1995; CC, *University College Chester Undergraduate Prospectus 1998*.

43   CC, Minutes of Academic Board, 1993–95: 17 February, 24 March, 30 June 1993, 18 May, 29 June 1994; CC, Minutes of Academic Board, 1995–96: 29 November 1995, 27 March 1996; CC, Minutes of Academic Board, 1996–98: 19 March, 18 June 1997; CC, *Insider Bulletin*, 16 September 1996, January 1997, May 1997; Dunn, *Bright Star*, p. 33.

44   CC, Minutes of Academic Board, 1993–95: 29 June 1994; CC, Minutes of Academic Board, 1996–98: 23 October 1996; *pers. comm.* Canon E.V. Binks, who pays tribute to the work of Stan France in recruiting Hong Kong students for the provision in Education.

45   CC, Minutes of Governors, 1990–99: 15 June 1993; CC, Minutes of Academic Board, 1989–93: 19 November 1991; CC, Minutes of Academic Board, 1993–95: 23 March, 29 June 1994; CC, Minutes of Academic Board, 1995–96: 24 April 1996; CC, *Insider Bulletin*, March 1996; *pers. comm.* Revd R. Ackroyd.

46   CC, Minutes of Academic Board, 1993–95: 24 March, 30 June 1993, 23 March 1994, 25 October 1995; CC, Minutes of Governors, 1990–99: 1 March 1994; *pers. comm.* Canon E.V. Binks. The School of Nursing & Midwifery's 'outreach' work with the St Petersburg students was a source of considerable pride, and the Principal of the city's Medical College No.1, Dr Irina Bublikova, was made a visiting fellow of the School: see also Dunn, *Bright Star*, p. 32 and CC, Minutes of Governors, 1990–99: 24 November 1999.

47   CC, Minutes of Governors, 1975–89: 12 May 1989; CC, Minutes of Governors, 1990–99: 2 June, 3 November 1992; CC, Minutes of Academic Board, 1982–89: 8 June 1988; CC, Minutes of Academic Board, 1989–93: 12 June 1991, 1 July 1992, 8 December 1993; CC, *Campus* 2 (June 1990), pp. 1, 4; CC, *Insider Bulletin*, October 1994, 12 May, 4 October 1995. Princess Margaret's Molloy Hall stone-laying ceremony took place at a spot convenient for photographs; the stone was later moved inside the building and may be seen in the entrance foyer (*pers. comm.* Canon E.V. Binks).

48   CC, Minutes of Academic Board, 1989–93: 23 October 1991; CC, Minutes of Governors, 1990–99: 25 February 1998; *VCH Cheshire*, V (ii), p. 288; CC, *Insider Bulletin*, October 1994, 25 January 1995, September 1995, 4 October 1995, January

1997, May 1997, September 1997; B. Ing, 'The Natural History of the College Campus' in White, *Perspectives*, pp. 51–54, at pp. 53–54.

49 CC, *Insider Bulletin*, 16 September 1996, September 1997.

50 CC, Minutes of Academic Board, 1982–89: 11 May 1988; Harrop, *Decade of Change*, pp. 126–27.

51 CC, Minutes of Academic Board, 1989–93: 21 February 1990, 20 May 1992, 12 May 1993; CC, Minutes of Academic Board, 1995–96: 27 March 1996; CC, Minutes of Governors, 1990–99: 2 June 1992; *pers. comm.* Canon E.V. Binks.

52 CC, Notes of a meeting held 15 December 1988 between Bill Hughes (Chester College) and David Hooper (Chester College Association); a student-run magazine entitled *Contact* had also been in existence since 1984 (*Collegian*, 2003, p. 4).

53 CC, *Insider Bulletin*, May 1997.

54 CC, Minutes of Academic Board, 1982–89: 1 March 1989; cf. CC, *Chester College Prospectus 1990,* where the Principal's Foreword describes the College as offering an opportunity 'to study for a University degree within a community which, at a personal level, is on a manageable scale'.

55 CC, *Insider*, First Edition, 1993.

56 CC, Minutes of Academic Board, 1989–93: 1 April 1992; CC, Minutes of Governors, 1990–99: 15 June 1993; see Chapter 9.

57 ZCR 86/7928: *Union Handbook '85–'86*, p. 19; CC, Minutes of Governors, 1990–99: 3 November 1992, 15 November 1994, 30 June 1999 ('Rag had not been as successful as in previous years because of organisational difficulties and bad weather'); CC, Minutes of Governors, 2000–05: 28 February 2002; CC, Minutes of Academic Board, 1998–2000: 28 October 1998; CC, *Chester College Prospectus 1990* and *University College Chester Undergraduate Prospectuses 1998, 1999*; *pers. comm.* R. Dawson. The 'Millennium Volunteers' scheme, part of a national initiative, was launched in 1999-2000 and co-ordinated by the Student Enterprise Manager within SGSS; in its first year it sent students to help in youth and children's clubs, Dr Barnardo's and residential care homes, as well as on projects within College (CC, *Annual Report, 1999–2000*, p. 9). According to CC, *Annual Report 2002–2003*, p. 28, the 'Millennium Volunteers' scheme, then in its last year, had grown to over 8,000 hours of community service by students, reckoned as worth over £45,000 to various local organisations, a sum greater than was ever raised in one year by the Rag. The 'Millennium Volunteers' were then replaced by the 'Chester Volunteers' run on similar lines, and volunteering has been a vibrant student activity ever since.

58 CC, *Insider Bulletin*, September 1997; CC, *Insider*, n.d. (1997).

59 CC, *Campus* 8 (June 1992), pp. 6, 7; CC, *Campus* 11 (Spring 1994), p. 4; CC, *Insider*, First Edition; CC, *Insider Bulletin*, 16 January 1996; CC, *Insider Bulletin*, February 1998, June 1998; *Chester First* 25 June 2012, accessed online 13/8/13.

60 CC, Minutes of Academic Board, 1989–93: 13 March, 12 June 1991, 1 July 1992; CC, Minutes of Governors, 1990–99: 18 February, 2 June 1992; *pers. comm.* C.C.

Taylerson. The revised job description agreed at this point for the Deputy Principal, which included formally deputising for the Principal in his absence and having an enhanced management and planning role, is described in Binks and Roberts, 'A Productive Partnership', p. 75.

[61] CC, Minutes of Academic Board, 1982–89: 1 February 1989; CC, Minutes of Academic Board, 1989–93: 21 February 1990, 30 January, 13 March 1991.

[62] CC, HEFCE Assessment of the Quality of Education, 1993, Chester College History Department: Institutional Self-Assessment and Letter of Response; CC, Minutes of Governors, 1990–99: 21 June, 15 November 1994, 5 July 1995; CC, *Insider Bulletin*: 25 January 1995. In *Learning from Subject Review, 1993-2001: Sharing Good Practice* (QAA, 2003), p. 8, the 1993 events were described as 'pilot reviews' from which lessons were learned about the process.

[63] CC, Minutes of Governors, 1990–99: 28 February 1996; CC, Minutes of Academic Board, 1996–98, 19 December 1997, 11 February 1998.

[64] CC, Minutes of Academic Board, 1989–93: 16 December 1992; CC, Minutes of Academic Board, 1993–95: 27 October 1993, 23 March 1994 (when further PhD studentships were allocated); CC, *Insider Bulletin*, February 1998. Spivey's successful completion is noted in CC, Minutes of Governors, 1990–99: 18 November 1997.

[65] CC, Minutes of Academic Board, 1993–95: 24 March, 8 December 1993, 29 June 1994, 15 February 1995; CC, Minutes of Academic Board, 1995–96: 29 November 1995, 27 March 1996.

[66] CC, *Insider Bulletin*, January 1997.

[67] Ceremonies were carefully choreographed to take account of the University of Liverpool's secular foundation, with the introductory hymn and prayer placed before the formal opening of the degree congregation. It is fair to say that University of Liverpool participants were consistently impressed by the Chester ceremonies, initially orchestrated by Jo Sykes (formerly Catchpole) of Registry and her colleague Maureen Sands. Mrs Sykes, who had first served the College as secretary to Bradbury in his capacity as Deputy Principal, retired from the University as Director of Registry Services after 43 years' service in 2003 (CC, Minutes of Governors, 2000–05: 5 March 2003) and received an honorary MA from the University of Chester in 2009.

[68] CC, Minutes of Academic Board, 1977–82: 4 October, 1 November 1978; CC, Minutes of Academic Council, 1972–81: 18 October 1978; CC, Minutes of Academic Board, 1982–89: 23 April 1986.

[69] CC, Programme of Events, 1989.

[70] Wotton, a Health & Community Studies graduate who went on to become a Sky Sports TV presenter, was commended by the Principal at the end of his term of office for having 'set a new standard of student participation in the affairs of the Governing Body and Academic Board': CC, Minutes of Academic Board, 1989–93: 1 May 1991; CC, Minutes of Governors, 1990–99: 16 May 1991. He wrote a lively

account of his exploits for *Collegian*, 1999, pp. 19–22. A College prize he donated is still awarded annually at the valedictory ceremony.

71 CC, Minutes of Governors, 1975–89: 2 December 1986; CC, Minutes of Governors, 1990–99: 16 May 1991, 26 June 1992, 1 March 1994; CC, Minutes of Academic Board, 1989–93: 8 March, 8 November 1989, 31 October 1990, 23 October 1991, 24 March 1993; CC, Minutes of Academic Board, 1993–95: 27 October, 1 December 1993, 16 February 1994; CC, Minutes of Academic Board, 1996–98: 18 March 1998; *pers. comm.* C. Lynas, P. Gallagher; Binks and Roberts, 'A Productive Partnership', p. 78. The original intention was to plant two trees; a second was planted later but died.

72 CC, *Campus* 8 (June 1992), p. 2; CC, Minutes of Academic Board, 1989–93: 12 December 1991, 1 July 1992.

73 CC, Minutes of Governors, 1990–99: 2 November 1993.

74 CC, Minutes of Academic Board, 1989–93: 16 February 1992; CC, Minutes of Governors, 1990–99: 15 November 1994, 27 February 1995; the DES had been re-named the Department for Education in 1992.

75 CC, Minutes of Governors, 1990–99: 28 February, 25 June 1996; CC, Minutes of Academic Board, 1995–96: 29 November 1995, 27 March 1996; CC, *Insider Bulletin*, 25 January 1995, reported a recent visit by Prof. Graeme Davies, Chief Executive of HEFCE, at which he said that the 'University College' title would not be officially recognised, but encouraged the College instead to ensure that 'its quality assurance procedures were equivalent to those required for independent degree awarding powers'.

76 CC, Minutes of Academic Board, 1982–89: 8 June, 2 November 1988; CC, Minutes of Academic Board, 1993–95: 29 June 1994; CC, *Insider*, September 1995; CC, *Insider Bulletin*, 4 October 1995; CC, *Insider Bulletin*, January 1997; CC, Minutes of Governors, 1990–99: 23 November 1998. Intranet links to off-campus nursing sites across Cheshire were not installed until after the successful retendering for the NHS contract in 1999.

77 CC, Minutes of Governors, 1990–99: 19 November 1996, Principal's Report; CC, *Insider Bulletin*, 16 January 1996, January 1997; the lease of the School from the Blue Coat Foundation had been suggested and facilitated by a governor, Canon Joseph White, who was also clerk to the foundation.

78 CC, *Insider Bulletin*, 4 October 1995; Caroline Sinclair, a great-great-granddaughter of John Coppack, the mid-nineteenth-century 'Blue Coat boy' whose statue adorns the front of the building, studied History in the School as part of her BEd course between 1997 and 2001 (*Collegian*, 1999, p. 18).

79 QAA: *Institutional Audit Report, University of Chester* (May 2005), pp. 7–8; *pers. comm.* K. Fisher. The Academic Quality Unit changed its name to Academic Quality Support Services (AQSS) around the turn of the millennium and moved offices six times between 1999 and 2011.

80 R. Anderson, British Universities Past and Present (London, 2006), p. 176; *Dearing Report: Higher Education in the Learning Society* (HMSO, London, 1997).

81 <<http://www.leeds.ac.uk/educol/ncihe/sumrep.htm>> accessed 7/8/13.

82 Student Loans Company: Facts & Figures: Maintenance Loans Take Up Figures, 1991–2005:<<http://www.slc.co.uk/statistics/national-statistics/facts-and-figures.aspx>> accessed 7/8/13.

83 CC, Minutes of Governors, 1990–99: 14 November 1995; CC, *Insider Bulletin*, March 1998.

84 CC, Minutes of Governors, 1990–99: 4 October 1990, 3 November 1992, 5 July 1995, 24 June 1997; CC, Minutes of Academic Board, 1989–93: 31 October 1990, 30 January, 1 May 1991, 1 April 1992; CC, Minutes of Academic Board, 1993–95: 8 December 1993.

85 CC, Minutes of Governors, 1990–99: 18 November 1997 (5,325 compared to 5,003).

86 CC, *Campus*, 15 (December 1997).

CHAPTER 12

TOWARDS A UNIVERSITY

The tradition that a late-twentieth-century Chester College Principal should come into office just as the government was conducting its latest shake-up of the sector – as de Bunsen, Seaborne and Binks had all done – was continued at the beginning of April 1998, when the baton passed to Timothy Wheeler. The publication of the Dearing Report in July 1997 had set a new agenda and the passage of the Teaching and Higher Education Act one year later would implement many of its proposals. Even the cheerily upbeat *Campus* broke out of its customary public relations mode to acknowledge that this was a difficult time:

> With increasing competition, particularly from new universities, against a backdrop of static student numbers nationally, and a cautious public funding structure, the new Principal will face a considerable challenge.[1]

But Wheeler was, and is, a man to seize opportunities and thrive on challenges. It has been a collective effort but the theme of his time in charge has been the triumphant surmounting of one obstacle after another in order to enhance the institution's prospects and prosperity.

Less than two years after the new Principal's appointment, the Secretary of State for Education and Employment, David Blunkett, set out his own vision for the future of British higher education, in a speech at the University of Greenwich.

> In the knowledge economy, enterpreneurial universities will be as important as entrepreneurial businesses, the one fostering the other. The 'do nothing' university will not survive – and it will not be the job of government to bail it out. Universities need to adapt rapidly to the top-down influences of globalisation and the new technologies, as well as the bottom-up imperatives of serving the local labour market, innovating with local companies and providing professional development courses that stimulate economic and intellectual growth. Above all, quality will be paramount. Diversity with quality will be the benchmark by which UK higher education will be seen and judged by those making choices, as businesses, individuals and nation states across the globe.[2]

Wheeler was taking over a college not a university, but it was an institution which would shortly be on the road from one to the other. And from the perspective of the 175th anniversary in 2014, Blunkett's agenda reads like a very fair description of what has since been achieved.

Wheeler was the first Principal not required to live on or immediately adjacent to the campus: within a 15-mile radius was deemed sufficient.[3] He was appointed after a three-day selection process from 9 to 11 December 1997. A series of meetings on the first day with different interest-groups, including the Students' Union, led on to interviews by a group of Foundation governors and a governors' panel on the second; those still in the running gave a presentation on the third morning on the challenges facing the College post-Dearing, with an afternoon interview to follow with the full Governing Body.[4] Representatives of both academic and support staff attended the presentations and were highly impressed by Wheeler's dexterity with PowerPoint, which had only recently advanced to allow a variety of transitions and effects. By this means, and through his interviews, he demonstrated a clear grasp of how institutional aspirations could be realised, including how to retain the University College title – in the face of the government's acceptance of Dearing's recommendations – and ultimately to advance to university status. His only competitor on the second day of selection was the Deputy Principal, Patricia Roberts. Although unsuccessful on this occasion, she went on in 2000 to be appointed as Principal of Whitelands College within Roehampton Institute of Higher Education, then in the process of becoming part of the federal University of Surrey.[5]

Wheeler had a Bachelor's degree and a doctorate from the University College of North Wales, Bangor, and had subsequently pursued a varied academic career which equipped him very well for the task now in hand: lectureships in Psychology and Communications at Sheffield Hallam University; Dean of the Faculty of Communication and Human Studies at Dublin City University; Professor and Head of the School of Social Studies at the Robert Gordon University, Aberdeen; Head of the Department of Communication and Media at Bournemouth University; and finally Acting Director and Chief Executive of Southampton Institute of Higher Education, destined like Chester to become a University in its own right (Southampton Solent) in 2005. He had a wide range of research publications to his name, in areas as diverse as psychopharmacology, dyslexia, communications and safety, and had experience of academic and industrial consultancies on three continents, as well as having spent time as a Senior Visiting Research Scholar at St John's College, Oxford. Not only was he the first Principal of the College to have a PhD at the time of his appointment, he also became the first permanent member of staff to hold a Professorship, criteria for which (along with those for Reader) had been agreed during his predecessor's last months in office as part of the drive to raise the profile of research within the institution. The new Principal had the title conferred upon him shortly before he came into office, but he was soon followed by the Dean of Science & Health, David Cotterrell, the recently appointed Head of Biology, Sarah Andrew, and the Director of the Centre for Victorian Studies, Roger Swift.[6]

At Binks's last meetings of both the Governing Body and Academic Board, in February and March 1998 respectively, two possible routes towards retention of the title University College Chester under the Dearing criteria had been discussed. One was for 'College governance to be subsumed under the University's Governing Council', effectively a sacrifice of autonomy. The other was for 'the College to acquire taught degree awarding powers' (TDAP), through an application to and subsequent visits from the QAA, although at this stage there was no conviction that the powers, if granted, would actually be used: it was sufficient that they would allow the College to keep the title it had adopted, leaving open the question of whether to continue teaching for Liverpool degrees.[7] The TDAP route was favoured and the elaborate process which followed – which took far longer than was foreseen in 1998 – dominated the thinking of College management, at all levels, for the next five years. But 'business as usual' in a highly competitive environment – when across the sector students were increasingly being seen as 'clients and customers purchasing an expensive service … and expecting in return a quality product'[8] – had to carry on in the meantime. So it is right first of all to consider developments on other fronts.

An immediate priority facing the new Principal was the issue of student numbers and funding for the forthcoming academic year. Higher than usual failure and withdrawal rates in 1996–97 had led HEFCE to cut the College's allocation of funded places for full-time BA and BSc programmes by some 150 and this, combined with a fall in income from the Teacher Training Agency because of a cap on BEd and PGCE numbers, meant that the College faced a serious drop in its receipts from these sources for 1998–99 compared to 1997–98. Binks had been arguing for a more generous settlement before he retired but it was his successor whose hard negotiation secured the restoration of the 150 lost HEFCE-funded places.[9] Having fended off the threat of a potential downward spiral in allocated numbers and funding, Wheeler was always keen to push for expansion thereafter. That summer, the Marketing & Recruitment department was reorganised as an integral part of Registry Services, shorn of its general public relations duties so that it could focus on attracting undergraduates and processing their admission; more resources were put into ensuring a high quality prospectus and attractive web pages, alongside more targeted marketing to prospective students, especially through good rapport with their schools.[10] The Principal was also determined to develop a fifth School, covering Business & Management, for which he thought – correctly – that HEFCE would grant additional numbers; Computer Science & Information Systems led the way with the launch in September 1998 of a BSc in Business Information Systems, and its Head Dennis Holman was tasked with developing a suite of related programmes, to include sub-degree courses leading to HNCs and HNDs awarded by Edexcel. All this led to new Business provision coming onstream in 1999 and to the formation of a new department, formally that of 'Business & Management' but marketed as the 'Chester Business School', one year later.[11]

Meanwhile, important steps were taken to enhance the attractiveness of the traditional portfolio. A lingering restriction on academic development was removed when subject departments were allowed from 1999 to introduce Single Honours BA or BSc programmes, provided that they conformed to a framework which aligned with the long-established Combined Subjects; those which did not, such as a BA in History & Heritage Management and a BSc in Animal Behaviour, both approved in the same year, were regarded as 'specialised degree programmes' instead.[12] Combined Subjects itself ceased to be the designation of awards, which from 2000 were being advertised according to the disciplines and weightings involved: 'Art and Biology' meant that the two were studied in equal proportions, 'Mathematics with Social Sciences' meant a preponderance of modules in Maths, especially in the final year. The allocation of UCAS codes to each of these named combinations led to over 500 separate ones appearing in the undergraduate prospectus of 2000, a signal to even the most casual reader that Chester 'had a lot to offer'.[13] Besides all this, with the contract for Nursing & Midwifery education due for retendering in 1999, Wheeler encouraged a bid for more work than was currently undertaken, embracing Halton and Warrington as well as the familiar centres in Cheshire. To have lost the bid would have been a severe financial blow but when it was successful, in the face of stiff competition from other HEIs, it not only brought some longer-term financial stability but added a further 120 or more students per annum from early 2000.[14]

One area not currently sharing in this expansion was Education, which notwithstanding its central role in the College's history was suffering a reduction in allocated numbers and funding from the Teacher Training Agency consequent upon disappointing Ofsted results. Academic staffing in the School had to be reduced by six in summer 1999, through a mixture of early retirement, redeployment and redundancy, and there was even talk among the governors of the possibility that 'Education could have to be phased out'. However, the College invested in some key leadership posts within the School, Ofsted scores improved and a policy of developing HEFCE-funded programmes to complement those financed by the TTA, such as a BA in Early Years Education – a policy started under Elaine Barnes as Dean and continued by her successor from 2003, Anna Sutton – meant that numbers recovered sufficiently for there to be a need to recruit additional staff by 2004. The School also celebrated its first PhD completion that year.[15]

All this meant that around the turn of the millennium the College had some 4,900 undergraduates (just over 1,000 of them part-time) and a further 2,500 (mostly part-time) postgraduates. The distribution of undergraduate enrolments – making no distinction between full- and part-time students – showed 38% in the School of Science & Health, 28% in both Arts & Humanities and Nursing & Midwifery and the remaining 6% in Education. Even if Nursing & Midwifery is not counted, but postgraduate registrations are taken into account, Education's share of all full- and part-time modular enrolments still amounted to only about 15%, against much larger proportions in the two other Schools. The relative decline of Education in little over a decade is striking: its total FTE of 476 at March 2000 was not far short of the 518 of October 1986, but back then it had represented almost half the institutional total.[16] There could hardly be a clearer demonstration of the significance for the College of diversification beyond the original purposes of its foundation.

Within these totals, Biology, which had recently been very active in expanding its portfolio, had become the largest single department as measured by its share of all student registrations for the modules it delivered. On this calculation, it accounted for 10.4% of all work outside Nursing & Midwifery; PE & Sports Science came next with 9.3% and English third with 8.0%. Business & Management, in its first year of operation, already had 84 FTE and at 2.7% was on a par with Languages, which having fought its way back into the undergraduate curriculum was facing fresh difficulties in recruitment – although the new Head of subject, Terry McWilliams, had begun to turn this round through the addition of modules in Spanish, which in 2000 became a full Combined Subjects pathway.[17] Further curriculum development, sometimes facilitated by partnerships[18] and often accomplished through successful bids to HEFCE for additional numbers, pushed the totals up even more. For example, Archaeology, already taught as a component of the History programme, was launched in September 1999 as a distinct pathway within Combined Subjects; critical to this was the input of archaeologists employed by Chester City Council, with whom a Memorandum of Co-operation had been signed.[19] Further Combined Subjects pathways in Business, History of Science, Communication Studies and International Development Studies followed in the next two years, stretching the capacity of the computerised timetable to accommodate so many combinations but enhancing the College's appeal to applicants.[20] A part-time Master's in Business Administration was also introduced in September 2000, raising the profile of the nascent Business School.[21] Within the Humanities, a BA in Literature & Film and a DipHE in Christian Youth Work were launched in 2001; over subsequent years, the latter was consistently awarded the highest possible grading in the annual validation it had to face from the National Youth Agency.[22] The Biology department – re-named Biological Sciences – was successful in a bid to the NHS to run programmes in Nutrition and Dietetics, which began to be delivered in September 2002; with Forensic Biology also added to its portfolio, it could boast no less than 14 undergraduate programmes by the end of that academic year.[23] Two-year Foundation Degrees, a government priority for which dedicated funding was available, were developed in areas such as Business & Management, Information & Communications Technology and Social & Health Care, mostly for delivery at partner FE colleges though with the hope that some students would progress to a full degree at Chester. A Director of Foundation Degrees and a Foundation Degree Advisory Group were in place to offer guidance on quality assurance and logistical issues by the spring of 2004.[24]

The net result of all this development was that whereas the undergraduate prospectus of 1999 had advertised just over 40 subjects for study, with an explanation that many of them could be taken either as Single Honours or in combination with another, that for 2005 was listing not far short of 2,000 different UCAS codes, the great majority being the myriad permutations possible within Combined Subjects.[25] As a demonstration of expansion this was impressive but it is worth adding that, amongst it all, there was one significant withdrawal of provision, in Health & Community Studies. The decision was taken in June 2000 to cease undergraduate recruitment and the Master's programme was also withdrawn two years later; the department was re-named 'Social & Communication Studies' with the intention of giving greater emphasis to the Social Sciences.[26] Health & Community Studies had played an important part in the diversification of the College's overall curriculum for over 20 years, both in its own right and as a precursor to the development of nurse education, but it was now time to bow to shifts in market demand. Fortunately, its staff expertise could readily be absorbed elsewhere.

Meanwhile, Work Based Learning (WBL) – a key component of the Chester undergraduate experience since the mid-1980s – had been undergoing developments of its own. TRS, ever willing to challenge convention, had secured permission for work experience to be a voluntary rather than compulsory component of the Bachelor of Theology in 1995 and, once this principle had been established, it was hard to resist its application elsewhere. By 1996–97, across the BA/BSc provision as a whole – outside Nursing & Midwifery where the College scheme had never operated – WBL had been extended from a standard four-week block to eight weeks, occupying the entire second half of the second semester for second-year students (effectively the full summer term). This apparent expansion had, however, been balanced by an opportunity for subject departments to offer their own alternative 'experiential learning' modules in the same eight-week slot. As a result, modules such as 'Methodology and action learning in Theology & Religious Studies', 'Experience into words: varieties of writing', 'Applied research experience in Psychology' and 'The applications and context of Art' now appeared, a common thread being that students applied their discipline in a context other than academia and engaged to some extent with relevant employers or practitioners.[27] There was now competition for 'employment-related' enrolments but the release from the obligation to find placements for every HEFCE-funded second-year student gave WBL staff a chance to try something different, to break free from the narrow confines of 'Work Based Learning' to embrace the broader concept of 'work related studies'.

Capitalising on the work done in the early 1990s to establish the entitlement of work based learners to academic credit, further optional modules were developed with an emphasis on critical reflection, such as 'Work Related Learning and Career Planning', available to first-year students from 2000. By then, a complete Work Based and Integrative Studies (WBIS) Framework had also been approved, in time for launch in 1998–99. This enabled students to negotiate their own customised programmes, from sub-degree to Master's level, based upon their workplace experiences; it also allowed employers to have their in-house training programmes accepted as earning academic credit. A Credit and Accreditation Panel was established in 2002 to provide the necessary quality assurance. Meanwhile, a Centre for Work Related Studies, headed by David Major, formerly of TRS and the person who had led these recent developments, was set up in summer 2000 and installed at one end of the Blue Coat School, assisted by funding from the Higher Education Reach Out into Business and Community Initiative. It soon established separate units covering different aspects of its work: a Professional Development Unit to manage WBIS; a WBL unit to run the Work Based Learning scheme and its associated modules; a Global Perspective Unit which handled students' placements in developing countries; and a Business & Community Development Unit which helped unemployed graduates to find employment and also ran a Learning & Enterprise Centre in the Blue

Coat basement teaching basic computing and employability skills to members of the public. The Centre proved to be very successful in winning bids for its work, including from the European Social Fund, and its student numbers rose appreciably. By March 2000, Work Related Studies in its various guises was responsible for the equivalent of 4% of all module enrolments, outside Nursing & Midwifery – more than that for departments such as Fine Art and Mathematics, and almost as many as Geography. Among its most noteworthy developments was a Foundation Degree in Government for members of the civil service, in place by 2004.[28]

All these initiatives, allied to vigorous marketing, led to a steep upward curve in student recruitment in the first half of the decade. In November 2000, for example, Wheeler reported 'an alarmingly massive 100% increase' in applications for 2001 entry compared to twelve months before. They stabilised thereafter, but by June 2001 he was still able to report a 9% increase over the previous year in UCAS applications compared to a 2% fall nationally, and a 20% increase to Nursing & Midwifery programmes against national growth of 7%. 'Chester College is the most popular higher education college in the country, according to statistics published by the Universities Council for Admissions Service' proclaimed the *Collegian* in 2001, and Wheeler repeatedly used good recruitment figures one year to argue for higher targets in the next.[29] The assimilation of a new campus at Warrington, to be discussed below, brought in a further 900 or so students, so that by 2002–03, overall numbers had risen to 6,119 full-time and 1,835 part-time undergraduates, along with 235 full-time and 1,391 part-time postgraduates – a grand total of 9,580, representing a remarkable 29% increase on three years earlier. In 2003–04 they were down slightly to 9,383 but in 2004–05, aided by the permission now given to institutions to recruit above allocated numbers albeit at lower cost, they reached a new record: 6,441 full-time and 2,269 part-time undergraduates, 218 full-time and 1,306 part-time postgraduates, amounting to 10,234 in all. So in its last year as a College rather than a University, Chester reached a five-figure total! There were some significant trends within this, notably the increasing popularity of Single Honours, which in 2002–03 had lagged behind Combined Subjects with 928 students against 1,244, at a time when the 'specialised degree programmes' had 1,985. By 2004–05 there were 2,137 students enrolled for Single Honours, 1,565 taking Combined Subjects and only 713 on 'specialised degree programmes', some of which had been withdrawn. It is also worth noting that ongoing commitment to postgraduate research had seen the number of research students rise from 47 in 1999–2000 to 109 by 2004–05, although most of this increase had been through self-funded part-time registrations.[30]

Growth in numbers was accompanied by changes in the conduct of everyday life. The *Collegian*, which following its demise in 1987 had occasionally appeared in different formats as a student-run magazine,[31] was revived in 1998 as a glossy annual publication edited by the Communications Officer, featuring the Principal's report, stories of staff and student activities and reminiscences from the past; re-named *The Cestrian* in 2006 (because the institution was no longer a college) and now produced biannually by Corporate Communications, it still serves this purpose. Then in 1999 came the closure of the General Office; since every academic department now had its own administrative, secretarial or clerical support, the service it had performed since the early 1970s was no longer required and its staff were dispersed to other support departments.[32] From 2000, academic staff were encouraged to apply for membership of the Institute for Learning and Teaching (ILTHE, later incorporated into the HE Academy), and both they and support staff were also given plenty of opportunity to obtain the European Computer Driving Licence.[33] A Learning Support Service to provide professional study skills advice to students began in 2001, coinciding with a phased programme to improve learning resources and upgrade Information Technology (IT) support for students with disabilities or other special needs.[34]

These developments were followed in autumn 2003 by the appointment of the College's first Teaching Fellows, born out of a concern that, while outstanding research was being acknowledged through the award of professorships and readerships, equivalent merit in teaching was not.[35] At the same time, Allan Owens, already a National Teaching Fellow and one whose work in the performing arts straddled the Schools of Education and Arts & Humanities, was recognised as the institution's first Distinguished Teaching Fellow. The following year, a Learning & Teaching Institute was established primarily to disseminate good practice and oversee pedagogical staff development. A Graduate School to manage the affairs of postgraduate research students was also set up, formally from 1 January 2004, with Roger Swift as the first Director and Elizabeth Christopher as Deputy Director.[36] Meanwhile, Chester Academic Press was launched in 2001 as a vehicle for the publication of books by staff and others associated with the College. Its first title was *Crime: Fear or Fascination?*, edited by Anne Boran of Social & Communication Studies, and it was quickly followed by *Physical Education Teachers on Physical Education* by Ken Green; his departmental affiliation on the back cover – Sport & Exercise Sciences – signalled yet another change of name for what had until recently been PE and Sports Science.[37]

Among the students, this was the period when, as we have seen, the annual College Rag was finally replaced by alternative volunteering initiatives: the 65,440 hours reckoned to have been spent by students in volunteering work between 2002 and 2007 was deemed equivalent to over £300,000, had payments been made at the minimum wage.[38] The Students' Union became increasingly active in mounting campaigns to safeguard communal health and welfare: in 2001–02, for example, it hosted an anti-racism evening, publicised meningitis awareness, and prioritised the prevention of spiking drinks on the campus. At a time when average student debt on graduation was some £12,000, the Union was also prominent in demonstrations and parliamentary lobbies. As for the College's traditional love of sport, at one level there was the customary story of outstanding achievement, with Michelle Daltry representing Wales at hockey, Steven Ravenscroft becoming British judo champion, and Kevin Kipling winning the British Welterweight Kickboxing Championship, all around the turn of the millennium. However, this was also a phase when the College sports teams were generally less successful than they had been in the past. The SU President reported to the governors in March 2003 that nine College sports teams had been relegated that season (compared to four promoted); both the men's and ladies' football teams had reached the quarter-finals of the British Universities Sports Association competitions but that seems to have been the pinnacle of achievement. This was so at variance with the traditions of the College that the Head of PE & Sports Science was moved to introduce 20 sports scholarships – amounting mostly to free kit and complimentary use of facilities – 'in an attempt to halt the decline of sports performance by College teams, which had impacted on recruitment to the department'.[39]

To cater for increased numbers, the College was as busy as ever in the field of property development. In 1999, Fisher and Astbury Houses, largely unchanged since their opening in the 1950s, were provided with wheelchair access and fitted with en suite facilities for each study-bedroom.[40] Major changes followed to the west end of the Chapel, with disabled access being provided through a reconstructed entrance leading from the Cheyney Road/Parkgate Road corner; a start was made on the creation of a 'memorial garden' in this corner to mark the millennium, but ultimately an alternative was provided in 2010 when a garden designed by staff for the previous year's RHS Tatton show, where it had won a silver-gilt medal, was replanted in front of the Beswick building (see Plate 6).[41] Abbey Court, a hotel close to the campus on Liverpool Road, was bought to house the new Business School in 2001; most of the premises, used as teaching and office accommodation, took the name of the first Principal, Rigg, while an annexe providing student rooms was named after (and opened by) John Milton, the Deputy Principal of the late 1960s and 1970s.[42] Further houses were purchased on and near Liverpool Road and in 2002 the College acquired Bache Hall, a listed nineteenth-century mansion north-east of the campus beside Countess Way, for use by what was re-named in February 2003 the School of Nursing, Midwifery & Social Care; this had most recently been serving as a school for beauticians.[43] The much-refurbished fitness centre within the Old Gym of 1939 was opened by the Liverpool and England footballer Michael Owen in 2003, six years after a previous version had been opened by (former) Manchester United and England footballer Sir Bobby Charlton.[44]

A continuing lack of residential accommodation for overseas students was eventually addressed through the building of 'Hollybank Court' opposite the Exton Park entrance to the Chester campus, ready by summer 2005. This was described by the Vice-Chancellor two years later as 'of high quality, marketable internationally. Having international students in one area facilitates student support and allows for the provision of the specific facilities required by particular groups'.[45] By 2003–04 the Small Hall – as the Gladstone Hall was now called – was also supposed to have been upgraded and enlarged to include offices for the Students' Union alongside an enhanced rehearsal and events space, not unlike the scheme mooted in the 1980s before the Molloy Hall was erected instead. Once again, however, the development did not come to pass, being superseded by plans for a brand new Union building at the southern end of the campus, eventually opened in 2008. So the cheaply constructed but cherished and much-used Hall yet again survived intact, still looking much as it had done when opened in 1959. In a statement of faith in its future, it was at last given its upgrade, with a new roof and windows, in 2013.[46]

However, the major building project of these early years of the new millennium was the construction of what became known as the Binks building, in space vacated by the demolition of Bradbury and Morrell houses and the removal of some portakabins. The provision of 'a significant teaching facility with staff offices' was under consideration before the close of 1999. This was to be financed partly from a bid to the HEFCE 'Poor Estates' fund, which ultimately contributed some £1.1 million (about a fifth of the total cost), but mainly from the College's own resources, including income from additional students; as Wheeler explained to the governors, it was intended as a 'landmark' building 'at a focal point on the campus' on which it was worth spending about 20% more than a 'mundane' structure would cost. Representatives of the architects and quantity surveyors presented the plans to the governors in January 2002 and, given that this was soon to become one of the most familiar buildings to anyone who lived or worked on the main Chester campus, it is worth quoting some of what they are reported to have said.

> The ground floor of the building would be accessed via a pedestrianised frontage into the main internal corridor, which would be built to resemble a street. The focus would be a three-storey glass atrium, which would light the internal areas. The ground floor would house a 300 seat lecture theatre and conference space together with a Brasserie and coffee area which would be the hub of the building … An open access computer suite would also be on the ground floor and it was noted that the building would have full disabled access and facilities … The first floor would continue the street theme around the glass void. Student Guidance and Support would occupy space to the front of the building, with a Careers suite, Student Information Centre, Counselling Service and Chaplaincy being contained within. This floor would also house Language Laboratories and satellite television rooms together with a 160 seat lecture theatre and break out areas … The second floor would be entered via the lift on to a glazed balcony area over the glass atrium. This floor would mainly be used for office space, with a Computing Laboratory with flexible space also contained therein … The third floor was planned as storage for plant.[47]

Most of this is recognisable today (see Plate 7). The building went up on schedule and largely to these specifications, although the third floor had to be pressed into service to accommodate the teaching of Journalism and the structure had to be slightly realigned because of objections from the resident of a nearby house in private occupation; it had originally been intended – as a 'town and gown' statement – to offer views from its first- and second-floor landings directly along the terrace towards the town hall.[48] The various rooms were in use by the beginning of the 2003–04 academic year, over twelve months before the building was formally opened on 4 November 2004 by yet another royal visitor, this time HRH the Princess Royal.[49] It was the most striking addition to the campus since the erection of the Price Tower in the late 1960s and one which, because of its position beside the main access road, continued to dominate the first impressions any visitor had of the University until the new student hostel, Grosvenor House, arose to take over this role in 2013.

Another highly significant event during these years was the assimilation of the Higher Education Faculty of Warrington Collegiate Institute, dating officially from 1 August 2002. In some of the literature of the time this was described as a 'merger', but unlike most of its fellow colleges founded in the Victorian period Chester had never at any stage merged with another institution and it did not do so now. From a strict constitutional standpoint, the College of 1839 continued as before, absorbing the assets and academic provision of Warrington as it had those of the local Nursing & Midwifery College a decade earlier, but remaining the same legal entity as a Church of England educational foundation. One manifestation of this was the branding of the Warrington campus for publicity purposes as 'Chester College at Warrington'. Another was its adoption of the Chester house style for its prospectus. Yet another was the appointment of an Anglican chaplain for the campus, where there had previously been an ecumenical chaplaincy provided by local churches and chapels.[50]

The Warrington story[51] had begun with the foundation in 1946 of an emergency training college for ex-servicemen wishing to become schoolteachers, based in a 39-acre site (larger than the campus at Chester) formerly used by Canadian troops at Fearnhead on the outskirts of Warrington. This had been transformed in 1949 into a permanent college for women, Padgate Training College, whose first Principal, Joyce Martin, had overseen the building of new halls of residence from 1955 onwards, the admission of the first male students in 1957, and even the advent of a College Rag in 1960. Under her successor, Lance Dobson (Principal from 1963 to 1972), the College had rebuilt much of its accommodation for teaching and administration and, in common with the rest of the sector, had introduced a four-year BEd course, in this case validated by the University of Manchester. The 1970s, however, had been as challenging here as anywhere else – arguably more so, since, as a local authority college, Padgate had found itself being transferred from Lancashire to Cheshire as part of the boundary changes of 1974. There had been diversification into a BA (Humanities) in 1975 but this had not been sufficient to allow the College to retain its separate identity and in 1979 it had merged with Warrington's Art College and Technical College into a new institution, North Cheshire College, offering both FE and HE courses. Teacher training had eventually ceased in 1987 but by then a varied HE curriculum leading to Manchester awards had been developed, among which Media Studies, in particular, had begun to gain a national reputation. Under yet another name, the Padgate Campus of Warrington Collegiate Institute (the title from 1993), the establishment had increased its HE numbers to almost 900 by the mid-1990s and had gone on – with Manchester's permission – to adopt the name 'University College Warrington' before being obliged to drop this for the same reasons as at Chester. Eventually, a decision to reorganise Warrington Collegiate Institute so as to focus on FE provision led to overtures being made for the transfer of the HE faculty and its Padgate campus to another HEI.

Given that the meeting in January 1839 which had taken the decision to found Chester College had been held in Warrington, and that Chester's sister diocesan college for women – forerunner of S. Katharine's Liverpool which went on to become part of Liverpool Hope University – had been based there until 1924, there was a certain historical symmetry in the arrangements now being proposed. Moreover, Chester College had recently acquired a stake in the town through its Nursing & Midwifery provision. However the two institutions had had few dealings over the years and in certain subjects had been competitors for students, especially during the tense 1970s when Padgate's reprieve from the threatened loss of teacher training numbers had been very annoying to Chester.[52] Warrington's loss had also been Chester's gain in 1992 when the Cheshire Micro Unit, a specialist IT facility where local teachers as well as College staff and students could try out computer applications, was transferred from one institution to the other, being housed just off campus at Rockmount at the junction of Parkgate and Liverpool Roads.[53] The approach from Warrington Collegiate Institute was entertained – after a full risk assessment – because it offered the prospect of extending the College's presence across the county, at a time when some established North West universities were interested in claiming a stake in Cheshire, and because it added at a stroke the best part of 1,000 students to institutional numbers, along with capital assets and income (see Plate 8).

The result was that provision at Warrington in Media Studies (which included three Master's programmes), Performing Arts, Leisure & Sport, Business & Management and Information Technology, together with a part-time Certificate in Education, all validated by the University of Manchester, became the responsibility of Chester College of Higher Education; under the new managerial arrangements, only Media Studies remained a separate department administered from Warrington, the rest being added to the portfolios of existing Chester-based departments. A complicated process followed, involving the phasing out of Manchester awards, introducing those of Liverpool and finally switching to Chester, all carefully managed by Registry Services. In theory the transition was relatively straightforward, since those graduating in 2004 were supposed to do so with Manchester, those in 2005–07 with Liverpool and those from 2008 onwards with Chester but in practice there were several individuals who fell behind their cohort and whose specific circumstances had to be tracked.[54] The model followed was that students would complete their studies entirely on one campus but staff in the relevant departments might have to travel between the two; provision already validated for delivery on one campus was in some cases approved to run on the other as well, with Journalism, already well-established at Warrington, becoming a notable addition to the undergraduate offering at Chester. Conversely, the Education department extended the BEd to Warrington, with the result, as proudly reported to Academic Board, that 'Initial Teacher Education … returned to "Padgate campus" for the first time for over 25 years'. The Students' Unions at the two campuses soon established friendly relations and amalgamated without difficulty.[55]

Part of the appeal of the assimilation of the Warrington campus, at least to some of the governors, was that it could be seen to strengthen the College's case for becoming the 'University of Cheshire'.[56] This was never the favoured title among those who knew that universities which declined to name their home town or city forfeited a clear identity. However, the promise of an enhanced regional, or at least county-wide, role was well-founded, even though projections of a doubling of student numbers at Warrington within five years[57] were not. By the close of 2002, for example, discussions were in train with Warrington Collegiate Institute – now purely an FE college – over student progression to higher education and with Warrington Borough Council over offering an MBA to its staff; joint proposals with the Institute to establish 'incubator units' to help start small businesses in the town were also being formulated by the following spring, although ultimately these did not come to pass.[58] Chester College's reach would certainly not have extended this far twelve months earlier.

As for University status itself, the journey towards this was to be peppered with hopes raised, dashed and raised again, en route to ultimate triumph. Under threat of an enforcement notice being served by the government if the 'University College' title was not given up by 1 February 1999, the institution reverted to its former name, Chester College of Higher Education, one month early on New Year's Day. What Wheeler described as 'subtle re-branding' devised by the Deputy Principal allowed the College to be presented for publicity purposes as 'Chester: a College of the University of Liverpool' which, through the use of the old lettering and of the familiar claret and blue logo minimised the visual impact of the change; there were embarrassing headlines about a loss of status in the local press but, as we have seen, student recruitment held up remarkably well.[59] It was hoped that the speedy acquisition of taught degree awarding powers would allow the previous title to be resumed with little delay: June 1999 was initially seen as an 'optimistic assessment' as the date for their conferment, sometime in 2000 as more realistic.[60] In the event, for reasons shortly to be explained, it was not until August 2003 that they were formally granted, allowing the institution officially to adopt the title University College Chester once again, in time for the 2003–04 academic year. Two years later it became the University of

Chester, a title agreed upon by the governors – assuming a successful outcome to the scrutiny process – in November 2004, with a Warrington member seconding the chair's proposal. A student applying to Chester College in autumn 1995 entered University College Chester in September 1996 but left Chester College (or 'Chester: a College of the University of Liverpool') in June 1999. An applicant to 'Chester: a College of …' in autumn 2002 was admitted to University College Chester one year later but found herself studying at the University of Chester in her final year before graduating in 2006 with a different university's degree. One has only to read the prospectuses of this period, with their amendments to institutional title from one year to the next, to appreciate something of the complexity involved in all this (see Plate 10). It is only fair to say that the College – notably staff in Registry Services and Marketing & Admissions who had to track students and prospective students and keep them informed – managed the implications of these frequent changes of status and title with considerable skill and professionalism.[61]

These developments were played out under scrutiny from the QAA, which had responsibility for assessing Chester's fitness, initially for degree awarding powers and then for the university title. The QAA has had a bad press in several accounts of higher education in this period, its inspection methodology being accused of promoting 'a bureaucratized "dumbing into the middle"' which removed 'whatever spontaneity and flexibility might otherwise have remained in the system'.[62] The experience at Chester, however – which between 1998 and 2005 had more visits from the QAA, in the guise of subject reviews, an institutional audit, and scrutiny for TDAP and the university title, than most institutions in the country – scarcely bears this out. It is true that subject reviews, which distilled the various aspects of an academic department's provision into a series of numerical scores, were unduly stressful and resource-intensive before and during each visit and, through their reliance as evidence on documents and exploratory meetings rather than direct observation of work in practice, were not always convincing measures of quality and standards as staff and students perceived them. It is also true that scrutiny for TDAP was more elaborate and long-drawn-out than was really necessary for a judgment to be made – as the QAA itself acknowledged a few years later by streamlining the process – although this was partly a reflection of prevailing caution within the sector over the extension of degree awarding powers to more institutions. Not every QAA visit in the years down to 2005 was a happy occasion.[63] But the majority of reviewers, assessors and auditors were professional and constructive, with an acceptance of the College's ethos. A great deal was learned from successive visits about the importance of clear communication and of consistency, both in the implementation of procedures and between one document and another, and this has been beneficial overall, especially to the student community. The requirement that academic work should be couched in the language of programme and module aims and of level-related learning outcomes was seen as an encouragement to artificiality by some but as a helpful design framework by others; there was no reason at all why this mode of expression, if inclusively phrased, should inhibit creativity in learning, teaching or assessment. Nor was it allowed to do so, as the vibrant curriculum development of the years down to 2005 makes clear: from the innovative, design-your-own-programme facility of the WBIS framework, to the practice pioneered in the BTh programme 10 years earlier of joint-teaching of modules at levels 3 (that is, final-year undergraduate) and M (Master's),[64] to the various collaborative partnerships forged by subject departments, especially TRS. All this was destined to be successfully defended before the QAA assessors.

The College's detailed application for TDAP was submitted to the Privy Council on 10 November 1999 and considered by the QAA's DAP committee in February and June 2000. This led on 31 July 2000 to a visit from a preliminary assessment panel, which took particular interest in actions following the 1996 audit and in the handling of the validation of the new Business & Management programmes; the cautious approach adopted to their initial approval, which had been for only one year pending revalidation ahead of the 2000–01 academic year, certainly paid off at this critical moment. This set the ball rolling for a series of visits by a panel of two institutional assessors and a QAA Assistant Director between November 2000 and July 2001, which involved observations of committees, assessment boards and validations, meetings with governors, staff and students, and study of documentation including a plethora of statements, minutes and the Quality Assurance Handbook.[65] The panel's report was considered in October 2001 by a scrutiny panel appointed by the DAP committee. It concluded 'that the institution's scholarly community had [not] yet achieved the strength and maturity looked for in the grant of taught degree awarding powers' but acknowledged that many of the criteria had been 'broadly satisfied' and that the College was clearly moving in the right direction:

> The Panel considered that the College should be invited to temporarily defer its application … [so that] … the various initiatives that had been set in train by the College … [could] … be taken forward to a point where satisfactory outcomes could be demonstrated. The Panel considered that a period of

approximately nine months should elapse before the College entered into discussion with the Agency regarding the re-activation of its application.[66]

In other words, the College was not quite ready to be awarded the powers but was sufficiently close to merit a suspension of activity rather than outright rejection, which would have sent the process back to square one.

Disappointing though this delay was – especially when the University of Liverpool's other college of HE, Liverpool Hope, successfully obtained its powers in August of the following year[67] – feedback from the QAA at least gave the College a picture of what was required. One issue was that the invaluable Quality Assurance Handbook, which had seen the College through the 1996 audit as a carefully updated compendium of procedures, had become a collection of statements which were sometimes regulatory, sometimes for guidance, sometimes for information and (very occasionally) contradictory. The assessors wanted a clearer exposition of the regulatory regime which would prevail once the College had its own degree awarding powers and several senior members of staff, alongside colleagues in AQSS and Registry, had a hand in drafting a fresh set of 'Principles & Regulations' for this purpose, supported by Handbooks dealing with procedures in more detail. This exercise, begun before the assessors finished their 2000–01 visits and substantially completed before they returned after the suspension of scrutiny, also allowed the College to address any quality assurance processes on which the assessors had expressed reservations.[68]

By the time the College formally reactivated the engagement with the QAA, in October 2002, it had also assimilated the campus at Warrington, a move which only added to the assessors' agenda when they made two further extended visits, in November 2002 and January 2003, obliging them to inspect the site, meet staff and students there and explore a raft of new issues. Indeed, the College governors had themselves been concerned at the potential upset to the TDAP application when debating the acquisition of the Warrington campus early in 2002. Paradoxically, however, the move worked in the College's favour: staff and students at Warrington acquitted themselves very well and the assimilation was so skilfully managed that it increased the assessors' confidence in the institution as a whole. As their Updating Report of February 2003 put it:

> the institutional assessors … were initially concerned at this potentially major addition to the already significant agenda the College's senior management team was seeking to address. However … the assessors conclude that careful and sensitive management of the merger [sic] has demonstrated the capacity of the College to manage change. The assessors were also struck by the quality of the staff and the body of good practice which the Warrington

Campus has brought to the College. As a consequence, the assessors are of the firm opinion that the College now finds itself in a much stronger position than it was in July 2001.[69]

With this recommendation behind them, the full scrutiny panel visited the College on 25 April. It confirmed the assessors' opinion and, after this confirmation had made its way through the necessary hierarchy of committees, the Privy Council's authorisation to award taught degrees was duly issued on 5 August. Success was all the sweeter for the arduous process which had led up to it. Along with the Dean of Arts & Humanities, Glyn Turton, whose institution-wide brief was for quality assurance once Patricia Roberts had left her Deputy Principal post, and also Louise Chaddock and others from AQSS, the present writer had enjoyed the privilege of co-ordinating the College's response to the TDAP scrutiny; an important role had also been played by the Dean of Higher Education at Warrington, Malcolm Rhodes, who had joined the senior management team as Assistant Principal (Planning) and Provost of the Warrington campus once the assimilation had gone through. He would make an immense contribution to the delivery of a series of critically important projects for the College and University in years to come. But really the achievement was one in which every section of the institutional community, in Warrington as well as Chester, could take pride: students who had spoken positively of their experiences and had consistently assured the assessors that a degree from the place where they had studied would be preferable to one from a prestigious but 'remote' university; housekeeping, maintenance, catering and IT-support staff who, along with porters, had ensured that the visits had gone smoothly; administrative support staff in AQSS, Registry and academic departments, several of whom were required to meet the assessors and whose collective expertise and attention to detail had enhanced the quality of paperwork submitted for review; senior managers and academic staff, of various grades, who had convinced the assessors of their fitness to be entrusted with the award of degrees. Essential to the outcome had been the success of one academic department after another in the subject review process: between 1999 and 2001 a string of subject areas – Biological Sciences, Business & Management, Fine Art, Nursing & Midwifery, Psychology, Health & Community Studies, Mathematics, PE & Sports Science and TRS – had undergone reviews, with the last four achieving 'excellent' scores, and crucially none had recorded less than a '3' for any aspect of provision. To have done so would have suggested that 'significant improvement' was needed in this area and, with the TDAP application in train, would have brought a halt to the process. Commendably, those Warrington departments which had experienced these reviews in the run-up to the assimilation had nothing less than a '3' on their record either.[70]

As noted already, Chester had originally embarked on the journey towards TDAP so that it could recover its University College title. There was no formal requirement to use the powers if granted, but very early in the process the QAA had intimated that there was a better chance of success if this was the declared intention. Accordingly, it had been assumed that there would be a period in which Chester students would be graduating with degrees from a university college rather than a university. Under the criteria prevailing at the turn of the millennium, an institution was expected to have held degree awarding powers for at least five years, and to have discharged them effectively, before advancement to university status could be entertained. Accordingly, back in 1999, the Principal had spoken of a five-year gap between the award of TDAP and the achievement of a university title and this timescale had been repeated in the *Collegian* three years later.[71] A more detailed schedule had been given to the governors early in 2001, when it had been envisaged that the College would move on from the acquisition of TDAP to obtain research degree awarding powers in 2006–07, by which time it should have generated sufficient research activity and have gained the critical mass of PhD completions to qualify; with possession of powers to award both taught and research degrees being essential criteria for university status, 2008 had been pencilled in as a possible date for this to be attained. By October 2002, as a result of the temporary suspension of TDAP scrutiny, the forecast date had been put back to 2010.[72] Such an interval would clearly have been fraught with risk, since for all the loyal words of those students who had met the TDAP assessors, no-one could predict the impact on recruitment of offering college, not university, awards.[73] Remarkably, and to considerable surprise, it was a prospect the College scarcely had to face. For, with one exception, by the time degree awarding powers were first implemented – for the intake of September 2005 – the institution had become a University in its own right. Awards of the Universities of Liverpool and Manchester, available to students entering in 2004, were replaced by awards of the University of Chester without any intermediate phase: the consequence of an unexpected, but most welcome, turn of events.[74]

On 22 January 2003 – while the TDAP assessors were at the College conducting their final visit – the Secretary of State for Education, Charles Clarke, introduced the Labour government's White Paper *The Future of Higher Education* in the House of Commons. This announced some major policy shifts. One was to concentrate yet further government funding for research in selected, 'world-class' units and institutions: not good news for a college such as Chester which was trying to raise its profile in this area. But alongside this went recognition that universities also had important roles to play in knowledge transfer and in the teaching of a much higher percentage of the age-group – by now some 43% – than at the beginning of the previous decade, and that these activities should also be valued. As he told the Commons:

> Our universities have to identify more clearly than they do now the way in which they address the great missions on the basis of which they were created. Those missions are research, knowledge transfer and, perhaps most important of all, teaching. These are the central themes of this white paper, and we start from the basis that over the years the emphasis on research has, for understandable reasons, been at the expense of teaching and knowledge transfer.

Accordingly – and crucially for Chester at this juncture – 'we will recognise excellent teaching as a University mission in its own right by making the award of university title dependent on undergraduate teaching degree awarding powers only'.[75]

There was much else of significance in Clarke's speech and in the White Paper itself, encouraging the development of Foundation Degrees largely through FE colleges, promoting widening access through a 'postcode premium' to institutions recruiting students from poorer backgrounds, and promising variable fees of up to £3,000 per annum, the latter duly introduced in the following year's Higher Education Act under a scheme which replaced upfront payments with repayable loans. But on the specific issue of university criteria, never was a government policy announcement better timed for Chester College, nor a cause for more rejoicing: all the more so for having come out of the blue, without any leak in advance.[76] There were of course objections from traditionalists, although in reality the teaching role of a university has an honourable history of far greater longevity than major involvement with research.[77] The government stuck to its position and revised guidance for applicants was published in August 2004. Henceforth,

> an organisation wishing to apply for approval to use the title 'University' must have been granted powers to award taught degrees, normally have at least 4,000 full time equivalent higher education students, of whom at least 3,000 are registered on degree level courses (including foundation degree programmes), and be able to demonstrate that it has regard to the principles of good governance as are relevant to its sector.

Particular attention would be paid to the 'scholarship and the pedagogical effectiveness of academic staff', although the previous expectation that a university must cover a wide range of disciplines disappeared.[78]

The governors, briefed on the criteria on the basis of a Department for Education & Skills consultation document, formally decided to apply for university title in March 2004. The College's application, drafted by Glyn Turton with input from a host of academic and administrative colleagues, was ready to be sent off in August, almost as soon as the new criteria were officially published. The application opened with a statement that the minimal criteria were fulfilled – 7,116 FTE students of whom 4,321 FTE were on degree level courses – and argued the institution's case through commitments to 'enrich students personally and … facilitate their employment', to engage in research and scholarship which both informed teaching and promoted knowledge transfer, and to contribute economically, intellectually and culturally to a sub-region which transcended county (and national) boundaries. Indeed, much was made of the fact that the College was 'the only higher education institution serving the County of Cheshire that has its principal site within the county' but one whose impact stretched beyond this to include the Manchester-Liverpool corridor, Wirral, the Welsh Marches and the 'North Wales coastal strip'. 'The College's strategic location is consistent with its strategic aim – that of becoming a university whose academic services meet the needs of a definable geographical zone.' The point was also made that teaching and research were seen as interlinked, part of a 'learning continuum' which embraced wider communities, nationally and internationally, beyond those within the North West.[79]

The application is also of interest as providing yet another statistical snapshot of the institution, this time in the closing phase of its life as a College. The number of academic staff in 2003–04 was given as 345, of whom 267 were permanent full-time employees; using the structure in place at that time, 145 of the 346 (42%) were in the School of Science & Health, 28 (8%) in Education, with the remaining 50% shared almost equally between Arts & Humanities and Nursing, Midwifery & Social Care. 31% of all academic staff currently held a UK doctorate, a higher percentage than in HE colleges and post-1992 universities at large, and a further 41 (12%) were working towards one. About a quarter – fairly evenly distributed across the four schools – had experience as an external examiner or moderator elsewhere. As evidence of its outreach towards 'applied research, consultancy, knowledge transfer and facilitation', the College was able to cite the existence of six Centres – Work Related Studies, Public Health Research, Victorian Studies, Christian Ministry, Religion & the Biosciences and Exercise & Nutrition Science, plus a further five Practice Development Units within the School of Nursing, Midwifery & Social Care. Indicative of its postgraduate work were no less than 37 taught Master's programmes, 36 PhD completions and 55 staff active as research supervisors, already a healthy basis for a future application for research degree awarding powers.[80]

In reality, data based on four Schools was already out of date when the application was submitted, since some major structural changes were approved for the start of the 2004–05 academic year: destined to be the institution's last as a College, though the new structure proceeded to serve it well as a University thereafter. There had already been some adjustment to the Senior Management Team, where the departure of the Deputy Principal in summer 2000 had led to Dorothy Marriss of Nursing & Midwifery stepping up to this position and several of the duties attached to the post being redistributed among others; what had originally been temporary arrangements were now confirmed as permanent four years later, though with the Bursar named as Vice-Principal, Rhodes taking on further corporate responsibilities alongside the oversight of his former Warrington campus, and his fellow Assistant Principals, Cotterrell and Turton, no longer being expected to combine their institutional duties with those of being Dean of a School. At the same time, the four Schools were reorganised into seven, with several new Deans being appointed internally, vacating their positions as Heads of Subject to create fresh opportunities for promotion below. The Schools of Education and of Nursing, Midwifery & Social Care remained intact, though the latter was re-named Health & Social Care. However Arts & Humanities now became Humanities on the one hand, Arts & Media on the other, while Science & Health was divided up into Applied & Health Sciences, Social Sciences, and Business, Management & Law: 'Business' at last became a separate School, as envisaged by the Principal soon after his arrival, but as one of seven not five, and with a new subject, Law, within its remit. The seven Deans of School, and a further three now appointed for Students, Learning & Teaching and Academic Quality & Standards, were to meet monthly with senior management and the heads of some key services on a new body, the College Executive Group, intended as a vehicle for strategic planning and decisions on actions to proceed; a wider group of service managers were to meet with the Executive as the College Management Group. Alongside all this went revised committee arrangements, with some delegation of powers to the Boards of Studies of the various Schools, each of which had a full-time administrator appointed to manage quality assurance at the local level.[81]

So it was a somewhat differently-structured College which on 15 and 16 November 2004 faced two further QAA assessors, whose task was to test the institution's fitness to become a university. They met the usual cast of Principal, governors, students and staff and sent their report to the QAA's

Advisory Committee on Degree Awarding Powers the following January. A positive recommendation from the QAA was duly accepted by the Department for Education & Skills in March. The May General Election would almost certainly have led to a change in government policy had there been a different result and the prize might yet have been snatched away. But with Labour successful once again the formal grant of university title by the Privy Council was duly issued on 22 July and took effect from 1 August 2005.[82] This grant has rightly been described as being 'as momentous as the Founding Resolution of 25 January 1839'[83] and a few extracts from the assessors' report are worth quoting as a fitting tribute to what had been accomplished, not only in the past decade and a half when there had been increasing focus on this ultimate goal, but in the century and a half which had gone before.

> The institution presents itself with conviction as a teaching-led, research-informed institution ... [with] ... a coherent and consistent vision of how it wishes to develop ... [It] is committed to sustaining its central mission of service to the community, infused by the spirit of its founding Christian ethos. It intends, despite potential tensions created by rapid expansion and split sites, to maintain what it sees as its key strengths: cohesiveness and singleness of purpose; adherence to national standards; and commitment to being a caring institution offering higher education 'on a human scale' ... [It]... has recognised research strengths ... [and] ... has demonstrated that it has the confidence and capabilities to exercise responsibly the duties that would be placed upon it were it to be granted university title.[84]

The QAA, which now had enough information on the College to write its own book on the subject, was not quite finished yet and followed up with an institutional audit – the first since 1996 – in May 2005. This found a few points on which to make advisable recommendations but again was very positive.[85] The battle had been won. After 166 years, the College could make way for the University with its head held high.

---

1   CC, *Campus* 15 (December 1997), p. 9.

2   Speech in February 2000, quoted in L. Bosetti and K. Walker, 'Perspectives of UK Vice-Chancellors in Leading Universities in a Knowledge-Based Economy', *HEQ*, LXIV, 1 (January 2010), pp. 4–21.

3   CC, Minutes of Governors, 1990–1999: 7 October 1997; CC, Minutes of Academic Board, 1998–2000: 23 June 1999. Wheeler did in fact live in the Principal's house on Parkgate Road from April 1998 to August 1999, before it took on a new role as student accommodation; the rear garden was incorporated into the grounds of the campus and became a 'peace garden' until built over in 2013.

4   CC, Minutes of Governors, 1990–99: 7 October 1997.

5   University of Surrey Roehampton, as the institution was known from 2000, became the independent Roehampton University in 2004, with Roberts as Pro-Vice-Chancellor.

6   CC, Minutes of Academic Board, 1993–95: 18 May 1994; CC, Minutes of Academic Board, 1996–98: 11 February 1998; CC, Minutes of Governors, 1990–99: 30 June, 23 November 1998; the first Readers, appointed in 1999, were Roy Alexander (Geography), Celia Deane Drummond (TRS), Neville Ford (Mathematics), Peter Gaunt (History) and John Williams (Biology), all of whom later became Professors (*Collegian*, 1999, p. 2).

7   CC, Minutes of Governors, 1990–99: 25 February 1998; CC, Minutes of Academic Board, 1996–98: 18 March 1998.

8   D. Hopkin, *The Role of Universities in the Modern Economy* (Cardiff, 2002), pp. 42–43.

9   CC, Minutes of Academic Board, 1996–98: 18 March, 17 June, 28 October 1998; CC, Minutes of Academic Board, 1998–2000: 17 June 1998; CC, Minutes of Governors, 1990–99: 30 June 1998.

10 Wheeler gave these as reasons for the College's relatively high application numbers when asked by the governors in June 2000, but also acknowledged 'the pleasant campus and city' as key factors: CC, Minutes of Governors, 2000–05: 29 June 2000; cf. CC, Minutes of Governors, 1990–99: 24 February 1999.

11 CC, Minutes of Academic Board, 1998–2000: 17 June, 14 July 1999; CC, Minutes of Governors, 1990–99: 30 June, 23 November 1998, 30 June 1999; CC, Minutes of Governors, 2000–05: 23 February 2000.

12 CC, Minutes of Academic Board, 1998–2000: 28 October 1998, 23 June 1999; the introduction from 1997–98 of a centralized and computerized timetable system, further refined in 1999, facilitated the simultaneous delivery of modules within several different programmes, whatever their designation as 'Single', 'Combined' or 'Specialised' (CC, Minutes of Academic Board, 1996–98: 19 March, 18 June 1997; CC, Minutes of Academic Board, 1998–2000: 14 July 1999) .

13 CC, *Undergraduate Prospectus 2000*, pp. 136–42.

14 CC, Minutes of Academic Board, 1998–2000: 17 June, 28 October 1998, 14 July 1999; CC, Minutes of Governors, 1990–99: 24 February, 30 June 1999; CC, Minutes of Governors, 2000–05: 23 February, 28 November 2002 (where the importance of income from Nursing & Midwifery in subsidising other areas of College activity is emphasised).

15 CC, Minutes of Governors, 1990–99: 30 June, 24 November 1999; CC, Minutes of Academic Board 2001–03: 20 March 2002; CC, Minutes of Academic Board, 2003–04: 2 July 2003, 24 March 2004.

16 CC, *Annual Report 1999–2000*, p. 23 (where the precise figures as returned to the Higher Education Statistics Agency for that year are 4,903 undergraduates and 2,501 postgraduates); *VCH Cheshire*, V (i) p. 288; CC, Minutes of Academic Board, 1998–2000: Third Report, Student Loading, March 2000; cf. Chapter 10.

17 CC, Minutes of Academic Board, 1995–96: 27 March 1996; CC, Minutes of Academic Board, 1998–2000: Third Report, Student Loading, March 2000; CC,

Minutes of Academic Board, 1998–2000: 22 March 2000; CC, Minutes of Governors, 1990–99: 23 November 1998, 24 November 1999.

18 By the time university title was granted in 2005, the College had developed collaborative programmes with 13 partners, including six FE colleges and three dioceses (QAA, Institutional Audit Report, 2005, paras. 12, 90; QAA, Institutional Audit Report, 2010, para. 57).

19 CC, *Annual Report 1999–2000*, p. 11. For examples of early work in archaeology by History students, see *Medieval Settlement Research Group Annual Report* 6 (1991), pp. 25–26; *Medieval Settlement Research Group Annual Report* 7 (1992), pp. 21–23; *Cheshire Past* 3 (1994), p. 19; *Cheshire Past* 4 (1995), pp. 14–15; *Cheshire History* XXXVII (1997–98), pp. 23–25.

20 CC, Minutes of Governors, 2000–05: 27 November 2001; CC, Minutes of Academic Board, 2000–01: 21 June, 1 November 2000, 27 June 2001.

21 CC, Minutes of Academic Board, 2000–01: 10 July 2000.

22 CC, Minutes of Academic Board, 2000–01: 21 March 2001; *The Cestrian*, 2008, p. 13.

23 CC, Minutes of Governors, 2000–05: 27 November 2001; CC, Minutes of Academic Board, 2001–03: 26 June 2002; CC, *Annual Report 2002–03*, p. 20.

24 CC, Minutes of Academic Board, 2001–03: 26 June, 30 October 2002; CC, Minutes of Academic Board, 2003–04: 12 February, 17 December 2003, 11 February, 24 March, 27 April 2004.

25 CC, *Undergraduate Prospectus 2005*, pp. 120–56.

26 CC, Minutes of Academic Board, 2000–01: 21 June 2000; CC, Minutes of Academic Board, 2001–03: 26 June, 17 July 2002.

27 CC, Minutes of Academic Board, 1995–96: 29 March 1995, 24 April, 23 October 1996.

28 CC, Minutes of Academic Board, 1996–98: 19 March 1997; CC, Minutes of Academic Board, 1998–2000: 17 June 1998, 10 February 1999, 22 March 2000; Third Report Student Loading, March 2000; CC, Minutes of Governors, 2000–05: 29 June 2000, 3 March 2004; CC, Minutes of Academic Board, 2001–03: 26 June, 30 October 2002; CC, Minutes of Academic Board, 2003–04: 11 February 2004; CC, *Annual Report 1999–2000*, p. 14, CC, *Annual Report, 2002–2003*, p. 17; CC, *Annual Report, 2003–2004*, p. 15. For a critique of the type of provision facilitated by the WBIS framework (casting the university in the role of 'a modern-day "spinning-jenny", turning the base metal of tacit knowledge … into gold … in an employer-led education sector'), see M. Bellamy, 'Valorisation and the Role of the University under New Labour: Reclaiming the Commons in a Knowledge-based Economy' in A. Green, ed., *Blair's Educational Legacy: Thirteen Years of New Labour* (New York, 2010), pp. 65–99 at p. 83; Bellamy wrote as Director of Postgraduate and Undergraduate Programmes for the Institute of Work Based Learning at Middlesex University.

29 CC, Minutes of Academic Board, 2000–01: 1 November 2000, 27 June 2001; *Collegian*, 2001, p. 1.02.

30 CC, *Annual Report, 1999–2000*, p. 23; CC, *Annual Report, 2002–03*, p. 30; CC, *Annual Report, 2003-04*, p. 30; CC, *Annual Report, 2004–05*, p. 29.

31 E.g. the Freshers' Edition of 1993.

32 CC, Minutes of Academic Board, 1998–2000: 10 February 1999.

33 CC, Minutes of Governors, 2000–05: 23 February 2000; the application for university title (p. 31) showed that by August 2004, 92 permanent members of staff (27% of the total) had been accepted into the HE Academy.

34 CC, Minutes of Academic Board, 2003–04: 23 June 2004; CC, *Annual Report, 1999–2000*, p. 9.

35 Those selected as the first Teaching Fellows were John Cartwright, Kate Irving and Jac Potter from the School of Science & Health, Derek Alsop and (Warrington-based) Helen Baron from Arts & Humanities, Linda Rush (Education) and Jan Gidman (Nursing, Midwifery & Social Care).

36 CC, Minutes of Academic Board, 2003–04: 12 February, 2 July, 29 October 2003; CC, Minutes of Academic Board, 2005: 22 June 2005; CC, Annual Statement to the University of Liverpool under the Instrument of Accreditation (March 2004), p. 7.

37 *Collegian*, 2003, p. 4.

38 UC, *Annual Report 2006–07*, pp. 11–12.

39 CC, *Annual Report 1999–2000*, p. 15; *Collegian*, 2001, p. 1.03; CC, Minutes of Governors, 2000–05: 28 February, 28 November 2002, 5 March, 27 November 2003.

40 CC, Minutes of Governors, 1990–99: 23 November 1998; *The Old Collegian*, 1998; *Collegian*, 1999, p. 6.

41 CC, Minutes of Academic Board, 1998–2000: 27 October 1999; CC, Minutes of Governors, 2000–05: 28 February 2002; *Collegian*, 1999, p. 26; *Chester Chronicle*, 22 July 2009. The Tatton garden had been designed by staff of Corporate Communications and Graphics, supported by Grounds & Gardens; an inscription accompanying the reconstructed version on the campus records its dedication by the Bishop of Chester on 11 September 2010 in memory of past students and staff.

42 CC, Minutes of Governors, 2000–05: 28 June 2001, 28 February 2002 (reporting the intention that Sir Howard Davies, Chief Executive of the Financial Services Authority, would formally open the Business School on 27 May); *Collegian*, 2002, p. 1.

43 CC, Minutes of Governors, 2000–05: 27 November 2001, 18 January, 28 February, 27 June 2002; CC, *Annual Report, 2002–03*, p. 26.

44 *Collegian* 2003, p. 8.

45 CC, Minutes of Academic Board, 2005: 29 April 2005; UC, Minutes of Senate, 2005–07: 28 February 2007; UC, *Staff News*, January 2005, pp. 6–7.

46 CC, Minutes of Academic Board 2001–03: 17 July 2002; CC, Minutes of Academic Board 2003–04: 12 February 2003; CC, Minutes of Governors, 2000–05: 28 February 2002, 5 March 2003, 30 June 2005; see Chapter 10.

47 CC, Minutes of Academic Board, 2000–01: 27 June 2001; CC, Minutes of Governors, 1990–99: 24 November 1999; CC, Minutes of Governors, 2000–05: 29 June 2000, 28 June, 27 November 2001, 18 January 2002; *Collegian*, 2002, p. 3.

48 *Pers. comm.* J.D. Stevens; the neighbour lived in the semi-detached house adjacent to 'Longfield'. The third floor later became a computing laboratory, besides continuing to house a network of pipes.

49 CC, *Annual Report 2002-03*, p. 8; CC, *Annual Report 2003–04*, pp. 20, 25; CC, *Staff News*, November 2004; *Collegian* 2005, p. 4.

50 CC, Minutes of Governors, 2000-05: 18 January, 27 June 2002, 5 March 2003.

51 This paragraph is based on E. Newton, *The Padgate Story: 1946–2006* (Chester, 2007).

52 See Chapter 10.

53 CC, Memo Bursar to K. Thompson, 16 December 1992.

54 CC, Minutes of Academic Board, 2001–03: 18 December 2002; the last Manchester-registered student at the Warrington campus graduated in 2007 (UC, Minutes of Senate, 2005–07: 4 April 2007).

55 CC, Minutes of Academic Board, 2003–04: 12 February 2003, 27 October 2004; CC, Minutes of Governors, 2000–05: 27 June 2002, 5 March 2003.

56 CC, Minutes of Governors, 2000–05: 27 November 2001; cf. 27 June 2002 for the admission of two Warrington representatives to the Governing Body, although in a personal rather than *ex officio* capacity.

57 CC, Minutes of Governors, 2000–05: 19 August 2003, cf. 26 June 2003.

58 CC, Minutes of Governors, 2000–05: 28 November 2002, 5 March 2003.

59 CC, Minutes of Governors, 1990–99: 23 November 1998, 24 February 1999.

60 CC, Minutes of Academic Board, 1998–2000: 28 October 1998; CC, Minutes of Governors, 1990–99: 23 November 1998.

61 Because of the early printing deadlines for prospectuses, they inevitably lagged behind events and there was much reliance on mailshots and the College website to keep information up to date. Those of 2000 (undergraduate and postgraduate) were the first to use 'Chester: a College of the University of Liverpool', which continued as the institutional title until 2004, although in the last year the traditional coat of arms appeared instead of the claret and blue logo; the 2005 prospectuses had 'University College Chester' (without reference to Liverpool in the title), as did the undergraduate prospectus for 2006; the postgraduate prospectus for 2006 was the first to show 'University of Chester' which of course continued in all prospectuses thereafter. All prospectuses since 2004 have displayed the coat of arms. On the title of the University, see CC, Minutes of Governors, 2000–05: 3 March 2004 (which reports substantial student support for the 'University of Cheshire' name) and 30 November 2004 (where the chair of governors of Warrington Collegiate Institute, Colin Daniels, seconded the proposal for 'University of Chester', after debate on whether 'The' should be part of the title).

62 R. Taylor and T. Steele, *British Labour and Higher Education, 1945–2000* (London, 2011), pp. 140–41, quoting A. Ryan, 'New Labour and Higher Education' in G. Walford, ed., *Education and the Labour Government: an Evaluation of Two Terms* (Oxford, 2006), pp. 85–98, at p. 96.

63 QAA, Foundation Degree Review, University of Liverpool, University College Chester, Warrington Collegiate Institute, West Cheshire College: Business and Management, July 2005; CC, Conduct of QAA in reviewing the Foundation Degree Programme in Business & Management, 2005.

64 CC, Minutes of Academic Board, 1995–96: 29 March 1995; joint teaching of levels 3 and M became popular in some curriculum areas, especially in TRS and nurse education, partly as a way to sustain low-recruiting options, but was not adopted in all departments or schools.

65 CC, Minutes of Academic Board, 1998–2000: 4 November, 15 December 1999, 16 February 2000; CC, Minutes of Academic Board, 2000–2001: 22 March, 10 July, 1 November 2000; CC, Minutes of Governors, 2000–2005: 30 November 2000, 21 February 2001.

66 QAA Advisory Committee on Degree Awarding Powers: Application for Taught Degree Awarding Powers – Chester College of Higher Education, Institutional Assessors' Updating Report (February 2003), p. 1; although it was to be 12 rather than nine months before the College formally reactivated its application, it was ready to approach the QAA on the subject informally by March 2002.

67 CC, Minutes of Governors, 2000–05: 28 November 2002; LIHE had been re-named Liverpool Hope in 1995.

68 CC, Minutes of Academic Board, 2000–01: 27 June 2001; CC, Minutes of Academic Board, 2001–03: 12 December 2001; CC, Minutes of Governors, 2000–05: 31 October 2001; QAA Institutional Assessors' Updating Report (February 2003), pp. 5–10, 15–31.

69 QAA Institutional Assessors' Updating Report (February 2003), p. 14; cf. CC, Minutes of Governors, 2000–05: 28 February 2002.

70 The sequence of subjects is not given in chronological order: Business & Management was the last. PE & Sports Science achieved the highest score of any, with 23 out of 24. Student Support and Guidance was awarded the highest grade of 4 ('the aims set by the subject provider are met') in every review, although according to the QAA's report, *Learning from Subject Review*, p. 36, almost 90% of subject providers nationally earned the top grade for this aspect. The same report, *passim*, shows that, other than in 'Quality Management and Enhancement' where the proportion was a little higher, '2' grades were normally awarded in well under 10% of cases, although when this was multiplied across six aspects and then across several different subjects, the statistical chances of eventually being awarded a '2' grade were considerably higher.

71 CC, Minutes of Academic Board, 1998-2000: 10 February 1999; *Collegian* 2002, p. 1; cf. CC, Minutes of Governors, 1990–99: 30 June 1998: 'the College had no immediate plans to use taught degree awarding powers if granted'.

72 CC, Minutes of Governors, 2000–05: 21 February 2001; CC, Minutes of Academic Board, 2001–03: 30 October 2002.

73 The possible implications of a delay in the award of university status until 2010 are discussed more fully at the end of the next chapter.

74 The exception was a BA in Social Work, approved to start in September 2004 under the new regulations which accompanied the College's degree awarding powers; in the event, these students, also, were able to be awarded University of Chester, rather than University College Chester, degrees on successful completion (CC, Minutes of Academic Board, 2003–04: 17 December 2003, cf. 29 October 2003). In March 2004, Academic Board accepted that 'all students entering the College from September 2005 would be registering for awards of University College Chester', a decision superseded by the grant in the meantime of the university title (CC, Minutes of Academic Board, 2003–04: 24 March 2004).

75 <<http://www.theguardian.com/education/2003/jan/22/highereducation. accesstouniversity>>, accessed 2/9/13.

76 Intelligence received by the Principal and reported to Academic Board just before Christmas 2002 suggested that the forthcoming White Paper might include a change to the criteria for TDAP, but there was no hint of any similar change affecting the grant of a university title (CC, Minutes of Academic Board, 2001–03: 18 December 2002).

77 E.g. House of Commons Education and Skills Committee: *The Future of Higher Education: Fifth Report of Session 2002–03: Vol. I, Report and Formal Minutes* (London, 2003), para 86: 'We have serious concerns about the decision to award university status to institutions without research degree awarding powers' which risked impacting adversely on 'the perception of the quality of the UK, and specifically the English, higher education sector in Europe and elsewhere'. But cf. A. Ryan, *Liberal Anxieties and Liberal Education* (London, 1999), p. 33.

78 Department for Business, Innovation and Skills: *Applications for the Grant of Taught Degree Awarding Powers, Research Degree Awarding Powers and University Title: Guidance for Applicant Organisations in England and Wales* (August 2004), pp. 20, 24–25. Cf. for a balanced assessment of the issues involved, including a forecast that 'narrowly focused commercial enterprises' might now establish universities, B. Bekhradnia, *Implications of the Government's proposals for university title: or What is a University?* (Higher Education Policy Institute, Oxford, 2003). During a visit to the College on 20 February 2004 Charles Clarke reaffirmed his commitment to the creation of 'teaching-led universities' (CC, Minutes of Academic Board, 2003–04: 25 February 2004; cf. CC, Minutes of Governors, 2000–05: 3 March 2004).

79 CC, Minutes of Governors, 2000–05: 3 March 2004; CC, Application to the Privy Council for the Title of University (August 2004), pp. 1, 2; the Department for Education and Skills had become the responsible government department in 2001.

80 CC, Application for University Title (August 2004), pp. 4, 12, 23, 25 (88 staff in Arts & Humanities, 85 in Nursing, Midwifery & Social Care), 27, 33, 39, 46.

81 CC, Minutes of Governors, 2000-05: 29 June 2000; CC, Minutes of Academic Board, 2003–04: 23 June, 27 October 2004; CC, Application for University Title (August 2004), pp. 15–16 and Appendix A.

82 CC, Minutes of Academic Board, 2005: 23 February, 29 April 2005; the College was sufficiently confident to notify the press in late March (e.g. *Chester Evening Leader*, 22 March 2005: 'University City Honour for Chester').

83 Dunn, *Bright Star*, p. 40.

84 QAA: Advisory Committee on Degree Awarding Powers, Application for University Title: Paper by the Agency-appointed institutional assessors, University College Chester (January 2005), p. 8.

85 QAA, *Institutional Audit Report, University of Chester* (2005), p. 1.

UNIVERSITY STATUS, 2005–14

CHAPTER 13

THE YOUNG UNIVERSITY

It is tempting to say that the University of Chester began with a bang – or rather a spectacular series of bangs, as firework displays lit up the city skies following a Grand Ball on the Chester campus on Friday 23 September 2005 and a banquet on Saturday 24. In fact, there had already been a gala luncheon on the Warrington campus the previous Monday to celebrate the new status and the town of Warrington had been rather quicker than the city of Chester to advertise the presence of a University through a change to the road signs. Even so, the last weekend of September should properly be regarded as the occasion of the new University's formal inauguration, with a service in Chester Cathedral on the afternoon of Sunday 25. A new silver-gilt mace, crafted by Mappin & Webb and sponsored by MBNA Europe, was ceremonially carried into the Cathedral; the Lord Lieutenant of Cheshire read the edict from the Privy Council authorising the use of the university title (ending with 'Fiat Universitas Cestriensis'); the Duke of Westminster was installed as the first Chancellor, and he in turn conferred official titles on senior members of staff. New University gowns were also worn by the senior officers, designed by Ede & Ravenscroft with an emphasis on gold and red, matching the colours on the coat of arms.[1]

Elevation to a university naturally brought some changes of nomenclature – within the Instruments & Articles of Government, within the regulatory regime, and within the physical and organisational structure. Academic Board met for the last time on 22 June 2005 and reconvened as the University Senate on 2 November, though it kept the same minute book. In a strategic decision to cease operating the Gladstone Conference Centre as an all-year-round facility, its residential accommodation was converted into student rooms and the original Old College buildings were subsequently converted into 'Senate House', ready for full use by the close of 2006.[2] Timothy Wheeler became the University's first Vice-Chancellor, while retaining the additional title of Principal for legal reasons associated with the previous Collegiate foundation. Dorothy Marriss translated from Deputy Principal to Deputy Vice-Chancellor, with the Assistant Principals becoming Pro-Vice-Chancellors. Their duties were reshuffled when the Senior PVC, Glyn Turton, who had done more than anyone to advance the institution to its new status, retired at the end of September. The conferment that summer of an Emeritus Professorship, the first awarded by Chester, was a recognition both of his scholarship and of his immense contribution during a momentous

13 years, and he took the opportunity presented by his professorial lecture eight days before his retirement, on 'The Strange Death of Liberal Education', to set out his thoughts on how, in an ideal world, he would have liked to see the University develop.

> Universities today are under enormous pressure from government, from students and from parents to equip young people with the skills which they will need in their working lives. It is perfectly right that universities should have that as one of their functions. But they also serve higher ends. There is a danger that, if we become too fixated on skills alone, we shall lose our sense of the basic values of academic debate and critical thinking.[3]

The hosting by his former department, English, of a biannual public lecture in his honour, always by distinguished academic and literary figures, would go some way towards fulfilling his hopes.

There would be further changes to the personnel of the senior management team over the next five years. In September 2008 came the retirement of David Cotterrell, by then Senior PVC (Research), who could look back on 14 successful years both shaping what had since become three Schools and overseeing the progress in research which is highlighted below. Another redistribution of duties led to his place as a PVC being taken by Chris Haslam, who had come to know the institution well as the QAA's Assistant Director during the TDAP and University application processes and who had joined the staff as Dean of Corporate Planning at the beginning of 2006. Two further PVCs were added through internal promotions in summer 2009: the Director of Legal Services and Academic Secretary Adrian Lee, whose advice on matters of law and contracts was invaluable, and the former Dean of Arts & Media Peter Harrop, whose remit was to manage and develop the Warrington campus. Another followed a year later when Michael Thomas became PVC (Academic), though he was to hold the position in conjunction with that of Dean of Health & Social Care, the post in which he had succeeded Dorothy Marriss in 2006. Marriss herself, who had relinquished her Dean's office so as to focus full-time on her other position as Deputy Vice-Chancellor, retired in summer 2010; appointed as Dean by Principal Binks as part of the absorption of the local College of Nursing & Midwifery in the early 1990s, she had become a respected ambassador for the institution, as shown in her early years through the link with nurse education in Russia and most recently through her visits to the Church of Uganda Kisiizi Hospital, where the University was able to establish a partnership for nursing and midwifery education in collaboration with the Countess of Chester Hospital. During her last year at the University there were in fact two DVCs, the Bursar

David Stevens having received the title in summer 2009; he effectively succeeded Marriss as sole holder of the position.[4]

Despite these comings and goings at senior level, Chester's early years as a University were in many ways a continuation of what had gone before. The revised committee structure set up in August 2004 carried on, although it did not take long for the University Executive to establish a Curriculum Advisory Group to give proper scrutiny on its behalf to new programme proposals. The Group was certainly kept busy: encouraged by a Vice-Chancellor anxious that the institutional portfolio should keep ahead of student demand, the ingenuity of academic staff in devising new programmes, at all levels, was reminiscent of the 1970s. Conversely, the Management Group was soon withdrawn for lack of useful business.[5] There were some departmental name changes in time for September 2005, with Geography becoming 'Geography & Development Studies' and History 'History & Archaeology', but these were reflections of recent developments in the curriculum which had already been shown to be successful. Earlier in the year, TRS had reconstituted its teaching-focused Centre for Christian Ministry as a separate entity outside the department; in the summer, the Centre for Work Related Studies was recognised as a 'department' in its own right. But these were matters of organisation and status rather than fundamental changes to the good work being accomplished. Another structural alteration in time for 2005–06 was the division of what had grown into a large Business & Management department into a separate Business department on the one hand and of Leadership & Management on the other, but again this did not significantly change the overall portfolio on offer. New programmes in Law, notably Single Honours leading to an LLB, were launched in September 2005 but the department had been created a year earlier under a newly appointed Head, Roger Kay, to allow time for their development and validation. Other new provision which heralded the birth of the University, a BA in Graphic Design and a pathway in Popular Music within the Combined Subjects (or Combined Honours) programme, had also been prepared during Chester's last year as a College.[6] Further reorganisation in 2006, whereby Business divided yet again to spawn a discrete Marketing, Tourism & Services Management department, and Art & Design split into separate Design and Fine Art departments,[7] can be seen as logical extensions of this process, accommodating the need to manage a more diverse suite of programmes. A change of title for the various Schools – they became 'Faculties' from 2007–08 – made little difference in practice, but the addition of 'Children's Services' to the name of the School of Education, in January 2007, was of more significance, since it reflected an interest in a broader workforce under the government's 'Every Child Matters' initiative.[8]

The infant University also witnessed the opening of several new buildings, but they had been planned in the days of the College. Fresh premises for Health & Social Care, designed to run roughly parallel to the railway embankment at the north end of the Chester campus and built during the course of 2005, had been approved early the previous year, although they had originally been intended to have one more storey; planning permission for a four-storey building had been refused because this could have been seen over-topping the embankment when viewed from the Parkgate Road approach. Shortlisted for a Chester City Council 'Built in Quality' Award, and incorporating a Deli Café Bar which according to *The Cestrian* 'specializes in healthy food', it was eventually opened by the Duke of Westminster (after whom it was named) on 25 May 2007.[9] The purchase of Kingsway High School in the Chester suburb of Newton, where the former comprehensive had closed, had also been approved in principle by the governors in June 2005, just before the advent of the University. This brought the College a major site 20 minutes' walk from the main Chester campus, including some much-needed playing fields, and after costly conversion (including the time-consuming removal of asbestos) had become a fine base for the various departments within Arts & Media by 2008; Performing Arts, Dance, Graphic Design, Fine Art and Journalism all moved into premises which now provided an extensive range of studios and IT laboratories (see Plate 11).[10] Even the new Students' Union building at the Cheyney Road end of the main campus, also opened in 2008, was being discussed as a better alternative to the remodelling of the Small Hall as early as spring 2005.[11] In their turn, the additional buildings released space for other departments. Law, for example, moved into the library extension vacated by Health & Social Care – before eventually relocating to premises on Liverpool Road in 2013 – while Geography came to occupy much of the area in the Best building which had previously housed Fine Art.

Meanwhile at Warrington, a major rebuilding scheme, largely financed by HEFCE, had similarly begun to enhance the appearance of the campus before the grant of University status in summer 2005. The refectory had been modernised and the theatre overhauled (later to be called the North West Media Centre) during 2004, and a new Students' Union building was built the following year. The demolition of pre-war and war-time buildings on the campus, though not accomplished until the closing months of 2005, had long been intended.[12] Both a Business Centre at Warrington, which bears the name of the former Principal of Warrington Collegiate Institute, Hilary Tucker, and a thoroughly refurbished and extended library given the name of another former Principal, Steven Broomhead, were also agreed in the last months of the College. These were both begun late in 2006 and came into use during 2007–08, with the Broomhead Library being formally opened by HRH the Duke of Kent on 8 February 2008.[13]

Another important area where the grant of University title represented a milestone but certainly not a change of direction was that of research. The College had adopted a more selective approach than in the past to the RAE of 2001, submitting only 15% of academic staff – just over 35 FTE – in six key areas, all of which had achieved scores which, though modest by national standards, did represent a step forward; indeed, though Chester was now ranked 123rd out of the 170 institutions entered in terms of its average grade, it could claim 'to have made the second largest improvement in grading'. Among the six units of assessment, TRS and 'Other Studies & Professions Allied to Medicine' – the latter an amalgam of expertise in different departments – had both achieved '3a' grades which entitled them to HEFCE funding; within TRS, internationally important research led by Celia Deane-Drummond in the field of Ecology and Theology had been 'flagged' for special recognition.[14] Building on this, a research Centre in Religion & the Biosciences had been set up in 2002 and others had followed in Stress Research, in Practice as Research in the Arts and in the Sociology of Sport, the latter involving the transfer to Chester of a team of researchers from the University of Leicester.[15] Accordingly, with a healthy record of PhD completions and the Graduate School in place to manage the postgraduate research student experience, the application for university title in 2004 had been able to describe Chester as 'an institution committed to research on a scale proportionate to its resources, and in a manner wholly consistent with its primary commitment to teaching' which 'has already reached that platform, from which the capability to oversee the award of its own research degrees is a realistic prospect'.[16] In its first full year as a University, Chester reckoned to have received £865,000 in research income, while its academic staff were responsible for 535 publications including 34 authored books.[17]

So although university status was achieved without research degree awarding powers (RDAP), there was never any intention of soldiering on without them. They became the next goal to be achieved, as proof against anyone who might be inclined to assert that institutions which lacked these powers were not 'proper' universities. An application was duly submitted in the spring of 2006, prompting a positive initial response from the QAA and a programme of scrutiny visits between October 2006 and March 2007; new regulations governing postgraduate research (PGR) programmes and awards were drafted as part of the process. Coincidentally there had already been a very good outcome to a separate audit by the QAA of the University's PGR provision for Liverpool awards early in 2006: a sound platform for the launch of the RDAP application which, allied to the considerable experience of handling audits and reviews acquired over recent years, stood the institution in good stead. The formal grant of the powers by the Privy Council duly followed in August 2007, when Chester became the first of the new universities created in 2005 to attain them. They came into force for all PGR students registering at Chester from 1 January 2008, while those already registered remained on course for Liverpool degrees.[18]

Yet for all the continuity between College and University, it was important to demonstrate that the elevated status was well deserved. The introduction in 2005 of the National Student Survey, canvassing the opinions of final-year degree students across the UK, led to the publication of results which, from the outset, showed levels of student satisfaction which compared very favourably with those in established universities.[19] There were also some benefits from a new structure to the academic year based on 20-credit rather than 15-credit modules, introduced for undergraduates from September 2007 and for postgraduates one year later, with undergraduate provision being obliged to move to year-long delivery: an end to the semesterisation introduced between 1993 and 1995 but one which inevitably involved an intensive process of programme rewriting and re-approval. The rationale for the change included encouragement towards more formative assessment and more in-depth study within a reduced number of modules; the opportunity for first-years to become more accustomed to HE before facing any major summative assessment; and the abandonment of what was perceived as a wasteful mid-year period between semesters. Together with an adjustment to the methodology for calculating degree classifications, introduced from 2006–07 in the light of practice across the sector, the reforms led to improved assessment results, with 58% of first-degree students graduating with First or Upper Second degrees in 2010 compared to 54% in 2007 and 46% in the first full year as a university.[20]

Meanwhile, the Learning & Teaching Institute (LTI) had a key role to play in enhancing the quality of teaching, running annual staff conferences on pedagogical issues and also a Postgraduate Certificate in Learning and Teaching accredited by the Higher Education Academy (HEA, successor since 2004 to the ILTHE); enrolment for this became a requirement for all newly appointed academic staff unless they already held the qualification or were Fellows of the HEA.[21] Geography, a department which had been at the forefront in using information technology in the late 1980s and of the Enterprise initiative in the early 1990s, again showed its innovatory spirit by experimenting with the use of podcasting as a vehicle for teaching; one of its exponents Derek France became the University's second National Teaching Fellow in 2008 for his work in this and other pioneering ventures in the field of e-learning.[22] Alongside advances in pedagogy went the 2008 RAE, which – though presenting its conclusions differently from previous exercises – confirmed the progress being made in academic research. Over 60 staff spread across ten units were entered and every unit was judged to be producing some 'internationally excellent' work; 15% of the work submitted in History, and 5% in each of Drama, Dance & Performing Arts, English Language & Literature and Sports-Related Studies was reckoned to be 'world-leading'.[23] There was still a need to develop high-quality research across a broader range of subjects but these results did much credit to the young University. So did some of the initiatives in the related area of Knowledge Transfer, established with the help of grants from the Higher Education Innovation Fund. Among these were an international project to combat malnutrition, in collaboration with Action Against Hunger and UNICEF, and work with an environmental consultancy to promote reductions in the carbon footprint, building on the University's existing work in the Cheshire village of Ashton Hayes. Meanwhile, the University's New Technology Initiative, founded in 2003 to offer external training in project management and technology applications, was accredited in 2007 to deliver highly regarded Prince 2 courses.[24]

League tables are a crude way of measuring the relative merits of different universities, begging all sorts of questions about methodology and reliability,[25] but the developments outlined in the two previous paragraphs did reflect positively on Chester's standing. Early in 2005 *The Guardian* had placed the College 113th in its league table of 122 degree-awarding institutions[26] but by the end of the decade the University was ranked about 80th.[27] *The Sunday Times* and the *Complete University Guide* also had it around that position.[28] Crucially, the institution benefited from its new status in terms of student recruitment, despite fears that the introduction for the intake of September 2006 and their successors of so-called 'top-up fees' of £3,000 per annum, to be paid retrospectively via the Student Loans Company, would have a deterrent effect.[29] Enrolments for a first degree at the University remained consistent, between 2,900 and 3,000, through the years from 2005 to 2009, although the figures contain an increasing number of registrations for full-time Foundation Degrees (FDs), provision where HEFCE was still willing to countenance growth.[30]

It was largely through its collaborative partnerships and through its awarding of FDs that Chester was able to fulfil an institutional commitment to widening access and participation. The University managed to secure additional numbers for FDs through a successful Lifelong Learning Network bid in 2005 and this led to the number of such programmes – delivered either by the University or by one of its partner FE colleges – leaping from 11 in 2005–06 to 26 in 2006–07 and 34 in 2008–09, by which time some 986 students were enrolled on them. All this required some careful quality assurance as well as staff development for those responsible for delivery and assessment at partner institutions; AQSS and the LTI, along with Claire Blanchard who moved on from being Director of FDs to become the University's Partnerships Advisor, all had their part to play here. In the event, partner colleges consistently fared well under scrutiny from the QAA's more enlightened Integrated Quality & Enhancement Review scheme, introduced in 2008, and the University's handling of FDs was warmly commended by a new chief external examiner appointed to oversee them. Among the most innovative of these programmes was an FD in Mortuary Science, the first in the UK, launched in January 2008 and primarily intended for funeral workers; it was soon followed by the country's only BSc in the subject. Among the more prestigious were an FD in Health Care Sciences, which received a 'quality' endorsement from the national co-ordinating body Foundation Degree Forward and was delivered by University staff online mainly to employees of the National Blood Service, and an FD in Early Years Practice endorsed by the Children's Workforce Development Council, taught for the University by staff of West Cheshire College.[31]

With its established reputation for work related studies, allied to the setting up of a Business Development Unit under Charlie Woodcock to seek opportunities for new work in the field, the University was well placed to respond to incentives to engage with what became known as 'employer-responsive provision'. This followed a call in the Leitch Report of 2006 for more employer- and employee-funded HE study and by summer 2007 the University had become one of only three institutions in the country to be successful in a bid for additional student numbers to pursue this endeavour. The WBIS framework was ideal for much of this work, and as its activity increased in both volume and complexity – it had over 1,000 registered students by 2007–08, on short courses as well as degree programmes, and embraced work with a variety of commercial and other training organisations – so the quality assurance had to be ratcheted up: a purpose for which the WBIS Approval Panel, serviced by AQSS, meeting monthly and chaired by the Dean of Academic Quality & Standards, duly replaced the Credit & Accreditation Panel. This was one area where the institution could fairly claim, alongside universities such as Middlesex and Derby, to be a sector leader. It was a claim acknowledged, for example, in the long-term secondment of Pandy Brodie from Work Related Studies to work on the skills development of decision-makers within the Pension, Disability and Carers Service; in the publication for HEFCE of a 30-page booklet *Facilitating Employer Engagement through Negotiated Work Based Learning* based on the Chester experience and largely written by the Professional Development Unit Manager, David Perrin; and in the launch of the UK's first Postgraduate Certificate in Work Based Learning Facilitation, which allowed successful students to proceed to Fellowships of the HEA. In addition, invitations from both the QAA and the national Quality & Strategy Network were issued to the Dean of Academic Quality & Standards to disseminate the processes by which all this was quality-assured. It was gratifying, but no real surprise, that when the QAA conducted yet another institutional audit, in March 2010, 'the effectiveness of the Work Based and Integrative Studies framework in providing flexible, responsive and relevant educational opportunities to work based learners' was identified as one of the features of good practice.[32]

As for collaborative partnerships generally, these almost doubled in the first five years of the University, from 13 on the eve of the new status being granted to 24 in 2009–10, by which time they accounted for over 1,000 students (or over 750 FTEs). TRS, which had been actively developing external links since the late 1980s, had 11 different partners, ranging from dioceses such as Chester and Manchester (including the Roman Catholic diocese of Shrewsbury) to training organisations and the Committee for Ministry of and Among Deaf and Disabled People, the latter a commitment which led to relevant members of staff learning sign-language. The Faculty of Social Science negotiated a prestigious partnership with Cheshire Constabulary, leading to the launch in 2007–08 of a FD in Policing which incorporated the force's initial training programme; other programmes followed – Neighbourhood Policing in 2008–09, Criminal Investigation in 2009–10 – all delivered at the Warrington campus where the presence of large numbers of police in uniform became a familiar sight. Links with nursing in the Isle of Man, which dated back to the earliest phase of this provision at Chester, continued through partnerships with the island's Nurse Education Centre and with its Department of Health & Social Security Education and Training Centre. And by 2009 seven FE colleges (Isle of Man, Mid-Cheshire, Reaseheath, South Cheshire, Warrington Collegiate, West Cheshire and Wirral Metropolitan) were delivering programmes leading to Chester awards.[33]

All this can be seen as a reflection of the major regional impact which the College had claimed it wished to make in its application for University status: among all the dioceses, colleges and other training organisations with whom the University had established formal collaborative partnerships, only three (all linked with TRS)[34] were based outside Cheshire, Lancashire (including Manchester) or the Isle of Man. Three local FE Colleges were also accorded Associate College status – Warrington Collegiate in 2006, West Cheshire and Reaseheath in 2007 – and Isle of Man College followed in 2010; the arrangement carried a commitment to the joint strategic development of the colleges' future HE provision alongside privileged access to the services of AQSS and the LTI. There were of course a variety of other 'partners', including the employers and commercial organisations with whom the Professional Development Unit was working and a growing number of institutions overseas with whom links of one sort or another were established. But the University continued to be cautious over how much autonomy was devolved to these bodies. By retaining control of at least some of the delivery and of all student assessment, it kept these arrangements outside the formal definition of collaborative provision as seen by the QAA. Accordingly, 'the systematic and supportive processes and management which underpin collaborative arrangements with key partners' became another feature of good practice identified in the audit of 2010.[35]

All this activity led to a further increase in overall student numbers, although the government's cap on most full-time recruitment meant that, in quantifiable terms and despite the enthusiasm for new programme development, these early years as a university are better characterised as a period of consolidation than as one of growth. There were 6,653 full-time undergraduates taught at or from the Chester campus in 2006–07 and 6,465 taught either from there or from the new Kingsway site by 2008–09; an increase in full-time taught postgraduates, from 216 to 409, was the main reason why overall numbers remained virtually the same. At Warrington, despite all the investment in new buildings and the launch of new programmes, 1,257 full-time undergraduates in 2006–07 had risen to no more than 1,306 by 2008–09. Part-time student numbers, at both undergraduate and postgraduate level, increased at Chester between the years, from 4,535 to 5,732, but fell at Warrington from 449 to 365. The net result was that, in terms of FTEs, 8,334 students at both Chester and Warrington in 2006–07 had become 8,307 in 2008–09, a slight contraction to set against a near-doubling in the meantime of collaborative numbers (398 to 768 FTEs), from which the University did derive a share of the income. This was certainly the main reason why the institution could claim modest expansion overall between these two dates: from 13,813 to 15,560 individual students, or from 8,732 to 9,075 FTEs.[36]

It is worth dwelling on these figures a little longer for the insights they give into the character of the University in the late 2000s. They confirm yet again the long-term significance for Chester of diversification beyond teacher training. From a peak in 1972–73 of over 900 students undertaking certificate of education, BEd or postgraduate certificate courses – when the only other provision was some in-service work – the institution now had less than 600 on equivalent BEd or PGCE programmes, although various part-time and postgraduate initiatives, including collaborative partnerships, brought the total FTE for which the Faculty of Education & Children's Services was responsible by 2008–09 to 1,058. Among the other Faculties that year, again if partner numbers are included, Applied & Health Sciences was the largest, with 1,702 FTE, followed by Health & Social Care (1,518), Social Science (1,508), Arts & Media (1,272), Humanities (1,035) and Business, Enterprise & Lifelong Learning (901), the last a rebranding of the School previously known as Business, Management & Law.[37] In round figures, some 3,500 full-time undergraduates were studying on Single Honours programmes but the enduring importance of Combined Subjects is reflected in the fact that a further 2,000 were registered for combinations within this framework.[38] Indeed, the availability of 'hundreds of possible options for combined honours courses' was often cited as a reason to apply to Chester,[39] and Marketing, Recruitment & Admissions repeatedly argued against restrictions on permitted combinations despite pressures on the timetable structure.[40]

The figures also chart the gradual phasing out of registrations for awards of the University of Liverpool, which had renewed the accreditation for taught programmes in 2003 and for research degrees in 2006.[41] Most of the entrants of 2004, the last cohort to be registered for Liverpool degrees, graduated in 2007, leaving only part-time students, those on longer programmes and those who, for whatever reason, had fallen behind their year-group to be accounted for. There were 3,601 Liverpool-registered students in 2006–07, over two-thirds of whom were full-time, but this number had come down to 488 by 2008–09, most of them taking a postgraduate taught or research degree on a part-time basis. Although small numbers of Liverpool students remained on Chester's books for some years yet – even at the end of 2013 there were still nine part-time research students yet to complete – Liverpool was last officially represented at a Chester graduation ceremony in March 2008.[42] After that, their graduates were invited to Liverpool's own ceremonies, though with provision for them to be congratulated at a Chester event through a handshake from Wheeler as the Vice-Chancellor which, to most observers, was indistinguishable from the conferment of a degree.

Embedded in these statistics are other messages about the composition of the student body. Of the 5,046 who graduated with Bachelor's degrees between 2007 and 2009, all but 252 (or 5%) were recorded as ethnically 'white' – although it is fair to add that a ground-breaking initiative by TRS, a BA in Muslim Youth Work taught at the Warrington campus which recruited 13 ethnic-minority students to its first cohort, does not appear in these figures since it was not launched until September 2007. This limited ethnic diversity was a reflection partly of geographical context – about 97% of Cheshire's population was 'white' according to the 2011 census – and partly of the slow progress made so far in internationalising the student intake despite various initiatives around the world: by 2008–09 there were still only 559 registered overseas students (3.6% of the total) including postgraduates, and at least a fifth of them came from the Isle of Man. Meanwhile, 362 (just over 7%) of those who achieved Bachelor's degrees between 2007 and 2009 had a declared disability.[43] There is nothing in the figures to suggest that any of these sub-groups was performing disproportionately and it is a credit to the University's disability support systems that students in this category were not far behind the others in the percentages of Firsts and Upper Seconds awarded. There were however some grounds for concern – noted by the Vice-Chancellor in his report to Academic Board early in 2006 – in the continuing imbalance between the sexes. This had first been regarded as an issue at Chester when female numbers had forged clear in the late 1960s; the addition of nurse education had predictably increased the preponderance of women over men and the ratio by 2006–07 was about 5:2, both among full-time undergraduates and within the student population generally. Male recruitment did improve in the next couple of years, so that by 2008–09 there were 5,771 full-time undergraduate women (and 11,158 women in total) compared to 2,609 (4,402) men, but perhaps the most significant matter was the 'gender split' when it came to academic performance. In 2006–07 58% of women but only 45% of men gained First or Upper Second Bachelor's degrees; by 2008–09 the figures were 60% and 48%.[44] Whatever conclusions may be drawn from this, the discrepancy itself was nothing new. Taken as a whole, female students had already been outperforming their male counterparts in the days of certificates of education four decades earlier.[45]

This mixed community was well served by the University's support services, although – in common with the rest of the sector – part-time and collaborative provision students made less use of them than did full-timers based on the Chester and Warrington campuses. Early in 2007 Student Support & Guidance (SSG), which had recently changed its name from SGSS, gained Matrix accreditation for the quality of its information advice and guidance service.[46] In April 2008 the careers service, by now known as Careers & Employability, became a separate support department outside SSG but together they became the first UK University service to be awarded by the British Quality Foundation both a 5-star Recognition for Excellence award (in 2008) and a UK Excellence Achievement award for Employee Satisfaction (in 2009). Although these accolades related specifically to the management of staff (who by now totalled 50 across the two departments), the indirect benefits to students were acknowledged when the University was runner-up for the *Times Higher* Outstanding Student Support award, also in 2009. Alongside this went the personal academic tutor system, still the bedrock of the University's pastoral care provision half a century after its introduction under Principal Price, and now more carefully managed than ever, with an annual report and action points being submitted to the Learning & Teaching Committee by the Director of Undergraduate Programmes, Diana Dunn. For its part, the chaplaincy retained a high-profile presence both at Chester and at Warrington, with a resident chaplain on both campuses still supported by local clergy and a team of staff and students as first devised in the 1980s. A 'faith space', located in a mobile building on the Chester campus, had come into use at the beginning of 2005 to cater for those who wanted an alternative to the University Chapel, while Warrington – which lacked a chapel – had a dedicated 'worship space' provided in one of the hostels, Aiken Hall, in summer 2006; this was subsequently refitted into a recognisable chapel, with a separate 'faith space' created elsewhere on the campus. Meanwhile, the University's Learning Support Services were kept busy, running study skills seminars and workshops and providing tuition for students with dyslexia and specific learning difficulties; a total of about 2,000 student attendances in 2005–06 rose to some 3,500 by 2008–09, spread across the campuses at Chester and Warrington and also two of the Cheshire hospital sites.[47] The institution had made much in its application for university title of a commitment to 'student-centredness' and of its 'strong, coherent network on which students may rely for help and advice'.[48] Its conduct in the years which followed amply justified these claims.

The Students' Union itself benefited considerably from the provision of new premises in 2008 and spent £400,000 from its own reserves on furnishing the building. The previous year – as if seeking to demonstrate that laments for the 'death of the Student Society' in the 1960s had been premature – it could claim to be overseeing over 60 clubs and societies with a membership in excess of 2,000, so the availability of extra meeting rooms was timely.[49] Volunteering continued to be a popular activity within the student community, nowhere better exemplified than by Holly Shaw, an Early

Childhood Studies graduate in 2009 who had had a kidney transplant a year earlier and whose campaigning and fundraising in the cause of organ donation led to her receipt of a national vInspired 'Shout' award as an 'ultimate campaigner'.[50] As the institution regained its reputation for sporting prowess, Tracey Neville, who had over 80 England caps at netball, graduated in Nutrition & Sports Science in 2007, the same year that Jon Clarke, a part-time Sport & Exercise Science student, made two rugby league appearances for Great Britain. In 2010, the men's basketball team won the British Universities & Colleges Sport Northern Conference Cup; Derval O'Rourke, a part-time distance learning student on the MSc in Sociology of Sport & Exercise, won silver in the 100 metres hurdles at the European Championships; and Rebecca Romero MBE, the first British woman to win Summer Olympics medals in two different sports, enrolled for the MSc in Sports & Exercise Nutrition.[51] In a different sphere, *The Cestrian* of 2009 was also able to report a victory for a group of Chester students over BBC2's renowned *Eggheads* quiz team; that of 2010 applauded the award of an MBE to Annette Rushton, a Diploma in Counselling student with nearly 40 years' experience in Nursing Management.[52] Meanwhile, Duffy – who as Aimee Anne Duffy had studied both Commercial Music Production (at Warrington) and Performing Arts (at Chester) before deciding to leave without completing her degree in 2006, topped the UK pop music charts in 2008 with a single, 'Mercy', and her debut album, 'Rockferry'.[53]

Yet for all the positivity associated with the student experience at Chester, there was an acknowledged difficulty in the area of residential accommodation. As we have seen, this had originally been identified as a problem by Principal Thomas: having wanted a hostel built before the First World War, he had had to fight the proposed closure of the College partly because of over-reliance on lodgings in 1933, and was dead by the time Fisher and Astbury Houses opened in the 1950s. Notwithstanding the provision of some off-campus residential blocks, such as Powys Court and John Milton Hall, either side of the millennium, and the new one at Hollybank opened in 2005, very little student accommodation had been built on the main Chester campus since the hostels for women in the 1960s; there had only been the small student village opened by Princess Margaret in 1989, at a time when the total College FTE was scarcely into four figures. The issue was on the agenda of a senior management team conference in November 2006 and by June 2008 preliminary plans had been drawn up for a £30-million 'student village' capable of housing over 900 students, to be built on the land immediately north of the old railway embankment which Binks had tried to acquire, and which had now at last been purchased. However, this low-lying site, known as 'Glenesk', suffered from drainage problems and there were objections from local residents whose houses were on the opposite side of Parkgate Road. Although these issues were not insurmountable, to have addressed them would only have added to the enormous cost; once the latest government enquiry – the Browne Committee – had begun its review of HE funding in November 2009 there were added concerns about future demand, in a context where more students might choose to live at home. In the end, although Glenesk remains earmarked for future development by the University, it was decided to switch to a building scheme on the main campus instead. By December 2010 the plan was for an £8-million hostel for 200 students. Initial problems over planning consent led to a delay in completion by 12 months from its original intended date of summer 2012, but at an eventual cost of about £10 million it was ready a week early – under the name of Grosvenor House and actually with 202 study-bedrooms – for the intake of September 2013.[54]

There were of course some disappointments, in this as in every other phase of the institution's history. Despite the best efforts of those charged with its development, the projected increase in the student population at the Warrington campus did not fully materialise. The student experience there was enhanced through new programmes and a much-improved learning environment; high-profile shirt sponsorship and joint training facilities with Warrington Wolves rugby league club brought good publicity and television exposure. But except in specially tailored fields such as the work with the Cheshire Constabulary, recruitment continued to be a challenge. Elsewhere, an ambitious project in collaboration with Wirral Metropolitan College to establish a university presence in Birkenhead, under the Labour government's 'higher education cold spot' initiative of 2008, was dropped when funding for the additional numbers was not forthcoming. A scheme to take over Burton Manor, a conference centre on Wirral, was not carried through, although the artisan workshops which the University established in the grounds did persist.[55] Even so, writing in *The Cestrian* of 2010, Wheeler could still look back on the first five years of the institution's new status with considerable satisfaction: 'the University is in excellent heart and despite the current economic challenges is looking forward to the future with confidence'.[56] The number of Single Honours programmes taught at the two campuses, as advertised in the 2010 prospectus, stood at 67, compared to 55 five years earlier; postgraduate and continuing professional development programmes had gone up from around 50 to over 70 in the same period.[57] The Faculty of Education & Children's Services received its best result to date from an Ofsted inspection in summer 2010, with an 'outstanding' grade for its

Primary provision and commendations for such matters as 'high levels of academic and pastoral care for trainees', 'very good use of school and college-based colleagues to deliver training' and 'very good use of resources to support training and promote good attainment'.[58] The QAA also gave Chester a ringing endorsement in its 2010 Audit report, highlighting such features of good practice as 'the strength of the partnership approach between faculties and Academic Quality Support Services in the assurance of quality and standards', 'the supportive relationships that underpin learning and working in the institution' and 'commitment to preparing students for study as demonstrated by its pre-enrolment activities and its extended induction arrangements'.[59] Alongside the verdict from Ofsted, and as the first QAA report since the grant of University status, it was evidence that some of the

Figure 36: HRH the Prince of Wales signs the visitors' book on the occasion of the conferment of an honorary degree in 2007, watched by (from left to right) the Duke of Westminster (University Chancellor), HRH the Duchess of Cornwall and the Vice-Chancellor.

best features of the College – especially its supportive environment and sense of common purpose – lived on in the new context.

Yet as we saw in the previous chapter, a QAA visit in 2010 could so easily have been for the purposes of scrutinising the institution's fitness to be a university at all. Through most of the TDAP process, until the government's decision early in 2003 to promote teaching-led universities, Principal, governors and staff had all been expecting Chester to spend some years recruiting for its own degrees as a university college. Acquisition of research degree awarding powers in 2007 meant that, even under the old criteria, Chester would have been in a position to secure university status around the end of the decade, as Wheeler had originally predicted. But what if the years 2005–10 had been spent as University College Chester rather than as the University of Chester? What difference would it have made?

There is one obvious answer, since the power to award honorary degrees came with the grant of University status, not that of taught degree awarding powers. The first recipient of an honorary doctorate – or for that matter any award – of the University of Chester was the Lord Lieutenant, William Bromley Davenport, who had read the proclamation from the Privy Council at the launch in September 2005 and returned to the Cathedral a few weeks later for the conferment of his degree.[60] He was followed by an impressive array of honorary graduates, including the cricketer and charity fund-raiser Ian Botham in 2006, HRH the Prince of Wales (and Earl of Chester) and the broadcaster Joan Bakewell in 2007, the poet laureate Andrew Motion and former archiepiscopal envoy Terry Waite in 2008, the Archbishop of York John Sentamu and composer Edward Gregson in 2009. None of them would have graced a degree ceremony of University College Chester.[61]

Beyond this, we are into the realms of institutional self-confidence and public esteem. There was already an intention to invite applications from local FE colleges for Associate College status on the strength of degree awarding powers alone,[62] but it was clearly more attractive for them to affiliate to a university than to a university college. Difficult though this is to quantify, some of the high-calibre academic staff recruited in this period, already holding a permanent post at another university or with good prospects of obtaining one, would not have applied to Chester had it not itself attained a university title. With scrutiny for university status still in the future, not the past, there might have been a little more caution in streamlining the processes associated with a 'belt and braces' approach to quality assurance, necessary in the first half of the decade but criticised for elements of duplication in the QAA audit of 2005.[63] It is unlikely that, as a university college, Chester would have been so confident in developing professional doctorates, of which the first three, in Professional Studies (via the WBIS framework), Business Administration and Practical Theology, were all launched in 2010.[64] Most important of all, the institution would almost certainly have struggled to sustain its full-time undergraduate recruitment in the age of £3,000 per annum tuition fees in the later years of the decade, when it could offer only university college, not university, degrees. Lower student numbers would have had a knock-on effect on income, on staff morale and employment prospects, and on the money available to spend on new equipment, new buildings and new sites. As it celebrated its 175th anniversary, even if by then it had become the University of Chester, the institution would have been smaller, in terms of enrolments and the size of its estate, poorer financially and with much further to climb in institutional league tables. But this is to indulge in 'counter-factual history'. What had actually happened was that fortune had smiled on the College in 2003 and Chester had seized its chance to become a university with minimal delay. In the new decade, there would be opportunities to take it to the next level.

---

1   CC, *Staff News*, July 2005, pp. 1, 3; *The Cestrian*, 2006, p. 5.
2   UC, Minutes of Governors, 2005 to date: 1 November 2006.
3   *The Cestrian*, 2006, p. 4.
4   UC, Minutes of Governors, 2005 to date: 27 June 2006, 29 November 2007, 24 June, 27 November 2008, 24 June 2009, 17 March 2010; *The Cestrian*, 2009, p. 20.
5   The Curriculum Advisory Group, better known as CAGE, was originally established in 2006–07 under the name of the Outline Planning Proposal Working Group (UC, Mid-Cycle Follow-Up to QAA Institutional Audit, October 2007, p. 8; UC, QAA Institutional Audit 2010 Briefing Paper, p. 5). As an example of curriculum development, the new programmes approved for delivery in 2009 included BA English Language, BA/BSc Accounting & Finance, BA International Business, MA Art Therapy, MSc Endodontics and BSc Zoo Management, the last two with collaborative partners (UC, Minutes of Executive Group, 4 November, 9 December 2008, 20 January 2009).
6   CC, Minutes of Academic Board, 2003–04: 27 October 2004; CC, Minutes of Academic Board, 2005: 15 December 2004, 23 February, 29 April 2005; UC, Minutes of Senate, 2005–07: 2 November 2005; CC, *Staff News*, July 2005, pp. 4–5.
7   UC, Minutes of Senate, 2005–07: 1 November 2006.
8   UC, Minutes of Senate, 2005–07: 13 December 2006.
9   *Pers. comm.* J.D. Stevens; the governors queried whether there was a possibility of 'subterraneous development' to create a basement instead of the intended top storey but were told that because the building was on a landfill site – the consequence of the successive levelling schemes – 'the cost of going down would be considerable' (CC, Minutes of Governors, 2000–05: 3 March 2004). On this

building, see also CC, Minutes of Academic Board, 2005: 29 April, 22 June 2005; UC, Minutes of Academic Board, 2005–07: 14 December 2005; CC, Minutes of Governors, 2000–05: 30 June 2005; *Collegian*, 2005, p. 5, *The Cestrian*, 2006, p. 8; *The The Cestrian*, 2008, p. 7; UC, *Annual Report 2006–07*, p. 50.

[10] CC, Minutes of Academic Board, 2005: 22 June 2005; UC, Minutes of Senate, 2005–07: 2 November, 14 December 2005, 21 June, 1 November, 13 December 2006, 28 February 2007; CC, Minutes of Governors, 2000–05: 30 June 2005, 6 March 2007; *The Cestrian*, 2007, p. 8; *The Cestrian*, 2008, p. 7. An initial idea had been to include Sport & Exercise Sciences among the provision to be relocated to Kingsway but this was when there were plans to build a new Performing Arts Centre on the main Chester campus; the relocation of Performing Arts to Kingsway led to the abandonment of this costly scheme (UC, Minutes of Governors, 2005 to date: 27 June 2006).

[11] CC, Minutes of Governors, 2000–05: 2 March 2005; UC, Minutes of Senate, 2005–07: 13 December 2006; *The Cestrian*, 2008, p. 7; *The Cestrian*, 2009, p. 21.

[12] CC, Minutes of Academic Board, 2003–04: 23 June 2004; CC, Minutes of Academic Board, 2005: 22 June 2005; UC, Minutes of Senate: 2 November 2005, 5 April 2006. UC, Minutes of Senate, 2005–07: 1 November, 13 December 2006, 28 February 2007; UC, Minutes of Governors, 2005 to date: 29 November 2007; UC, *Staff News*, February/March 2008, pp. 1, 3; *The Cestrian*, 2008, p. 6; UC, *Annual Report 2006–07*, pp. 11–12.

[14] CC, Minutes of Governors, 2000–05: 28 February 2002; *RAE Submissions 2001: Chester College of HE, Theology, Divinity & Religious Studies* (HEFCE, 2002). The definition of a 3a grade was 'quality that equates to attainable levels of national excellence in over two-thirds of the research activity submitted, possibly showing evidence of international excellence'; the other gradings were Applied Mathematics, Art & Design and History all 3b, and English Language & Literature 2.

[15] CC, Minutes of Governors, 2000–05: 27 November 2003.

[16] CC, Application to the Privy Council for the Title of University (August 2004), p. 11; see Chapter 12.

[17] UC, *Research that Makes a Difference, 2005–06*.

[18] UC, Minutes of Senate, 2005–07: 15 February, 5 April, 21 June, 20 September, 11 December 2006, 28 February 2007; UC, Minutes of Governors, 2005 to date: 29 November 2007; UC: Mid-Cycle Follow-Up to QAA Institutional Audit, October 2007, p. 6; UC, QAA Institutional Audit 2010 Briefing Paper, p, 2; *The Cestrian*, 2008, p. 14.

[19] See e.g. <<http://www.theguardian.com/education/students/tables/0,,1574395,00.html>>, accessed 22/9/13; in the first year of the NSS, Chester ranked 18th out of 140 institutions and it has repeatedly performed strongly since then (UC, Minutes of Senate, 2005–07: 2 November 2005, 1 November 2006; UC, Minutes of Governors, 2005 to date: 29 November 2005). In 2006–07, Chester's Fine Art students were reckoned to be 'the most satisfied in Great Britain' and Geography

was the only UK department in that subject to score 10/10 for teaching quality (UC, *Annual Report 2006–07*, p. 15).

20   *Complete University Guide: University League Tables, 2008, 2009, 2012* (using data for degree classifications from two years earlier); UC, QAA Institutional Audit 2010 Briefing Paper, pp. 4, 10; UC, Minutes of Senate 2005–07: 21 June, 20 September, 1 November, 13 December 2006.

21   UC, QAA Institutional Audit 2010 Briefing Paper, pp. 16, 24–25; the Learning & Teaching programme could also be taken to an MA.

22   UC, *Annual Review 2009*, p. 43; C. Ribchester, D. France and A. Wheeler, 'Podcasting: a Tool for Enhancing Assessment Feedback?' in E. O'Doherty, ed., *The Fourth Education in a Changing Environment Conference* (Santa Rosa, California, 2008), pp. 119–36; D. France and C. Ribchester, 'Podcasts and Feedback' in G. Salmon and P. Edirisingha, eds, *Podcasting for Learning in Universities* (Milton Keynes, 2008), pp. 70–79.

23   <<http://www.rae.ac.uk/results>> accessed 23/9/13: RAE 2008 Quality Profile, University of Chester. Thirty per cent of work in both History and TRS, 25% in Drama, Dance & Theatre Studies, 20% in Sports-Related Studies, 15% in each of Allied Health Professions & Studies, Applied Mathematics, Social Work & Social Policy Administration, and English Language & Literature, 10% in Geography & Environmental Studies and 5% in Art & Design was rated 'internationally excellent'.

24   *The Cestrian*, 2008, p. 18; Ashton Hayes had set itself the goal of becoming the UK's first carbon neutral village and the University received a good deal of national and even international publicity from this initiative (e.g. UC, *Annual Review 2009*, p. 12; UC, *Annual Report 2006–07)*, p. 16. Prince 2 was an internationally recognised project management method, developed by the Office of Government Commerce.

25   See e.g. M. Tight, 'Do League Tables Contribute to the Development of a Quality Culture? Football and Higher Education Compared', *HEQ*, LIV 1 (January 2000), pp. 22–42. Liverpool and Manchester are included among the places where the football club is rated more highly than the university, Oxford and Cambridge as places where the opposite is the case. Chester appears as one of 37 towns with a football league club but no university, but the situation has in fact been reversed since 2009.

26   CC, Minutes of Academic Board, 2005: 29 April 2005; <<http://education.guardian.co.uk/universityguide2005>> accessed 22/9/13.

27   <<http://www.theguardian.com/education/table/2009/may/12/university-league-table>>, billed as the University Guide 2010 but published 12 May 2009, gives Chester as 80th for the previous year and 90th for the current one. <<http://www.theguardian.com/education/table/2010/jun/04/university-league-table>>, the 2011 Guide published on 4 June 2010 has Chester at 79th. (Both accessed 23/9/13.)

28 *Complete University Guide: University League Tables, 2008* (84th), *2009* (90th), *2010* (90th), *2011* (81st), *2012* (80th), but based on data from the two previous years; UC, Minutes of Governors, 2005 to date: 24 November 2009.

29 Chester decided like most universities to charge the full £3,000 annual fee, but with a bursary scheme for poorer students (see e.g. UC, Minutes of Senate, 2005–07: 13 December 2006).

30 UC, Institutional/Strategic Level Key Performance Indicators, updated November 2009, p. 3; cf. UC, Minutes of Senate, 2005–07: 15 February, 13 December 2006.

31 UC, QAA Institutional Audit 2010 Briefing Paper, pp. 4, 13 and List of Evidence Da, Db; *The Cestrian*, 2008, p. 13; *The Cestrian*, 2010, p. 17; UC, Minutes of Foundation/Mission Committee, 2003 to date: 10 October 2007.

32 UC, Minutes of Governors, 2005 to date: 21 June 2007, 11 March 2008; QAA: *Institutional Audit Report, University of Chester* (2010), p. 4; UC, Student Enrolments by Mode and Course Type, 2006–09; D. Perrin, P. Weston, P.A. Thompson and P. Brodie, *Facilitating Employer Engagement through Negotiated Work Based Learning: a Case Study from the University of Chester* (n.d.); UC, *Annual Review 2009*, p. 20.

33 UC, QAA Institutional Audit 2010 Briefing Paper, pp. 28–29; UC, Student Enrolments by Mode and Course Type, 2006–09; *The Cestrian*, 2009, p. 19; *The Cestrian*, 2010, p. 17; on Isle of Man nurse education, see Chapter 11.

34 These were Education for Ministry and the Committee for Ministry of and among Deaf and Disabled People, both national bodies, and the Southern Theological Education Training Scheme.

35 UC, QAA Institutional Audit 2010 Briefing Paper, pp. 29–30; QAA: *Institutional Audit Report, University of Chester* (2010), p. 4; UC, Minutes of Senate, 2005–07: 20 September 2006; UC, Minutes of Governors, 2005 to date: 21 June, 29 November 2007; *The Cestrian*, 2008, p. 17. On overseas links, see e.g. *The Cestrian*, 2009, p. 20; *The Cestrian*, 2010, pp. 19–20; UC, *Annual Report 2006–07*, p. 46; UC, Register of University of Chester's Collaborative Arrangements 2012/13. The delivery of an MSc in Cardiovascular Rehabilitation at the Asian Heart Institute, Mumbai, is a good example of the limited devolution granted to an overseas institution; staff of the University's Centre for Exercise & Nutrition Science retained close control of teaching and assessment, though supported by local tutors. This model had already been applied with The National Training Centre, Dublin (arrangements established in 2004) and would later govern the link with Donau University, Austria (2013).

36 UC, QAA Institutional Audit 2010 Briefing Paper, p. 1; UC, Student Enrolments by Mode and Course Type, 2006–09. Figures for the 'Chester campus' include students at hospital sites across Cheshire and also those taught overseas through staff visits and by distance learning.

37 Lifelong Learning had briefly been a separate Faculty in the early years of the University, overseeing Work Related Studies, but it had been absorbed once again into the Business Faculty by 2008–09.

38 UC, Student Enrolments by Mode and Course Type, 2006–09; numbers for Single Honours (3,489 plus a further 16 on a specialised degree programme) and for Combined Honours (2,019) are for 2008–09; a slight discrepancy between totals from the various Faculties and the overall University FTE is accounted for by small numbers registered on freestanding modules and with the LTI, outside the Faculty structure.

39 E.g. *The Sunday Times University Guide 2008* (21 September 2008), p. 18.

40 UC, Minutes of Senate, 2005–07: 28 February 2007.

41 UC, Minutes of Academic Board, 2001–03: 26 March 2003; UC, Minutes of Academic Board, 2003–04: 2 July 2003; UC, Minutes of Senate, 2005–07: 5 April, 21 June 2006.

42 UC, Student Enrolments by Mode and Course Type, 2006–09; UC, Minutes of Senate, 2005–07: 13 December 2006 (when the Vice-Chancellor had estimated 1.5% of the student body to be made up of international students, including 0.5% from the Isle of Man), 28 February 2007.

43 <<http://www.doriconline.org.uk/Viewdata>> 2011 Census KS201Ethnic Group, accessed 26/9/13; UC, Student Enrolments by Mode and Course Type, 2006–09; *The Cestrian*, 2008, p. 13; and for initiatives in Bahrain, Congo, Palestine, Saudi Arabia, South Africa, Uganda and elsewhere, UC, Minutes of Foundation/Mission Committee, 2003 to date: 29 January 2009; *The Cestrian*, 2009, p. 20; UC, Minutes of Senate 2005–07: 28 February 2007. 'Overseas' students were those whose home was outside the EU. The University's 'Global Perspective' scheme, administered from within Work Related Studies, was reluctantly closed in 2008 following a (successfully handled) critical incident, but for several years it had given students an opportunity of work experience in places such as Brazil, Costa Rica, Kenya and Uganda (UC, Minutes of Foundation/Mission Committee, 2003 to date: 8 October 2003, 1 October 2008; UC, Minutes of Executive Group, 14 October 2008).

44 UC, Student Enrolments by Mode and Course Type, 2006–09; UC, Minutes of Senate, 2005–07: 15 February 2006.

45 See Chapter 9.

46 UC, Minutes of Governors, 2005 to date: 6 March 2007. Both Student Support & Guidance and Careers & Employability also secured Matrix accreditation in 2013.

47 UC, QAA Institutional Audit 2010 Briefing Paper, pp. 20–23; UC, 2009 BQF Achievement Award Employee Satisfaction: Submission; UC, 2009 BQF Achievement Award for Employee Satisfaction Report; UC, Learning Support Services Summary Report 2008–09; UC, Minutes of Foundation/Mission Committee, 2003 to date: 13 October 2004, 16 December 2004, 17 May 2006; UC, *Annual Review 2009*, pp. 25–26.

48 CC, Application for University Title (August 2004), pp. 7–8.

49 *The Cestrian*, 2007, pp. 2, 8.

50 *The Cestrian*, 2010, p. 15; <http://www.lltgl.org.uk/Content/Holly-Shaw>> accessed 28/9/13; UC, *Annual Review 2009*, pp. 36–38.

51 *The Cestrian*, 2008, p. 32; *The Cestrian*, 2010, pp. 31–32; UC, Minutes of Governors, 2005 to date: 2 December 2010; Romero (whose medals were a silver for rowing in 2004 and a gold for cycling four years later) is only the second woman of any nationality to achieve this double-medal-winning feat.

52 *The Cestrian*, 2009, p. 12; *The Cestrian*, 2010, p. 15.

53 *The Cestrian*, 2008, p. 8; cf. UC, Minutes of Foundation/Mission Committee 2003 to date: 15 May 2008.

54 UC, Minutes of Governors, 2005 to date: 6 March, 21 June 2007, 24 June, 27 November 2008, 11 March, 24 November 2009, 24 June, 2 December 2010, 16 March, 30 June, 29 November 2011, 21 March 2012; UC, Minutes of Senate, 2005–07: 13 December 2006; UC, *University of Chester Development Framework* (March 2012), p. 42; *pers. comm.* J.D. Stevens, M. Rhodes. For the Browne Committee, see Chapter 14.

55 UC, Minutes of Governors, 2005 to date: 29 November 2007, 24 June, 27 November 2008, 11 March 2009, 24 November 2009, 24 June 2010, 29 November 2011 (which records a decision not to purchase Burton Manor); *Times Higher Education*, 6 March 2008; *The Cestrian*, 2010, pp. 13, 17; UC, *Annual Review 2009*, p. 14.

56 *The Cestrian*, 2010, p. 2.

57 UC, *Undergraduate Prospectus 2005*, p. 230; UC, *Postgraduate Prospectus 2005*, pp. 124–27; UC, *Undergraduate Prospectus 2010*, p. 57; UC, *Postgraduate Prospectus 2010*, p. 33.

58 UC, Minutes of Governors, 2005 to date: 24 June 2010; UC, Annual Statement to Senate on Quality Assurance and Quality Enhancement during the Academic Year 2009–10.

59 QAA: *Institutional Audit Report, University of Chester* (2010), p. 4.

60 UC, Minutes of Senate 2005–07: 14 December 2005; cf. UC, Minutes of Governors, 2000–05: 30 June 2005.

61 Prince Charles's award of a Doctorate of Letters *honoris causa* took place in the Binks building on 19 July 2007; other awards were made as part of the degree ceremonies in Chester cathedral. See UC, *Annual Report 2006–07*, pp. 6–10.

62 CC, Minutes of Academic Board, 2003–04: 15 December 2004.

63 QAA, *Institutional Audit Report, University of Chester* (2005), pp. 14, 36; UC, QAA Institutional Audit 2010 Briefing Paper, p. 5.

64 UC, *Annual Review, 2010*, p. 36.

CHAPTER 14

ADVENTURE AND ACCLAIM

Between 2005 and 2010, Chester had consolidated its position and proved itself a worthy member of the 'university club'. It had continued to enjoy sound recruitment despite the challenges posed by increased tuition fees. It had maintained its reputation for good teaching and support, for high levels of student satisfaction and for the promotion of work related learning. It had made an increasing regional impact through its collaborative partnerships. It had also made some headway in raising the profile of research and knowledge transfer. However, most of this could have been said of the College before 2005. With due credit to advances made since then, including better overall degree classifications, an improved RAE result, the proliferation of regional partnerships and the acquisition of the Kingsway site, it would not be unfair to describe the first five years as a university as 'Chester College in new clothes'. Some of the problems faced by the College continued to beset the University, including limited student accommodation and comparatively low income from international students.[1] It was now time to move on, to retain the best of what had gone before but to venture beyond this and develop as an institution which would be a match for long-established universities: in the quality of its buildings and other facilities, in the attainments of its students and research-active staff, in its specialist and expert contribution to the local and regional economy, and in its international reach. As Chester celebrated its 175th anniversary, there was still some way to go towards the achievement of these goals but it was impossible not to recognise the progress being made.

The University's Corporate Plan of 2012, covering the period to 2016, was a blend of the old and the new. The declared 'Strategic Objectives' included several rooted in institutional tradition:

> To ensure that the University's Christian values of honesty, integrity and respect for all, its underpinning ethos and traditions, and the supportive people-centred culture continue to play an appropriately prominent and facilitative role ...

> To continue to deliver high quality, actively supported and highly regarded teaching within a curriculum framework which is responsive to emerging developments and improvements in programme design and delivery, including work based learning and technology enhanced learning ...

> To continue to act as a regional University committed to employer and community engagement which is successful in attracting students with a range of backgrounds and experiences …
>
> To further enhance provision at the University's Warrington Campus targeted at meeting the needs of the public services and the professions …
>
> To ensure that students obtain appropriate graduate level employment.

With its emphasis on high-quality teaching and support and on service to the region, the Plan echoed the 2004 application for university title. But alongside all this there now went some significant statements of intent: 'to further explore appropriate international development opportunities', 'to promote an environment within which staff are able to translate … research and entrepreneurial activities into effective technology, knowledge transfer and exchange services to business and industry' and 'to continue the journey to become a centre of excellence in teaching, learning and research'. In the more detailed teasing-out of these objectives there were commitments 'to develop and strengthen the position of University of Chester in the international higher education and business markets', 'to develop and market a measurable research profile, both in the UK and internationally, and support and extend … research' and 'to maintain and enhance an innovative and agile teaching, learning and study environment'. The 'built' aspect of this 'agile environment' was the subject of a separate *Development Framework*, also issued in 2012, which explained the University's strategy for enhancing its teaching and residential accommodation so as to 'meet or exceed the changing requirements of our students and staff'.[2]

The extent to which the University succeeds in meeting the objectives set out in the Corporate Plan will help to determine the verdict of a future historian on the institution's fortunes during the second decade of the twenty-first century. The nature of any adventure is that the outcome is uncertain. But, at the very least, substantial development of the University's physical estate seems certain to figure prominently in any retrospective analysis. In summer 2010 the Faculties of Education & Children's Services and of Health & Social Care, alongside some support departments including the Business Development Unit and Marketing, Recruitment & Admissions, moved away from the Parkgate Road campus to occupy Cheshire's former County Hall; the inauguration in April 2009 of separate authorities, Cheshire West & Chester on the one hand and Cheshire East on the other, had meant that the building was no longer required for local government purposes. These were grand, prestigious premises, incorporating both the earlier Shire Hall of 1792–1814 (described in the 2011 edition of Pevsner's *Buildings of Cheshire* as 'one of the most powerful monuments of Neoclassicism in the whole of England')

and the later County Hall opened in 1957.[3] Bought for £10,275,000 in the closing months of 2009, what became known as the Riverside Campus revolutionised the University's profile within the city: no longer confined to its old College campus and the new Kingsway site – both away from the centre and off the tourist trail – but now incorporating a prominent structure adjoining the river and the racecourse, close to restaurants and shops, at a key intersection on the inner ring road (see Plate 15). An adjoining building was converted into a business incubation hub, the 'Riverside Innovation Centre' the following year.[4]

The acquisition of Riverside released some premium space on the Parkgate Road campus and a scheme to erect a new teaching block where the de Bunsen Centre had stood was cancelled.[5] This remains a site for possible future development but for the moment most of the Faculty of Business, Enterprise & Lifelong Learning could relocate to the Westminster building vacated by Health & Social Care, although the Centre for Work Related Studies moved to the Bache building instead. In turn, History & Archaeology transferred from the Blue Coat School to occupy much of the area of the Binks building previously used by Education & Children's Services. There were several other moves during the summer of 2010, including the establishment of a new department – which became known as Clinical Sciences & Nutrition – at Rockmount at the intersection of the Parkgate and Liverpool Roads, modernisation of Hollybank for TRS, and the re-launch of upgraded dining halls on the main Chester campus as 'White's Dining Rooms', so named after the catering manager. Indeed, Malcolm Rhodes, who as the Senior PVC (Resources) successfully oversaw these projects, wrote that the summer of 2010 witnessed 'the largest and most complex' refurbishment programme 'ever undertaken within the University' requiring 'a series of logistically complex and time-critical relocations … involving some 450 academic and support staff across nearly 20 departments and locations'.[6] This is as good an indicator as any that one phase of the institution's history was giving way to another.

There was, however, much more construction work to come. By summer 2012, the 1960s tower block – one of the most dominant buildings on the main campus – had been thoroughly overhauled, with the installation of new lifts, solar control glazing and external cladding which disguised the concrete structure and transformed its appearance. A three-year upgrade of the Seaborne Library, incorporating more space for group work and facilitating 24-hour access, was also completed by this time.[7] In 2013, ready for the September intake that year, came the opening of both the newly built Grosvenor House on the Parkgate Road campus and the recently purchased

Sumner House, a former Travelodge adjacent to Chester's Fountains roundabout on Northgate Street. Between them, these two large hostels added 362 modern, exceptionally well-equipped study-bedrooms to the accommodation the University could offer its students: a substantial contribution towards addressing a long-acknowledged weakness. At the beginning of February 2014 the North West Food Research Development Centre building was also finished, occupying the eastern side of what became in effect a courtyard with the Best and Chritchley buildings to the west and Westminster building to the north. Backed by the European Regional Development Fund, the Exchange was intended as a business incubator and advisory hub serving both new and established companies in the food and drink sector.[8]

The cover of the 2012 Corporate Plan had quoted the Vice-Chancellor to the effect that 'study at the University of Chester has always been, and will continue to be, a journey of exploration, discovery and fulfilment'. As we have seen, the Plan itself had described the institution as on a 'journey to become a centre of excellence'. There was no claim that the University would soon be as eminent across as wide a range of fields as the best-regarded institutions in the land. Research, for example, was expected to improve in quality and volume, as measured by external awards, REF gradings and PhD completions, but insofar as any numerical targets were set they were realistically modest. Research was still seen as linked closely to teaching and knowledge transfer, in keeping with other institutional priorities; the creation in 2013 of a new Sport & Community Engagement department at Warrington, for example, separate from Sport & Exercise Sciences at Chester, was intended to encourage the promotion of 'knowledge transfer activities'.[9]

There was, however, no doubt about the overall direction of travel and in a number of areas the University was coming to occupy a prominent place within the sector. In 2010, for example, TRS set up a series of partnerships with theological colleges – St John's College (Nottingham), the Wales Evangelical School of Theology (Bridgend), Westminster Theological Centre, the Irish Baptist College (County Down), Spurgeon's College (Croydon) and King's Evangelical Divinity School (Kent); Regents Theological College (West Malvern) and Mattersey Hall College (Doncaster) were added a year later. Although revisions to the Church of England's arrangements for theological training meant that not all these partnerships would be long-lasting, cumulatively they took the department beyond its previous (though not exclusive) focus on the North West, so that the University became a major UK player in this field.[10] Sustained commitment to the promotion of new forms of education academies, beginning with a secondary academy in Ellesmere Port in 2009 and embracing no less than nine primary and secondary schools by the close of 2013, from Kidsgrove to Liverpool, made Chester, through its Academies Trust (formed in 2011), one of the first significant University sponsors of this type of school in the country. This in turn helped to burnish the institution's long-cherished reputation in the field of education, recently enhanced from 2010 onwards through the receipt of 'Outstanding' grades from Ofsted.[11] The Centre for Work Related Studies continued to be in the vanguard of national developments, increasingly attracting applicants for postgraduate rather than undergraduate study; a negotiated Work Based Learning programme leading to an MBA, approved in summer 2013, was the first of its kind in the UK.[12] The University also showed that it could compete with the best for research funding. During 2012, for example, the European Research Council awarded over €1.2 million to the History & Archaeology department for a joint project with the University of Exeter on changing perspectives of memory in medieval and modern England and Wales; there were also six-figure grants to Biological Sciences from the National Centre for the Replacement, Refinement and Reduction of Animals in Research for two major projects, one of them in collaboration with the University of Liverpool.[13] These were awards of which any university in the country would have been proud.

Meanwhile, there was a concerted effort to raise the international profile. By August 2013 the number of institutions on the University's Partnerships Register – excluding those involved simply in exchange agreements, all set up between 1993 and 2007 – had risen to 69, and among them were several new overseas partners: Bhaktivedanta College (a Vaishnava college in the Ardennes region of Belgium), approved in 2011; the Florence Institute of Design International, HELP University (Kuala Lumpur), Dimensions International College (Singapore) and Southville Foreign University (Manila), all in 2012; the Department of Health & Social Services of the States of Jersey and Yildirim Beyazit University, Turkey, in 2013.[14] Thirty-two students were recruited from Wuhan University (China), mostly to further their degrees in Business, for the start of the 2012–13 academic year and a link with Globe Education Services, specialists in international recruitment, boosted enrolments on the BA in Business Administration and the MBA one year later.[15] The 2014 postgraduate prospectus was able to claim that Chester's students were 'drawn from over 90 countries globally'.[16]

Some exceptional results in the National Student Survey for 2012 led to the University winning a *Times Higher Education* award for 'The Most Improved Student Experience' in the UK; English was rated first in the whole country for overall student satisfaction, with History & Archaeology also in the top ten. By the same measure, on the specific issue of teaching, Chester was placed 12th in the whole country; Geography & Development Studies topped the ratings for its own subject area and another five departments – English, TRS, Law, Nursing and Sport & Exercise Sciences – were placed between second and ninth for their subjects.[17] *The Times and Sunday Times Good University Guide 2014*, using a wider range of measures including research quality, entry standards and graduate employment prospects placed three disciplines taught at Chester in the top 20 nationally: two long-established ones (Theology & Religious Studies at 20 out of 34, Sports Science at 13= out of 73) and one relatively recent arrival (Hospitality, Leisure, Recreation & Tourism at 7= out of 49).[18]

As usual, there were several other achievements to celebrate, not least because of the opportunities presented by the 2012 London Olympics and Paralympics. Chester was not one of over 30 universities to provide accommodation for national squads,[19] but it did co-ordinate the volunteers who lined the route of the Olympic torch relay through the city; supplied one of the torch-bearers in the person of first-year General Primary Creative Communication student Hannah Jones, a highly successful fundraiser for brain tumour charities; and provided four students for the 'London Prepares' events to test sporting facilities in advance, plus a further five 'Games Makers' who supported the festival itself. James Roberts, a postgraduate student in Sociology of Sport & Exercise was a member of the Team GB Paralympian sitting volleyball squad, while third-year Sport & Exercise Sciences student Yana Radcliffe, herself a black belt kick-boxer, recorded footage from several competitions, including Taekwondo, wrestling, boxing and weightlifting, for analysis by Team GB coaches. Most notable of all was the achievement of David Brailsford, who had studied PE & Sports Science and Psychology at Chester between 1988 and 1991 and had been awarded an honorary doctorate by the University in 2009; as Performance Director of British Cycling, he deserved much of the credit for the nine medals (including seven golds) secured by Team GB's cyclists at the London Olympics, plus a further 22 Paralympic cycling medals, as he had when there had been a similarly impressive return from Beijing four years earlier. He was voted Coach of the Year (for the second time) in the BBC's Sports Personality of the Year event and went on to be knighted in the New Year's Honours of 2013.[20]

In the year before the Olympics, final-year Geography & Development Studies students had won a 'best poster and presentation' award at the first-ever British Conference of Undergraduate Research, while Cat 1251, the University's student radio station at the Warrington campus, had been crowned 'Most Improved Student Radio Station' at the 'I Love Student Radio'

Awards.[21] During 2012 itself, outgoing SU President Dechlan Jarrett presented HM Queen Elizabeth II with a Loyal Address and Humble Petition as part of her visit to Warrington for her Jubilee celebrations. The subsequent academic year, 2012–13, would be the first in which the senior offices in the Students' Union, carrying entitlement to a sabbatical, were all held by women; that year's National Student Survey led to the Union being rated 'best in the North West'.[22] Then in February 2013 the University Rowing Club's new boat was launched, bearing the name 'David Stevens' in honour of the Deputy Vice-Chancellor who had retired at the end of 2012; he had served the institution with great distinction for 35 years, most recently as both Bursar and DVC, always bringing courtesy, assurance and insight to a most demanding role. He was succeeded as Bursar by Bill Stothart, who joined from Wirral Metropolitan College where he had been Vice-Principal and Director of Finance and Resources.[23]

By the close of 2013, Chester had become a University of some 17,800 students, just under two-thirds of whom were women. About 9,000 were undergraduates (mostly full-time), 5,000 postgraduates (mostly part-time) and the remainder were on programmes leading to a qualification less than a full degree. The highest proportion, some 6,600, was based at the Parkgate Road campus, with a further 3,400 at Riverside and 700 at Kingsway; outside Chester, the Warrington campus catered for another 1,500. Beyond this, there were around 1,400 students at hospital sites associated with the Faculty of Health & Social Care and no less than 4,200 studying by distance learning or with partner institutions in the UK or abroad. It is some indication of the University's extended reach that – having begun as an institution serving its local diocese – it now recruited two-thirds of its undergraduates from beyond a 30-mile radius; some 6% came from outside the UK and 9% were of 'non-white- European' ethnic origin. Almost a quarter of the undergraduates were aged 21 or over at the commencement of their studies and 98% had been educated at state schools; the last figure was several points higher than the national average, although similar to that for about half the institutions in the sector. Among the faculties, Health & Social Care was now the largest, with 22% of all module registrations, followed by Humanities (17%), Business, Enterprise & Lifelong Learning (14%), Social Science (13%), Education (10%) and Arts & Media (7%); a new Faculty of Science & Engineering, created for 2013–14, had 3%, almost entirely students of Mathematics and Computer Science which had moved into it from the Applied Sciences Faculty. The rest of Applied Sciences had been rebranded Life Sciences, accounting for 12%.[24]

Despite the diversity of experience represented by these figures – different origins, different goals, different locations of study – the Students'

Union statement on the *Which University 2013* website chose to emphasise the University's 'amazing community spirit'. It was obviously a different sense of community from the one which had prevailed until the beginning of the 1960s – all men, all training to be teachers – or that which had characterised the period until the 1980s, when there had been less than 1,000 students all based on a single campus. But within the confines of what students and staff now chose to regard as their own smaller communities, it is fair to say that a caring and supportive ethos continued to be widespread. The Union explained this as 'due to smaller lecture groups and excellent support services, so you are always a name not a number' and there is no doubt that higher-than-average levels both of student satisfaction and of graduate employability were major factors in pushing Chester to its best-ever ranking – 46th out of 119 – in *The Guardian* league tables of 2013. It also figured in the middle band in other tables. The *Complete University Guide* had it 71st out of 124.[25] *The Times and Sunday Times Good University Guide 2014* put Chester 52nd-equal overall, third-equal among the 'modern universities' (the former polytechnics and colleges which had become universities since 1992) and fourth in the North West behind only Lancaster, Manchester and Liverpool.[26] For their part, staff also stressed 'community' when asked what was best about the University[27] and there was some confirmation of this in the grant in summer 2013 of both an Investors in People silver award and a Health@Work Workforce Wellbeing Charter.

Meanwhile, there was a good deal of emphasis in corporate publications of the period on the 'distinctiveness' of the Chester experience. It featured, for example, as one of the institution's 'Core Values' approved in 2006, where it was defined as 'a high-quality, caring and supportive learning experience, including work related learning, that equips [students] with the necessary personal and academic skills to engage confidently with the wider world'.[28] 'Distinctiveness' was also a matter which repeatedly exercised the minds of the Mission Committee,[29] in a context in which there was increasing thought nationally about whether universities with a Christian foundation, such as Chester, had any particular qualities to offer the sector.[30] 'The Chester Difference' was also a theme of the 2013 Annual Review.[31] It is worth pausing briefly to reflect on the relevance of all this, as the University charted its course through the second decade of the twenty-first century.

The institutional Mission Statement, as redrafted in 2006 and from which a Vision and a series of Core Values and Key Strategic Objectives followed, was tweaked in time for the 2012 Corporate Plan and by the 175th anniversary it read as follows.

The University was established by the Church of England in 1839 and, within an open, inclusive and supportive environment guided by Christian values of honesty, integrity and respect for all, we seek to provide our students and staff with the education, training, skills and motivation to enable them to develop as individuals and have lives of service in the communities within which they live and work. This Mission, which has helped shape our development and diversification, continues to inform our future planning and enrichment as a University.

This had shifted somewhat from the Mission Statement of 1992, with its commitment to giving students 'opportunities to give systematic consideration to the personal and social challenge of Christian teachings' but the guidance offered by 'Christian values' and an emphasis on service to others remained in modified form, alongside greater emphasis on inclusivity and individual personal development.[32]

Tempting though it is to be sceptical about the impact made by statements of this nature, they were not empty words. As a member of the 'Cathedrals Group' of universities and university colleges (16 in number by 2013), Chester had signed up in 2009 to a memorandum of understanding which included commitment to 'the enhancement of Christian principles in higher education' and 'the development of strong ethical principles in all aspects of higher education'. The Vice-Chancellor – who had become a lay canon of Chester Cathedral in 2003 – chaired the Group for two years beginning in November 2010, during which the Leadership Foundation for Higher Education undertook a HEFCE-funded enquiry into the distinctive characteristics of its institutional members. The report, which was printed at Chester and carried a foreword by Wheeler, concluded that 'faith-based institutions do indeed have distinctive features and a definable identity', summarising these features as follows.

- Lived out core values which reflect the history and provenance of the institutions.
- A special approach to students, centred on the development of the whole individual.
- A particularly strong tradition of volunteering and external community engagement.
- A strong sense of internal community based on personal values of trust and respect.
- Vibrant Chaplaincies which are an integral part of the university or college structure and which have a very positive effect on both staff and students.
- An acute sensitivity in handling change.

- An approach to staff reflecting core values of individuals in a supportive community.
- A distinctive approach to partnerships with other faith-based institutions.

There was no suggestion that institutions outside the Cathedrals Group did not display some of these characteristics but the argument was that all of them were in evidence among those surveyed and that, collectively, they set the Group's members apart.[33]

It would be an exceptional institution which consistently lived up to all these ideals and Chester was far from immune to the tensions and conflicts of interest which beset UK higher education in the early twenty-first century: like the rest of the sector, it faced very occasional industrial action, with one national pay dispute by the University and College Union ongoing at the time of the 175th anniversary of the foundation meeting in January 2014. But there can be little doubt that, among these bullet-points, the third and fourth represented particular institutional strengths. Student volunteering had been a prominent activity since the demise of the Rag around the turn of the millennium and by 2013 was reckoned to contribute over 23,250 hours of community service per annum, with an office in the Beswick building and a presence on Facebook to assist with the co-ordination.[34] A supportive community spirit, as we have seen, was widely acknowledged by students and staff alike, even though in reality the institution had been composed of several communities, not one, for at least a quarter of a century. Apart from this, there was certainly a strong chaplaincy presence. Chester was one of the first Cathedrals Group institutions to raise the status of the senior chaplain to that of 'Dean of Chapel'; with echoes of the rationale behind the remodelling of the chaplaincy in the mid-1980s,[35] this redesignation was a deliberate affirmation of the centrality of the faith-based ethos of the University with an expectation upon the postholder to be more than simply part of the student support network.[36] The creation of a distinct Chaplaincy Centre at the beginning of 2012 was an indication of this new emphasis, since in place of a single room in the Binks building adjacent to Student Support & Guidance it was given prominently signposted premises in most of the house called 'Longfield' on the access route on to the main Chester campus. This happened at the same time as the appointment of Peter Jenner as the second Dean of Chapel, the post to be held in conjunction with a Residentiary Canonry of Chester Cathedral. With, in addition, a full-time chaplain for Warrington and the various healthcare sites, another colleague on the Chester campus who divided her time between chaplaincy duties and a lectureship, a chaplaincy co-ordinator, the equivalent of one full-time chaplaincy assistant, an ecumenical group of 'associate chaplains' (six at Chester, two at Warrington) drawn from local clergy and ministers, and the support of a chaplaincy team of volunteer staff and students, there was a considerable investment of resource both by the University and by local churches.[37]

Whatever attributes collectively defined the University of Chester by 2014, they embraced an ever-more-diversified academic portfolio. The undergraduate prospectus for that year listed some 62 Single Honours programmes, about half in disciplines also available within Combined Honours, and another 16 subjects offered only as a Combined Honours component. Recent additions included Single Honours in Creative Media, Music Journalism and Social Work at the Warrington campus, part of a strategic focus here since Harrop had become Provost in 2009 on provision in the Public Services and Creative Industries. At Chester, Chinese Studies appeared for the first time within Combined Honours.[38] The same year's postgraduate prospectus advertised over 100 programmes, including five professional doctorates. The presence among them of an MA in Restorative Dentistry, utilising both the University's Riverside campus and the Manchester Dental Education Centre, an MSc in Digital Marketing, delivered at Warrington, and a Postgraduate Certificate in Applied Wildlife Forensics taught at the main Chester campus,[39] illustrates how far the institution had travelled since it had broken the bounds of teacher training some four decades earlier. The November 2013 graduation ceremonies embraced more events than ever before and included the award of 14 honorary degrees, with former Secretary of State for Education & Science Lord (Kenneth) Baker, the campaigning Labour MP for Birkenhead Frank Field, Olympic gymnast Beth Tweddle, and the Warrington-based peace campaigner Colin Parry among those honoured with doctorates.[40]

An expanding academic offering, modern residential and teaching accommodation, high levels of student satisfaction: all were vital to the continuing attractiveness of the University of Chester in an age of intensified competition within the HE sector. In 2011 the institution received a record number of UCAS applications, well over 22,000, compared to some 19,000 the year before.[41] But yet another change to the funding regime meant that there was no room for complacency. The Browne Committee, set up during prolonged economic recession in November 2009 to 'analyse the challenges and opportunities facing higher education and their implications for student financing and support', reported eleven months later – like Dearing in 1997 – to a different government from the one which had commissioned it. It recommended that universities should be free to charge whatever fees they chose (though with levies to support poorer students which would act as a disincentive to pitching too high), that the loans taken out to meet these fees be repaid by graduates once they obtained adequately remunerated employment, and that within some overall parameters set by the government (through a new Higher Education Council) institutions should be free to compete for students and their fees rather than be subject to centrally imposed maximum numbers. 'Our proposals are designed to create genuine competition for students between HEIs … a surer way to drive up quality than any attempt at central planning'.[42]

To the embarrassment of the Liberal Democrats, who had promised to abolish HE tuition fees in their 2010 General Election manifesto only to find themselves part of a Conservative-led Coalition intent on putting them up, all this was introduced in modified form in time for the 2012–13 academic year. The government's White Paper of June 2011, *Higher Education: Students at the Heart of the System*, borrowed its title from a phrase in the Browne report but made some adjustments to its proposals. It did set a 'cap' on what institutions could charge in fees, at £9,000 per annum, and it did retain the concept of centrally allocated 'core student numbers', while leaving one margin for competitive bidding and another to allow those with the best A-level grades to apply wherever they wished without any numbers 'cap' to restrict them. Existing bodies such as HEFCE and the QAA were also permitted to continue, rather than being rolled up into a new Higher Education Council. Yet despite these adjustments in matters of practice, it was clear that overall policy was now based on the principles behind the Browne report: yet more intense competition for students and for the fee-income they brought with them and an expectation that, with fees at an exalted level, the quality of the student experience would be bound to improve in response. Indeed, in percentage terms, UK universities operating a 'mass higher education system' in the second decade of the twenty-first century found themselves as reliant on students' fees as their predecessors had been in the 'elitist' context of the interwar years.[43] Only time will tell us the long-term consequences of these reforms, but a reasonable forecast is that we are once again in an era of 'the survival of the fittest': popular universities will thrive and become even more successful, others will be condemned to a downward, self-perpetuating spiral of falling recruitment, income and reputation, with a sadly predictable result.[44] Hence the importance of league tables, for all the reservations which critically minded academics ought to entertain about them.

Chester's response to all this was to pitch the 'headline' (or standard) fee level for 2012 undergraduate entrants at just under £8,000 and to increase this to £9,000 – in line with virtually the whole of the sector – for 2013, although waivers in the interests of widening access brought the average to £8,133.

Undergraduate applications did fall ahead of 2012–13, to just over 19,000, but for the September 2013 intake they were up to 21,000, suggesting that yet another period of uncertainty caused by the latest government directive had been successfully negotiated. Alongside effective marketing and the University's enduring reputation for good teaching and student support, the major investment in new buildings and facilities since the turn of the decade must take much of the credit.[45]

However, a thriving institution never stands still and the undergraduate and postgraduate prospectuses for September 2014 carried new information of profound significance for the future of the University. Among the provision advertised for the first time were BEng and MEng programmes in Electronic/Electrical Engineering, Geotechnical Engineering and Mechanical Engineering, following the establishment of the new Faculty of Science & Engineering the previous summer.[46] This in turn was a response to what the Vice-Chancellor has described as 'one of the biggest things to happen to the university in our 175-year history', and it is a fitting event, therefore, on which to bring this narrative to a close. Shell UK decided during 2011 to move out of its 66-acre Technology Centre at Thornton, where research and development work had been going on for three-quarters of a century. It subsequently agreed to donate the site, including all 48 buildings and nearly all the specialist equipment, to the University of Chester, a gift estimated to be worth £240 million. From Shell's perspective, this was explained as 'the perfect opportunity to give something back' to a local community apprehensive about sweeping job losses. As Shell UK's chairman put it, the donation to the University 'will ensure that innovation and technology will remain a key contributor to the local and regional economy and community … [building] … on Shell's long history of manufacturing and technical innovation in the region'. For the University, in the words of the Vice-Chancellor:

> Our commitment at Thornton could bring up to 2,000 jobs to the area over the next five years, together with perpetuating Shell's distinguished reputation. [Our] vision is to build on the excellent foundations laid by Shell to create an internationally-recognised, financially self-sustaining and multi-disciplinary campus that targets and stimulates private sector growth through employment, education and inward investment. It will integrate students with employers and employees.[47]

As Wheeler explained to the governors and to Senate, the intention was to retain three key buildings for teaching, research and students' own projects, but to let the remainder to local businesses so that the site would become a

Science Park in which the worlds of academia and of commerce would interact to their mutual benefit.

By any measure, this development is a game-changer in the institution's history. As the governors acknowledged when first discussing the proposal in March 2012, 'with such a unique opportunity which could transform the University came very high risks', and the offer was not accepted without a thorough, independent, due diligence assessment.[48] But it represents a spectacular vote of confidence in the University from the UK arm of one of the biggest companies in the world. It is far too early to assess the long-term importance of this venture but of one thing we can certain. With its emphasis on engineering and technology, it is an initiative of which the first College Principal, Arthur Rigg, 'founder of the first English School for Technical and Practical Engineering',[49] would have thoroughly approved.

---

1   As noted by a University and College Union report on institutional finances (UC, Minutes of Senate, 8 December 2010).

2   UC, *Defining the Future: Corporate Plan* (2012–16), esp. pp. 12–26; UC, *University of Chester Development Framework* (March 2012), esp. p. 11.

3   Hartwell *et al.*, *Buildings of England: Cheshire*, pp. 245–47.

4   UC, Minutes of Governors, 2005 to date: 24 November 2009; UC, *Annual Review 2009*, p. 44; UC, *Annual Review 2010*, p. 11; *The Cestrian*, 2010, p. 12; UC, *Annual Review 2011*, p. 56; *The Cestrian*, Spring 2011, pp. 8–9.

5   UC, Minutes of Governors, 2005 to date: 24 June, 27 November 2008, 11 March, 24 June 2009.

6   UC, *Annual Review 2010*, pp. 11–13; the department of Clinical Sciences & Nutrition subsequently moved into the tower.

7   UC, *Annual Review 2011*, p. 57; UC, *Annual Review 2012*, p. 43; *The Cestrian*, Autumn 2012, p. 7.

8   UC, Minutes of Governors, 2005 to date: 16 March, 30 June 2011, 21 March, 28 June 2012, 20 March 2013; UC, *Annual Review 2012*, p. 44; *The Cestrian*, Spring 2013, p. 4.

9   *Defining the Future*, p. 17; UC, Minutes of Senate: 19 June 2013. The REF (Research Excellence Framework) was successor to the RAE.

10 UC, Minutes of Partnerships sub-Committee: 21 June 2010, 9 November 2011, 6 March 2013; UC, Annual Statement to Senate on Quality Assurance and Quality Enhancement for 2009–10.

11 <<http://ucat.chester.ac.uk/Content/AboutUs/Default.aspx>> accessed 25/10/13; UC, Minutes of Governors, 2005 to date: 30 June, 29 November 2011. The director of teaching and learning for the University's Academies Trust, David Cracknell, was awarded an OBE in the New Year's Honours of 2014.

12 UC, Annual Monitoring Report for WBIS postgraduate modular programme for 2011–12: '[the year] has seen a major shift within WBIS, arguably the most seismic

in its history. This is the move towards significantly increased postgraduate recruitment but noticeably declining undergraduate student numbers'; cf. UC, Annual Monitoring Report for WBIS undergraduate modular programme for 2012–13, which attributes the decline in undergraduate enrolments to increased student fees. By 2013, around 70% of WBIS enrolments were for postgraduate provision, including for a Doctorate in Professional Studies (*pers. comm.*, D. Perrin).

13 UC, *Annual Review 2012*, p. 55.

14 UC, Minutes of Partnerships sub-Committee: 9 November 2011, 16 May 2012; UC, Minutes of Senate: 19 June 2013; UC, Register of Collaborative Arrangements 2012–13.

15 UC, Minutes of Governors, 2005 to date: 28 June, 27 November 2012; <<http://www.geducation.co.uk/index.php>> accessed 17/10/13.

16 UC, *Postgraduate Prospectus 2014*, p. 12.

17 UC, *Annual Review 2012*, p. 3; UC, *Forum*, Edn 2, 2012–13, p. 3; *The Cestrian*, Spring 2013, p. 5.; cf. *The Cestrian*, Spring 2012, p. 4, where the previous year's results included Geography 1st, Archaeology 2nd, English 4th, Social Work 6th and Subjects Allied to Medicine 10th for 'overall student satisfaction' compared to their equivalents in other HEIs, according to the *Complete University Guide*.

18 *The Times and Sunday Times Good University Guide, 2014* (Glasgow, 2013), pp. 141–42, 193–94, 196.

19 'Sharing the podium', *Times Higher Education*, no. 2,059 (19 July 2012), pp. 35–39.

20 UC, *Annual Review 2012*, pp. 10–14; *The Cestrian*, Autumn 2012, pp. 5; *The Cestrian*, Spring 2013, p. 8.

21 UC, *Annual Review, 2011*, pp. 7–10; *Warrington Guardian*, 27 August 2010; <<http://www.barclays.co.uk/TakeOneSmallStep/Meetour2011winners/P12426 09377971>> accessed 10/10/13.

22 UC, *Annual Review 2012*, pp. 4–5, 16–17; *The Cestrian*, Spring 2013, p. 3; UC, *Forum*, Edn 1, September 2013, pp. 2–3.

23 UC, *Forum*, Edn 2, 2012–13, p. 5; *The Cestrian*, Spring 2013, p. 4.

24 <<<http://www.hesa.ac.uk/index.php?option=com_content&task=view&id=2397 &Itemid=141>>, accessed 16/1/14; figures supplied by the University's Management Information Systems and Corporate Communications. Among the qualifications 'less than a full degree' were Foundation Degrees and various diplomas and certificates. Figures for faculties total 98%; the remaining 2% were registered outside faculties, e.g. on courses run by the Learning & Teaching Institute. The Faculty of Business, Enterprise & Lifelong Learning (marketed externally as the University of Chester Business School) was restructured at the end of 2013, with rebranded Schools and Departments within it, but overall student numbers were as shown.

25 <<http://university.which.co.uk/university-of-chester-c55>> accessed 27/9/13 and 14/10/13. Ninety-four per cent of graduates were reported as either in work or in further study.

26 *The Times and Sunday Times Good University Guide 2014* (22 September 2013), pp. 17, 28, 52.

27 *The Cestrian*, Spring 2011, p. 19.

28 E.g. UC, *Annual Review 2009*, p. 5; UC, *Annual Review 2012*, p. 7.

29 UC, Minutes of Foundation/Mission Committee, 2003 to date: 17 May, 20 November 2006, 30 January, 28 April 2009, 11 February, 20 October 2010, etc.

30 See e.g. S. Heap, *What are Universities Good For?* (Cambridge, 2012), pp. 23–25, which laments 'an increasingly instrumentalist, individualistic and marketized view of higher education' and argues for 'a positive Christian vision of higher education' which 'will see it as being about holistic individual development and for the sake of the common good'.

31 UC, *Annual Review 2013*, e.g. p. 10.

32 See Chapter 11.

33 E. Wooldridge and E. Newcomb, *Distinctiveness and Identity in a Challenging HE Environment: a Unique Opportunity for The Cathedrals Group Institutions* (2011), esp. p. 6; the 'Cathedrals Group' was a re-branding in 2009 of the Council of Church Universities and Colleges, which (under a previous name) had succeeded the Association of Voluntary Colleges in 1988.

34 *University of Chester Student News*, Issue 1, 2013, pp. 6–7; UC, *Annual Review 2013*, p. 22; *pers. comm.* S. Griffiths.

35 See Chapter 10.

36 *The Anglican Identity of Church of England Higher Education Institutions: End of Year One Report* (September 2012), p. 15.

37 UC, *Annual Review 2013*, pp. 45–46.

38 UC, *Undergraduate Prospectus, 2014*, pp. 66–67, 74–75, 154–55, 180–81.

39 UC, *Postgraduate Prospectus, 2014*, pp. 40, 64, 113.

40 UC, *Forum*, Edn 3, December 2013, pp. 10–11.

41 UC, Summary of Undergraduate Applications, 2011, 2010; UC, Minutes of Governors, 2005 to date: 16 March, 30 June 2011.

42 *Securing a Sustainable Future for Higher Education: An Independent Review of Higher Education Funding and Student Finance* (12 October 2010), p. 8; Brown, *Everything for Sale?*, pp. 90–91.

43 V. Carpentier, 'Public-private Substitution in Higher Education: has Cost-sharing Gone too Far?', *HEQ*, LXVI, 4 (October 2012), pp. 363–90, at pp. 368, 372.

44 Brown, *Everything for Sale?*, pp. 92–94.

45 UC, Minutes of Governors, 2005 to date: 16 March, 29 November 2011; UC, Summary of Undergraduate Applications 2013, 2012; *The Times and Sunday Times Good University Guide 2014*, p. 17.

46 UC, *Undergraduate Prospectus 2014*, pp. 90–95; cf. UC, *Postgraduate Prospectus 2014*, p. 59; UC, Minutes of Senate: 13 March, 19 June 2013. The University website subsequently added programmes in Chemical Engineering and Natural Sciences.

47 <<http://www.itv.com/news/granada/story/2013-03-01/shell-donates-240m-science-centre-to-university/>>;

<<http://www.shell.co.uk/gbr/aboutshell/media-centre/annual-reports-and-publications/swuk/thornton-next-chapter.html>> accessed 13/10/13.

[48] UC, Minutes of Governors, 2005 to date: 21 March, 28 June, 27 November 2012, 20 March 2013.

[49] See Chapter 2.

CHAPTER 15

PAST, PRESENT AND FUTURE

In 1923, the Deeside Regional Planning Scheme, prepared by – among others – the future College architect Theodore Fyfe, summarised the city of Chester as 'a military centre … an ecclesiastical centre … a market town and shopping centre … an archaeological town … a riverside town … a large-house residential town … a workmen's residential town … a roadside town … a railway centre … a manufacturing town … an institutional and administrative centre'. Its prospects for future expansion were as 'a shopping town, a business centre, a social meeting ground, a recreation resort, and a focus for artistic effort and those features of civilization which [it] already possesses.'[1] Chester College was not mentioned at all. It was a teacher training college of about 150 students which, through its school, its employment of a small number of teaching and domestic staff and its growing need for lodgings to supplement on-campus accommodation, had some impact in the northern suburbs but whose most obvious contribution to the city at large was the annual students' Rag Day, then in its infancy.

Almost a century later, no assessment of the city of Chester, from a social, cultural, economic or environmental standpoint, could conceivably ignore the University's presence. Asked by the governors in 2006 to estimate the economic value of the University to the local community, the Vice-Chancellor had replied that under the methodology used by Universities UK the figure for Chester was about £100 million and for Warrington £18 million.[2] The University's *Development Framework*, published in 2012, stressed its role as:

> a major economic generator not solely by bringing academic, commercial and research interests into the city, but also by exporting the value of the city and its potential to the wider world. The University has also added to the vitality and cultural diversity of the city.

It put a figure of £298 million on 'the overall contribution to the economy',[3] a total which embraced the region as a whole but took no account of the subsequent impact of the Thornton Science Park.

For all this, the city of Chester remains curiously ambivalent to the presence of a University in its midst – far more so than the town of Warrington – with opinions ranging from the enthusiastic to the wary.[4] But to begrudge the city a university is to disparage its history down the centuries as host to a series of institutions of more-than-usual significance: the biggest legionary fortress in Roman Britain; a major medieval and early-modern port, which in the 1190s welcomed 'ships coming from Aquitaine, Spain, Ireland and Germany';[5] the administrative base for a medieval shire whose exceptional autonomy led to its designation as a 'county palatine'; the headquarters of a diocese which when established in 1541 became the third largest in area in England. All this has given the city regional, even national, importance and made it a hub for visitors with work to do and money to spend. The University is the latest expression of the city's traditional role.

Apart from anything else, the institution gives the people of Chester a grade II* listed early-Victorian Chapel and a range of buildings on the Parkgate Road campus which are an object lesson in the changing styles of educational architecture (see Plates 4, 5, 13 and 14). The latest edition of Pevsner's *Buildings of Cheshire* (2011) is, however, far less generous to this long-established campus than it is to the recently acquired one at Riverside.[6] The original College buildings are described as 'bleak and forbidding Educational Tudor' and the campus itself as 'a cramped muddle of buildings of wildly varying styles interspersed with good gardening'; 'each generation' is accused of having 'maltreated its predecessor'. The entrance added to the original buildings in the 1960s is dubbed 'barbarous', the tower is condemned because it 'upsets all balances and axes', and the insertion of the De Bunsen Centre between Astbury and Fisher Houses is blamed for blocking their 'central axis'; mercifully, the Binks and Westminster buildings are seen as 'markedly more ambitious in scale and finish'.[7] In fairness, this was written before the University demolished the De Bunsen Centre, refaced the tower and improved the entrance to what is now Senate House, but in any case these critical comments take no account of the circumstances in which successive Principals and governors have had to operate, often having to accommodate growing numbers of staff and students as economically as possible by adapting or extending existing structures, or by building to a tight budget without the luxury of architectural embellishment. In any case, from an aesthetic viewpoint there are far worse university buildings up and down the country than any of those at Chester. An institution which has occupied the same site for 175 years – unless its original buildings still fulfil all its needs today – is bound to display a mixture of architectural styles. What to some is a 'muddle' to others is a vivid illustration of changing tastes and requirements down the generations.

Yet back in 1851, when Rigg took his students to the Great Exhibition and they stayed overnight at Sumner's Lambeth Palace, there was no reason to think that, among the group of men's Church training colleges by then in existence in England, the institution at Chester would emerge as one of only two to retain a separate identity and go on to prosper as a twenty-first century university. In HMI Moseley's report that year to the Committee of Council on Education, it was accorded an earlier date of foundation than any of the others and was second only to Battersea in the number of students trained since its establishment, but on most quantitative measures it can best be seen as ranking in the 'upper-middle': larger than Durham and Exeter, for example, but smaller than Chelsea and Cheltenham and only fourth-highest as a recipient of government grant.[8] In its focus on 'industrial occupations' it did offer a distinctive approach to teacher training, but these provoked mixed reactions and Rigg's refusal to bend to government requirements during the 1860s led to the College's virtual collapse; the resurrected institution had a generally sub-standard reputation, at least until the late 1880s. But it is still with us, more vibrant than ever.

Most of Chester's fellow early-Victorian men's Church colleges were also to enjoy an honourable history but are no longer separate entities. St John's Battersea and St Mark's Chelsea merged as the College of St Mark & St John (Marjon), Chelsea in 1926, moved to Plymouth in 1973 and in 2013 became the University of St Mark & St John. Bishop Otter College Chichester merged in 1977 with Bognor Regis College to become the West Sussex Institute of Higher Education, which in 2005 became the University of Chichester. St Luke's Exeter was taken over by the University of Exeter in 1978. Bede College, Durham merged with the adjacent St Hild's College in 1975 and as the College of St Hild & St Bede became a full constituent College of the University of Durham four years later. The College at York merged with that at Ripon in 1974 to become the College of Ripon & York St John; this had transferred fully to York by 2001 and it went on to secure the title of York St John University in 2006. Cheltenham has an especially complicated history. One College became two, St Paul's and St Mary's, during the 1920s but they amalgamated in 1979 and later merged with the Higher Education Trust of Gloucestershire College of Art & Technology to form Cheltenham and Gloucester College of HE in 1990; this became the University of Gloucestershire in 2001. Even this briefest of summaries brings home the significance of the 1970s as a critical decade, as different colleges worked out their salvation in different ways, but rarely without a significant loss of autonomy.

The closest parallel with Chester is King Alfred's Winchester, and not only because its founding Bishop was the brother of Chester's own John Bird Sumner. This began life as a diocesan training school for masters in 1840 (though not occupying its present site until 1862), admitted its first female students in 1960, diversified into BA as well as BEd courses in the 1970s (initially with the CNAA rather than its local university, Southampton), acquired taught degree awarding powers in 2003, became the University of Winchester in 2005 and added research degree awarding powers in 2008.[9] Like Chester, it has never merged constitutionally with another institution. Although Chester has become a much larger University than Winchester in terms of student numbers and the breadth of its academic portfolio, as they approached their 175th anniversaries the two were vying with each other for leadership of the Church-colleges-turned-universities in published league tables: Winchester ahead in one, Chester in two others.[10] There is much for both Universities to be proud of here, although celebration is rather easier than explanation. Analysis of Winchester's achievements must be left to its own historians, but some attempt may be made here to summarise the reasons for Chester's remarkable story of survival and success.

Geographical location is certainly a major factor. Whatever its growing national and international reputation in recent times, the institution has traditionally been able to recruit healthily from the North West, partly because prospective students have seen the city as an attractive location which they have enjoyed visiting in the past. More than this, until the opening of S. Martin's Lancaster in 1964, Chester was the only Church of England men's college in a vast early-Victorian diocese covering the heavily populated North West. Despite its modest reputation under Critchley and the increasingly embarrassing and anachronistic absence of hostel accommodation throughout the first half of the twentieth century, there was a clear rationale for the College's presence and a large catchment area from which to recruit. This helped to ensure that it remained one of the larger institutions of its type, less vulnerable to closure – other than in the exceptional circumstances of 1932–33 – than some smaller Church colleges, such as those which once served the more rural dioceses of Peterborough, Truro, Norwich and Oxford.[11] Before the Cheshire local authority opened Crewe College in 1912 it was also the only teacher training college in the county.

These geographical circumstances have repeatedly been alluded to at critical moments, as in 1974 when the DES gave Chester's 'situation in an attractive city' as one of its advantages and hence among the reasons why, for the present, it should not be forced into closure or amalgamation; in 1975, when Principal Seaborne argued that there was 'no other college of education or polytechnic in the populous West Cheshire and Wirral area'; and in 2004, when the application for university title pointed out that Chester was 'the only higher education institution serving the County of Cheshire that has its principal site within the county'.[12] These claims, important as providing a strategic justification for Chester's continuing existence or advancement, could not have been made had Thomas's idea in 1921 of moving the College to Liverpool been taken up; assuming its survival till then, the College would almost certainly have been brought into a federation of Liverpool institutions during the 1970s, as happened to S. Katharine's when it became part of LIHE towards the end of that decade. Such claims could not have been made, either, had the new university mooted for Chester in the 1960s come about, although whether the College would have been absorbed into it (as at Exeter) or would have valiantly maintained its independence in a distinctive role (as at Lancaster and York) must remain speculation. At the very least, some of the geographical advantages enjoyed by the College would have passed to the new university and the institution on Parkgate Road would not have attained the size, range and influence which it commands today.

Another key factor in Chester's success has been its reputation. Judged purely in academic terms, this has obviously fluctuated over the best part of two centuries. When Principal Allen arrived in 1886, for example, he was taking on what was clearly a low-achieving College and he had only limited success in raising standards before making way for Best in 1890. Conversely, the intellectual quality of many students in the interwar period was a match for most universities of the time. The arrival of female students in the early 1960s certainly raised the academic tone of the institution and this was to be of critical importance in the following decade: the fact that by the 1970s Chester, then admitting more women than men, had a far higher proportion of students with two 'A' levels than most other colleges helped persuade the DES to advocate its survival and the University of Liverpool to permit diversification into teaching for BA degrees. More recently, generally healthy application figures have allowed the institution cautiously to raise its admission requirements and this in turn has contributed to improvements in degree classifications: in 2000, some 41% of students obtained a (Liverpool) Bachelor's degree with a First or Upper Second, in 2013 just over 62% did so, this time from the University of Chester. The percentage puts Chester just under halfway in the UK rankings on this specific measure, below most pre-1992 universities but above most of those created since: a respectable record for a University less than ten years old and a sound base for further advance.[13]

Reputation is of course based on much more than academic prowess and it seems fair to say that the majority of students down the decades have both enjoyed and appreciated 'the Chester experience', although the precise nature of this has obviously changed over time. The phrase embraces the nineteenth- and early twentieth-century *esprit de corps* bred by enforced dormitory living and Chapel attendance; the camaraderie of the College Rag from the 1920s to the 1990s; a strong and enduring culture of sporting endeavour and achievement (which predates, but has been sustained by, the prominence since the 1920s of Physical Education as a discipline, albeit under various names); and, in more recent times, increasingly diverse opportunities to express one's own identity within what may broadly be described as a 'caring environment' overseen by a high-profile student support service.[14] The attention paid since the 1970s to graduate employability, through initiatives ranging from dedicated careers guidance to embedded Work Based Learning, has also helped Chester to maintain an above-average record in this regard. To cite the University league tables yet again, Chester's position as high as 22nd for 'student satisfaction' in 2013, derived from National Student Survey returns[15] – by no means its best performance over the preceding decade – is in line with what one might have expected as a response from previous generations, based on the anecdotal evidence of the *Collegian* and the reminiscences of students from the past. One who spent her undergraduate years as a mature student at Chester during the transition from College to University – and who is now pursuing an academic career at the University of Western Australia – summarises her appreciation of the experience in these terms:

> I was extremely grateful for the nurturing environment that Chester afforded due to its size. Class sizes were small and there were always opportunities for debate during the lecture … I realise how fortunate I was not to have been an anonymous face in the crowd and for the kind of relationship I was able to form with the lecturers. There was always a lot of good-natured banter that went on in lectures, which added to the enjoyment of the overall experience. I think that being a small institution gave the students a real sense of 'community'. We ranged in age from 18 to 74 but there were never any divisions and we enjoyed each other's company both inside and outside of the University. I am still in contact with students and some members of staff today.[16]

In seeking to explain the College's good fortune over the years, all this matters. Generations of former students have recommended it strongly to prospective applicants, so helping to maintain sound recruitment. One of the first things Chritchley did when trying to revive the institution in 1869 was to organise a reunion of 'schoolmasters who have passed through the College', so that they could be recruiting agents on his behalf,[17] and their successors down the years have proved to be major assets in periods of uncertainty – such as the mid-to-late 1970s when the College sought to develop alternatives to the BEd, the late 1990s and 2000s as it had to adjust to various changes of title in a highly competitive market, and most recently in 2012–13 as it met the challenge of a steep rise in tuition fees. To add to all this, the College Club (inaugurated in 1882) and its successors (currently the Alumni Association) have kept alive an ongoing commitment to the institution, expressed periodically through donations but never more crucially than in 1933 when an intensive lobbying campaign helped persuade the Church Assembly to reject proposals to close the College down. As the institution increasingly makes its mark as a modern University, good reports from its former students will continue to be critical to its future.

The willingness of generations of academic and support staff to 'go the second mile' for the good of the institution and its students is another important factor in its survival and success. Of course, there has always been an element of self-interest in working extra hard to ensure the continuation of one's source of employment. It is also true that Chester is far from alone among the former Church colleges in generating a peculiar sense of institutional loyalty – one which, for most of their history, has been largely derived from a widely shared allegiance to the Christian values of the foundation, albeit varying from overt commitment to tacit sympathy. But the fact remains that, time and again, a quart has been poured from a pint pot and the College, now the University, has reaped the rewards. One thinks, for example, of the selfless devotion of Theodore Ardern in fostering a musical tradition and ensuring the success of the College Club in the years before the First World War; of the pains taken in 1954 by the lecturer in Art, Joseph Clarke, to design the coat of arms still used today; of the creative energy of all those members of staff in the 1970s who devised credible new programmes for the College to deliver; and of the patient, intelligent application of everyone who met the QAA assessors, alongside those who backed them behind the scenes, during the prolonged, demanding journey towards university status.

Much else of this nature is left unrecorded but one further example from recent times may be cited. Devolution of responsibility for the approval of new programmes and partnerships, first through accreditation by the University of Liverpool in 1994 and then through the grants of degree awarding powers and university title a decade or so later, has allowed the institution's portfolio to multiply on a scale comparable to that of the seed of Abraham.[18] But this has only been possible through the repeated willingness of support staff to work extra hours to produce paperwork to tight deadlines and of academic staff to sit on validation and partnership panels – increasingly overseas, as the twenty-first century wears on – in order to approve provision from which they and their own departments will derive no direct benefit. At the time of the application for university title, one-third of all academic staff had experience of serving on a validation or review panel,[19] and this tradition of drawing on a wide pool of expertise to underpin quality management has been maintained. There is scarcely any reason, other than corporate goodwill, why members of (for example) the Faculty of Humanities should devote time to overseeing the approval of new initiatives in (say) the Faculty of Health & Social Care, or vice versa, but it happens on a regular basis and the University could not thrive without it.

This institutional commitment has certainly been recognised by successive leaders of the institution. In the mid-1990s, the Principal and Deputy Principal, for example, jointly expressed their acute awareness that 'we must temper any personal passions in order to maintain the remarkable goodwill and staff enthusiasm that continues to exist throughout our particular college community', goodwill and enthusiasm which they saw as being fostered through allowing colleagues 'the freedom to make a distinctive personal contribution to the institution'.[20] At the turn of the millennium, Bill Hughes, an eloquent staff governor and esteemed member of the English department, whose long and devoted service to the College had included that of public relations officer in the 1980s, felt obliged to draw attention to mounting pressures in comments to the Governing Body.

> The more the College responded to initiatives and to guidelines to create a surplus, the greater the danger of a knock on effect with regards to the student experience and academic work. At the present time five teaching staff from the English Department were being asked to become members of the Institute of Learning and Teaching and to attend a course for the European Computer Driving Licence. Three of those staff had book contracts that were vital for the RAE and would bring in money for the College. The money available at other institutions to carry out research was not available at the College.[21]

Yet the reality was that he and his colleagues did continue to deliver strongly on all fronts, as the drive for further diversity as well as towards university status gathered pace. However, his fundamental point – with its implication that the institution was heavily dependent on the extraordinary commitment of its staff – remains as valid in the changed context of today as it did when it was made. As higher education continues to evolve, it will be a challenge for the future leadership of the University to retain the widespread goodwill on which the success of the institution has been built.

On the question of leadership, it is worth stressing that Chester College has been remarkably fortunate in the overall calibre of its Principals. Two of them, Chritchley – effectively the 'second founder' of the College in 1869 – and Astbury, deserve credit for their careful stewardship but their innate conservatism was arguably not in the institution's best long-term interests. This would also have been the verdict on Price, had his wish to refuse admission to women been granted. But they each made important contributions to the College's progress and all the others may reasonably be regarded as excellent holders of the office. Best, Thomas and Seaborne all led the institution wisely and had considerable knowledge of what was required at the time; the last two played key roles in helping the College to survive when there was a serious threat of closure. Allen and de Bunsen were, in very different ways, formidable and distinguished characters of a reforming disposition whose reigns were too short for their full potential to be realised. The last two leaders, Binks and Wheeler, in office when diversity of institutional mission was being encouraged, have, through their own vision and drive, put a personal stamp on the College and University; it may fairly be claimed that the institution would not be quite 'like it is' had someone else been in charge. The same could be said of the first Principal, Rigg, whose enthusiasm for 'industrial occupations' made Chester College unique and, in a sense, ahead of its time. He led the College in a period when teacher training was still at an experimental stage and different models were to be welcomed. There are comparable opportunities to take the University in its own distinctive direction today.

Notwithstanding the high quality of successive Principals, it remains the case that every holder of the office after Chritchley has built on what he inherited – an obvious statement but one which should remind us that there have been many others who deserve credit for shaping the institution's development and providing continuity from one regime to the next. Looking only at the period since the Second World War, the improvements to students' living conditions which came with an end to the dormitories under Price was the result of Astbury's patient efforts to have the two hostels completed; the tower block, an icon of de Bunsen's reign, was commissioned while Price was in post; diversification beyond teacher training, an achievement of Seaborne's time, was being planned before de Bunsen retired; nurse education and integrated work experience, key components of the College's portfolio under Binks, can trace their origins to the days of Seaborne; degree awarding powers and university status, attained by Wheeler, were under active discussion with Binks at the helm. Each one in their turn has paid generous tributes to the staff and students who have given character to the College or University and have promoted its cause during their time in charge, none more so than the present Vice-Chancellor under whom the institution has more than doubled its student numbers, spread from one campus to five[22] and been transformed from a well-regarded

College of Higher Education to an attractive, medium-sized and middle-ranking university with potential for further advance. Indeed, the most favourable of the published league tables for 2014, that in *The Guardian*, already has it ahead of two universities founded in the 1960s, when the city arguably missed its chance to take advantage of university expansion.[23]

Naturally, there are other factors which should be cited in any account of Chester's development. Status as a Church of England foundation undoubtedly shaped the College's ethos and, as discussed in the previous chapter, continues to influence that of the University today. The support of the Church, financially at various points (such as in the major building campaign of the 1960s) and through the commitment of time, effort and expertise on the part of several ecclesiastical governors, has been highly beneficial – not least the contribution of successive Bishops of Chester (most recently Baughen, 1982–96, and Forster since then) who have been dedicated to the success of the institution and have used their political influence on its behalf. It was certainly to Chester's advantage in the 1970s to be a 'voluntary' church college, outside the control of the local authority, because it could not simply be rolled up into whatever reorganisation scheme the county devised; its future could not be guaranteed and its continuing place alongside the local authority colleges had to be negotiated, but at least the Church of England – for whom Chester was of strategic importance in the North West – could bring pressure to bear on the decision-making process. As the HE sector sub-divides into clusters of like-minded institutions, the University's leading role within the Cathedrals Group may well have an impact upon the way it develops in years to come.[24]

The help and guidance offered by the University of Liverpool, corporately and through individuals as governors and academic advisors, should also be recognised, especially the support it offered as the validating body to repeated diversification initiatives from the 1970s onwards and also its genuine encouragement to the College in its early twenty-first century quest to become a University in its own right. Had the College decided in 1973–74 to diversify under the aegis of the CNAA rather than of Liverpool, as it almost did, there would have been a good deal of fence-mending to do with the University in 1992 when the CNAA was closed and colleges had to find new awarding bodies – a process of rapprochement which would surely have delayed the grant of accredited status and conceivably the subsequent applications for degree awarding powers and university title as well. In recent decades, the institution has also drawn heavily on support from local authorities and the business community, again through the contribution of individual governors and also as partners in joint initiatives. But while backing from all these quarters has been important, it is best regarded as of secondary significance. The Church of England has never had a blank cheque with which to underwrite all its educational foundations and most of its colleges are no longer with us. Quite rightly neither the Church, nor the University of Liverpool, nor the city and county authorities, nor various commercial enterprises would have given their support to an institution which had not shown, through its own endeavours, that it merited such support. 'God helps those who help themselves.'

It would be easy to conclude that Chester's success in the period between the 150th and 175th anniversaries has been built above all on astute opportunism: seen, for example, in the rapid ascent to university status following the government's change of policy in 2003, in the acquisition of substantial property – in the city centre and beyond – as it became available, and in a series of funding bids reflecting the latest ministerial priorities. This does less than justice to the strategic planning which has put the institution in a position to take these opportunities when they have arisen, and in any case the statement should be seen as compliment not criticism in an age when every college and university has had to respond nimbly to shifts in the political and economic climate. That quarter-century has witnessed a revolution in the governance and conduct of UK higher education, with increased state control eroding institutional autonomy and an expectation that universities will compete for the limited resources available to teach massively enlarged numbers of students. At a national level, it has been characterised as a period of greater commercialism, managerialism and bureaucracy, during which academic staff morale across the sector has declined.[25] But whatever individual regrets there may be at the passing of earlier ways, as an institution Chester has succeeded in turning most of this to its advantage – success which owes far more to good judgment than to good luck.

As it celebrated its 175th anniversary, the University looked forward to taking advantage of the government's removal of the 'cap' on undergraduate numbers, announced in the Chancellor's autumn statement of 2013; to the publication in December 2014 of the results of the REF exercise, which promised to enhance the institution's reputation in terms of the overall quality of its research; and to the development, with the support of Shropshire Council and HEFCE, of a university presence in the fellow-marcher town of Shrewsbury. The pace of change since the turn of the millennium has been breathtaking and it shows no sign of slackening. But all plans for the future will inevitably have to be tempered by the onward march of unpredictable 'events' and it will be for the University's next historian to describe and assess the outcome of initiatives such as these.

Yet if there is one lesson for the future to take from the past, it is that the institution has traditionally thrived on ambitious forward-thinking. Chester has repeatedly been at its most vulnerable when it has been most conservative and inclined to 'play safe'. Under Chritchley – who must never be denied his achievement in bringing the College back from the dead – Principal and governors alike seem to have been content with a cheaply run, second-rate establishment. Had this policy continued, Chester might well not have survived the competition from university day colleges and local authority colleges which so concerned Best in the years before the First World War. Procrastination by the governors in the 1920s meant that the College missed the opportunity to buy Abbot's Grange on the other side of Parkgate Road, where the construction of a modern hostel of study-bedrooms would have made it much harder for the Church of England Board of Supervision to make the case for closure in 1932–33. The near-unanimous view of Principal Price, his senior staff and his governors that Chester should remain an all-male College would have spelled disaster during the years of 'concentration' in the 1970s, had they not bowed to pressure from the Ministry to admit women students in return for funds to permit expansion. Conversely, calculated risk-taking – such as the purchase under Thomas of empty fields sloping down to the canal and railway line, using borrowed money and far beyond immediate requirements, and the progressive diversification of the curriculum since the 1970s, initially beyond teacher training and then beyond traditional subjects – has paid off handsomely. The acquisition in 2002 of a new campus at Warrington seemed at the time to be destabilising an application process for taught degree awarding powers which was then at a delicate stage, but in the event it strengthened the College's case and raised its profile within the county and region. The latest venture to establish an Engineering presence at Thornton also involves a leap into an uncertain future but it carries the promise of great reward. Every university in the early twenty-first century has to take risks, and the trick is to continue to assess them carefully and back winning initiatives while retaining integrity, maintaining and enhancing quality, upholding standards and remaining true to the institution's strategic priorities and corporate values.[26] On Chester On!

1   P. Abercrombie, S. Kelly and T. Fyfe, *The Deeside Regional Planning Scheme* (Liverpool, 1923), pp. 47–50; the 'military' role was a reference to the presence in the city since 1907 of the headquarters of Western Command.

2   UC, Minutes of Governors, 2005 to date: 28 November 2006.

3   UC, *University of Chester Development Framework* (March 2012), p. 16.

4   Reservations can be traced to long before the creation of the University. For example, in *Collegian*, 1973, p. 17, the Dean of Students comments that 'as the Rating and Valuation officer declared, Chester College is in no way different from any other University or College in the country, and if people live near an institution of this kind it is not unreasonable to suppose that they will occasionally hear a certain degree of noise. The College is most anxious to preserve good relations with its neighbours…'.

5   Lucian, *De Laude Cestrie*, reproduced in *Chester, 1066-1971: Contemporary Descriptions by Residents and Visitors*, ed. D.M. Palliser (Chester, 1972), p. 6.

6   See Chapter 14.

7   Hartwell *et al.*, *Buildings of England: Cheshire*, p. 277. On the 'good gardening', see the SU comment in the *Which University 2013* website that the main campus is 'beautiful' and the recurrent successes since the 1990s in the annual 'Chester in Bloom' competition: <<http://university.which.co.uk/university-of-chester-c55>>, accessed 10/10/13; CC, Minutes of Governors, 1990–99: 3 November 1992; CC, *Insider*, September 1995; CC, *Insider Bulletin*, 16 September 1996, September 1997; CC, *Annual Report 1999–2000*, pp. 16-17.

8   *Minutes of Committee of Council on Education, 1851–52*: vol. I (London, 1852), p. 282.

9   Rose, *History of King Alfred's College, Winchester, passim*; the name 'King Alfred's' was not adopted until 1928.

10 *The Guardian University Guide 2014* (published 3 June 2013) had Chester 46th, Winchester 66th; the *Complete University Guide: University League Table 2014* had Winchester 69th, Chester 71st; *The Times and Sunday Times Good University Guide 2014* put Chester 52nd, Winchester 57th.

11 St Peter's College, Peterborough and the diocesan training college at Truro closed in the late 1930s, Culham (Oxford) in 1979, Keswick Hall (Norwich) in 1981.

12 See Chapters 10, 12; Crewe College, having merged with Alsager in 1974, became part of Manchester Metropolitan University in 1992 and was rebranded as MMU Cheshire in 2003.

13 CC, Application for Degree Awarding Powers for Taught Courses, Update on Developments and Work in progress (October 2002), Appendix D, Annex D; *Complete University Guide: University League Tables 2014* (Good Honours).

14 Since it became as University, Chester has hosted a Diversity Festival every February or March – billed as 'a unique opportunity to learn and experience different cultures and perspectives' – open to the public as well as to students and staff.

15 *Complete University Guide: University League Table 2014* (Student Satisfaction).

16 *Pers. comm.*, L. Dolan (a Combined Honours student of 2002–06).

17   ZCR 86/12/21: *Report of the Chester and Manchester Diocesan Board of Education for year ending December 1869*, p. 5.

18   *Genesis* ch. 22, v. 17.

19   CC, Application for University Title (August 2004), p. 41.

20   Binks and Roberts, 'A Productive Partnership', pp. 72, 78.

21   CC, Minutes of Governors, 2000–2005: 29 June 2000; following his retirement in 2008 after 34 years at the College, Hughes was awarded an Honorary Fellowship in English (*The Cestrian*, 2009, p. 13).

22   For this purpose, the Kingsway site is reckoned a 'campus'.

23   Sussex (which received its charter in 1961) and Essex (1965) are ranked 50th and 63rd by *The Guardian* compared to Chester's 46th, although they are above Chester in other tables. It is only fair to add that Chester has some way to go to catch other 1960s foundations, such as Lancaster, Exeter, York and UEA (Norwich).

24   Under the University's 2007 Instrument of Government, the Vice-Chancellor and Deputy Vice-Chancellor are required to be 'practising members of a Church which is a member of Churches Together in Britain and Ireland, or its successor body'. This is a broader requirement than the traditional insistence on communicant-member status within the Church of England.

25   Shattock, 'Policy Making', p. 184.

26   See e.g. the advice of one Vice-Chancellor: 'to retire with a good conscience … now means being relentlessly strategic', quoted in Bosetti and Walker, 'Perspectives of UK Vice-Chancellors', p. 18.

BIBLIOGRAPHY

PRIMARY SOURCES

Cheshire Archives and Local Studies

ZCR 86/1/1: [Governing Body] Minute Book, 1854–67.

ZCR 86/1/2: [Governing Body] Minute Book, 1871–83.

ZCR 86/1/3: [Governing Body] Minute Book, 1883–90.

ZCR 86/1/4: [Governing Body] Minute Book, 1890–96.

ZCR 86/1/5: [Governing Body] Minute Book, 1896–1904.

ZCR 86/1/7: [Governing Body] Minute Book, 1872, 1877.

ZCR 86/1/8: [Governing Body] Minute Book, 1904–27.

ZCR 86/1/9: [Governing Body] Minute Book, 1927–44.

ZCR 86/1/10 [Governing Body] Minute Book, 1945–62.

ZCR 86/2/1: [Governing Body] General Purposes Committee Minute Book, 1891–95.

ZCR 86/2/2: [Governing Body] General Purposes Committee Minute Book, 1895–1900.

ZCR 86/2/3: [Governing Body] General Purposes Committee Minute Book, 1901–07.

ZCR 86/2/5: [Governing Body] General Purposes Committee Minute Book, 1911–33.

ZCR 86/2/6: [Governing Body] General Purposes Committee Minute Book, 1933–46.

ZCR 86/3/2: Ledger Book, 1865–72.

ZCR 86/5/1: Examination Class List Register, 1870–1906.

ZCR 86/5/2: Examination Record Book, 1912–45.

ZCR 86/6/1: Register of Staff Appointments, 1910–31.

ZCR 86/7/3: *Annual Report on Chester Training College, 1914.*

ZCR 86/7/4: *Annual Report on Chester Training College, 1915.*

ZCR 86/7/23: *Report of the College Council for the year ended 31 July 1937.*

ZCR 86/7/24: *Report of the College Council for the year ended 31 July 1938.*

ZCR 86/7/26: *Report of the College Council for year ended 31 July 1940.*

ZCR 86/7/28: *Report of the College Council for year ended 31 July 1942.*

ZCR 86/7/29: *Annual Report for 1946* (including summary 1942–45).

ZCR 86/7/42: *Annual Report and Accounts for 1959.*

ZCR 86/7/43: *Annual Report and Accounts for 1960.*

ZCR 86/7/44: *Annual Report and Accounts for year ended 31 July, 1961.*

ZCR 86/7/45: *Annual Report and Accounts for year ended 31 July 1962.*

ZCR 86/7/46: *Annual Report and Accounts for year ended 31 July, 1963.*

ZCR 86/7/47: *Annual Report and Accounts for year ended 31 July 1964.*

ZCR 86/7/48: *Annual Report and Accounts for year ended 31 July, 1965.*

ZCR 86/8/1: Chester College Club Minute Book, 1890–1906.

ZCR 86/9/10: File re coat of arms, 1953–54.

ZCR 86/11/1: Letters and papers re affiliation to University of Liverpool. 1920–55.

ZCR 86/11/2: Letters and Papers re new buildings, 1938–42.

ZCR 86/11/4: Letters and Papers re North Hostel, 1947–53.

ZCR 86/11/5: Letters and Papers re new buildings, 1948–49.

ZCR 86/12/1: Letters and Papers, 1839 (including *Verbatim Report of the Great Diocesan Meeting at Warrington*).

ZCR 86/12/4: Letters and Papers, 1842 (including *A Sermon preached in Chester Cathedral on the Opening of the Training College, September 1st 1842* by Rev. Canon Slade).

ZCR 86/12/12: Letters and Papers, 1850.

ZCR 86/12/21: Letters and Papers, 1869 (including *Report of the Chester and Manchester Diocesan Board of Education for the year ending December 1869*).

ZCR 86/12/22: Letters and Papers, 1870 (including *Report of a Public Meeting held in the Town Hall of Chester on Tuesday 27 September 1870*, reprinted from the *Chester Guardian*, and *First Report of the Chester Diocesan Board of Education for year ending December 1870*).

ZCR 86/12/23: Letters and Papers, 1871 (including *Second Report of the Chester Diocesan Board of Education for year ending December 1871*).

ZCR 86/12/24: Letters and Papers, 1872 (including *Third Report of the Chester Diocesan Board of Education for year ending December 1872*).

ZCR 86/12/25: Letters and Papers, 1873 (including *Diocese of Chester Report on the Diocesan Institutions for year ending December 1873*).

ZCR 86/12/27: Letters and Papers, 1875 (including *Diocese of Chester Report on the Diocesan Institutions for year ending December 1875*).

ZCR 86/12/32: Letters and Papers, 1885 (including *School Management Notes: Syllabus of Lectures in Psychology and in the Method Used in the Practising School at Chester College*).

ZCR 86/12/33: Letters and Papers, 1886.

ZCR 86/12/39: Letters and Papers, 1891.

ZCR 86/12/43: Letters and Papers, 1895.

ZCR 86/12/48: Letters and Papers, 1900.

ZCR 86/12/58: Letters and Papers, 1910.

ZCR 86/12/59: Letters and Papers, 1911.

ZCR 86/12/71: Letters and Papers, 1923.

ZCR 86/12/80: Letters and Papers, 1932.

ZCR 86/12/81: Letters and Papers, 1933.

ZCR 86/12/81: Miscellaneous papers re proposed closure of Chester College, 1932–33.

ZCR 86/12/85: Letters and Papers, 1936.

ZCR 86/12/89: Letters and Papers, 1940.

ZCR 86/12/94: Letters and Papers, 1945.

ZCR 86/12/95: Letters and Papers, 1946.

ZCR 86/13/1: Notes and Transcripts on the History of the College.

ZCR 86/13/4: Letters and Papers re Revd Arthur Rigg.

ZCR 86/13/5: Autograph book of Henry Norris.

ZCR 86/14/37: *Chester College Prospectus 1965–66.*

ZCR 86/14/37: *Chester College: Campaign for Expansion, 1965.*

ZCR 86/15/1: File of newspaper cuttings, 1842–43.

ZCR 86/15/2: File of miscellaneous newspaper cuttings.

ZCR 86/19/3: Lithograph headed 'Chester College, 1909–11'.

ZCR 86/19/4: Cartoons of 'Happy Memories of Chester College'.

ZCR 86/19/11: Notes on student opinion of community life, 14 April 1970.

ZCR 86/7928: Student scrapbook, 1880–81.

ZCR 86/7928: Student scrapbook, 1928–30.

ZCR 86/7928: *Annual Report to the Governors on the Year 1967–68.*

ZCR 86/7928: Minutes of Student Centre Committee.

ZCR 86/7928: Chester College of Higher Education, Outline Proposals for the Institution of Courses leading to the award of BEd (Ord.), BEd (Hons), BA in Combined Studies (Ord.) and DipHE, to begin in September 1975 (February 1974).

ZCR 86/7928: Carhart deposit: Reports on Restructuring of Church Colleges: Note (by M.V.J. Seaborne, 14 February 1985) of a Joint Meeting of Governors' Working Party and of Chaplaincy team, 8 February 1985.

ZCR 86/7928: *Union Handbook '85–'86.*

ZCR 86A/1: Minutes of the Educational Technology Committee, 1972–79.

ZCR 86A/227, 231, 232, 235, 236, 240: Surveys and plans.

ZCR 86A/327: *Prospectus 1966–67.*

ZCR 86A/329: *Prospectus 1968–69.*

ZCR 86A/330: *Prospectus 1979.*

ZCR 86A/331: *Prospectus 1980.*

University of Chester

CC, *Annual Report 1967–68.*

CC, *Annual Report 1999–2000.*

CC, *Annual Report 2002–03.*

CC, *Annual Report 2003–04.*

CC, *Annual Report 2004–05.*

CC, Annual Statement to the University of Liverpool under the Instrument of Accreditation (March 2004).

CC, Application for Degree Awarding Powers for Taught Courses, Update on Developments and Work in progress (October 2002).

CC, Application to the Privy Council for the Title of University (August 2004).

CC, *Campus* 2 (June 1990).

CC, *Campus* 5 (January 1991).

CC, *Campus* 8 (June 1992).

CC, *Campus* 11 (Spring 1994).

CC, *Campus* 15 (December 1997).

CC, *Chester College Prospectus, 1990.*

Bibliography

CC, *Chester College Songs*, 1913.

CC, Conduct of QAA in reviewing the Foundation Degree Programme in Business & Management, 2005.

CC, *Enterprise in Higher Education: Final Report* (November 1994).

CC, HEFCE Assessment of the Quality of Education, 1993, Chester College History Department: Institutional Self-Assessment and Letter of Response.

CC, Hooper deposit: *Training College Examinations Board: Regulations and Syllabus, 1935–1937.*

CC, Hooper deposit: *Prospectus, 1958–59.*

CC, Hooper deposit: *Calendar 1965–66, Michaelmas Term.*

CC, Hooper deposit: *Calendar 1966–67, Michaelmas Term.*

CC, Hooper deposit: *Calendar and Diary 1967–68.*

CC, Hooper deposit: *Handbook for Students*, September 1969.

CC, Hooper deposit: *Calendar and Diary 1969.*

CC, Hooper deposit: *Calendar and Diary 1970.*

CC, Hooper deposit: *Calendar and Diary, Michaelmas Term 1972.*

CC, *Insider* and *Insider Bulletin*, 1993–98.

CC, Memo Seaborne to Academic Council, 'Chester as a Church College', January 1976.

CC, Memo Bursar to K. Thompson, 16 December 1992.

CC, Minutes of Academic Board, 1966–70.

CC, Minutes of Academic Board, 1970–73.

CC, Minutes of Academic Board, 1973–77.

CC, Minutes of Academic Board, 1977–82.

CC, Minutes of Academic Board, 1982–89.

CC, Minutes of Academic Board, 1989–93.

CC, Minutes of Academic Board, 1993–95.

CC, Minutes of Academic Board, 1995–96.

CC, Minutes of Academic Board, 1996–98.

CC, Minutes of Academic Board, 1998–2000.

CC, Minutes of Academic Board, 2000–01.

CC, Minutes of Academic Board, 2001–03.

CC, Minutes of Academic Board, 2003–04.

CC, Minutes of Academic Board, 2005.

CC, Minutes of Academic Council, 1966–72.

CC, Minutes of Academic Council, 1972–81.

CC, Minutes of Course Planning and Academic Development Committees, 1977–85.

CC, Minutes of Governors, 1975–89.

CC, Minutes of Governors, 1990–99.

CC, Minutes of Governors, 2000–05.

CC, Minutes of Guild Council.

CC, Notes of a meeting held 15 December 1988 between Bill Hughes (Chester College) and David Hooper (Chester College Association).

CC, Programme of Events, 1989.

CC, Report on the Upkeep of the Great East Window by P. Kemp-Jones.

CC, *Staff News*, November 2004.

CC, *Staff News*, July 2005.

CC, The Future of the Colleges of Education (paper by Seaborne to Academic Board and Governors, February 1977).

CC, *Prospectus 1997*.

CC, *Undergraduate Prospectus 1998*.

CC, *Undergraduate Prospectus 1999*.

CC, *Undergraduate Prospectus 2000*.

CC, *Undergraduate Prospectus 2005*.

Chester College Song Book (1939).

Collegian, 1888–1987, 1999, 2002.

Collegian, Freshers' Edition, 1994.

The Cestrian 2006–13.

The Old Collegian, 1998.

UC, 2009 BQF Achievement Award Employee Satisfaction: Submission.

UC, 2009 BQF Achievement Award for Employee Satisfaction Report.

UC, Annual Monitoring Report for WBIS postgraduate modular programme for 2011–12.

UC, Annual Monitoring Report for WBIS undergraduate modular programme for 2012–13.

UC, *Annual Report 2006–07*.

UC, *Annual Review 2009*.

UC, *Annual Review 2010*.

UC, *Annual Review 2011*.

UC, *Annual Review 2012*.

UC, *Annual Review 2013*.

UC, Annual Statement to Senate on Quality Assurance and Quality Enhancement during the Academic Year 2009–10.

UC, *Defining the Future: Corporate Plan* (2012–16).

UC, deposit by Mr B. Thomas of Harborne, Birmingham, 2011.

UC, *Forum*, Edn 1, Sept 2013.

UC, *Forum*, Edn 2, 2012–13.

UC, *Forum*, Edn 3, December 2013.

UC, Institutional/Strategic Level Key Performance Indicators, updated November 2009.

UC, Learning Support Services Summary Report 2008–09.

UC, Mid-Cycle Follow-Up to QAA Institutional Audit, October 2007.

UC, Minutes of Executive Group.

UC, Minutes of Foundation/Mission Committee, 2003 to date.

UC, Minutes of Governors, 2005 to date.

UC, Minutes of Partnerships sub-Committee.

UC, Minutes of Senate, 2005–07 (subsequent minutes on University intranet).

UC, *Postgraduate Prospectus 2005*.

UC, *Postgraduate Prospectus 2010*.

UC, *Postgraduate Prospectus 2014*.

UC, QAA Institutional Audit 2010 Briefing Paper.

UC, Register of University of Chester's Collaborative Arrangements 2012/13.

UC, *Research that Makes a Difference, 2005–06*.

UC, *Staff News*, January 2005.

UC, *Staff News*, February/March 2008.

UC, Student Enrolments by Mode and Course Type, 2006–09.

UC, Summary of Undergraduate Applications, 2010, 2011, 2012, and 2013.

UC, *Undergraduate Prospectus 2005*.

UC, *Undergraduate Prospectus 2010*.

UC, *Undergraduate Prospectus 2014*.

UC, *University of Chester Development Framework* (March 2012).

University of Chester Student News, Issue 1, 2013.

Other Primary Sources

Abercrombie, P., Kelly, S. and Fyfe, T., *The Deeside Regional Planning Scheme* (Liverpool, 1923).

Board of Education: *Report of the Consultative Committee on Infant and Nursery Schools* ['Hadow Report'] (HMSO, London, 1933).

Cheshire Observer, 17 December 1932, 21 May, 14 June 1939, 20 June 1967.

Chester Chronicle, 27 June 2008, 22 July 2009.

Chester Courant, 15 September 1880, 14 July 1954.

Chester Evening Leader, 22 March 2005.

Church Assembly: Report of Proceedings 1932 (London, 1932).

Church Assembly: Report of Proceedings 1933 (London, 1933).

Church of England Training Colleges for Teachers: Report of the Committee of Enquiry (Westminster, 1933)

Church Times, 17 February 1933, 20 June, 3 October 1952.

Complete University Guide: University League Tables, 2008, 2009, 2010, 2011, 2012, 2014.

Dearing Report: Higher Education in the Learning Society (HMSO, London, 1997).

Department for Business, Innovation and Skills: *Applications for the Grant of Taught Degree Awarding Powers, Research Degree Awarding Powers and University Title: Guidance for Applicant Organisations in England and Wales* (August 2004),

DES: *Report of the Study Group on the Government of Colleges of Education* (Weaver Report, 1966).

Hansard, House of Commons, 23 October 1952, vol. 505, c. 1256.

House of Commons Education and Skills Committee: *The Future of Higher Education: Fifth Report of Session 2002–03: Vol. I, Report and Formal Minutes* (London, 2003).

Liverpool Daily Post, 10 July 1954, 14 June 1969.

Lucian, *De Laude Cestrie*, reproduced in *Chester, 1066-1971: Contemporary Descriptions by Residents and Visitors*, ed. D.M. Palliser (Chester, 1972), p. 6.

Manchester Guardian, 10 February 1933.

Minutes of the Committee of Council on Education, 1840–41 (London, 1841).

Minutes of Committee of Council on Education, 1851–52 (London, 1852).

Minutes of Committee of Council on Education, 1855–56 (London, 1856).

Picture Post, 14 March 1942.

Pupil-Teachers' Classified Examination Questions (London, 1895).

QAA Advisory Committee on Degree Awarding Powers: Application for Taught Degree Awarding Powers – Chester College of Higher Education, Institutional Assessors' Updating Report (February 2003).

QAA: Advisory Committee on Degree Awarding Powers, Application for University Title: Paper by the Agency-appointed institutional assessors, University College Chester (January 2005).

QAA: Foundation Degree Review, University of Liverpool, University College Chester, Warrington Collegiate Institute, West Cheshire College: Business and Management, July 2005.

QAA: *Institutional Audit Report, University of Chester* (2005).

QAA: *Institutional Audit Report, University of Chester* (2010).

RAE Submissions 2001: Chester College of HE, Theology, Divinity & Religious Studies (HEFCE, 2002).

Report of the Committee of Council on Education, 1893–94 (London 1894).

Report of the Committee of Council on Education, 1897–88 (London, 1898).

Robbins Report: Higher Education (HMSO, London, 1963).

The Ecclesiastical History of Orderic Vitalis, VI, ed. M. Chibnall (Oxford, 1978).

The Guardian University Guide 2014.

The Guardian, 27 August 2012.

The Times and Sunday Times Good University Guide, 2014 (Glasgow, 2013).

The Sunday Times Good University Guide 2014 (22 September 2013).

The Sunday Times University Guide 2008 (21 September 2008).

The Teacher, 7 January 1905.

Times Higher Education, 6 March 2008, 19 July 2012.

University of Liverpool Annual Reports, 1932 (Liverpool 1932).

Warrington Guardian, 27 August 2010.

Yorkshire Post, 10 February 1933.

WEBSITES

<<http://university.which.co.uk/university-of-chester-c55>>

<<http://www.barclays.co.uk/TakeOneSmallStep/Meetour2011winners/P12426093 77971>>

<<http://www.cheshire.mmu.ac.uk/aboutus>>

<<http://www.doriconline.org.uk/Viewdata>>

<<http://www.geducation.co.uk/index.php>>

<<http://www.hesa.ac.uk/index.php?option=com_content&task=view&id=2397&It emid=141>>

<<http://www.historyandpolicy.org/papers/policy-paper-61.html#students>>

<<http://www.itv.com/news/granada/story/2013–03–01/shell-donates-240m-science-centre-to-university/>>

<<http://www.leeds.ac.uk/educol/ncihe/sumrep.htm>>

<<http://www.lltgl.org.uk/Content/Holly-Shaw>>

<<http://www.rae.ac.uk/results>>

<<http://www.shell.co.uk/gbr/aboutshell/media-centre/annual-reports-and-publications/swuk/thornton-next-chapter.html>>

<<http://www.slc.co.uk/statistics/national-statistics/facts-and-figures.aspx>>

<<http://www.theguardian.com/education/2003/jan/22/highereducation.accessto university>>

<<http://www.theguardian.com/education/students/tables/0,,1574395,00.html>>

<<http://www.theguardian.com/education/table/2009/may/12/university-league-table>>

<<http://www.theguardian.com/education/table/2010/jun/04/university-league-table>>

<<http://www.theguardian.com/education/universityguide2005/0,15903,1455246,00.html>>

<<http://www.tolliss.com/gedview/family.php?famid=F4637>>

<<http://www.ucat.chester.ac.uk/Content/AboutUs>>

<<https://www.gov.uk/government/publications/teachers-standards>>

PRINTED SECONDARY SOURCES

Note the following abbreviations:

Bradbury, *Chester College*: J.L. Bradbury, *Chester College and the Training of Teachers* (Chester, 1975).

Dunn, *Bright Star*: I. Dunn, *The University of Chester 1839–2012: The Bright Star in the Present Prospect* (Chester, 2012).

HEQ: Higher Education Quarterly.

VCH: Victoria County History.

White, *Perspectives*: G.J. White, ed., *Perspectives of Chester College, 150th Anniversary Essays, 1839–1989* (Chester, 1989).

Alexander, R.J., Craft, M. and Lynch, J., 'Introduction' to R.J. Alexander, M. Craft and J. Lynch, eds, *Change in Teacher Education: Context and Provision since Robbins* (London, 1984), pp. xiii–xviii.

Alexander, R.W., 'Assessing a Group-Based Enterprise Project' in G. Clark, ed., *Geography and Enterprise in Higher Education* (Lancaster, 1991), chap. 8.

Allen, A.J.C., *The Christ of the Future: A Criticism and a Forecast* (London, 1920).

Allen, A.J.C., *The Church Catechism: Its History and Contents: A Manual for Teachers and Students* (London, 1892).

Anderson, R., *British Universities Past and Present* (London, 2006).

Andrews, P.J., 'The Making of a Victorian Schoolmaster: Peter Calvert at Chester College' in White, *Perspectives*, pp. 55–62.

Astbury, S., *A History of Chester College Chapel* (Chester, 1953).

Astbury, S., *A History of Chester Diocesan Training College* (Chester, 1946).

Bekhradnia, B., *Implications of the Government's Proposals for University Title: Or What is a University?* (Higher Education Policy Institute, Oxford, 2003).

Bellamy, M., 'Valorisation and the Role of the University under New Labour: Reclaiming the Commons in a Knowledge-based Economy' in A. Green, ed., *Blair's Educational Legacy: Thirteen Years of New Labour* (New York, 2010), pp. 65–99.

Binks, E.V., 'The Present State of Play' in White, *Perspectives*, pp. 85–87.

Binks, N. [E.V.] and Roberts, P., 'A Productive Partnership' in S. Weil, ed., *Introducing Change 'from the Top' in Universities and Colleges* (London, 1994), pp. 71–79.

Bosetti, L. and Walker, K., 'Perspectives of UK Vice-Chancellors in Leading Universities in a Knowledge-Based Economy', *HEQ*, LXIV, 1 (January 2010), pp. 4–21.

Bowen, J., *Right Place Right Time* (Lancaster, 2002).

Bradbury, J.L., *Chester College: A Brief Guide to the College Buildings* (privately printed, 1978).

Brown, R. and Carasso, H., *Everything for Sale? The Marketisation of UK Higher Education* (London, 2013).

Browning, O., *The Importance of the Training of Teachers* (Cambridge, 1906).

Bruce, A., *The Cathedral 'Open and Free': Dean Bennett of Chester* (Liverpool, 2000).

Carpenter, E., *Archbishop Fisher: His Life and Times* (Norwich, 1991).

Carpentier, V., 'Public-private Substitution in Higher Education: Has Cost-sharing Gone too Far?', *HEQ*, LXVI, 4 (October 2012), pp. 363–90.

Cheshire History XXXVII (1997–98).

Cheshire Past 3 (1994).

Cheshire Past 4 (1995).

Collins, B. and Morgan, R., *Celebrating a Centenary: Teacher Education at Sheffield Hallam University* (Sheffield, 2005).

Connell, L., *A Century of Teacher Training in Leeds, 1875–1975* (Leeds, 1994).

Dawtry, A.F., 'All Work and No Play … the Development of Student Leisure Activities at Chester College' in White, *Perspectives*, pp. 75–84.

de Bunsen, B., *Adventures in Education* (Kendal, 1995).

Dent, H.C., *The Training of Teachers in England and Wales, 1800–1975* (London, 1977).

Edwards, E., *Women in Teacher Training Colleges, 1900–1960: A Culture of Femininity* (London, 2001).

Evans, E., *Those Were the Days: Recollections of Chester College in the Fifties and Sixties* (privately printed, 1989).

Foden, F.E., 'The Rev. Arthur Rigg: Pioneer of Workshop Practice', *Vocational Aspect of Secondary and Further Education*, XI, no. 23 (1959).

Bibliography

Forfar, D., 'What became of the Senior Wranglers?', *Mathematical Spectrum*, XXIX (1996–97), pp. 1–4.

France, D. and Ribchester, C., 'Podcasts and Feedback' in G. Salmon and P. Edirisingha, eds, *Podcasting for Learning in Universities* (Milton Keynes, 2008), pp. 70–79.

Gardner, P. 'Higher Education and Teacher Training: A Century of Progress and Promise' in J. Furlong and R. Smith, eds, *The Role of Higher Education in Initial Teacher Training* (London, 1996).

Gay, J.D., 'The Churches and the Training of Teachers in England and Wales' in V.A. McClelland, ed., *Christian Education in a Pluralist Society* (London, 1988), pp. 207–29.

Gedge, P.S. and Louden, L.M.R., *S. Martin's College Lancaster, 1964–89* (Lancaster, 1993).

Geodiversity Trail: Walking through the Past on the University's Chester Campus (Chester, 2007).

Goldstrom, J.M., *Education: Elementary Education, 1780–1900* (Newton Abbot, 1972).

Gosden, P., 'The James Report and Recent History' in J.B. Thomas, ed., *British Universities and Teacher Education: A Century of Change* (London, 1990), pp. 73–86

Gosden, P., 'The Role of Central Government and its Agencies, 1963–82' in R.J. Alexander, M. Craft and J. Lynch, eds, *Change in Teacher Education: Context and Provision since Robbins* (London, 1984), pp. 31–45.

Greenbank, P., 'The Evolution of Government Policy on Widening Participation', *HEQ*, LX, 2 (April 2006), pp. 141–66.

Hargreaves, C., 'Chester College – Site and Setting' in White, *Perspectives*, pp. 19–28.

Harrop, S.A., *Decade of Change: The University of Liverpool, 1981–1991* (Liverpool, 1994).

Hartwell, C., Hyde, M., Hubbard, E. and Pevsner, N., *The Buildings of England: Cheshire* (New Haven and London, 2011).

Heap, S., *What are Universities Good For?* (Cambridge, 2012).

Hencke, D., *Colleges in Crisis: The Reorganization of Teacher Training, 1971–7* (Harmondsworth, 1978).

History of Education, XXXVIII, no. 1 (January 2009), pp. 1–4 (Seaborne obituary).

Hollinshead, J.E., ed., *S. Katharine's College, Liverpool Institute of Higher Education: In Thy Light, 1844–1994* (Liverpool, 1994).

Hopkin, D., *The Role of Universities in the Modern Economy* (Cardiff, 2002).

Horn, P., *The Victorian and Edwardian Schoolchild* (Gloucester, 1989).

Horn, P., *Education in Rural England, 1800–1914* (Dublin, 1978).

House of Commons Education and Skills Committee: *The Future of Higher Education: Fifth Report of Session 2002–03: Vol. I, Report and Formal Minutes* (London, 2003).

Hughes, T., *A Stranger's Handbook to Chester* (Chester, 1856).

Hursey, T. and Taylor, M., 'Where do Students Figure in your EHE Equation? The Development of the Role and Function of a Student Enterprise Manager' in J. Gold and R. Holden, eds, *Enterprise in Higher Education: Lighting the Blue Touchpaper* (Bradford, 1991), pp. 30–34.

Ianelli, C., 'Inequalities in Entry to Higher Education: A Comparison Over Time between Scotland and England and Wales', *HEQ*, LXI, 3 (July 2007), pp. 306–33.

Ing, B., 'The Natural History of the College Campus' in White, *Perspectives*, pp. 51–54.

Iremonger, F.A., *William Temple, Archbishop of Canterbury: His Life and Letters* (Oxford, 1948).

Kelly, T., *For Advancement of Learning: The University of Liverpool 1881–1981* (Liverpool, 1981).

Larsen, M.A. *The Making and Shaping of the Victorian Teacher* (London, 2011).

Layard, R., King. J. and Moser, C., *The Impact of Robbins* (Harmondsworth, 1969).

Learning from Subject Review, 1993–2001: Sharing Good Practice (QAA, 2003).

Lockett, T.A., 'The Government of Colleges of Education' in T. Burgess (ed.), *Dear Lord James: A Critique of Teacher Education* (Harmondsworth, 1971), pp. 170–88.

McGregor, G.P., *A Church College for the 21st Century? 150 Years of Ripon & York St John* (York, 1991).

McIntosh, P.C., *Physical Education in England since 1800* (2nd edn., London, 1968).

Medieval Settlement Research Group Annual Report 6 (1991).

Medieval Settlement Research Group Annual Report 7 (1992).

Montgomery, F.A., *Edge Hill College: A History, 1885–1985* (Ormskirk, 1985).

More, C., *A Splendid College: An Illustrated History of Teacher Training in Cheltenham. 1847–1990* (Cheltenham, 1992).

Newton, E., *The Padgate Story: 1946–2006* (Chester, 2007).

Osborne, J., ed., *Saltley College Centenary, 1850–1950* (Birmingham, 1950).

Oxford Dictionary of National Biography, VIII, XIV, XLV, L, LIII.

Parry, G., 'Patterns of Participation in Higher Education in England: A Statistical Summary and Commentary', *HEQ*, LI, 1 (January 1997), pp. 6–28).

Perrin, D., Weston, P., Thompson, P.A. and Brodie, P., *Facilitating Employer Engagement through Negotiated Work Based Learning: A Case Study from the University of Chester* (n.d.).

Pevsner, N., *The Buildings of England: Cambridgeshire* (2nd ed., Harmondsworth, 1970).

Ribchester, C., France, D. and Wheeler, A., 'Podcasting: A Tool for Enhancing Assessment Feedback?' in E. O'Doherty, ed., *The Fourth Education in a Changing Environment Conference* (Santa Rosa, California, 2008), pp. 119–36.

Rich, R.W., *The Training of Teachers in England and Wales during the Nineteenth Century* (Cambridge, 1933).

Ridley, S., 'Theological Perspectives over 150 Years' in T. Brighton, ed., *150 Years: the Church Colleges in Higher Education* (Chichester, 1989).

Ridley, S., 'Theological Perspectives over 150 Years' in White, *Perspectives*, pp. 7–18.

Robinson, W., *Pupil Teachers and their Professional Training in Pupil Teacher Centres in England and Wales, 1870–1914* (Lampeter, 2003).

Rose, M., *A History of King Alfred's College, Winchester, 1840–1980* (Chichester, 1981).

Ross, A., 'The Universities and the BEd Degree' in J.B. Thomas, ed., *British Universities and Teacher Education: A Century of Change* (London, 1990).

Ryan, A., *Liberal Anxieties and Liberal Education* (London, 1999).

Bibliography

Ryan, A., 'New Labour and Higher Education' in G. Walford, ed., *Education and the Labour Government: An Evaluation of Two Terms* (Oxford, 2006), pp. 85–98.

Seaborne, M.V.J, *Primary School Design* (London, 1971).

Seaborne, M.V.J, 'The College Buildings' in White, *Perspectives*, pp. 29–49.

Securing a Sustainable Future for Higher Education: An Independent Review of Higher Education Funding and Student Finance (12 October 2010).

Shattock, R., 'Policy Making in British Higher Education, 1980–2006', *HEQ*, LXII, 2 (July 2008), pp. 181–203.

Shaw, K.E., 'Exeter: from College of Education to University' in R.J. Alexander, M. Craft and J. Lynch, eds, *Change in Teacher Education: Context and Provision since Robbins* (London, 1984), pp. 203–14.

Snape, M.F., *The Royal Army Chaplains' Department: Clergy under Fire* (Woodbridge, 2008).

Stewart, W.A.C. and McCann, W.P., *The Educational Innovators, 1780–1880* (New York, 1967).

Stewart, W.A.C., *Higher Education in Postwar Britain* (Basingstoke, 1989).

Sumner, C., *On the Borderline* (Harefield, 1997).

Sutherland, G., *Policy-Making in Elementary Education, 1870–1895* (Oxford, 1973).

Sylvester, D.W., *Robert Lowe and Education* (Cambridge, 1974).

Taylor, R. and Steele, T., *British Labour and Higher Education, 1945–2000* (London, 2011).

Taylor, W. 'The National Context, 1972–82' in R.J. Alexander, M. Craft and J. Lynch, eds, *Change in Teacher Education: Context and Provision since Robbins* (London, 1984), pp. 16–30.

The Anglican Identity of Church of England Higher Education Institutions: End of Year One Report (September 2012).

Thomas, J.B., 'Victorian Beginnings' and 'Day Training College to Department of Education' in J.B. Thomas, ed., *British Universities and Teacher Education: A Century of Change* (London, 1990).

Tight, M., 'Do League Tables Contribute to the Development of a Quality Culture? Football and Higher Education Compared', *HEQ*, LIV, 1 (January 2000), pp. 22–42.

Trow, M., *The Expansion and Transformation of Higher Education* (New York, 1972).

VCH Cheshire, III, V (i), V (ii).

White, G.J, 'Three Great Tutors: Lovell, Ardern, Morrell', in White, *Perspectives*, pp. 63–74.

Wooldridge, E. and Newcomb, E., *Distinctiveness and Identity in a Challenging HE Environment: A Unique Opportunity for the Cathedrals Group Institutions* (2011).

INDEX

Only a minority of the individuals named in the text have been included below, in most cases under the appropriate category heading (e.g. 'Alumni', 'Principals').